Studies in Applied Economics

Studies in Applied Economics is an English translation of *Études d'économie politique appliquée* (1898) by Léon Walras (1834–1910).

Until now, *Éléments d'économie politique pure* (1874) was the only book by Walras available in English (*Elements of Pure Economics*, 1954). It contains the theory of general economic equilibrium under free competition, with the concept of utility maximization as its core. Walras's conclusion was that where free competition is possible, it should be the rule.

So, in the present book, he advocates protective regulation, within which economic agents may compete freely. For water, gas or railway transport, for instance, where free competition is impossible, rules are formulated to maintain its advantages. Issues such as money, capital, credit, banking and the stock markets are also dealt with. The book's final chapter recapitulates the themes of Walras's three main works: *Éléments, Études d'économie sociale* and this volume, *Études d'économie politique appliquée*.

Walras's aim was to provide an economic blueprint for a social ideal where poverty and similar evils could be banished. His three main books include all the elements necessary 'to complete the mathematical theory of economic equilibrium'. Unfortunately, this synthesis was never developed, but the current book sheds light upon this point, providing a unique insight into Léon Walras's mind and a better understanding of his *Éléments*.

This translation was prepared under the auspices of the Centre Auguste et Léon Walras, Université Lyon-2. Most of the annotations are translations of those by Jean-Pierre Potier (Centre Walras) in *Études d'économie politique appliqué* (Paris: Economica, 1992). These notes and the translator's introduction make the book independently readable.

Jan van Daal is an expert on the life and works of Léon Walras. A former member of the Econometric Institute of the Erasmus University Rotterdam, he is now at the Centre Walras. He has also written on such diverse subjects as the work of H. H. Gossen, traffic models in Dutch inland navigation, aggregation problems and demand systems.

Studies in Applied Economics

Theory of the production of social wealth

Volume I

Léon Walras

Translated and introduced by
Jan van Daal

Routledge
Taylor & Francis Group
LONDON AND NEW YORK

English translation first published 2005
by Routledge
2 Park Square, Milton Park, Abingdon, Oxon OX14 4RN

Simultaneously published in the USA and Canada
by Routledge
605 Third Avenue, New York, NY 10017

Routledge is an imprint of the Taylor & Francis Group, an informa business

British Library Cataloguing in Publication Data
A catalogue record for this book is available from the British Library

Library of Congress Cataloging in Publication Data
A catalog record for this book has been requested

ISBN 13: 9781041275411 (pbk) (volume I)
ISBN 13: 9781041275428 (pbk) (volume II)
ISBN 13: 9780415654296 (two-volume set)

Contents

Preface

Unlike French and Italian writings on Léon Walras's œuvre, English papers and books on this subject deal more often with issues based only on his *Éléments d'économie politique pure* (first published in 1874; for all bibliographical details see the References after the Introduction).[1] The *Éléments* is Walras's only book translated into English till now (by William Jaffé, under the title *Elements of Pure Economics*, 1954). Of course, this splendid and extremely important book may very fruitfully be studied on its own, but Walras had more to say. To place his *Éléments* in the context of his whole work, and to grasp the essence of his message, knowledge of his other writings is required, including normative and applied economics. In particular, this will give the reader an understanding of the *Leitmotif*, the final *raison d'être* of Walras's *œuvre*.[2] A good overview and a clear picture of all his work will reduce the risk of research on Walras becoming biased and unbalanced. This risk may be expected to increase rather than decrease, since worldwide knowledge of French is far from expanding. It seemed useful therefore to provide a translation of Walras's other two main books, *Études d'économie politique appliquée* (*Théorie de la production de la richesse sociale*) (1898) and *Études d'économie sociale* (*Théorie de la répartition de la richesse sociale*) (1896). Almost all of his research would then be available in English, enough to understand what he was trying to say.

1 Less than 10 per cent of the 136 papers in the four collections of papers in English on Walras published up to now (Walker 1983, 2001b; Blaug 1992; Cunningham Wood 1992; see the references to the Introduction, below) deal with other subjects. In somewhat more of these papers such other topics are mentioned but not further examined. The French papers presented at the first three colloquies (1999, 2000 and 2002) of the International Walras Association deal nearly 50 per cent with other subjects. I have the impression that this figure applies roughly to the whole French/Italian literature on Léon Walras. Jolink (1991, 1996), Walker (1996) and Bridel (1997), however, are examples of studies in English of Walras's *œuvre* based on more than Jaffé's translation of the *Éléments* only.

2 This has been made evident in Albert Jolink's Rotterdam thesis, *Liberté, égalité, rareté* (1991).

The idea of translating these volumes arose around 1994 in the Centre Auguste et Léon Walras, Université Lyon-2. There I was then working with three colleague-friends on Walras's translation (1879) of Hermann-Heinrich Gossen's book *Entwickelung der Gesetze des menschlichen Verkehrs und der daraus fließenden Regeln für menschliches Handeln* (1854; English translation: Gossen 1983). This French translation, considered as being lost, had been found again some years before in Turin. We edited it and had it published (Gossen 1995). Working on Gossen, I increasingly realized that making texts of our discipline's pioneers available and accessible is at least as important as contributing to the secondary literature and, moreover, I began to enjoy this kind of work. Thus, after talking to many people, I decided to plunge into this very deep water and started translating into English the second edition (1936) of Walras's *Études d'économie politique appliquée*, together with most of the notes, compiled by Jean-Pierre Potier from the most recent French edition (a variorum edition published in 1992 as volume X of *Auguste et Léon Walras: œuvres économiques complètes*, Economica, Paris, 1987–2004, prepared, introduced and annotated by Jean-Pierre Potier of the Centre Walras). The decision to try it myself, being an economist rather than a translator, was supported by the publisher, who preferred economics from an economist in economists' English ('proofread' afterwards by a professional translator) to bad economics in superior English. So I started the work by the end of 1995.

For translating a complicated book like Léon Walras's *Études d'économie politique appliquée* into English a number of conditions in terms of abilities, knowledge and circumstances have to be satisfied which can hardly be satisfied simultaneously by one and the same person. I mention: (1) working knowledge of French and English, (2) knowledge of the one of these languages at the level of a mother tongue, (3) knowledge of the theory and history of economic science, (4) knowledge of Léon Walras's work in particular, (5) knowledge of mathematics, (6) knowledge of the (economic) history of the nineteenth century, (7) material possibilities in terms of time and money, (8) eagerness to execute the work. A number of these conditions I do fulfil sufficiently. One, I believe, I do not meet at all and some others not adequately. So it was impossible to do the work without some aid. Fortunately I found Jean-Pierre Potier more than willing to read and comment on the whole translation. His suggestions have really improved the text. Then I was so fortunate as to meet Alison Coulavin-Simmers, a retired professor of English language at Grenoble. She helped me to change my English into real English, her native language, and went thereby much further than I dared hope. It is a pleasure to me to thank Alison and Jean-Pierre for their support, suggestions and friendship.

In this respect, I should not forget to mention the Economics Faculty of the Erasmus University Rotterdam. They were so generous as to finance my numerous trips all over the world and even continued to do so after I moved from the Netherlands to France in 1995 and only kept a (very) little part-time appointment. When I finally retired, in 2002, they surprised me with a handsome last grant to help finance the translation project. Grateful as I am for that, I must say there was one thing I appreciated still more. From the mid-1980s onwards, the Faculty gave me the opportunity to make my hobbies, the history of economics in general and Walras in particular, more and more the main subject of my professional research, for which they even changed my appointment. So I turned from an econometrician into a historian of economics. I remember this period of about ten years as a most fruitful and productive one, the best part of it being the work for Albert Jolink's PhD thesis, which I had the pleasure to supervise. One way or another we created a wonderful research environment which stimulated us to intensive, creative study of our subjects. The result was much more than a thesis only. I could never have brought the present translation to a conclusion without those ten Rotterdam years.

Of course, my thanks go further. Sophia Wunderink-van Veen (Technological University Delft), Nol Merkies (Free University, Amsterdam), Donald Walker (Indiana University, Pennsylvania) and Jean-Pierre Potier read and commented on the whole Introduction. Their comments and suggestions gave rise to many improvements in the text (and in some cases much extension). I thank them for this thoughtful interest in my work. I acknowledge also that I benefited from the know-how on Walras accumulated in the Centre Walras–Pareto of the University of Lausanne, where Léon Walras's manuscripts and his personal library are preserved. I remember with much delight the openmindedness and hospitality from the Centre's director, Pascal Bridel, and the other members.

This work has been executed under the auspices of the Centre Auguste and Léon Walras of the Université Lyon-2. I am very grateful for the sympathetic reception, hospitality and friendship I met with, both from the Centre's three subsequent directors, Pierre Dockès, Jean-Michel Servet, Gérard Klotz, and the other members. In addition to Jean-Pierre Potier, Pierre Dockès, Pierre-Henri Goutte and Claude Mouchot particularly were always willing to put their knowledge of Walras and his work, (economic) history, philosophy and methodology at my disposal. I like to imagine that Léon Walras would have been greatly satisfied that in 'his and his father's Centre' at Lyon the idea emerged and developed of an English translation of another of his three famous books. Let us hope that the last will soon follow.

Jan van Daal
La Chapelle en Vercors
31 March 2004

Abbreviations and notes on the text

Abbreviations

ŒEC	*Auguste et Léon Walras: œuvres économiques complètes*
Éléments	*Éléments d'économie politique pure*
EEPA	*Études d'économie politique appliquée*
EES	*Études d'économie sociale*

Notes on the text

Text within square brackets has been added by the translator.

Footnotes (with arabic numbering) are by Léon Walras himself.

Notes at the end of each chapter (with Roman numerals) are mostly translations of notes by Jean-Pierre Potier in the Potier edition of the *Études d'économie politique appliqué.* All other endnotes have been added by the translator; they are marked with an asterisk: *.

The numbers in bold type within square brackets in the text denote the pagination of the second edition (1936) of the *Études d'économie politique appliquée*, which is identical to that of the first edition.

The translator has adapted, or inserted, the numbering of formulae, graphs and tables where necessary; further he added captions.

Walras's graphs were originally printed on separate pages as plates. In *EEPA* there are three such plates. Here the graphs appear in context.

Introduction

This introduction is intended to serve two purposes; first, it will possibly help to understand how the *Études d'économie politique appliquée* fits within the whole of Walras's work. Second, together with the endnotes of each chapter it may perhaps make the book more or less self-contained. In Section 1 the reader will find some facts about Léon Walras himself and his time. In Section 2 his general ideas about science, social science and economics are briefly dealt with; here I also discuss how Walras's three main books fit into the framework of his economic ideas. Section 3 is intended to give an impression of Walras's pure and social economics. Section 4 contains the story of how the *Études d'économie politique appliquée* came into being. A summary of the book can be found in Section 5.

I added four appendices. Appendix A is on Walras's terminology concerning capital goods and services. Appendix B contains a chronological list of the papers forming the *Études d'économie politique appliquée*. Appendix C gives information on the fourteen volumes of *Auguste et Léon Walras: œuvres économiques complètes* (Économica, Paris, 1987–2004). Appendix D is a list of correspondences between the (identical) paginations of the first and second edition of the *Études d'économie politique appliquée* and the Potier edition. In the present translation I have indicated by bold numbers between brackets running from 1 to 495 the pagination of the first and second edition; this enables the reader to compare any passage of the translation with the corresponding passage in any French version.

1 Léon Walras

1.1 Facts of his life

Léon Walras was born in Évreux (Normandy) in 1834. Around 1853 he went to Paris, where, in 1854, he became a student at the École des Mines. Inspired by his father, the economist Antoine-Auguste Walras (1801–66), he was highly interested in the so-called 'Social Question', that is, the enormous problem of how to elevate the poor from their misery. This and his unconventional demeanour when he was young made him hardly fit to become a mining engineer, and so he was a student only in name. Instead he more envisaged a career as a man of letters. This, he thought, would be the best way to put himself at the service of the Social Question. Indeed, in the first six years of his residence in Paris he produced a novel, entitled *Francis Saveur* (Walras 1858; a long love story with a lengthy introduction on the Social Question and other topics), a short story, 'La Lettre' (Walras 1859), and several other pieces of writing expressing his ideas. In fact, he vainly tried to serve two masters at the same time, namely Literature and the Social Question. The reaction of the public was not encouraging, and, therefore, trying to make a living out of these activities appeared inappropriate.

The reaction of his father, Auguste Walras, an able literary man himself, was severe, but not altogether negative. On one hand, Auguste judged Literature (with a capital L) unsuitable for his son. On the other hand, however, he respected Léon's ambitions concerning the Social Question. So he suggested him to set up a career as a publicist on socio-economic matters and helped him to get a job as a sort of assistant editor of the *Journal des économistes*. Further, Auguste put his vast collection of books and unpublished writings at his son's disposal and started a comprehensive, broad correspondence on economic matters; so he provided Léon with a large number of subjects and ideas.

Twelve hard, laborious, studious years in Paris followed. From the very beginning, Léon was not only a prolific writer, but also tried to put his ideas into practice – for instance, his work for the co-operative movement (see Walras 1990). During this period, he wrote altogether about eighty books, articles, brochures and other papers (Walker 1987b). His preoccupation appears right from his very first book on an economic subject (Walras 1860), which started with a long, thorough introductory essay on the Social Question (see also Walras 2001: 77–143). Nevertheless, it was difficult to earn a living, because, to put it mildly, his writings did not always meet with general approval. There were several failures and only a few successes. One of these, however, was decisive for the rest of his career. In 1860 he participated in a conference on taxation in Lausanne, where he attracted some attention. There he came into contact with a young Swiss lawyer, Louis Ruchonnet. They became friends and met several times afterwards. Ruchonnet's career developed successfully and by 1870 he was head of the Vaud department of education in Switzerland, where he was in charge of the reorganization of the Academy (later, University) of Lausanne. He suggested Léon Walras should apply for the new professorship of economics. Indeed, Walras was nominated, in spite of the fact that he had no academic degrees and made no secret of his interest in the Social Question. So his accession to the professorship was not a walkover. The nominating committee (some members originated from elsewhere in Switzerland or abroad) had serious hesitations. Eventually, three of the seven members considered his allegedly socialist ideas and activities insurmountable for the function. So in the first instance he was nominated for only one year, with the lowest possible majority of the committee. On 16 December 1870, his thirty-sixth birthday, he started his lectures. In Lausanne itself the administrators were more open-minded, and a year later he was given tenure by a simple State Council decree. He was a dutiful but unexciting lecturer who wrote out all his lectures to read them in full (Walras 1996). In 1892 he retired from lecturing because of ill health. However, he continued his research until about 1900. He died in 1910.

1.2 Professional life

From his arrival in Lausanne onwards, Walras led the seemingly uneventful life of a man of learning. The intellectual climate there gave him enough freedom for independent research and teaching. With the exception of a number of trips to France, he travelled little. Nevertheless, his international contacts were wide and varied: during his career, he wrote or received about 8,000 letters, many of them to or from abroad.

His research brought him fame, in particular that on general economic equilibrium, though he did much more. In so doing he never forgot his point of departure: the Social Question, thereby mainly focusing upon his native country. Léon Walras was certainly not the only person in the nineteenth century to feel sorry for the people living in misery; nor was he the only man eager to contribute to the solution of this Social Question. The appalling living circumstances of the poor, not only in France, could not be ignored by anyone walking in his neighbourhood. Moreover, it was well known that the revolutions in France of 1789, 1830 and 1848 had found some of their roots in this misery (without having helped much, because the political system did, in fact, not change substantially). Workers' wages of two francs per day were quite normal at the beginning of Walras's career. (This was somewhat less than one-quarter of the (modest) salary he received in 1870 as an untenured professor.) More than half the workers' wages had to be spent on food, of which the major part consisted of bread and other cereal products. The price of bread fluctuated wildly at the time, with an average of about 0.30 F per kilogram of inferior quality (the *pain bis-blanc*).

Walras thought at first that he could help by acting upon the minds of people living in better circumstances. Apparently he hoped that by making their minds more open to the problem, people would be incited 'to do something'. However, the instrument of Literature appeared unsuitable in his hands and fortunately he was stopped right at the beginning. As such, in the hands of able novelists like Honoré de Balzac and Émile Zola, it was certainly not inappropriate. All these and other men of letters, whether *manqués* like Walras or not, had a vital point: misery (or, to call it by its proper name, pauperism) had already persisted so long, from generation to generation, that the poor themselves were no longer in a position to improve their situation by their own strength, given the low level of their mental attitude and physical condition and the political, social and economic circumstances at that time. Maintaining this basic idea, Walras changed his instrument and restricted the group to be approached. As a publicist on socio-economic subjects, and soon a social scientist in his own right, long before his arrival in Lausanne, even, he first addressed himself directly to scientists and students, and, more indirectly, to politicians to try to convince them that both economic conditions and social justice should be changed and improved.

In Walras's time there were, roughly speaking, two groups of social scientists in France who studied the same problems as he did: the 'Socialists' and the 'Economists', a typically French distinction; see Walras 1860 (2001: 101ff.). In the translation I have used the term 'the economists', where necessary, instead of 'economists'; see, e.g. pp. 14 and 53 below. Walras did not consider himself as belonging to either of them but took a middle position, although he did this in a way that caused both groups' disapproval.

The socialists were in general of the opinion that the existing social order was to be blamed for poverty; we would now perhaps call them anti-globalists in a sense. In particular they opposed freedom of trade (in nearly every sense of the term) and private ownership of all means of production.[1] Walras's problem with these people was that they all proposed actions to alleviate misery that were based on ideals rather than well considered, rational principles. They all tried to reform society in a way they believed to be beneficial to the poor by attacking free competition and private ownership of production factors.

The economists were the champions of the existing order; they occupied the chairs of economics in the French institutions of higher education, which 'they passed on from father to son, uncle to nephew or father-in-law to son-in-law' as Walras more or less rightly asserted (Walras 1965, Letter 428, to Jules Ferry, 9 February 1879). He also accused them of having a 'theory' of economics consisting of only four words: *laisser-faire, laisser-passer*, to be applied to every aspect of economic life; see, for instance, Chapter 8 below. According to the economists, all exchange should take place under free competition. Here too, the scientific underpinning was not impeccable, to say the least. Of course, they did not ignore the Social Question, but, in some sense, they seemed to lay the responsibility for solving the problem at the paupers' own door. They blamed them for lack of education and hygiene, for instance.

In the light of these considerations it is not surprising that Walras's most important scientific work can be summarized for the greater part as follows. First, he thoroughly investigated the conditions and characteristics of free competition. To that end he devised a series of mathematical models of increasing complexity where exchange and production are supposed to take place under a regime of free competition and capital is owned by private persons. The basic subjects of analysis are here the *individual* consumers. Walras believed that if one wants to elevate the poor to better conditions one must devise a theoretical economic framework in which each person, or at last each family is considered as a separate entity because everyone's happiness counts, happiness being largely determined by the degree to which a household is provided with consumer goods and services. This part of his research is well known and is set out in his *Éléments d'économie politique pure, ou théorie de la richesse sociale* (first edition, in two instalments, 1874–7; henceforth called *Éléments* for short). In the *Éléments* the theory of general economic equilibrium under the regime of free competition is presented, with utility maximization as a prominent element. His conclusion was that, indeed, free competition is so advantageous that it should be the rule, *if possible*; see Section 3 of this introduction.

Second, he investigated therefore where free competition is possible and where not. It is self-evident and right, he said, for free competition to be the rule if possible, i.e. when the goods are private goods and the number of suppliers is large. For such situations he advocated a kind of regulated free competition, a framework of rules in which the economic agents interact in relative freedom. Further, he investigated where free competition is impossible and monopoly appears a more plausible form of market organization. Such monopolies should be carefully regulated in order that the advantages of free competition be preserved as much as possible. This is dealt with in the *Études d'économie politique appliquée* (*Théorie de la production de la richesse sociale*) (1898), which also contains other issues whose correct establishment is necessary for a smooth course of the economic process: money, credit, banking and the stock exchange.

Third, Walras wondered whether private ownership of all means of production is in agreement with social justice. This study brought him to the conclusion that in the ideal situation the State owns the land and hires it out competitively to its users. So the State gets an income, and taxes can be abolished in the (very) long run. The *Études d'économie sociale* (*Théorie de la répartition de la richesse sociale*) (1896) is for a large part devoted to this topic.

Most economists have restricted their attention to Walras's *Éléments* only, in particular to its last edition (the posthumous one, 1926). There are several reasons for this nearly exclusive attention. First, Walras himself gave much care to it, as appears from the fact that during his lifetime he published four editions of the book (1874–7, 1889, 1896, 1900), altering, rearranging and supplementing it every time. He himself presented it as his most important book. Obviously, the issue of general economic equilibrium was never out of his mind. Second, the *Éléments* was until now Walras's only book translated into English (by William Jaffé 1954). Third, he ran out of time, like so many first-generation academic economists who felt obliged to provide an overall picture of the whole field. Starting with pure theory, he did not succeed in completing the other treatises he envisaged: *Éléments d'économie sociale* and *Éléments d'économie politique appliquée*. Based on his lectures on social and applied economics (see Walras 1996), these had to be just as comprehensive and systematic as the *Éléments d'économie politique pure*. Instead however, feeling his strength waving, he consolidated the substance of his other research in the *Études d'économie sociale* and the *Études d'économie politique appliquée*. Both volumes consist of a collection of existing papers. In that form they could not compete with the *Éléments d'économie politique pure* and therefore the latter book received most of the attention. The *four* editions of the *Éléments* and the two *Études* contain the essence of Walras's work.

2 General ideas about science, social science and economics

2.1 Social science

The society Walras aimed to study was simply the one in which he lived. He took it for granted and analysed, stylized and modelled it as such. The starting point of his research was therefore the fact that a person living in that society was so specialized that he or she was unable to obtain all the necessities of life independently. Hence people were dependent on each other because they had to exchange goods and services. According to Walras, there are then two main categories in society to be distinguished, studied, analysed and co-ordinated: (1) things worthwhile to be exchanged (called 'social wealth') and (2) persons, in particular their rights and duties *vis-à-vis* each other (*Théorie générale de la société. Leçons publiques faites à Paris*, 1867–68, second lesson; Walras 1990: 49ff.; see also Jolink 1996: 68). This may be elucidated by means of Figure 0.1.[2]

Pure economics, Walras said, deals with the nature, causes and laws of social wealth; applied economics deals with the production of this wealth. Social economics, also called moral economics by Walras, deals with the distribution of social wealth among the members of society and has to do with both social wealth and human rights (in particular social justice). From the 1870s onwards Walras concentrated on the first three topics of the fourth column in Figure 0.1. Furthermore, he brought in his reflections on science in general, which may be illustrated by means of Figure 0.2.

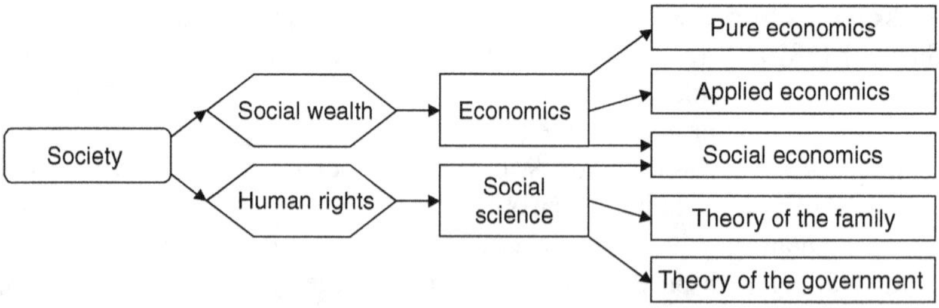

Figure 0.1 Society and its sciences.

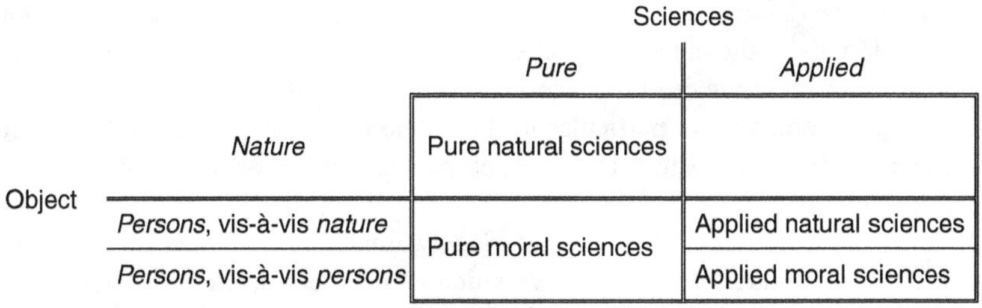

Figure 0.2 Walras's classification of science.

The idea expressed by Figure 0.2 is explained by Walras in several places throughout his work, inclusive of his *Éléments*. In his *Mélanges d'économie politique et sociale* (1987), for instance, the following passage, dating from 1879, can be read:

> *Pure* science establishes facts and relations; *applied* science prescribes rules of conduct. There exist *pure natural* sciences, studying facts and relations which have their origin in the play of the fatal forces of nature and *pure moral* sciences, studying facts and relations originating from the exercise of man's free will.... There exist *applied natural* sciences, providing rules of conduct for man *vis-à-vis* impersonal things and *applied moral* sciences, providing rules of conduct for people *vis-à-vis* each other.
> (1987: 414; Walras's italics)

The upper right cell of the figure is empty because it does not make sense to speak about rules of conduct for nature *vis-à-vis* persons or itself. Pure sciences are for instance mathematics, physics, chemistry and philosophy. Examples of applied natural sciences dealing with the relation Man–Things are geodesy, pharmacology and medicine. Applied moral sciences, dealing with relations Man–Man, are, for example, law, ethics and theology. Applied sciences must be preceded by and based upon one or more pure sciences. Considering Part I of the *Éléments*, it seems that Figure 0.2 has overridden Figure 0.1.

So, according to Walras, we have not simply the partition theory versus practice. There are rather three stages: (1) *pure theory*, (2) *applied theory, or theory of the art*, (3) *practical application of the art*, where the word 'art' is to be understood in the same meaning as in the word 'artisan'.

2.2 Economics

In economics, Walras says, the main fact to be explained is exchange of material or immaterial things which are both useful and limited in quantity. Walras reserved the adjective 'scarce' for such things, whose entirety he called 'Social Wealth'; see *Éléments*, Preface (1988: 11). In the first instance, Walras was not as explicit about the distinction between flows and stocks as Adam Smith was in the very first sentence of the *Wealth of Nations*, which begins with words that are most interesting, in particular to the econometrician: 'The *annual* labour of every nation . . . ' (Smith 1994: lix; emphasis added). Walras must certainly have read this.

The phenomenon of exchange is closely linked to (1) value in exchange (price), (2) production, or industry, which can be seen from both a technical and an economic point of view, and (3) property. In Walras's opinion, value in exchange is a natural fact because things are limited in quantity by nature, independent of our psychological freedom. This does not mean that we do not have any control over prices as natural facts. However, just as we respect gravity's laws, we should respect those of exchange, since we are unable to change them. In Walras's view, both property and industry arise from the exercise of human will. Industry belongs to the category of manifestations of human will over natural forces. Property is a manifestation of human will over other people's will or actions. See also *Éléments*, §19 (1988: 41–2). For economic science, Figure 0.2 can then be specified as shown in Figure 0.3.

Walras's principal scientific work as can be found in his three main treatises, *Éléments d'économie politique pure*, *Études d'économie sociale* and *Études d'économie politique appliquée* (*Éléments*, *EES* and *EEPA* for short, respectively), can be placed in Figure 0.4, deduced from Figure 0.3. These figures not only indicate the relationships between the various components of Léon Walras's research, but they also seem to impose a certain order with respect to their timing. If in certain applied work one needs some theory, then that theory must exist already. We shall see below that in the case of Walras's work on applied monetary theory, indeed, he made use of the theory he had developed previously. However, he used now and then elements (like the 'economic tides'; see Chapter 2 below) that lacked theory and he did not always revise applied work in the light of further development of his theory.

		Economics	
		Pure	*Applied*
Object	*Nature*	Pure natural economics	
	Persons, vis-à-vis *nature*	Pure moral economics	Applied natural economics
	Persons, vis-à-vis *persons*		Applied moral economics

Figure 0.3 Walras's classification of economics.

<table>
<tr><th></th><th></th><th colspan="2">Texts</th></tr>
<tr><th></th><th></th><th>*Pure economics*</th><th>*Applied economics*</th></tr>
<tr><td rowspan="3">Object</td><td>*Nature*</td><td>*Éléments d'économie politique pure*</td><td></td></tr>
<tr><td>*Persons*, vis-à-vis *nature*</td><td rowspan="2">*Études d'économie sociale*
Part I</td><td>*Études d'économie politique appliquée*</td></tr>
<tr><td>*Persons*, vis-à-vis *persons*</td><td>*Études d'économie sociale*
Parts II, III, IV</td></tr>
</table>

Figure 0.4 Walras's three main treatises within the framework of Figure 0.3.

3 Pure economics and social economics

A thorough comprehension of the *EEPA*, and, incidentally, the *EES*, requires some knowledge of Walras's pure theory of economics. He himself says as much in the last sentence of the *Éléments*: '[T]he general principles which we have considered here are more than enough for the elaboration of the theories of social economics and applied economics which we have in view' (*Éléments*, §408; 1954: 459).

In this section, I shall therefore sketch the main points of Léon Walras's pure theory. It must be observed that at the time of publication of *EEPA* (1898), the fourth edition (1900) of the *Éléments* did not yet exist, nor were there important pre-publications of this edition's new features or letters in which they were announced.[3] In the next subsection I try to elucidate what Léon Walras meant by 'free competition'. In subsections 3.2–3 I shall go somewhat deeper into the matter of general economic equilibrium; these subsections all lean heavily on the *Éléments*.

Finally, in subsection 3.4 I shall present a short outline of some of the main points of Walras's social economics: his plan for the nationalization of land and the abolition of taxes.

3.1 Free competition

According to Walras, free competition means that demanders and suppliers of goods and services are free to engage in processes of haggling in all markets, and that entrepreneurs are free to enter or withdraw from every branch of industry, guided by their expectations about profits or losses. All these activities take place simultaneously and influence each other. Free competition is so to speak a self-regulating mechanism that brings about equilibrium in the markets at unique prices for all goods and services, and equality of selling and cost prices of the products for all branches of industry. It should be noted that Walras's notion of production costs agrees completely with modern notions and comprises therefore a remuneration of everything that has contributed to production. Walras's enterprises are therefore quite able to make ends meet, both at present and in the long run when they sell their products just at cost price. Walras was interested both in free competition's final result, i.e. the equilibrium situation, and in the process of bringing about this equilibrium, i.e. what actually happens in the markets.

Regarding the question 'Was Léon Walras a proponent of unlimited free competition?' the answer should be: 'Not at all!' On the very first page of his very first analytical publication on the subject, a paper presented at a meeting of Parisian colleagues in 1873 (see Walras 1874a), he made his position clear. He said he was going to study theoretically how the production and exchange of goods and services take place 'under the regime of the most free competition, the most absolute *laisser-faire, laisser-passer*, not counting any consideration of interest or justice'. However, he continues, 'I am certainly not saying [that I am doing this] because free competition would be more useful or more equitable, but only to find out what would happen.' *Laisser-faire, laisser-passer*, i.e. free competition under all circumstances, was the order of the day among 'the economists' in Walras's time and was abhorred by the 'socialists'. Both groups restricted themselves to slogan-mongering instead of underpinning their opinions with arguments. Here Walras saw a task for himself. He compared thereby his position with that of a medical researcher who tries to learn everything about a certain drug, not because he wants it to be used in all circumstances, but in order to know when to prescribe it as a doctor and when not to do so. See, for instance, the letter to W. Lexis of 17 March 1883 (Walras 1965, letter 548). Therefore he set out to find the conditions and consequences of free competition, which were to become the core of his pure theory.

3.2 General economic equilibrium

To make things more comprehensible, Walras stylized the economic process as a sequence of periods of time in which production and trade take place as determined by the working of a carefully devised mathematical model that was to mirror reality as accurately as possible.[4] He did this for two reasons. First, he hoped to gain more insight into the working of the economic world of his time. Second, he hoped that it could serve as a theoretical basis for social reform, as we know.

At the outset of a period the quantities of capital of each individual capital owner are given, as well as the model's parameters, i.e. the technology (the production functions), consumers' preferences (the utility functions) and the composition of the population. Given this initial situation, the model tries to depict people's behaviour, which ends up in the period's equilibrium. New, endogenously determined quantities of capital goods result at the end of the period. Together with the (possibly changed) parameters, these capital goods form the initial conditions for the next period. A new equilibrium emerges, and this goes on from period to period. Apparently, capital endogenously transmits wealth to the next period.

Like his father, Léon Walras drew a distinction between consumer goods and capital goods, i.e. production factors. He thereby distinguished three types of capital: (1) 'land'; (2) 'human capital'; (3) 'capital Proper' (fixed capital: houses, machines, etc., and circulating capital: stocks of products and money). See Appendix A to this introduction for an overview of Walras's special terminology with regard to capital and its services. The entrepreneurs hire capital of all three types, or, to be more precise, they buy the services of this capital during the period in question. One of the entrepreneurs' tasks is to take care that the services thus bought are transformed into consumer goods and proper capital goods, though they are not necessarily the actual producers. The price for these services the entrepreneurs pay to the capital owners is used by the latter to buy consumer goods, from the former, or to save. Accordingly, there are four types of agents: (1) landowners; (2) workers; (3) capitalists; (4) entrepreneurs. Two or more of these types may be united in one person. The word 'capitalist' is used to indicate a person possessing proper capital (i.e. category 3 above), while the words 'capital owner' denote a person owning some capital of whatever category. Hence a capitalist is always a capital owner, but a capital owner is not necessarily a capitalist. Note that, in fact, every individual is a capital owner, because he disposes of physical or mental abilities.

Walras clearly pointed out that in the competitive markets of his most general model:

- Demanders will bid higher prices in the event of excess demand and suppliers will ask lower prices in the event of excess supply, which will eventually reduce excess demand and supply in all markets of goods and services to zero in equilibrium.
- In a branch where the cost price is higher than the selling price, entrepreneurs will decrease production or leave the industry, and the opposite will take place if the cost price is lower than the selling price, which will make each product's cost price equal to its selling price and bring profit rates to zero in equilibrium.
- The use of capital services will be shifted from one branch to another by the entrepreneurs and the quantities produced of new capital will be changed

until eventually the ratios of the net revenue per unit of each capital good and its selling (cost) price are the same for all capital goods, which will make the total amount of gross savings equal to the total value of newly produced capital and all capital goods equally profitable in equilibrium.
- This same ratio, finally, will be the equilibrium rate of interest that equalizes total demand and supply in the money market in equilibrium.

These four points together describe a situation of general economic equilibrium in its most comprehensive form. They result from the mathematical model.

This mathematical model consists of two parts, a static and a 'dynamic' one. The latter is very special and has to do with what Walras called *tâtonnement*, which literally means a process of trial and error to reach a certain goal; this French word has become standard in the literature. *Tâtonnement* will be dealt with in subsection 3.3. Let us first concentrate on the static part, a system of equations, together with their underpinning. The solution of these equations yields the aforementioned situation of general economic equilibrium: prices, wages and the rate of interest at which the markets clear (demand equals supply); further, they yield the market-clearing quantities of all goods and services.

In the remainder of this subsection I shall deal somewhat more with the details of the equations. In the underpinning of these equations, Walras paid most of his attention to consumers' behaviour. Since the capital goods are owned solely by the individual consumers (landowners, workers and capitalists), the entrepreneurs can provide themselves with capital services only by renting land from the landowners, employing workers or hiring capital proper. Of course, as we have already stated, combinations of two or more of the roles of landowner, worker, capitalist or entrepreneur in one person may exist.

Selling capital services procures the individual landowners, workers and capitalists an income, which enables them to buy consumer goods and capital services for their own use, and to repair or replace pieces of capital in order to keep their stock at the same level as at the beginning of the period. The rest of this income consists, by definition, of net savings (which can be positive, zero or negative). Léon Walras assumed that net savings would be used by the individual capital owner to buy newly produced capital proper, which assures him a future income increase. In the first three editions of the *Éléments* Walras did not work out this idea. He simply added the variable i to the variables of his equations, the inverse of i being the price of future additional income. In the fourth edition he was more specific on this point. Then, three kinds of arguments (instead of two) appear in his individual utility functions: first, the quantities of the various consumer goods; second, the quantities of the services of the various capital goods to be consumed by the individual himself;[5] third (the new element), the amount of expected additional future income, whose price equals $1/i$. By introducing present utility of the expectation of future additional income, Walras was able to bring himself 'as close as possible to the dynamic point of view . . . without abandoning the static point of view' (*Éléments*, fourth and fifth editions, §272; 1988: 441). Here 'inter-period dynamics' is meant, in contradistinction to the 'intra-period dynamics' of *tâtonnement*; see subsection 3.3). From these utility functions Walras derived individual demand and supply functions, by assuming that the consumers maximize utility, given their income and the prices. The theoretical refinement did not influence the final mathematical form of the equations, however. One may consider these demand and supply functions as schedules from which the consumer can infer, at every price configuration, the magnitudes of the various goods and services that will yield him maximum utility at these prices. With these schedules in mind, as it were, he enters the markets. The schedules are aggregated, i.e. summed up per good or service over all consumers, and these aggregates enter as equations into the model. (The aggregation problems involved are dealt with in van Daal and Walker 1990.)

The production side of the economy is less developed, because Walras simply supposed so-called *constant coefficients of production*. This means that he assumed that for the production of each unit of any product fixed quantities of the productive services are needed, irrespective of the level of production. It may be that in Walras's time this was not as arguable as it appears to be now. Anyway, the result is a set of relatively simple production functions.

These production equations and the (aggregated) demand and supply equations are combined with equations expressing the final result of free competition: market clearing for all goods and services and for money, equality of selling price and cost price of each product, equality of the interest rate to the ratio of net revenue and cost price of every capital good. The resulting equation system is in fact a macroeconomic model and thus not so big, or, at any rate surveyable; note that the demand and supply equations are meticulously derived from microeconomic theory. (For more details refer to van Daal and Jolink 1993: appendix IV.) The variables are prices (including the wages and the rate of interest) and the *aggregate* (total) quantities of the goods and services. Using the individual demand and supply equations, these quantities can be split up per individual consumer, indicating the amounts of goods and services that maximize his utility, given these equilibrium prices. Hence, in such a situation of general economic equilibrium, profits being zero, *all utility goes direct to the consumers to a degree depending for each individual on his initial situation and his eagerness to obtain goods*. For Walras this meant an ideal situation, provided that the initial circumstances are right. The real situation, however, was far from ideal at the time. Two things had to be done therefore. First, free competition should be maintained or established where possible, and in those markets where it was impossible such market organization and regulations should be applied that the outcome of the market process would resemble that of free competition (*EEPA*). Second, the initial situation of many individuals should be changed – not by giving them personally more or fewer endowments but by changing economic and social circumstances (*EES*).

For Léon Walras one of the most important issues concerning his mathematical models was the problem of the existence of a solution to his systems of equations. This existence is indeed important because it makes the coherence of Walras's theory more plausible. He considered it as guaranteed by the equality of the numbers of variables and independent equations of the model. This criterion was quite standard among economists and mathematicians at the time. Nowadays existence proofs have to meet the most rigorous standards of modern advanced mathematics; see van Daal (1998).

We have just described Walras's most complicated and complete model. He had a whole sequence of them, from simple to highly complicated, and was therefore one of the first economists to make use of the method of decreasing abstraction for pedagogical reasons. For Léon Walras the basic economic phenomenon was exchange, between freely competing parties, of scarce, useful goods, and therefore he saw as his basic task the explanation of the ratios of exchange, i.e. the prices. Consequently, neither the Robinson Crusoe economy nor the two-goods-two-exchangers economy was an appropriate starting point for his analysis. His assumption of free competition may look, indeed, more reasonable if each good or service be offered and demanded by groups of persons. Therefore the number of agents in his models is always arbitrary and supposed to be (considerably) more than one. After the introductory Part I of the *Éléments*, he started model building in Part II with a model with only two commodities, (A) and (B). One part of the people possess only commodity (A) and want to exchange this good partly or completely for some quantity of a commodity (B) owned by the rest of the people, who, in their turn, want to exchange this for commodity (A). These exchanges take place, of course, under a regime of free competition: prices are raised in the event of excess demand and lowered in the event of excess supply. See on this point Walker (1996), where, incidentally, it has been made clear that it is the people themselves who determine prices and not some authority above the groups; see also subsection 3.3. Adding up the individual demand curves, based on utility maximization, Walras obtained so-called aggregate demand functions for (A) and (B) with prices as variables, and from these he came to aggregate supply functions for (B) and (A), respectively. In equilibrium there is equality of aggregate demand and supply of both goods. This model was extended, in Part II of the *Éléments*, into a model of exchange of an arbitrary number of goods.

Walras's next step (Part IV of the *Éléments*) was building his so-called 'model of production', in which only consumer goods are produced, by using the services of land, human capital and proper capital goods (i.e. no circulating capital).[6] Production is, as we know, characterized by fixed coefficients of production. In this model all capital services are used up either in the production of consumer goods or in personal use by their owners (production factors being supposed everlasting in this model). The model of production was enlarged in Part V to the so-called 'model of capital formation' in which the production of capital goods proper was incorporated.[7] Finally, in Part VI the model of capital formation was expanded into two models, one with circulating capital and fiat money (paper money, for example) and one with circulating capital and commodity-based money (gold, for example). All these models, except the final one, were intended as pedagogical devices, to explain the last one, which was to be used for policy recommendations.

3.3 Tâtonnement

Though *tâtonnement* is only twice mentioned in the *EEPA* (103, 338), I believe I should deal with it here, for completeness's sake. Moreover, where the *EEPA* deals mainly with markets, we cannot neglect a so important an element of Walras's notion of them. There is considerable difference between Walras's *tâtonnement* and what is called Walrasian *tâtonnement* in the literature. As it stands now, Walras would hardly have recognized modern *tâtonnement.* For instance, Walras's *tâtonnement* has nothing to do with inter-period dynamics. This latter kind of dynamics deals with the transition from one period to the next, in particular how the events of past periods influence those of future periods. In my opinion, it is often in the context of inter-period dynamics that *tâtonnement* has been (mis)understood in the literature. Where this interpretation seems to be incorrect, it is not surprising that *tâtonnement* has started its own life and evolved in a direction that, however interesting, has nothing to do with Walras's work itself. Walras himself did not explicitly elaborate inter-period dynamics, though it was at the back of his mind. He was rather dealing with what may be called *intra*-period dynamics. He devised his *tâtonnement* as a means 'to establish that the theoretical solution and the solution of the market are identical' (*Éléments*, §124; 1988: 187, 189). In other words, his intention was to show that the outcome of the equations of the model is, indeed, the same as the outcome of the market process in the period under consideration. The essence of the process of *tâtonnement*, as developed by Walras, is that buyers will bid up the price in cases of excess demand and sellers will underbid each other in cases of excess supply, and that entrepreneurs will withdraw from industries in which they incur losses and enter those where benefits may be expected. *Tâtonnement*, for that reason, is something that takes place entirely within a period and has to do with the existence and the nature of equilibrium in that period.

The idea of Walras's *tâtonnement* is as follows. For simplicity's sake we restrict ourselves mainly to the case of simple exchange, the only one that is generally known to present-day economists. In some way or another a set $\boldsymbol{S}_1$ is announced of m prices of the various goods, numbered $1, 2, 3, \ldots, m$, to be exchanged (Walras used the word 'cried'). These prices will generally not produce equality of demand and supply in all markets. Hence they are not the equilibrium prices and no trade will take place. Starting from this set $\boldsymbol{S}_1$, Walras devised a procedure to find a second set $\boldsymbol{S}_2$ of prices that are closer to the equilibrium prices than those of the initial set. He did this in several steps. The first step was to determine another value for the first price of $\boldsymbol{S}_1$. He replaced it by one that, together with the other prices of $\boldsymbol{S}_1$, would bring about market clearance in the first market; by a mathematical argument based on the demand functions' negative slope he made it plausible that such a new price for the first good exists. The second step was replacing the second price by one that, together with the changed first price and the rest of the prices of $\boldsymbol{S}_1$, brings about equality of demand and supply in the second market; this change will most probably upset the equilibrium of the first market. The third step was replacing the third price by one that, together with the changed first and second prices and the rest of the prices of $\boldsymbol{S}_1$, brings about equality of demand and supply in the third market; this change will most probably not restore equilibrium in the first market and it will upset the just achieved equilibrium of the second market. After m steps a new set $\boldsymbol{S}_2$ is obtained. In this procedure, each equality just fulfilled is again offset by the next step. Hence $\boldsymbol{S}_2$ will in most cases not bring about general equilibrium. However, Walras gave mathematical arguments that $\boldsymbol{S}_2$ is closer to equilibrium than $\boldsymbol{S}_1$. He introduced thereby so-called primary and secondary effects on prices. The change of price i in step i of the construction of $\boldsymbol{S}_2$ he called the primary effect on price i; the changes of price i in the next steps he called the secondary effects on that price. The secondary effects on a price may be expected to be of a lower degree than the primary effect on it, Walras argued; moreover, they will not all have the same sign and may, therefore, more or less cancel each other. This brought Walras to the conclusion that $\boldsymbol{S}_2$ lies nearer to the equilibrium than $\boldsymbol{S}_1$, convinced as he was that equilibrium exists whatever the case may be.

Similarly, starting from $\boldsymbol{S}_2$, a set $\boldsymbol{S}_3$ of prices can be obtained that will bring the inequalities of demand and supply still nearer to equality, and so on. Hence, Walras concluded, there are prices that will bring about exact equality. These prices – obeying the equations of the model – are the equilibrium prices and the transactions may start. This is the process of *tâtonnement*, as Léon Walras baptized it from the first edition of the *Éléments* onwards. As he said, it reflects reasonably well outbidding and underbidding as happens in well organized markets. He was thinking thereby possibly of the Bourse de Paris, but it must be observed that the organization of this stock exchange was in reality a far cry from what has just been described above; see, for instance, Walker (2001b), who argues that what happens on the Bourse rather looks like a 'continuous market', which, in its turn, resembles Walras's 'permanent market' (*Éléments*, §322; 1988: 579–80). In particular, it is not true that on the Paris stock exchange no trade outside equilibrium occurred, or trade at different prices for the same security. It might be, however, that on the whole, and in normal circumstances, the final result of trading was approximately equilibrium in Walras's sense. Anyway, however, *tâtonnement* may at most be considered as a highly idealized representation of the functioning of freely competitive markets.

For the models with production Léon Walras developed very complicated *tâtonnement* processes. Now the initial situation was not a set of prices only, as $\boldsymbol{S}_1$ above, but a set of prices of productive services plus quantities of products to be produced in first instance. In the first three editions of the *Éléments* Walras admitted disequilibrium production. The goods produced in disequilibrium were exchanged according to a *tâtonnement* process of exchange as described above. The result was almost never a situation of general economic equilibrium, but Walras was able to derive from it a new situation closer to equilibrium. This situation was then used as a new initial situation to find a third situation still closer to equilibrium, and so on. The details are highly complicated and, unfortunately, mathematically dubious.

In first instance, *tâtonnement* was really intended to reflect the dynamics of daily economic life during a certain period. Consumers work, earn money, buy goods, consume them; producers/entrepreneurs hire workers, buy raw materials and intermediate products, produce products, sell them; capitalists save and the money saved is invested in capital goods. Some order does exist among all these elements, and this is what Walras tried to model by means of the *tâtonnement* in the first three editions of his *Éléments*. It is this *tâtonnement* that Walras had in mind when writing the papers that eventually found their place in the *EEPA*. For a comprehensive and authoritative discussion of *tâtonnement* and of Walras's way of trying to embed his markets in an institutional framework see Walker (1996). See also van Daal (2000).

All this changed dramatically from the fourth edition of the *Éléments* onwards, where Walras removed disequilibrium production from his models, possibly because it might lead to inconsistencies. Presumably for that same reason, Walras discarded from the first edition of the *Éléments* onwards the possibility of disequilibrium transactions in the case of exchange only. About the nature of these inconsistencies there is much controversy, not to say uncertainty, in the literature. Walras himself was silent on the issue. In the new, fourth edition's set-up the agents in the models respond with written 'pledges' (Walras's French word was *bon*). These pledges represent actions that the agents would undertake in answer to the prices and quantities announced and would be binding in the event that these prices and quantities entailed equilibrium. Generally, this is not the case in the first instance, and then the pledges give rise to the announcement of new prices and quantities, followed possibly by new pledges. The play of announcing and pledging continues until equilibrium prices are reached, after which production and exchange were permitted to take place according to the 'equilibrium pledges'. As a consequence of this unhappy modification of his models Walras had to make another change: he had to suppose that the whole economic process of a period, in all its complexity, had to take place instantaneously. This changed the models fundamentally and meant an enormous decrease in their degree of reality. The whole matter was even more blurred after mid-twentieth-century commentators on Walras's work introduced the 'auctioneer', an omniscient, unselfish individual supposed to organize and oversee the market, in particular *tâtonnement*; Walras himself never spoke of such an element.

The way Walras amended *tâtonnement* in the fourth edition of the *Éléments* has reduced it, in fact, to another mathematical device for proving the existence of equilibrium – no more, no less. This fourth edition's *tâtonnement* is the one which is familiar nowadays, but it is not that of *EEPA*. That is Walras's original *tâtonnement*, of the preceding editions of the *Éléments*, characterized by the occurrence of disequilibrium production. This is in my opinion much more realistic than its successor. However, the earlier *tâtonnement* has remained so unknown that it was reinvented later, as so many wheels, under the name of *non-tâtonnement*, of all names! Alternatively, some authors went as far as associating *tâtonnement* with the problem of stability of equilibrium, which Walras had taken up only in the case of exchanging two goods; in fact, this is nothing more than studying the stability of *tâtonnement* itself and does not say anything about other things.

3.4 Social economics

Walras's applied natural economics established conditions for abundant production of wealth, as we shall see below in the present book. His applied social economics dealt with the conditions for a just distribution of this wealth. This distribution has been discussed in a number of separate studies collected in his *Etudes d'économie sociale*.

It was never Walras's intention to prescribe the details of the allocation of money or certain commodities to specific persons or groups of persons. He was convinced that the distribution of wealth as such would take place properly in the markets if certain general conditions were fulfilled. Here we are back to the problem of how to make sure that the initial situation with which an individual is confronted when entering the economics scene is the right and just one, given his own endowments in terms of personal abilities and property, and here the problem has to be located. So Walras's applied theory of the distribution of social wealth consists of two components coupled to each other like the two sides of the same coin: one dealing with property and the other with taxation. His point of departure in dealing with the notion of property was that the 'owner of a thing is the owner of the service of both the thing itself . . . and its [money] price' (*EES*: 206, 207; 1990: 178). Consequently, the property rights of the products result, through exchange, from the property rights of the capital goods land, personal faculties and capital goods proper. The latter kind of capital, however, consists of products as well. Those who have manufactured them should therefore own them. Hence the problem appears to be reduced to the ownership of land and personal faculties.

Personal faculties are clearly the property of the individuals concerned themselves; the times of slavery belong to the past. Land, according to Walras, belongs to all of us and not only to this generation but to all generations. Since all people have equal rights to pursue their destiny, they should all profit equally from the resources offered by nature to accomplish their destinies. Land, Walras argues, will therefore belong to the community, i.e. to the State. The State as owner of the land will then be the owner of its services and products, or the rent obtained from it. This provides the State with an income of its own and in that (ideal) situation all taxes should be abolished. The rent received will enable the State to meet its expenses and pay back the former landowners, because the rent will increase considerably, land becoming increasingly scarce in the future. As a matter of fact, the increase of rent due to increasing scarcity belongs to the community as a whole and not to the individuals who happen to be the owners of the land in question; in Walras's opinion this was another argument for putting all land in the hands of the State.

Taxation, either on income or on capital other than land, either direct or indirect, is in Walras's view to be considered as unjust, since it would be a claim of the State on something that it does not possess. Taxes or subsidies therefore lead always to some kind of disturbance of the ideal of giving each economic agent what is rightfully his. Wealth is the reward of labour and savings; poverty is the consequence and penalty of idleness and prodigality. Walras put it as follows:

> Individual moral will have its natural sanction and the State may leave it to individuals to ask freely of religion or philosophy the aid they need to endure the hardships of nature or to overcome their own weakness. Taxation will bar the way to that ideal.
>
> (*EES*: 438; 1990: 404)

According to Walras, the State could consider either a land tax or the expropriation of the land. In the first case, the State would operate as a kind of co-proprietor. The alternative would be the *rightful* repurchase of the land; this could take place only over a long period. The actual situation in Walras's days was one in which the land was privately owned, as it had been for centuries. Unfortunately, the French Revolution wasted the opportunity to change this situation. The complicated operation of bringing the land into the hands of the State should be carefully executed *vis-à-vis* the present landowners; they are, of course, not responsible for the present unjust situation, Walras said. One cannot remove an injustice by committing another one, and therefore he considered merely confiscating the land as much an injustice as maintaining the present situation. (Taking future expectations connected with land ownership from the landowners was not considered by Walras as an injustice.) The question was then how the State could obtain the privately owned land. Gossen (1854, 1995, chapter 23) had already dealt with this question.[8] On similar grounds to those of Walras, Gossen proclaimed the nationalization (or, as he called it, the repurchase) of the land by the State. The latter would buy the land from the landowners and obtain the rent in return from the farmers and other users of the land. Gossen's idea was that it would be profitable for the State to purchase the land, since the value of it would increase continually.

In Chapter 16, §IV below, Walras himself deals with the repurchase of the land by the State.

4 Genesis of *Études d'économie politique appliquée*

4.1 History

In November 1893 Walras abandoned the idea of publishing the *Éléments d'économie politique appliquée* and the *Éléments d'économie sociale*. As mentioned above, it had always been his intention to do this on the basis of his lectures on applied and social economics at the University of Lausanne (collected in Walras 1996). Now he decided to confine himself to regrouping a certain number of texts under the titles *Études d'économie politique appliquée* and *Études d'économie sociale*. He developed a number of successive projects, each time reshuffling and changing his choice of texts. In contradistinction to the *EES*, none of the projects for the *EEPA* provided for a preface, though seven short notes have been found with points for it. These notes are so uncohesive that it is impossible to get an idea of what introduction Walras could have had in mind. For the details refer to the 'Avertissement' in the Potier edition of the *EEPA* (Walras 1992: xxi) and to Walras 2000: 575–8.

Eventually, the *EEPA* appeared in August 1898, published by F. Rouge, Lausanne, and F. Pichon, Paris, bringing together the booklet *Théorie de la monnaie* and various papers, sometimes already several times edited, presented in public and published. The oldest work dated from about twenty-five years before. For a good overall understanding, one should know these pieces' order. Therefore, I listed them chronologically in Appendix B. In the next section I shall discuss them in the order Walras gave them in this book.

No second edition appeared during Walras's lifetime. However, by 1902 he had finished a complete revision, inserted in the manuscript of the book. (Likewise, he had revised the *EES* and the fourth edition of his *Éléments*.) The changes are all of minor importance (just like those he made in the first publications of the papers before inserting them in *EEPA*).

4.2 Bibliography

In 1906 Walras composed a bibliography of his writings; see Walker (1987). The manuscript is preserved in the Fonds Walras of Lausanne in box 7, section IVa.

This autobibliography was composed with a view to a long cherished desire, namely publication of his father's and his own complete economic works. Since the 1890s he had set up a number of schemes for such a publication; see the editors' general introduction to Auguste Walras (1990). For a number of reasons none of these plans was very successful. Some time after his death in 1910, Léon Walras's children donated his personal library, his archives and his own and his father's manuscripts to the University of Lausanne with the stipulation that the university should initiate and sponsor the publication of the complete economic works of Léon and Auguste Walras, included some manuscripts unpublished so far. Unfortunately, it cannot be said that the University of Lausanne took this moral obligation seriously at the time.

Walras's daughter Aline in particular was much concerned by the attitude of (some members of) her father's university.[9] Consequently, she and some of her friends took the initiative to try to bring out such a publication on their own. In 1924 she conveyed part of her father's papers and books to the University of Lyon on the basis of which the publication of the economic works of her father and her grandfather could be brought about. Etienne Antonelli, at the time Professor of Economics at the University of Lyon, had taken upon himself the task of editing the twofold work. Unfortunately, illness and, later, political engagements prevented him from starting the project. Having recourse to other friends (in particular Gaston Leduc, Professor of Economics at the University of Caen), however, Aline Walras finally succeeded in having the fifth edition of the *Éléments* published (1926, the so-called *édition définitive*), a second edition of the *EES* (1936) and a second edition of the *EEPA* (1936), with the corrections made by Léon Walras himself. Further, his *Abrégé des éléments d'économie politique pure* was brought out (1938); this book is a previously unpublished, simplified version of the *Eléments*, finished in 1903.

Aline Walras died during the Second World War and from that time the attempts to publish the remaining works ceased for many decades. The Lyon archives fell into obscurity until 1984, when they were rediscovered under a thick covering of dust at the bottom of a bookcase in one of the university buildings. This discovery was a reminder that a task still needed to be carried out. A team from the Faculty of Economics of the Université Lyon-2 (headed by Pierre Dockès) decided that Antonelli's commitment could not be ignored and founded the Centre Auguste et Léon Walras, in which they organized themselves to start the activities which would lead to publication. After making a first inventory and creating a data bank with respect to the two authors they decided to prepare a fourteen-volume publication entitled *Auguste et Léon Walras: œuvres économiques complètes*, to be published by the Paris publishing house Economica (see Appendix C).

So far Economica has brought out eleven volumes. The remaining volumes are in a stage of preparation such that we may safely presume that 2004 will at last see the publication of the Walrases complete economic works. All volumes have been made much more understandable by extensive editorial work in the form of introductory texts and explanatory notes and, indeed, readability has been enormously enhanced, since the editors put at the reader's disposal their great knowledge of nineteenth-century general history, the history of science and the history of economic facts and theory. They refrained thereby from interpretation, since, as they said, 'Walras's work is everlasting and our analysis of it will stay fresh for at most a matter of decades.'

As I said, the translation in the present book is based on the main text and the notes of the so-called Potier edition: Volume X of the above series, published in 1992, which is a variorum edition edited by Jean-Pierre Potier. I chose to translate the text of the second edition (1936) because that is, I believe, what Walras would have wished. I translated most of the editor's notes, skipping only those that are of no importance to readers of an English version. Further, I added a number of notes (indicated by an asterisk), some of a more technical nature and some that may be uninformative for French but not for English readers.

5 Contents of *Études d'économie politique appliquée*

What follows may be used as a reader's guide, though I did not intend to write such a thing. I wrote this section simply because I believe that a reader must know what a book is about. Nevertheless, some considerations of how to read a book like the present one seem appropriate. It can be read by an economist who places all he reads immediately within the context of twenty-first-century economic theory and facts. The harsh reader will then find a lot of theorizing that is 'primitive', 'incomplete', 'dubious' or 'no longer applicable' (I omit references). Knowing the history of the theory and facts of their science, other economists will read the book in retrospect, putting the things they read in their proper place in history. These readers may ask how useful some pieces of the books still are for present-day economics, for instance because 'history repeats itself'. They can also recognize and appreciate Walras's originality and creativity. Personally, I should suggest to the reader another way of reading. Why not trying to put all modern knowledge aside or at the back of the mind and read the book as the interested 'educated layman' of Walras's time would have done?

The papers and the booklet *Théorie de la monnaie*, inserted in *EEPA* and listed chronologically in Appendix B to this introduction were all written after Walras's arrival in Lausanne; the oldest dates from 1873. (A substantial part of the papers in *EES*, however, date from the 1860s.) Looking carefully at his previous papers on similar topics, one might conjecture why Walras did not select one of these for the *EEPA*: being nearly all exclusively descriptive and often politically oriented, they were considered not analytical enough for such a theoretical book; see also Baranzini (2000). During the 1860s Walras became more and more an independent author on the subjects concerned, making use of experience picked up in several jobs ((assistant) editor of a number of periodicals, railway clerk, co-director of a co-operative discount bank which went bankrupt and bank employee, subsequently); moreover, his father, his most important adviser, died in 1866. From 1870 onwards he had to teach economics, which obliged him to accelerate his thinking even more and go as deep as possible, not without success, as we know now.

The *EEPA* consists of seven parts, all having their own theme. Each part consists of one or more chapters, some of which consist of two or more of the papers of the list in Appendix B. In total there are thirteen, unnumbered chapters, counting the *Théorie de la monnaie* as one chapter (the third of Part I). In the present translation I split this booklet into four chapters, which could be done in a logical way. It makes all the chapters more or less the same length. Of course, I have retained Walras's division into parts. This means that *Studies in Applied Economics* contains sixteen chapters in seven parts; I have numbered these chapters consecutively.

Part I is entitled 'Money' and contains seven chapters; their order is not so easily understood. It deals primarily with the question of how to organize the monetary system so that prices do not fall or rise too much, because price variations generated by economic life itself, mostly inevitable, should not be aggravated by a badly functioning monetary system. Although one can also find other, remarkable issues in it, a good deal of this part is a long plea for Walras's own system of general price control. Some repetitiveness cannot be denied. The subject of Part II (entitled 'Monopolies') is clearly indicated by its title and that of its single chapter: 'The State and the railways'. Part III, 'Agriculture, industry and commerce' (three chapters) deals with theoretical and practical aspects of the regulation of all sorts of competitive markets. At this point it should be observed that by the expression 'regulation of competitive markets' Walras did not mean interventions in the process as such that lead to market equilibrium, let alone organize or direct those processes. Walras was convinced that the market parties themselves bring about equilibrium through bidding up or underbidding. By 'regulation' he meant taking measures so that bidding and underbidding can take place freely and unhampered, undisturbed by those who have dishonourable intentions. Parts IV ('Credit', one chapter), V ('Banks', two chapters) and VI ('Stock markets', one chapter) deal mainly and very generally with topics that are vital for smooth settlement of transactions between parties active in the capital market. The nature, organization and regulation of this special market always had a great deal of Walras's attention. The longest chapter of the book is the one forming Part VII, which remained untitled in the original. In the English version I have given it the title 'Outline of a doctrine'. Here Walras presented an interesting reflection on what he had done during his long career as a social scientist. It can be considered as a sort of afterthought, perhaps even a 'farewell address', were it not that two years later he came up with his last substantial publication, the fourth edition of the *Éléments*. It must be observed that, in spite of their length, Parts I and VII seem to be a bit less directly connected with the subject in hand than the other ones. All subjects of the book's first fifteen chapters belong to the domain of applied economics as Walras defined it. The sixteen chapters will now pass under review.

5.1 Part I: Money (seven chapters)

Chapter 1 (paper 7 in the chronological list in Appendix B, further to be called simply 'list') is entitled 'Gold money with regulating silver token'; its topic is the regulation of the value of money. Where a stable monetary system is of the utmost importance for all kinds of business, it is, after all, not amazing that Walras inserted this material in his *EEPA*, but one may wonder why he started *EEPA* with this paper as the first chapter.

As he did so often, Walras took a middle position regarding this issue. He did not want to be considered as a supporter of either monometallism or bimetallism, but he had his own system:

> Monometallism based on gold, combined with a silver token, distinct from coins for small change, to be introduced into the circulation or withdrawn from it in such a way that the value of this multiple standard would not vary.
>
> (p. 3 below)

This system is not the same as bimetallism because the role of silver is not the same as that of gold. Gold can be minted on demand, but the quantity of silver token as legal money in the country of issue is regulated by the State. The silver token could very well be the existing *écus* with a value of 5 F, Walras proposed, and could therefore readily be used for paying wages and for most of the daily expenses of private persons. The system looks rather like a kind of 'open-market policy' *avant la lettre*. The theory of the system, Walras explained at length, is based, on one hand, on the properties of the individuals' *raretés* (marginal utilities) and, on the other hand, at the monetary level, on the quantity theory. (Walras already had that notion, and its name.) The system cannot really be rejected on theoretical grounds, but many French economists raised political, technical and practical objections, sometimes unfriendly in tone. Walras discussed most of these objections, some more thoroughly than others, and showed thereby great confidence in scientific development.

The practical problem of how to effect such an introduction or withdrawal, however, he did not mention at all. Introducing silver token into the monetary circulation is easier said as done. Government cannot expect the money value to change by simply expanding the quantity of silver token and keeping it in its own or the bank's stock. The token does not enter automatically into circulation. It must be brought in purposely, for instance by buying something which otherwise would not be bought by private persons so that there will be no crowding out, or other economic effect. It is difficult to imagine such a thing. Hiring unemployed people to do work that would otherwise remain undone, or increasing civil servants' salaries, is an other possibility. Withdrawing silver token seems even more difficult. Firing civil servants or reducing their salaries seem to be inelegant methods. Selling government property or bonds appears better. Payment for such property or bonds will mostly take place in gold, but government may then use this gold for payments it normally makes in silver. The losses incurred should be compensated for by the profits made before by issuing token. None of these or other options was discussed by Walras, his critics or the reviewers of the *Théorie de la monnaie* or the *EEPA*. This lack of interest in the details of the practical execution of the system on the part of its critics indicates clearly how sceptical most of them were at the time.

Walras remained optimistic and said that, in fact, the system was already in existence and functioning. He referred to the so-called Latin Union, a monetary union between Belgium, France, Italy, Switzerland and Greece, existing from 1864 till the First World War. (For more information about this predecessor of the European Monetary Union see below, note i to Chapter 1.) The Latin Union started with a regime of bimetallism which, however, soon ceased to exist with the limitation in 1874 and complete suspension in 1878 of minting silver coin on demand. So Walras concluded that his system existed already in the Latin Union. It sufficed to make sure that it would not be renounced. He expressed it as follows:

> Well, what was done for copper or nickel was done for silver the very day it was decided to limit minting silver at will, just as minting copper or nickel is regulated . . . .
>
> So the only necessity is to note the rise, fall or stability of prices most carefully, and decrease or increase the quantity of silver écus, or leave it untouched. In a nutshell, doing rationally what has always previously been done empirically.
>
> (pp. 11–12 below)

This situation was the closest ever to his ideas; he never saw them truly applied in practice. Throughout the whole of Part I Walras returned to the subject. He thereby discussed and gave his opinion on alternatives as regulating the production of precious metals, returning to bimetallism or the silver standard. None of these found favour in his eyes.

Chapter 2, 'Measuring and regulating variations in the value of money', is mostly devoted to (statistical) points regarding the measurement of prices; it contains three papers on the list (1, 8 and 9). The first deals with the index problem, as we would now call it. The second contains a recapitulation of Walras's system of regulating the variation in the value of money in which he tried to base his arguments solely on his own theory of marginal utility. The third consists of Walras's only piece of empirical work, an attempt to measure price variations for France and Switzerland.

Chapters 3–6 form the *Théorie de la monnaie*, or, rather the *Theory of Money* (paper 10 on the list). Chapter 3 consists of a preface (untitled in the original) and an introduction. The preface contains an overview of Walras's early work on money and an explication of the reasons why and how he revised it completely, basing it now on 'the subjective theory of value' and the notion of a 'desired cash balance'. Further, he compared his work with that of famous colleagues of the period. In the introduction he first revisited once more his previous articles on money to illustrate his change of mind. Then he dealt with his critics on many of the points mentioned above. We may say that in the preface the work of a number of foreign economists is discussed who were in large measure in agreement with Walras's results, and that the introduction is devoted mostly to unkind French critics.

Chapter 4, Part I of the *Theory of Money*, is devoted to monetary theory. It would have served wonderfully as the opening chapter of Part I. Entitled 'Exposition of the principles', it starts with Walras's theory of general economic equilibrium in a nutshell. This is applied to money and its roles. To this end Walras introduced the notion of cash balance, which made it possible to formulate a more or less sophisticated version of the quantity theory. The chapter ends with some considerations of the nature and measurement of variations of the *numéraire* and money.

Chapter 5 (Part II, 'Critical discussion of the systems') starts with a discussion of the varied monetary regimes, with much attention paid, of course, to Walras's own system, culminating in nice, original pictures of the general price curves under the gold and silver standards compared with bimetallism.[10] By means of these graphs he illustrated when and how one system may shift into another, thus showing these systems' limitations. Then a brief survey of the world's monetary history followed, which led Walras to the conclusion that 'the only thing left to do is: make a special, or complementary, token: a *regulating* token'. He warned against optimism in the sense of expecting too much from 'automatism' in monetary affairs. Too many people were of the opinion that simply putting the newly produced gold and/or silver into circulation was enough to maintain the price level. The chapter ends with a section on problems regarding the realization of Walras's scheme. These problems relate to political and social implications rather than practical execution.

Chapter 6 (Part III, 'Statistical desiderata') starts with a discussion of the varied types of price indices that may be used for measuring the 'variation in the money price of social wealth', illustrated with some English and German material. Then Walras went on with a more general discussion of the problem, ending with some beautiful graphs illustrating the (macro) working of his system. The chapter ends with a note 'On the quantity theory'. This note contains an interesting, albeit somewhat dubious, deduction of the quantity theory from Walras's theory of utility and that of cash balances.

Chapter 7 ('The monetary problem') concludes Part I. It collects four papers dealing with monetary matters in India, Europe and the United States (papers 11, 12, 13 and 14 on the list). The chapter shows, again, Walras's lively interest in the subject. The conclusion is always that adopting his system would solve a good many of the world's monetary problems. This ends Part I.

5.2 Part II: Monopolies (one chapter)

In the next parts Walras discussed several markets and proposed detailed regulations. It appears appropriate to deal first with some general points regarding his ideas about market regulation. As so often, the point of departure was his discontent about the existing opinions and their lack of underpinning:

> Until now, regarding the way in which they drew their conclusions, it is not clear whether economists of the new school [the 'socialists of the chair' are meant] are much superior to those of the old one. The old economists proclaim *Laisser-faire, laisser-passer*; the new proclaim State interventionism; but none of them demonstrates anything at all. Now we are thoroughly tired of gratuitous assertions and above all we demand rigorous demonstrations. In spite of everything, we blame Mr Chevalier [see chapter 8, note iii] not so much for concluding in favour of freedom of trade and labour in matters of railways and banknotes as for not establishing it on any particular basis, whether rational or experimental. It would not suffice, either, to hear socialists of the chair assuring us that they would let the State intervene in railway matters somewhat more than the economists do, without, however, allowing it to the same degree as real socialists do.
> (p. 163 below)

In order to make out exactly in which cases and to what degree the State has to do something, Walras would like to know: by what right may or must the State intervene in cases of monopoly? This brings the problem into the field of science.

So it is important to describe what we have to study. For Walras this is, on the one hand, the products' demand and supply circumstances and, on the other hand, the State's right to intervene. Economic science learns that under free competition the products are of a nature and in quantities sufficient to procure greatest possible individual satisfaction of needs, in other words, the best use has been made of services. So, Walras said, it is self-evident and right that free competition be the rule if possible, i.e. when the goods are private goods and the number of suppliers is large. For such situations he advocated nevertheless a kind of regulation of free competition, a framework of rules in which the economic agents interact in relative freedom. These rules concern prohibitions, obligations or prescriptions with regard to a wide variety of issues: minimum prices, mutual price agreements between enterprises, advertising, product information, consumer credit, production factor mobility between markets, etc. In the case of private goods demanded by a large number of consumers which cannot be produced by a great number of relatively small enterprises, it is highly disputable whether a monopolist really has the right to take a profit over and above his duly calculated production costs (see the first paragraph of subsection 3.1 above); only some privileges may be granted in this respect to certain inventors wholly or partly 'masters of the secret' (p. 166 below). There are products, like water, gas, transport by canal and over highways or railways, for example, which cannot be brought under regulations of free competition; for these, production under monopoly appears evident. Under uncontrolled monopoly, however, the consumers' amounts of maximum utility would be lower than possible because monopoly prices restrict their budgets. Therefore, in general all kinds of price fixing, like monopoly pricing and price discrimination, should be the subject of State intervention to ensure equality of the, single, selling price of each product to its cost price. Walras is quite specific about how this should be done in practice and what kind of exceptions may be admitted; see, e.g. pp. 167 and 184–5 below. So these monopolies are reduced to regulated monopolies, called 'economic monopolies' by Walras. It should be noted here that he considered only two cases with regard to the number of producers: free competition and monopoly. Cases of few – say, two or three – producers in one branch he considered as transient, short-lived because of mergers or take-overs.

Besides the private goods and services, there are the public goods and services. These give rise to what Walras called 'moral monopolies', in which, generally, the State itself produces the public goods and services to put them at the disposal of individuals.

So Walras's ideas about market regulation may well be illustrated by Figure 0.5. Under free competition, the entrepreneurs' entry into or exit from

		Goods and services supplied by	
		Many producers	*One producer*
Goods and services demanded by	*Many consumers*	Free competition	Economic monopoly (Natural monopoly)
	The State (*public goods*)		Moral monopoly (State monopoly)

Figure 0.5 The cases for free competition and for monopoly.

a certain branch and the decrease or increase of their production will lead to zero profits in equilibrium. This is not the case under unregulated, pure monopoly with a single monopoly price because then there is, by definition, no entry or exit. Those monopolistic entrepreneurs who understand their position will change production to increase profit until they have obtained a situation of maximum profit ('maximum net product', p. 215 below). From Walras's numerical examples it can be concluded that his conception of monopoly pricing may be expressed by the graph presented in Figure 0.6. The clever monopolist tries to find the quantity yielding him maximum profit. He may do so by trial and error until he has found out that once having reached the quantity OQ*, a further change of the quantity will decrease his profit. Maximum profit is equal to AB, the difference between total revenue AQ* and total costs BQ*. (The revenue curve is derived from the market demand curve by multiplying each quantity demanded by its price.) In regulated monopoly, the production will be OQ′ and total revenue will equal total costs. In this case, Walras said, the situation will be similar to that of free competition. However, he neglected the complication caused by fixed costs. Where Walras insisted upon market regulation in a case of single monopoly prices, it is clear that he was, generally, not in favour of the practice of further increasing monopoly profit by price discrimination either.

In Chapter 8 ('The State and the railways', paper 4 on the list) the ideas set out above are applied to the case of the railways. This text dates from the mid-1870s, when there was much discussion about who should be the owner of the railways: the State or private enterprise. The chapter starts with this issue. It is argued that the railways, i.e. the tracks, certainly must be subject to State intervention. Walras mentioned two reasons. First, just as is the

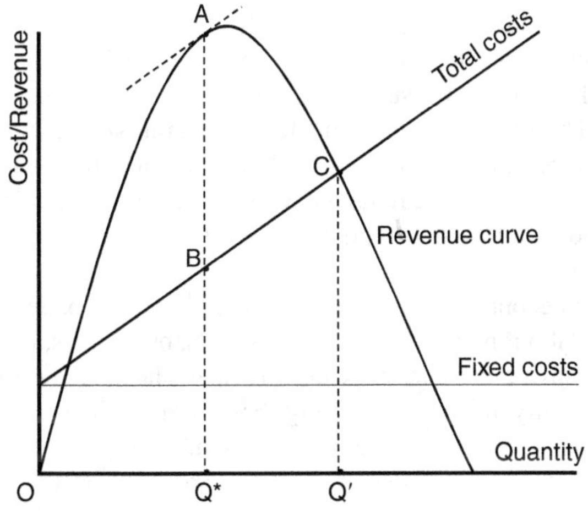

Figure 0.6 Single monopoly price fixing.

case with pipelines for water or gas, one cannot permit an indefinite number of enterprises to cover the ground with railways. Second, being a means of communication, instrumental for national defence, the administration of justice and national cohesion, the railways form at the same time a public good. Hence there is enough reason to bring them, i.e. the tracks, under State control. The same applies to the exploitation of the railways. One cannot permit an indefinite number of enterprises to transport passengers or freight over a certain network; in this respect the situation differs from that of canals and roads.

At the time all this was the subject of debate in parliaments, (learned) societies and elsewhere. Walras hinted at these discussions at many places; see also the relevant notes to Chapter 8. In spite of these discussions, however, the railways were then run by private enterprises acting as pure monopolists. On the basis of an impressive number of annual reports and other literature, Walras demonstrated that no clever monopolist as meant above could be found among the railway entrepreneurs. He gave thereby a nice picture of the railway business in the third quarter of the nineteenth century.

5.3 Part III: Agriculture, industry, commerce (three chapters)

The main point of Chapter 9 ('The influence of communication between markets on the situation of rural communities', paper 3 on the list) is the fact that many people were generally better-off around 1870 than some decades before as a consequence of economic progress, accelerated by the rise of the railways and free competition: wages and rents increased in general, while the rate of interest decreased; communication between regions made prices more similar between those regions; prices of industrial products decreased on the whole, but those of agricultural products remained relatively high. (In discussing price and income changes and their effects on consumer behaviour Walras appeared already familiar with the notion of the substitution effect of price changes, which was rare at the time.) The statement Walras made was that this situation cannot be the end of the development because in agriculture still many improvements can be made if some rigidities can be removed with respect to the organization and execution of the work and the state of mind of some (groups of), sometimes selfish, people.

Chapter 10 ('Applied economics and the protection of wages', paper 17 on the list) deals with the labour market, as the title suggests, but Walras, being in a talkative mood, let many other topics pass under review. The main message is that there should be mobility of labour: 'To bring about or maintain equilibrium of production as far as wages are concerned labour must be diverted from enterprises where the wages tend to decrease to enterprises where the wages tend to increase' (p. 224 below).

Small variations in wages in some branches may therefore be tolerated as indicators that such shifts of labour have to take place in order to prevent unemployment or more considerable increases or decreases in wages. The main argument Walras put forward is theoretical and typically Walras's. In the *tâtonnement* of production ('the equations which solve the mechanism of free competition', ibid., see also *Éléments*, lesson 21) he derived the following equation:

$$(O_t - D_t)p_t + \cdots + (O_p - D_p)p_p + (O_{p'} - D_{p'})p_{p'} + \cdots \\ + (O_k - D_k)p_k + \cdots = 0$$

a kind of Walras's law *avant la lettre* in the market of production factors, where $O_t \cdots O_p, O_{p'} \cdots O_k \cdots$ are the quantities offered, $D_t \cdots D_p, D_{p'} \cdots D_k \cdots$ the quantities demanded and $p_t \cdots p_p, p_{p'} \cdots p_k \cdots$ the prices of the productive services (T) $\cdots$ (P), (P′) $\cdots$ (K) $\cdots$ If one of the equation's factors in brackets is, say, positive, then at least one of the others must be negative, prices being considered always positive. If it concerns factors of a different nature, like the services of land and capital, we may have, for instance, $O_t > D_t$ and $O_k < D_k$. The mechanism of free competition will then achieve equality by decreasing p_t and increasing p_k. If the services are more or less similar, like, for instance, the work of different persons in not too different occupations, there is a second possibility. If, say, $O_p > D_p$ and $O_{p'} < D_{p'}$, equality may be achieved without price variation, by directly transforming (P) into (P′), which will decrease O_p and increase $O_{p'}$. We call this labour mobility. (Of course, the modern reader sees all sorts of quibbles, but he should be aware of the fact that Walras was the very first to try out this way of thinking in terms of equilibrium.) If it could be made a normal, accepted habit to move labour from branches where a surplus of labour is to be expected to where extra labour will be needed, much conflict between labourers and entrepreneurs could be prevented and strikes, so detrimental to both parties, would be a thing of the past.[11] Walras wonders:

> Why are there no strikes between entrepreneurs and capitalists? It is because the markets in fixed capital (the Bourse) and circulating capital (the banks) have been organized somewhat better than the labour market, which is not organized at all.
>
> (p. 224 below)

Before going on with these capital markets, in Chapters 12–15, Chapter 11, 'Theory of free trade' (paper 15 on the list), has to pass review. Walras says: 'Free trade is none other than the extension of the regime of free competition to the whole world, in matters of economics' (p. 240 below).

The main point of this chapter is that if free trade is given the time and opportunity to come completely put into operation in all its aspects then it is profitable to many consumers without harming other consumers or the owners of productive services. The arguments run in both real and monetary terms;

the individuals' utility functions also play their part. Under the conditions that would make this all possible, Walras's scheme for nationalization of land and the abolition of taxes is not lacking, nor the necessity of peace among the nations. This long plea for free trade is possibly somewhat over-idealistic, but quite comparable with similar pleas such as Smith's, in the chapter of his *Wealth of Nations* where the invisible hand is explicitly mentioned (Book IV, chapter II), and Ricardo's, in chapter VII of his *Principles*.

5.4 Part IV: Credit (one chapter)

Chapter 12, 'Theory of credit', is the second paper of our chronological list. It deals with a special type of capital, as Walras explained in the chapter's first paragraph:

> *Credit* is borrowed capital. What is capital [here]? Strictly speaking, it is that part of social wealth that is rented out in the form of money. The word *capital* (like the word *revenue*) has therefore two different meanings in economics, easily distinguishable with a little expertise. When we speak of landed, personal or proper *capital*, it concerns valuable goods that can be used more than once; when we speak of fixed or circulating *capital*, it concerns borrowed commodities [goods bought with borrowed money are meant] that have to be returned in money, not in kind.
>
> (p. 249 below)

That this terminological explanation is only given in the twelfth chapter of the *EEPA* is one of the consequences of the fact that we have here to do with a collection of essays, instead of the never published textbook Walras had in mind.

Where money is the means of exchange of real goods and services, credit, in its turn, is the means of exchange of money as capital. In both cases the transactions can take place more quickly and smoothly than without a well organized means of exchange and an efficient branch of special mediators, the banks.[12] The type of credit Walras had in mind in this chapter is so-called *productive credit*: existing, saved money is lent to entrepreneurs to be invested in the production and sale of products.

Credit lent to individuals or the State for consumption purposes should not exist because consumption should be financed by means of current income, in Walras's opinion. In the case of money as a means of exchange it is of the utmost importance that the monetary system is well organized, stable and secure. Credit as a means of exchange of money capital between capitalists and entrepreneurs should meet similar conditions. These conditions form an important part of the chapter. One of the most important conditions concerns the security given to lenders to be certain that interest payment and redemption take place as contracted. This differs highly with the type of credit, in particular whether it concerns long-term or short-term credit, or, in Walras's terms, loans of fixed or circulating capital. All this is extensively dealt with in the chapter, which gives it at first sight a rather descriptive character in spite of its title. The theory, however, is not lacking but is interspersed with the exposition of practical matters.

5.5 Part V: Banking (two chapters)

Chapter 13 ('Mathematical theory of banknotes', paper 6 on the list) dates from 1879 and is a piece of work by Walras at the peak of his creative powers. His point of departure is:

> Should banknotes be issued by the State, a single bank empowered with a monopoly under special conditions, or by an indefinite number of free banks? Here we have a question of applied economics that has hitherto been controversial and has divided economists into two equally large and authoritarian camps.
>
> (p. 273 below)

Credit in general is a private service, Walras said, and where banknotes are a form of short-term credit it seems at first sight that we are talking about a business between private banks and entrepreneurs, the first granting credit to the latter, the latter receiving banknotes. In a situation where there is only metallic money, a bank is solely an intermediary between capitalists and entrepreneurs; the first deposit their money savings at the bank and the second receive it as credit, giving due security. If the bank pays with banknotes, and if these banknotes, reimbursable in metallic money at sight to the bearer, are not fully covered by saved metallic money, then the quantity of money has increased. So it appears that an issue of banknotes may widen credit limits by allowing banks and bankers to make loans to entrepreneurs without borrowing from capitalists. In Walras's day (and before) it was not so clear what was happening here. Economists differed in their opinions regarding to explain the phenomenon of banknotes, just as bankers did. The latter did not know how far they could go in issuing banknotes and behaved sometimes as the famous sorcerer's apprentice did. Walras tried to bring some order into the matter by dealing with three special effects of the issue of banknotes which undermine the conclusion that it concerns here a private matter.

First and foremost, he discussed the monetary depreciation caused by the issue of banknotes, which is the topic of the chapter's first section. Here we encounter Walras's macro-monetary model for a closed economy (which may be the whole world). By means of formulae and beautiful graphs, he investigated how the value of money, measured in goods, changes when the money good – silver, for instance – serves both as merchandise and as *numéraire* and money, and how this value further changes on account of the issue of banknotes. Such an issue causes a noticeable depreciation of the money metal and, therefore, an important rise of the prices of all goods and services. In spite of its rigidities (the mass of the money good remains unchanged and the quantity theory of money plays a prominent role), the model provides a useful global framework for understanding the general rise in the price level owing to the issue of banknotes. Second, the issue of banknotes has the twofold temporal effect of an additional demand for capital goods and an extra price increase, as Walras explained in the second section of the chapter. To understand this, it should be borne in mind that in Walras's view the banknotes issued by banks are in the first instance put into the hands of entrepreneurs, who bring them into circulation. They do what entrepreneurs normally do, i.e. provide themselves with capital goods. This will mainly be fixed capital because it does not make much sense to buy only circulating capital, as this does not extend the economy's production capacity. In other words, according to Walras, the banknotes create an additional demand for capital goods without a compensating decrease in demand for consumer goods. The situation of equilibrium between the production of consumer goods and capital goods will then be disturbed, with the double effect that the production factors' prices, and therefore all prices, will rise and that more capital goods are produced to the detriment of consumer goods. This price rise, to be added to the one discussed above, will stop at the end of the period of issue (i.e. when all banknotes have been absorbed by the circulation), together with the extra production of capital goods. The third effect Walras indicated (in section 3 of this chapter) is a more or less permanent result of the second one: the practical impossibility of liquidating the issue of banknotes. The banknotes, intended to represent circulating capital, after all represent fixed capital. This made Walras afraid of what could happen if the public asks for reimbursement of the banknotes in metallic money. A crisis might occur. Banknotes have no value as such, as metallic money has, in Walras's opinion. His conclusion in the fourth section of the chapter is therefore that the issue of banknotes is a dangerous instrument that has more disadvantages than advantages.

Chapter 14, 'The Post Office Savings Bank of Vienna and *comptabilisme social*' (paper 18 on the list) goes on discussing what a bank should do or not do. Issuing banknotes is not the only way by which a society sells its metallic money at a reduced price as metal merchandise and creates new capital. One could also execute transfer payments from accounts created by giving credit on securities and not on money, or clear cheques secured by available deposits bearing interest.

Walras was not a supporter of either mode, although he was aware of the positive aspects of transfer banks as far as they facilitate payments. Using the working of the recently founded office of cheques and transfers of the postal savings bank of Austria as an example, he gave his opinion on this kind of extension of banks' activities. The last section of this chapter is in particular interesting because it recapitulates once more Walras's pertinent ideas.

5.6 Part VI: Stock markets (one chapter)

Chapter 15, entitled 'The stock exchange: speculation and *agiotage*', paper 5 on the list, was prepared when Walras was also working on the second instalment of the *Éléments*' first edition. Capital formation is an important part of this instalment and so, while finishing it and writing the article, pure and applied theory of capital formation went hand in hand.

The stock exchange is the place where capitalists' money savings are transformed into fixed capital. (See Appendix A for the double meaning of the term 'fixed capital'.) The capitalists receive shares or bonds of enterprises or local or national government bonds in exchange for their money, for which government and these enterprises buy capital goods. This exchange takes place through the intermediary of stockbrokers; see Walker (2001b). Often this occurs with the purpose of placing capitalists' money in shares and bonds to be kept by them to benefit from dividends and interest. (That is why these buyers of shares are called share*holders*.) This is one part of the activities taking place on the stock exchange; normally it concerns bonds and shares issued by established firms and stable governments. The other part is speculation, or rather financial speculation. From Walras's viewpoint speculation is simply buying a thing, not with the purpose of holding it but to sell it again, thereby making a profit, or incurring a loss. Financial speculation is therefore buying and selling obligations and bonds in the stock market, not to hold these securities but to make a profit in dealing in them. Carried out by specialist, professional institutions, this may be a quite legitimate matter, Walras argues, because it mostly concerns shares and bonds of newly established, developing enterprises, whose business results are not yet certain. The aim of speculation is then, first, providing those enterprises with capital and, second, by means of all sorts of techniques, among which bulling and bearing the market, giving the enterprises concerned the time to let the value of their securities tend to a normal value, in proportion to their then stabilized revenues. The thus stabilized securities will then be added to those already available for placement among capitalists wanting to invest their money saved. So the increase of money savings will find its way to the entrepreneurs asking for it in an expanding economy. The speculators, therefore, run the risk of losing money when such an enterprise fails. When it succeeds, however, they usually make a profit.

All this is right enough, but there are also abuses. Walras's name for them is *agiotage*. Large-scale abuses are mostly committed by unscrupulous people, relying on other people's greed; they drive up a security's quotation by means of false rumours and mismanagement in the sense of pushing up short-term profits to the detriment of the enterprise's future. Walras argues that it is difficult to rule these abuses out by legislation; he is rather in favour of good public information on what is happening with the big enterprises and extensive discussion in newspapers, professional journals combined with openness at shareholders' meetings. Further he proposes that financial *speculation* will be permitted only to specialist, licensed persons or institutions. This may also preclude another evil, namely speculation by private persons who try to make a benefit, but instead lose their fortune, or at least a lot of money, because they lack knowledge and experience.

5.7 Part VII: [Outline of a doctrine] (one chapter)

The last chapter of *EEPA* is the last one on the list, prepared during the five years preceding its publication. Entitled 'Esquisse d'une doctrine économique et sociale', it is a résumé of his ideas on science in general (§I), pure, moral and applied science versus practical application (§II), pure science of social wealth (§III), the theory of the distribution of social wealth (§IV), the theory of the production of social wealth (§V) and a final section (§VI) divided into two parts, first a very personal account of French economic policy in the eighteenth and nineteenth centuries and then a somewhat perplexing last part entitled 'A freethinker's prayer'. In sections II to V, Walras's pure, applied and social economics are adequately summarized. As such they convey useful information.

The beginning and the end of the chapter are more puzzling, but not uninteresting. In §I Walras takes as point of departure the ideas of Franklin H. Giddings as set out in the latter's 1896 book, in particular chapter II: 21–51, and in a couple of earlier articles by Giddings. The reader will observe that reading Giddings perhaps changed Walras's basic ideas on science somewhat; see also Potier (1994). I do not go into that matter here because Walras did not incorporate these new ideas into the rest of his work (as he did with his new ideas on *tâtonnement*), for the simple reason that he lacked the time and energy; see Walker (1996: 1–13).

The first subsection of §VI is a plea for a proper foundation of policy, with more pure and applied social science, which would enable politicians to guide society's entering into the industrial and commercial state. The second subsection, 'A freethinker's prayer', fills the last two pages of the *EEPA* (two pages difficult to translate). I think this piece is rather a vision, a dream, than a prayer, as may appear from the following passage, on the book's last page:

> What light this sheds! The real, absolute being manages to make himself 'me', spirit in humanity; by art and science he loves and knows himself, both as nature and humanity. By Family, Government and Ownership he preaches humanity to himself; by Industry he exploits himself as nature.

> Beauty, Truth, Justice, Well-being: this is divinity, the 'category of the ideal'! The fulfilment of all this means the reign of God. Adveniat! [May it come soon.] . . . Conscience tells [him]: 'Make your ideal come true'. Reason adds: 'Working like this you will achieve the universal ideal.'
>
> (p. 385 below)

6 Conclusion

So we are back at the point of departure, the Social Question, whose solution goes hand in hand with the realization of the (social) ideal. Walras did not present a clear, complete description of that ideal, but he provided all its elements, as we have seen above. In this ideal situation all people will be allowed to provide themselves with what they need to meet their wants, freely using their own capacities and property, in free competition with other individuals without infringing upon others' rights; the role of the State will be restricted to guaranteeing this freedom. The State will own all the land and the individuals will freely compete for its use, which will lead to optimal utilization of the land and provide the State with an income, making taxation needless.

Everything Walras developed in his *Éléments* and his two *Études* had undoubtedly its proper place in the master plan he had in mind 'to complete the mathematical theory of economic equilibrium' (*EES*, first edition: 433; 1990: 400 n). Walras was good at synthesis but, as already indicated above, he paid so much attention to his *Éléments d'économie politique pure* that he ran out of time and this synthesis was never put down on paper. However, a broad design for the economic framework of the completion envisaged by Walras has been suggested, combining the model of subsection 3.2 with the following elements: (1) the production structure of both private goods (whether produced under free competition or (regulated) monopoly) and public goods is supposed to be that of fixed coefficients of production; (2) all goods (both private and public) are supplied at cost price, under free competition as well as under monopoly; (3) the State acts as an individual with a role which does not differ mathematically from that of an individual. The abolition of taxation, combined with State ownership of land and the fiction of a social welfare function with quantities of public goods as variables, has the effect that the State has a real budget constraint, with rent as income and a utility function, with quantities of public goods as arguments, just as the individual consumers have utility functions with quantities of private goods as arguments. See van Daal (1999), where this complete design has been expressed in a system of equations whose consistency has been demonstrated.

At the end of this introduction the reader may permit me two remarks. First, Léon Walras's *Études d'économie sociale* also ends where it started: the last section of the book is entitled 'France and the Social Question'. Second, Walras was not the only idealistic author to end a book somewhat elatedly. Gossen, who was not only a precursor of Walras but also a source of inspiration, had similar passages. What to think of the following, at the end of his book?

> Mankind, once you have recognized completely and entirely the beauty of this plan of the Creation, steep yourself in adoration of the Being, which in its incomprehensible wisdom, power, and goodness has been able, by means apparently so insignificant, to bring about on your behalf something so enormously incalculably beneficial. Make yourself worthy of all that this Being has showered upon you, organizing your actions for your own benefit in such a manner that this most desirable result is brought about as quickly as possible!
>
> (Gossen 1983: 299)

This sort of assertion should not deter us from studying Walras's works (or, for that matter, Gossen's book). One should not forget that scholars like Walras worked, pioneered in isolation, trying to find their way in to yet undiscovered territories of the scientific world. They had no colleagues of the same standing, with their offices just down the corridor, whom they could ask to read and comment on their writings. They had no referees, editors or proof readers (and certainly no ghost writers). This, however, means that their texts are entirely their own work, which gives it eternal freshness, one of the many attractive features of the old masters' writings.

Appendices

A Walras's terminology with regard to capital

In Walras's pure theory, individual capital owners are the owners of all capital goods and they rent these out to the entrepreneurs, or, in other words, they sell the services of these capital goods to the entrepreneurs. Making abstract theory on the basis of this supposition is one thing; another thing is that in practice one cannot abstract so easily from the facts of life. Indeed, there are markets where capital services, land services or labour, for instance, are offered and demanded and exchanged directly, but capital goods proper, like machines or factory buildings, paid for by money saved by individuals, are almost never bought by these individuals themselves and rented out to an entrepreneur. They prefer to lend the money saved to an entrepreneur, who buys himself the capital goods in question. The entrepreneur pays interest and at the agreed time he will refund the capitalist in money and not in kind. Hence there are capitalists who own capital in the form of money lent out. The word 'capital' may therefore have two different meanings: capital goods, i.e. valuable things that can be exchanged and mostly can serve more than once, and capital in the form of money. If the money is lent out for a short term, it is generally used for commercial purposes

Capital Goods: types, services in kind, remuneration in money

Type of Capital				*Service in Kind (sometimes called 'revenue')*			*Remuneration in Money*		
French	*English*	*Examples*	*Owners*	*French*	*English*	*Symbols*	*French*	*English*	*Symbols*
Capitaux fonciers or Terre	Landed capital or Land	Agricultural land, Forests, Ground beneath buildings	Landowners	Rente or Rente foncière or Services fonciers	Land-services or 'Rente'	O_t, $O_{t'} \ldots D_t$, $D_{t'} \ldots$	Fermage	Rent (of land) or Ground rent	p_t, $p_{t'} \ldots$
Capitaux personels or Personnes	Personal capital or Persons	Coachmen, Servants, Cooks, Judges, Doctors, Artists	Workers	Services personnels or Travail	Services of persons or Labour	O_p, $O_{p'} \ldots$ D_p, $D_{p'} \ldots$	Salaire	Wages	p_p, $p_{p'} \ldots$
Capitaux mobiliers or Capitaux propre-ments dits	Capital proper	Dwelling-houses, Factory-buildings, Furniture, Machines, Tools, Circulating capital, Fixed capital	Capitalists or Capital owners	Revenues mobiliers or Services mobiliers or Profits	Capital services or 'Profits'	O_k, $O_{k'} \ldots D_k$, $D_{k'} \ldots$	Intérêt	Interest charge or Interest	p_k, $p_{k'} \ldots$

as financing the entrepreneur's stocks till these are sold or for other bridging purposes; Walras speaks then of 'circulating capital'. If the money is lent out for a long term, for financing machinery for instance, Walras speaks of 'fixed capital'. Here, however, the double meaning of the word 'capital' is quite noticeable: for the capitalist the terms 'fixed capital' or 'circulating capital' mean simply a certain amount of money lent out, for the entrepreneur they may also mean the goods or services bought by means of that money.

B Chronological order of the contents of EEPA

1 'Examen critique de la doctrine de M. Cournot sur les changements de valeur absolus et relatifs' (1872)

- Translated as: 'Critical examination of Mr Cournot's doctrine on changes in relative and absolute value', Chapter 2, §I below.
- First publication: lesson 28 of the first edition of the *Éléments d'économie politique pure*, Lausanne: Corbaz/Paris: Guillaumin/Basle: Georg, 1874: 163–8.
- *EEPA* 1898: 20–6.

2 'Théorie du crédit' (1872–3, afterwards slightly changed several times)

- Translated as: 'Theory of credit', Chapter 12.
- First publication (except parts three and four): *Revue d'économie politique* (Paris), 12 (2), February 1898: 128–43.
- *EEPA* 1898: 307–36.

3 'De l'influence de la communication des marchés sur la situation des populations agricoles' (1874)

- Translated as: 'The influence of communication between markets on the situation of rural communities', Chapter 9.
- Public presentation: Société vaudoise d'utilité publique, Lausanne, 29 April 1874.
- First publication: *Journal de la Société vaudoise d'utilité publique* (Lausanne), no. 5, May 1874: 103–16, and no. 6, June 1874: 121–35.
- *EEPA* 1898: 239–64.

4 'L'État et les chemins de fer' (1875; rejected by the *Journal des économistes* in 1876)

- Translated as: 'The State and the railways', Chapter 8.
- First publication: *Revue du droit public et de la science politique en France et à l'étranger* (Paris), vol. VII (May–June 1897): 417–36; vol. VIII (July–August 1897): 42–58; 'Note': 58–61.
- *EEPA* 1898: 193–232; 'Note': 233–6.

5 'La Bourse, la spéculation et l'agiotage' (1874–9)

- Translated as: 'The stock exchange. Speculation and *agiotage*', Chapter 15.
- First publication: *Bibliothèque universelle et revue suisse* (Lausanne), 86th year, 3rd period, vol. V (March 1880): 452–76; vol. VI (April 1880): 66–94.
- *EEPA* 1898: 401–45.

6 'Théorie mathématique du billet de banque' (1879)

- Translated as: 'Mathematical theory of banknotes', Chapter 13
- Public presentation: Société vaudoise des sciences naturelles, Lausanne, 19 November 1879.
- First publication: *Bulletin de la Société vaudoise des sciences naturelles* (Lausanne), 2nd series, 16 (83), May 1880: 553–92, one plate.
- Second publication: in *Théorie mathématique de la richesse sociale,* Paris: Guillaumin/Lausanne: Corbaz, 1883: 145–75, one plate.
- *EEPA* 1898: 339–75, one plate.

7 'Monnaie d'or avec billon d'argent régulateur. Principes proposés à la Conférence monétaire pour la prorogation de l'Union latine' (1884; rejected by the *Journal des économistes* in 1884)

- Translated as: 'Gold money with regulating silver token', Chapter 1.
- First publication: *Revue de droit international et de législation comparée* (Brussels and Leipzig), 16 (6), 1 December 1884: 575–88.
- *EEPA* 1898: 3–19.

8 'D'une méthode de régularisation de la variation de valeur de la monnaie' (1885)

- Translated as: 'Of a method of regulating the variation in the value of money' Chapter 2, §II.
- Public presentation: Société vaudoise des sciences naturelles, Lausanne, 6 May 1885.
- First publication: *Bulletin de la Société vaudoise des sciences naturelles* (Lausanne), 2nd series, 21 (92), August 1885: 71–92.
- *EEPA* 1898: 26–49.

9 'Contribution à l'étude des variations de prix depuis la suspension de la frappe des écus d'argent' (1885)

- Translated as: 'A contribution to the study of price variations since the suspension of silver écu minting', Chapter 2, §III.
- Public presentation: Société vaudoise des sciences naturelles, Lausanne, 3 June 1885.

- First publication (with Alfred Simon as co-author): *Bulletin de la Société vaudoise des sciences naturelles* (Lausanne), 2nd series, 21 (92), August 1885: 93–103, one plate.
- *EEPA* 1898: 49–61, one plate.

10 *Théorie de la monnaie* (1886)

- Translated as *Theory of Money*, Chapters 3, 4, 5 and 6.
- First publication: *Revue scientifique* [*Revue rose*] (Paris), 3e série, 23e année, 37 (15), 10 April 1886: 449–57 (Part I); 37 (16), 17 April 1886: 493–500 (Part II). Part III was rejected.
- Complete publication, as a booklet: *Théorie de la monnaie*, Lausanne: Corbaz/Paris: Larose & Forcel/Rome: Loescher/Leipzig: Duncker & Humblot, 1886, xii + 123 pages, four plates, with an introduction ('Introduction : réponse à quelques objections'), an untitled preface and an appendix ('Note sur la "théorie de la quantité" '; see 16 below on this list).
- *EEPA* 1898: 63–151, four plates.

11 'Note sur la solution du problème monétaire anglo-indien' (1887)

- Translated as: 'A note on the solution of the Anglo-Indian monetary problem', Chapter 7, §I.
- First publication: in English, translated by H. S. Foxwell as 'On the Solution of the Anglo-Indian Monetary Problem', Report of the fifty-seventh meeting of the British Association for the Advancement of Science, held at Manchester in August and September 1887, London: John Murray, 1888, Transactions of Section F, Tuesday, 6 September: 849–51.
- Second publication (in French): *Revue d'économie politique* (Paris), 1 (6), November–December 1887: 633–6.
- *EEPA* 1898: 159–61.

12 'Le problème monétaire anglo-indien' (1893)

- Translated as: 'The Anglo-Indian monetary problem', Chapter 7, §II.
- First publication: *Gazette de Lausanne*, 94th year, no. 172, 24 July 1893: 1.
- *EEPA* 1898: 162–7.

13 'Le problème monétaire' (1894; in 1897 this title became 'Le problème monétaire en Europe et aux États-Unis', for the republication in the *Études d'économie politique appliqué*)

- Translated as: 'The monetary problem in Europe and the United States', Chapter 7, §III.

- First publication: *Gazette de Lausanne*, 95th year, no. 49, 27 February 1894: 1.
- *EEPA* 1898: 168–74.

14 'Le péril bimétalliste' (1895)

- Translated as: 'The bimetallist danger', Chapter 7, §IV.
- First publication: *Revue socialiste* (Paris), 22 (127), 15 July 1895: 14–25.
- *EEPA* 1898: 175–90.

15 'Théorie du libre échange' (1895)

- Translated as: 'Theory of free trade', Chapter 11.
- First publication: *Revue d'économie politique* (Paris), 11 (7), July 1897: 649–64.
- *EEPA* 1898: 286–304.

16 'Note sur la "théorie de la quantité" ' (1897; prepared to be added as an appendix to *Théorie de la monnaie* in *EEPA*)

- Translated as: 'On the "Theory of quantity" ', Chapter 6, Note.
- *EEPA* 1898: 153–8.

17 'L'économique appliquée et la défense des salaires' (1896–7)

- Translated as: 'Applied economics and the protection of wages', Chapter 10.
- First publication: *Revue d'économie politique* (Paris), 11 (12), December 1897: 1018–36.
- *EEPA* 1898: 265–85.

18 'La Caisse d'épargne postale de Vienne et le "comptabilisme social" ' (1897–8; provisional titles in 1896–7: 'Le compensationnisme' and 'La Banque de compensation')

- Translated as: 'The Post Office Savings Bank of Vienna and "*comptabilisme social*" ', Chapter 14.
- First publication: *Revue d'économie politique* (Paris), 12 (3), March 1898: 202–20. The third part ('Le comptabilisme social : l'unité fixe de valeur') was reprinted in the *Annales de l'Institut des sciences sociales* (Bruxelles), 4th year, 1898: 257–62, and in the brochure *A propos du comptabilisme social* (offprints of the *Annales de l'Institut des sciences sociales*), Brussels, 1898.
- *EEPA* 1898: 376–98.

19 'Esquisse d'une doctrine économique et sociale' (1893–8, rejected by the *Revue de métaphysique et de morale* and the *Revue socialiste*)

- Translated as: 'Outline of an economic and social doctrine', Chapter 16.
- First publication: Section 6 only, in two parts: 'Politique française', *Gazette de Lausanne*, 101st year, no. 162, 14 July 1898: and 'La prière du libre penseur', *Gazette de Lausanne*, 101st year, no. 166, 18 July 1898: 1. The first article was reprinted as 'Esquisse d'une doctrine économique et sociale' in *L'Association catholique. Revue des questions sociales et ouvrières* (Paris), 23rd year, vol. XLVI, 15 December 1898: 571–6.
- *EEPA* 1898: 449–95.

C Auguste et Léon Walras: œuvres économiques complètes

Auguste Walras

I *Richesse, liberté et société* (1990, edited by Pierre-Henri Goutte and Jean-Michel Servet)
II *La Vérité sociale* (1997, Jean-Michel Servet and Pierre-Henri Goutte)
III *Cours et pièces diverses* (2004, Pierre-Henri Goutte and Jean-Michel Servet)
IV *Correspondance* (2004, Claude Hébert)

Léon Walras

V *L'Économie politique et la justice* (2001, Pierre-Henri Goutte)
VI *Les Associations populaires coopératives* (1990, Jean-Pierre Potier)
VII *Mélanges d'économie politique et sociale* (1987, Claude Hébert and Jean-Pierre Potier)
VIII *Eléments d'économie politique pure ou théorie de la richesse sociale* (variorum edition, 1988, Claude Mouchot)
IX *Etudes d'économie sociale (Théorie de la répartition de la richesse sociale)* (variorum edition, 1990, Pierre Dockès)
X *Etudes d'économie politique appliquée* (*Théorie de la production de la richesse sociale*) (variorum edition, 1992, Jean-Pierre Potier)
XI *Théorie mathématique de la richesse sociale* (*et autres écrits mathématiques et d'économie pure*) (1993, Claude Mouchot)
XII *Cours* (2000, Pierre Dockès, Jean-Pierre Potier and Pascal Bridel)
XIII *Oeuvres diverses* (2001, Pierre Dockès, Claude Mouchot and Jean-Pierre Potier)
XIV *Tables et index* (2004, prepared by a group of members of the Centre Walras, Lyon, or the Centre Walras–Pareto, Lausanne)

D Correspondence between (A) editions 1 and 2 and (B) the Potier edition of the EEPA

- '*x* : *y*' means that page *x* of A begins at the top of page *y* of B.
- '*x* : *y*, *z*' means that page *x* of A begins at page *y* of B at the left-hand side of line *z* from above.
- 'b' after a line number means that the lines have to be counted from below.
- '*x* : *y*, *z* bla' means that page *x* of A starts at page *y* of B in line *z* with 'bla'.
- Running titles, notes, figures and tables are ignored in counting lines.
- Every line of an equation or bloc of equations counts as one line.

3 : 5
4 : 5, 1b -culation
5 : 6, 12b -ports
6 : 7, 19 -mes
7 : 8, 9 -stances
8 : 8, 2b -times
9 : 9, 8b serait
10 : 10, 16b consommation
11 : 11, 15 -loppais
12 : 12, 5 bien
13 : 12, 6b qu'il
14 : 13, 14b -lateur
15 : 14, 17 et
16 : 15, 7 facile
17 : 15, 5b acheminé
18 : 16,6b banque
19 : 17, 17b double
20 : 19
21 : 19, 4b points
22 : 20, 12b
23 : 21,13 AC
24 : 22, 16 parler
25 : 23, 7 Ainsi
26 : 24, 4 un
27 : 24, 5b blé
28 : 25, 16b $\frac{1}{2}$
29 : 26, 16 sert
30 : 27, 7 *d'*
31 : 28, 3 du tableau I
32 : 28, 1b les observations
33 : 29, 3b et
34 : 30, 8b donnant
35 : 31 figure
36 : 32, 7b théorème
37 : 33, 8b
38 : 34, 14b -riation
39 : 35, 6b on
40 : 36, 10b et la
41 : 37, 7b de
42 : 38, 14b -minué
43 : 39, 13 théorie
44 : 40, 15 25
45 : 41, 8
46 : 41, 3b -vantageuse
47 : 42,13b pourrait
48 : 43, 19 -tance
49 : 44, 11 -nouvellée
50 : 45, 5 sa
51 : 46
52 : 46, 9b
53 : 47, 17b
54 : 48, 15 plus
55 : 49, 5 exactement
56 : 49, 1b faut
57 : 50, 1b
58 : 51, 9b l'autre
59 : 52, 9b -teur
60 : contient le *Tableau* I
61 : contient le *Tableau* II
62 : blanche
63 : 57
64 : blanche
65 : 57, 4
66 : 57, 1b lequel
67 : 58, 4b
68 : 59, 4b valeur
69 : 60, 14b à
70 : 61, 10b théoriquement
71 : 63
72 : 63, 4b *journal*
73 : 64, 12b la courbe
74 : 65, 16b -pris
75 : 66, 15 -tistique
76 : 67, 16 *combustibles*
77 : 68, 7 -drait
78 : 68, 2b économique
79 : 69, 9b du *Procès-verbal*
80 : 71
81 : 71, 7b n'est
82 : 72, 17b mais
83 : 73, 14b *Théorie*
84 : 74, 15b -vahissement
85 : 77
86 : 78, 2 On

87 : 78, 4b de l'égalité
88 : 79, 12b effective
89 : 80, 19 Pour
90 : 81, 10 $p_b =$
91 : 82, 71 :p_b
92 : 83, 14 $Oq_{d,2}r_{d,2}\delta_{r,2}$
93 : 84, 12
94 : 85, 8 soit
95 : 86, 5b une
96 : 88, 10 Et
97 : 89, 11 toujours
98 : 90, 7b
99 : 91, 6b banquiers
100 : 93, 8 terme
101 : 94, 10
102 : 95, 15 la monnaie auxquelles
103 : 96, 7 ce
104 : 97, 9 entrepreneurs
105 : 98, 10 permis
106 : 99, 5 et
107 : 101
108 : 101, 1b N[']importe
109 : 102, 7b n'augmenterait
110 : 103, 12b l'autre
111 : 104, 18 l'or
112 : 105, 13
113 : 106, 9 la
114 : 107, 1 elle
115 : 107, 5b rare
116 : 108, 10b de 1881
117 : 109, 8b -ganisation
118 : 110, 19b -siblement
119 : 111, 11 marchandise
120 : 112
121 : 112, 4b ne
122 : 113, 9b monometallisme-or
123 : 114, 12b une
124 : 115, 18b
125 : 116, 12 la monnaie
126 : 117, 6 cette
127 : 119
128 : 119, 2b qu'elle
129 : 120, 7b remédierait
130 : 121, 15b quantité
131 : 122, 7b -ticulier
132 : 123, 8b fournir
133 : 124, 12b
134 : 125, 11b
135 : 126, 11 anglaises
136 : 127, 4
137 : 127, 2b -gent
138 : 128, 6b une
139 : 129, 3b
140 : 130, 6b
141 : 131, 13b
142 : 132, 9b
143 : 133, 6 variation
144 : 134, 14 de la
145 : 135, 8 qui
146 : 136, 2 d'or
147 : 137, 2 -ait
148 : 137, 3b
149 : 138, 4b -gal
150 : 139, 11b -lisme
151 : 140, 16 moi
152 : blanche
153 : 146
154 : 146, 7b
155 : 147, 4b α
156 : 148, 7b
157 : 149, 6b
158 : 150, 10b
159 : 153
160 : 153, 1b proportion
161 : 154, 4b en
162 : 156, 3
163 : 157, 4 grande
164 : 157, 9b -nétaire
165 : 158, 13b
166 : 159, 20b *yeux*
167 : 160, 14 à 1
168 : 161, 5
169 : 162, 6 *dépit*
170 : 163, 10 octobre
171 : 164, 17 d'espérer
172 : 165, 10 de la
173 : 166, 5 le
174 : 166, 4b entre
175 : 167, 9b
176 : 168, 16b -leurs
177 : 169, 15
178 : 170, 1 -tion
179 : 170, 4b l'ignorance
180 : 171, 9b vendeurs
181 : 172, 14b fait
182 : 173, 18 de
183 : 174, 8 -doption
184 : 174, 1b de ces
185 : 175, 12b commerciales
186 : 176, 18 vu
187 : 177, 12 valeur
188 : 178, 7 sauf
189 : 179, 4 ne
190 : 197, 4b une
191 : 181
192 : blanche
193 : 183
194 : 183, 8b l'État
195 : 184, 14b -versaire
196 : 185, 17 la
197 : 186, 8 un
198 : 187
199 : 187, 11b -ces
200 : 188, 14b
201 : 189, 16 eux
202 : 190, 11 -vention
203 : 191, 5 concédait
204 : 191, 1b de la
205 : 192, 5b encore
206 : 193, 10b l'exploitant
207 : 194, 14b *Par*

208 : 195, 14 l'on
209 : 196, 8 des routes
210 : 196, 2b -munication
211 : 197, 11b conduite
212 : 198, 16b dit-il
213 : 199, 17 habitudes
214 : 200, 8 à la
215 : 200, 2b ou
216 : 201, 12b dans
217 : 202, 20 plaisir
218 : 203, 11 de
219 : 204, 4
220 : 204, 7b -pagnies
221 : 205, 11b n'ont
222 : 206, 19
223 : 207, 9 conditions
224 : 208, 6 dernier
225 : 208, 6b –leurs, que
226 : 209, 12b puissant
227 : 210, 18b 2 ou 3
228 : 211, 13 de vue
229 : 212, 3 de la
230 : 212, 8b -ploitation
231 : 213, 15b -poles
232 : 214, 17 devra
233 : 215
234 : 215, 1b -cernent
235 : 216, 12b exploitation
236 : 217, 22 l'Orléans
237 : 219
238 : blanche
239 : 221
240 : 222, 3 des
241 : 222, 5b comme
242 : 223, 12b reconnaître
243 : 224, 19 en raison
244 : 225, 12
245 : 226, 11
246 : 227, 9 -tenant
247 : 228, 4 dépréciation
248 : 229
249 : 230
250 : 230, 6b difficiles
251 : 231, 6b -on
252 : 232, 12b
253 : 233, 18 la
254 : 234, 14b
255 : 235, 17 -sistences
256 : 236, 8
257 : 236, 1b avancée
258 : 237, 8b des
259 : 238, 16b -me dans
260 : 239, 16 centimes
261 : 240, 7 -ducteurs
262 : 240, 3b construisant
263 : 241, 8b fâcheux
264 : 242, 17b -sité
265 : 245
266 : 245, 6b -ditions
267 : 246, 14b
268 : 247, 15 -neurs
269 : 248, 9
270 : 249, 3 aucun
271 : 249, 7b trop
272 : 250, 15b produisant
273 : 251, 17 mécanisme
274 : 252, 8 -pliquée
275 : 253, 4 serait
276 : 253, 2b -turel
277 : 254, 13b d'une
278 : 255, 17 de même
279 : 256, 14 services
280 : 257, 9 des prix
281 : 258, 2 -quilibre
282 : 258, 8b nom
283 : 259, 11b qu'on
284 : 260, 18 toute
285 : 261, 12 comme
286 : 263
287 : 264, 9s' effectuer
288 : 265, 1 perdu
289 : 265, 5b -rents
290 : 266, 8b
291 : 267, 9b
292 : 268, 9b
293 : 269, 15b
294 : 270, 14 propriétaires
295 : 271, 8 -tats
296 : 271, 5b producteurs
297 : 272, 10b
298 : 273, 18b
299 : 274, 14 à
300 : 275 6 -taire
301 : 276, 1 *baissant*
302 : 276, 3b -tions
303 : 277, 6b est une
304 : 278, 13b croît-on
305 : 281
306 : blanche
307 : 283
308 : 283, 3b une
309 : 284 11b, -tion
310 : 285, 20 puis
311 : 286, 12 -bles
312 : 287, 9 y a
313 : 288
314 : 288, 8b -ter
315 : 289, 15b réalise
316 : 290, 16 aux
317 : 291, 9 -tions
318 : 292, 6 chaques
319 : 292, 3b entrepreneurs
320 : 293, 13b ou
321 : 294, 18 -ités
322 : 295, 8 -priété
323 : 295, 1b désintéressé
324 : 296, 4b
325 : 297, 17b réclamer
326 : 298, 16 capitaux

327 : 299, 7 *-che*
328 : 300, 10 -quée
329 : 301, 6 -cipe
330 : 301, 4b se
331 : 302, 12b monnaie
332 : 303, 20b à
333 : 304, 11 créances
334 : 305, 1 *-tières*
335 : 305, 5b
336 : 306, 8b
337 : 309
338 : blanche
339 : 311
340 : 311, 3b individu
341 : 312, 19b suffisait
342 : 313, 16b divers
343 : 314, 17 banque
344 : 315, 8
345 : 316, 9
346 : 317, 4 celle
347 : 317, 5b existante
348 : 318, 10b
349 : 319, 20 de
350 : 320, 11 les
351 : 321, 1 dans
352 : 321, 3b
353 : 322, 5b
354 : 323, 9b –tal fixe
355 : 324, 14b
356 : 325, 16
357 : 326, 12
358 : 327, 4 leçon
359 : 328, 6 cet
360 : 329, 4 fermages
361 : 329, 2b *-nution*
362 : 330, 6b relativement
363 : 331, 14b *une*
364 : 332, 16 de
365 : 333, 11 -rable
366 : 334, 4 tous
367 : 334, 6b
368 : 335, 14b élève
369 : 336, 18 -demanderaient
370 : 337, 15 faut
371 : 338, 6 -mission
372 : 338, 1b des
373 : 339, 9b Quant
374 : 340, 14b -taire
375 : 341, 16b exclusivement
376 : 343
377 : 343, 4b sont
378 : 344, 9b
379 : 345, 16b il
380 : 346, 16 capitaux
381 : 347, 6 assez
382 : 348
383 : 348 3b d'or
384 : 349, 13b
385 : 350, 19 chiffres
386 : 351, 9 l'étranger
387 : 352, 3 chacun
388 : 353
389 : 353, 3b
390 : 354, 8b
391 : 355, 14b fictive
392 : 356, 14
393 : 357, 7 fur
394 : 357, 3b florin
395 : 358, 8b les
396 : 359, 19b On
397 : 360, 12 -talistes
398 : 361, 9 prix
399 : 363
400 : blanche
401 : 365
402 : 365, 4b
403 : 366, 11b
404 : 367, 20 -quebots
405 : 368, 9 annuelles
406 : 369
407 : 369, 9b -tions et
408 : 370, 16b nous
409 : 371, 16 égalité
410 : 372, 8 France
411 : 373, 1 un
412 : 373, 10b
413 : 374, 18b lui
414 : 375, 14 baisse
415 : 376, 7
416 : 376, 3b -chandise
417 : 377, 14b terme
418 : 378, 17 son
419 : 379, 12
420 : 380, 2 à
421 : 380, 6b
422 : 381, 11b
423 : 382, 18 tous
424 : 383, 10 en constructions
425 : 384, 3
426 : 384, 7b -nu-
427 : 385, 16b -tant
428 : 386, 16
429 : 387, 7 producteurs
430 : 388, 1 à rien
431 : 388, 4b
432 : 389, 13b donnée
433 : 390, 19 -saire
434 : 391, 9
435 : 392, 9 elle-même
436 : 392, 10b à
437 : 393, 19b croyait
438 : 394 12
439 : 395 10, de
440 : 396, 2 par
441 : 396, 6b plus
442 : 397, 13b sans
443 : 398, 17b sur une
444 : 399, 15 mesures
445 : 400, 13 -mettent
446 : est en blanche
447 : 403
448 : est en blanche
449 : 405
450 : 405, 3b instant
451 : 406, 8b -thique

452 : 407, 14b ses
453 : 408 17 -manité
454 : 409, 8 pure
455 : 410, 3
456 : 410, 9b -gences
457 : 411, 15b
458 : 412, 14 soi-même
459 : 413, 5 que
460 : 413, 5b dans
461 : 414, 13b le
462 : 415, 17b les
463 : 416, 13 ils
464 : 417, 4 -mais
465 : 417,7b
466 : 418, 17b diminue
467 : 419, 14 -matique
468 : 420, 7 confirmer
469 : 420, 4b existe
470 : 421, 13b tout
471 : 422, 19 verra
472 : 423, 7
473 : 424, 4 aux
474 : 424, 7b -sisterait
475 : 425, 14b
476 : 426, 16 les
477 : 427, 6 un
478 : 427, 6b -formes
479 : 428, 17b du
480 : 429, 15 libre
481 : 430, 4 normal
482 : 430, 8b ils
483 : 431, 19b la
484 : 432, 13 doit
485 : 433, 3
486 : 433, 8b solution
487 : 434, 10b l'industrie
488 : 435, 17b rupture
489 : 436, 14 aux
490 : 437, 7 bulletin
491 : 437, 3b
492 : 438, 8b des
493 : 439, 17b touchent
494 : 440, 15 ces
495 : 441, 8 temps

Notes

1 Remarkably, Karl Marx declared himself in favour of free exchange already in 1846! Perhaps he was not a socialist by the narrow French standards at the time.

2 All material about classification of (economic) science was first developed within the framework of the research for Jolink's doctoral dissertation (Rotterdam 1991, particularly chapter 3). Walras did not draw diagrams like Figures 0.1–0.2; they reflect our interpretation of his ideas.

3 There are, after all, only two, unimportant, pre-publications. Moreover, many chapters of *EEPA* were written (long) before 1898.

4 This point has become somewhat controversial; see, for instance, Bridel (1997), Bridel and Huck (2002) and Rebeyrol (1999). This was mainly through Donald Walker's seminal *Walras's Market Models* (1996), where he discussed realism saying that all Walras's notions are firmly rooted in reality, or at least are meant to be so. Personally, I have never understood how some of our colleagues could believe that economists living and working around the middle of the nineteenth century were interested in ununderstandable abstractions about exchange, money, time, virtual processes and things like impossible auctioneers. The first economists had other things to do. They had to found a new profession and were called to occupy themselves with real things, like money, trade, remuneration, poverty, wealth, etc. It would have been very stupid if they had started with abstract philosophies while the solution of concrete problems was waiting. It is true that some of them felt obliged to study the whole field or part of it instead of giving immediate, but ill considered answers. Walras was such a person and it is not difficult to mention other examples. All those economists invested some time in order to be able to give better, but still realistic, answers; in other words, they built what we now call models.

5 He may keep some of the services of his own capital goods for himself (taking leisure, living in his own house, riding his own horse, etc.) and he may even buy services from other capital owners.

6 So it can happen that sometimes when Walras was speaking about 'production' he only meant production of consumption goods.
7 Walras's French term was *capitalisation*; I have translated it as 'capital transformation'.
8 When reading it for the first time, in early 1878, Walras must have been amazed at finding in Gossen's book, systematically worked out, his own scheme for land reform, advanced from the beginning of his career onwards (1859; see Walras 1881, 1885).
9 This attitude belongs now to the distant past.
10 It seems that making this kind of fine graph was the only thing Walras had learnt at the École des Mines.
11 Some factual information on strikes in France in Walras's days seems relevant here. Since 1864 individual strikes were no longer illegal and since 1884 a coalition of workers to organize a strike was no longer a crime. This, indeed, made strikes less violent, but no less frequent. In the 1880s there were on average about 150 strikes per year. In 75 per cent of the cases the main motivation was a claim for a wage increase on the part of the workers refused by the employers or a protest on the workers' side against a wage cut proposed by the employers. On average 250 workers participated in these strikes, but there were also some strikes with 10,000 or 20,000 participants. Twenty-one per cent ended favourably for the strikers, but even in the case of a wage increase obtained by the strike, the extra wage earned in one year and two months, on average, was needed to compensate for the costs in terms of non-paid wages during the strike. See also Michel (1893) and Turquan (1893).
12 Walras often used the term 'bankers and banks', which sounds now somewhat pleonastic. At the time, however, the profession of banking often was still a one-man business, particularly in small cities.

Bibliography

Allais, M. (1943) *Traité d'économie politique pure*, 2 vols, Paris: Imprimerie Nationale.

Baranzini, Roberto (2002) 'Léon Walras, l'épargne, le crédit et les crises', in *L'économie walrassienne*, Actes du Colloque de l'Association Internationale Walras, 16 September 1999, *Les Cahiers du CERAS* (Reims), Hors série no. 1: 147–63.

Blaug, Mark, ed. (1992) *Léon Walras 1834–1910*, Aldershot: Edward Elgar.

Bridel, Pascal (1997) *Money and General Equilibrium Theory*, Cheltenham: Edward Elgar.

—— and Elisabeth Huck (2002) 'Yet another look at Léon Walras's theory of *tâtonnement*', *European Journal of the history of Economic Thought*, 9 (4): 513–41.

Cunningham Wood, J., ed. (1993) *Léon Walras: Critical Assessments*, 3 vols, London: Routledge.

Giddings, Franklin Henri (1896) *The Principles of Sociology*, third edition, New York: Macmillan.

Gossen, Hermann Heinrich (1854) *Entwickelung der Gesetze des menschlichen Verkehrs und der daraus fließenden Regeln für menschliches Handeln*, Braunschweig: Vieweg.

——(1983) *The Laws of Human Relations and the Rules of Human Action Derived Therefrom*, translated by Rudolph Blitz, with an introductory essay by Nicholas Georgescu-Roegen, Cambridge, MA: MIT Press.

——(1995) *Exposition des lois de l'échange et des règles de l'industrie qui s'en déduisent*, translated (in 1879) by Léon Walras and Charles Secrétan, introduced and annotated by Jan van Daal, Albert Jolink, Jean-Pierre Potier and Jean-Michel Servet, under the auspices of the Centre Auguste et Léon Walras, Université Lumière Lyon-2 and the Tinbergen Instituut, Erasmus Universiteit Rotterdam, Paris: Économica.

Jolink, Albert (1991) 'Liberte, égalité, rareté', doctoral dissertation, Erasmus Universiteit Rotterdam.

——(1996) *The Evolutionist Economics of Léon Walras*, London: Routledge.

Michel, George (1893) 'Grèves. Examen théorique des grèves, de leur légitimité et de leurs conséquences', in Léon Say and Joseph Chailley, eds, *Nouveau dictionnaire d'économie politique*, Paris: Guillaumin, I: 1109–11.

Morishima, M. (1977) *Walras' Economics*, Cambridge, MA: Cambridge University Press.

Potier, Jean-Pierre (1994) 'Classification des sciences et divisions de l' "économie politique et sociale" dans l'oeuvre de Léon Walras: une tentative de reconstruction', special issue 'Walras' of *Économies et sociétés. Cahiers de l'ISMEA*, 28 (10–11), October–November, series 'Oeconomia. Histoire de la pensée économique', P.E., no. 20–1: 223–77.

Rebeyrol, Antoine (1999) *La Pensée économique de Léon Walras*, Paris: Dunod.

Smith, Adam (1994) [1776], *An Inquiry into the Nature and Causes of the Wealth of Nations*, New York: Modern Library.

Turquan, V. (1893) 'Grèves. Statistiques des grèves', in Léon Say and Joseph Chailley, eds, *Nouveau dictionnaire d'économie politique*, Paris: Guillaumin, I: 1111–15.

van Daal, Jan (1998) 'Léon Walras's general economic equilibrium models of capital formation: existence of a solution', *Revue Économique*, 49: 1175–98. (Reprinted in Donald A. Walker, ed., *The Legacy of Léon Walras*, Cheltenham: Edward Elgar, 2001, II: 390–405.)

——(1999) 'Léon Walras et le capitalisme', *Revue européenne des sciences sociales*, 37 (116): 83–99.

——(2000) 'Les tâtonnements dans le modèle de la production chez Léon Walras. Bons à rien?' in *L'Économie walrasienne*, Actes du Colloque de l'Association Internationale Walras, 16 September 1999, *Les Cahiers du CERAS* (Reims), Hors série no. 1, June: 58–78.

——and Albert Jolink (1993) *The Equilibrium Economics of Léon Walras*, London and New York: Routledge.

——and Donald A. Walker (1990) 'The problem of aggregation in Walras's general equilibrium theory', *History of Political Economy*, 22: 489–505.

Walker, Donald A., ed. (1983) *William Jaffé's Essays on Walras*, Cambridge, MA: Cambridge University Press,

——(1987) 'Bibliography of the writings of Léon Walras', *History of Political Economics*, 19 (4): 667–702.

——(1996) *Walras's Market Models*, Cambridge, MA: Cambridge University Press.

——(2001a) *The Legacy of Léon Walras*, Cheltenham: Edward Elgar, 2001, II: 341–57.

Walker, Donald A., ed. (2001b) 'A factual account of the functioning of the nineteenth-century Paris Bourse', *European Journal of the History of Economic Thought*, 8 (2): 186–207.

——(2001c) *The Legacy of Léon Walras*, 2 vols, Cheltenham: Edward Elgar.

Walras, Auguste (1990) *Richesse, liberté et société*, edited by Pierre-Henri Goutte et Jean-Michel Servet, under the auspices of the Centre Auguste et Léon Walras at Lyon, vol. I of *Auguste et Léon Walras: œuvres économiques complètes*, Paris: Économica.

Walras, Léon (1858) *Francis Sauveur*, Paris: E Dentu.

——(1859) 'La lettre', *Revue française*, 16 (4): 193–206; 16 (5): 275–8.

——(1860) *L'Économie politique et la justice. Examen critique et réfutation des doctrines de M. J-P. Proudhon*, Paris: Guillaumin. (Republished in Walras 2001: 75–313.)

——(1868) *Théorie générale de la société. Leçons publiques faites à Paris. Première série 1867–1868*, Paris: Guillaumin. (Republished in *EES*: Walras 1990: 25–173.)

——(1874) 'Principes d'une théorie mathématique de l'échange', *Journal des économistes*, 34 (100), April: 5–21. (Republished in Walras 1987: 261–90.)

——(1874) *Éléments d'économie politique pure, ou Théorie de la richesse sociale*, first instalment, Lausanne: Corbaz/Paris: Guillaumin/Basel: Georg.

——(1877) *Éléments d'économie politique pure, ou Théorie de la richesse sociale*, second instalment, Lausanne: Corbaz/Paris: Guillaumin/Basel: Georg.

——(1881) 'Théorie mathématique du prix des terres et de leur rachat par l'Etat', *Bulletin de la Société vaudoise des sciences naturelles*, 2e série, vol. 17: 189–284. (Republished in *EES*: Walras 1990.)

——(1885) 'Un économiste inconnu, H. H. Gossen', *Journal des économistes*, 30: 68–90, 260–1. (Republished in *EES*: Walras 1990. Also in Gossen 1995: 41–58.)

——(1886) *Théorie de la monnaie*, Lausanne: Corbaz/Paris: Larose & Forcel/Rome: Loescher/Leipzig: Duncker & Humblot. (Republished in *EEPA*: 57–151.)

——(1889) *Éléments d'économie politique pure, ou Théorie de la richesse sociale*, second edition, Lausanne: Rouge/Paris: Guillaumin/Leipzig: Duncker & Humblot.

——(1896) *Études d'économie sociale* (*Théorie de la répartition de la richesse sociale*), second edition, Lausanne: Rouge/Paris: Pichon.

——(1896) *Éléments d'économie politique pure, ou Théorie de la richesse sociale*, third edition, Lausanne: Rouge/Paris: Pichon/Leipzig: Duncker & Humblot.

——(1898) *Études d'économie politique appliquée* (*Théorie de la production de la richesse sociale*), second edition, Lausanne: Rouge/Paris: Pichon.

——(1900) *Éléments d'économie politique pure, ou Théorie de la richesse sociale*, fourth edition, Lausanne: Rouge/Paris: Pichon.

——(1926) *Éléments d'économie politique pure, ou Théorie de la richesse sociale*, definitive edition, revised by the author, Paris: Pichon & Durand-Auzias/Lausanne: Rouge.

——(1936) *Études d'économie politique appliquée* (*Théorie de la production de la richesse sociale*), second edition, Lausanne: Rouge/Paris: Pichon & Durand-Auzias.

——(1936) *Études d'économie sociale* (*Théorie de la répartition de la richesse sociale*), second edition, Lausanne: Rouge/Paris: Pichon & Durand-Auzias.

——(1938) *Abrégé des éléments d'économie politique pure*, Lausanne: Rouge/Paris: Pichon & Durand-Auzias. (Republished in Walras 1988.)

——(1954) *Élements of Pure Economics, or The Theory of Social Wealth*, translated and annotated by W. Jaffé, Homewood, IL: Irwin/London: Allen & Unwin.

——(1965) *Correspondence of Léon Walras and Related Papers*, 3 vols, edited by William Jaffé, Amsterdam: North-Holland.

——(1987) *Mélanges d'économie politique et sociale*, edited by Claude Hébert and Jean-Pierre Potier, under the auspices of the Centre Auguste et Léon Walras, Lyon, vol. VII of *Auguste et Léon Walras: œuvres économiques complètes*, Paris: Économica.

——(1988) *Éléments d'économie politique pure, ou Théorie de la richesse sociale*, variorum edition of the editions of 1874–7, 1889, 1896, 1900 and 1926 (and of the edition of the *Abrégé* of 1938) augmented by a translation of the notes of William Jaffé in *Elements of Pure Economics* (1954), edited by Claude Mouchot, under the auspices of the Centre Auguste et Léon Walras, Lyon, vol. VIII of *Auguste et Léon Walras: œuvres économiques complètes*, Paris: Économica.

——(1990) *Les Associations populaires coopératives*, edited by Jean-Pierre Potier, under the auspices of the Centre Auguste et Léon Walras, Lyon, vol. VI of *Auguste et Léon Walras: œuvres économiques complètes*, Paris: Économica.

——(1990) *Études d'économie sociale: théorie de la répartition de la richesse sociale*, edited by Pierre Dockès, under the auspices of the Centre Auguste et Léon Walras, Lyon, vol. IX of *Auguste et Léon Walras: œuvres économiques complètes*, Paris: Économica. (First edition 1896, second edition 1938.)

——(1992) *Études d'économie politique appliquée* (*Théorie de la production de la richesse sociale*), edited by Jean-Pierre Potier, under the auspices of the Centre Auguste et Léon Walras, Lyon, vol. X of *Auguste et Léon Walras: œuvres économiques complètes*, Paris: Économica. (First edition 1898, second edition 1938.)

Walras, Léon (1996) *Cours*, edited by Pierre Dockès, Jean-Pierre Potier and Pascal Bridel, under the auspices of the Centre Auguste et Léon Walras, Lyon, vol. XII of *Auguste et Léon Walras: œuvres économiques complètes*, Paris: Économica.

——(2000) *Œuvres divers*, edited by Pierre Dockès, Claude Mouchot and Jean-Pierre Potier, under the auspices of the Centre Auguste et Léon Walras, Lyon, vol. XIII of *Auguste et Léon Walras: œuvres économiques complètes*, Paris: Économica.

——(2001) *L'Économie politique et la justice*, edited by Pierre-Henri Goutte and Jean-Michel Servet, under the auspices of the Centre Auguste et Léon Walras, Lyon, vol. V of *Auguste et Léon Walras: œuvres économiques complètes*, Paris: Économica.

ÉTUDES

D'ÉCONOMIE SOCIALE

(THÉORIE DE LA RÉPARTITION DE LA RICHESSE SOCIALE)

PAR

LÉON WALRAS

LAUSANNE
F. ROUGE, LIBRAIRE-ÉDITEUR
4, rue Haldimand, 4.

PARIS
F. PICHON, IMPRIMEUR-ÉDITEUR
24, Rue Soufflot, 24.

1896

Part I

Money

[3]

1 Gold money with regulating silver token[1,i]

The forthcoming expiration of the convention of 23 December 1865, which constituted the Latin Union, and the meeting in Paris of a conference to discuss and decide about the conditions of its prolongation bring me to reconsider a monetary system that I have already exposed very concisely, but explicitly enough for scientists, at the end of a memoir entitled 'Théorie mathématique du bimétallisme'. This memoir was published in the *Journal des économistes*, December 1876, May 1881 and October 1882, and reproduced in my *Théorie mathématique de la richesse sociale*.[ii] The system consisted of *monometallism based on gold, combined with a silver token, distinct from coins for small change, to be introduced into the circulation or withdrawn from it in such a way that the value of the multiple standard would not vary*.[iii] Three elements simultaneously determine the value of the metal that constitutes the money commodity: (1) the utility of this metal as a commodity; (2) its utility as money, in other words, as the 'desired cash balance'; (3) its total quantity. The increase or the decrease of the first two elements[iv] will increase or decrease its value; the increase or the decrease of the third element will decrease or increase its value. Consequently, if one or the other utility were to increase, or if the quantity should decrease, one would have to introduce the special token into the circulation, in order partially to supply the money metal and keep, at the same time, enough metal in the mode of commodity. If one or the other utility were to decrease, or if the quantity should increase, the special token would have to be withdrawn **[4]** from circulation, in order to leave the money commodity in its place and to avoid too much metal in the form of a commodity. In this way, we shall be able to regulate the variation in value of money. I shall again expose this system, making it in a way more complete, and more accessible. If possible, I shall put its principle beyond

1 Rules proposed for the International Monetary Conference [Paris, 1884] for the prolongation of the 'Latin Union'. *Revue du droit international*, December 1884.

contest. Finally, I shall develop its practical conclusion, applicable to the present circumstances.

I realize that the aim of my system, as I see it, will result in most economists, whether monometallists or bimetallists, denouncing it. To answer the latter, I have already hinted that their objection is not admissible: presenting the bimetallic standard for the whole world to adopt, because it would be a much stabler standard than the monometallistic standards, means giving everyone the right to claim for himself to seek the greatest stability of the monetary standard. However, I shall have to take on the monometallists' argument.

> Value – they will say – is a relative fact. When the price of corn increases from 20c to 25c, that is, from a fifth to a quarter of a franc (5 g) per pound (500 g), the price of silver in corn decreases by this very fact from 5 lb to 4 lb a franc. There is no reason to say that the value of corn has increased by one-quarter without saying at the same time that the value of silver decreased by one-fifth. Strictly speaking, the value of corn as such and the value of silver as such are things that do not exist; and, consequently there is no reason to seek their constancy or regulate their variation.

I accept their initial argument, but not what follows, and I shall undertake to demonstrate to those readers who are willing to pay a little attention that this consequence is not necessarily what it seems.

Strictly speaking, it is quite sure that value does not exist: there are only ratios of values or prices. But I have proved in my *Éléments d'économie politique pure*, or in the first four memoirs of my *Théorie mathématique de la richesse sociale*,[v] which resume it [i.e. the *Éléments*], that these **[5]** ratios of values or prices are mathematically equal to the ratios of the *intensities of the last wants satisfied*, i.e. of the *raretés* for each consumer. In the first two memoirs, I have established that this equality occurs in the exchange of two commodities as well as in the exchange of several commodities for one another. In the second two I have shown that it persists throughout all complications of production and the formation of capital, and that it is valid for productive services as well as products. We shall see, by the example of the problem of money, how the substitution of the ratios of *raretés* for ratios of values will bring absolute elements into our discussion instead of relative ones and provide us with the solution to the most important economic questions.

Likewise, when its price was 20c, the intensity of the last want for corn satisfied was, for every consumer, in the same proportion to the intensity of the last want for silver satisfied as 1 is to 5. At a price of 25c, this intensity of the last want for corn satisfied will be in the same proportion to the last want for silver satisfied as 1 is to 4. Both terms of these two proportionalities exist of their own accord. For each consumer facing whatever commodity, we may perfectly well conceive of wants decreasing in intensity, from the more or less intense want that solicits the first unity or fraction of a unity of the commodity, when consumption had not yet taken place at all, to zero want, called satiety, experienced after consuming the commodity extensively. This conception becomes completely clear by setting up utility or want curves or functions as have been formulated by Gossen, Jevons and myself. Consequently, we also understand quite well that, the ratio of the intensities of the last wants of corn and silver satisfied being switched from 1/5 to 1/4, either the intensities of the last wants of corn satisfied decreased by 25 per cent, where the *raretés* of silver did not change, or the intensities of the last wants of silver satisfied increased by 20 per cent, while the *raretés* of corn remained the **[6]** same. In the first case everybody stops at a want for corn somewhat more intense than before; in the second case everybody will be a little nearer to satiety with respect to silver. Now, we may agree that in the first case it will be said that the value of corn has increased by 25 per cent while silver has not changed. In the second, it will be said that the value of silver has dropped by 20 per cent while corn has remained stable.

For the sake of simplification, we may also proceed in the same way as we do with respect to sizes, as far as the intensities of the last wants satisfied or the *raretés* are concerned. When people say that, in a certain country, 'inhabitants' height has increased or decreased', they are speaking about the average height of a whole generation as compared with the average height of another generation. Similarly, when one says that, in a certain market, 'the *rareté* of some commodity has increased or decreased', it is clear that one is speaking about the average *rareté* of that commodity during a certain period as compared with its average *rareté* in another period. In this sense it could be stated, as an assertion that may be true or false but that everybody will understand, that 'for half a century the average intensity of the last want of corn satisfied has not changed, while the average *rareté* of silver is only four-fifths of what it was fifty years ago'. So let us imagine for a moment that these average *raretés* are directly measurable and that there are two types of goods, indicated in a general way by (A) and (B). If the average *rareté* of (A) is multiplied by α (α being greater than 1 or less), and if the average *rareté* of (B) is multiplied by β (β may also be superior or inferior to 1), one can prove mathematically that the price of (A) in (B) would be multiplied by α/β and that of (B) in (A) by β/α. One might therefore say, substituting the word *value* for *rareté*, that in the case of these price changes the value of (A) has been multiplied by α and that of (B) by β. So, finally, under the inexact expression 'variation in value of a commodity' lies a pertinent idea, namely that of considering the **[7]** circumstances of utility and quantity inherent in that commodity that have brought about the variation in its price in all the others or of the other prices in its own.

Money does not have any *rareté*;[vi] we do not feel a direct need with an intensity that decreases with the consumption of the metal as money but only as far as it regards the metal as a commodity. But under the regime of an unlimited coinage by the State on account of private individuals, precious metal as a commodity will command the same value as money. From this it follows that considering money as something whose value does not vary, or will only vary regularly, means considering precious metal as something whose average *rareté* does not vary, or will vary regularly. Pursuing the fixity or the regular variation in the value of money is the same as pursuing the fixity or the regular variation in the average *rareté* of precious metal. Is this pursuit impossible and chimerical?

> Obviously – our adversaries will say. The intensities of the last wants satisfied, or these *raretés* as you define them, are not, as you supposed, sizes that can be evaluated. How can we find the average? How can we know whether this average is greater or lesser than another is at a certain moment? So how then, can we fix it or get it to vary following such and such rule?

Well, this problem is no more insurmountable than the previous one.

If, by chance, there should exist a commodity whose *rareté* is fixed by its nature, whether or not the money commodity itself, the problem would be solved, since it would then suffice to ensure that the price of money in that commodity, or the price of that commodity in money, would not vary, or would vary regularly, so that the ratio of the *raretés* would not vary either, or would also vary regularly. This would be the final situation resulting from our manipulation of the respective quantities of the metal as a commodity and as money. For example, if corn was, by its nature, of fixed *rareté*, it would suffice to ensure that the price of corn in silver remained 20c **[8]** so that the *rareté* of silver would not vary; and it would suffice to ensure that the price of corn increased from 20c to 25c so that the *rareté* of silver would decrease by 20 per cent. Now, as a matter of fact, it is quite reasonable to believe corn, by its nature, of fixed *rareté*, at least when we consider it over rather long periods. Corn is a kind of commodity of which a given quantity is at the same time both necessary and sufficient for us, because it is an essential but dull foodstuff that is eaten only out of necessity and not for pleasure. Should we have less than we need, the intensity of the last want satisfied would be very high and its price very high; mortality would rise and the *rareté* decrease. When we have more than enough the intensity of the last want satisfied drops to nearly zero and the price is negligible; with a very high birth rate *rareté* will rise. It can therefore be seen that, to study the problem of money, a particular analysis of the utility curve of corn, with its elements and its principal specificities, would be extremely useful. Pure economics would much benefit from such a study, which has already been taken up by various authors and which I have no time to undertake here. I only notice, in passing, that we would probably have come very near a solution to the problem of stability or regular variation in value of money if we established stability or regular variation in[vii] the price of corn in money.

If corn, by its nature, were not of fixed *rareté*, Mr Cournot's solution would suffice. Let us suppose that, in the general fluctuation of prices from one period to another, the money prices of a certain number of commodities had all changed proportionally, which is to say that the prices of these commodities, measured by one of them, had remained the same. In that case two hypotheses could be formed. Either, by some particular chance, the *raretés* of these commodities had all changed proportionally; or, more naturally and more probably, all those *raretés* had remained the same, whereas **[9]** only the *rareté* of the money commodity changed, in the opposite direction. The second hypothesis would become the more certain as the number of commodities in question increased. Let us suppose that the prices of all these commodities had increased by 25 per cent. We could then take it for granted that the value of the money commodity would have decreased by 20 per cent and we could take appropriate action with regard to the quantity of money. Thus the issue of finding a commodity of fixed value or *rareté* is reduced to finding a large enough number of commodities whose prices all rose or fell in the same proportion. It is up to the statisticians to procure us such a list.

Finally, where the *rareté* and the value of money were not constant, but rather varied in the same way as the average *rareté* and value of social wealth, then Lowe and Poulett Scrope's system of the multiple standard as explained by Jevons in his *Money and the Mechanism of Exchange* [chapter XXV], would apply. Jevons adheres strictly to this system. According to Lowe and Poulett Scrope one should take a certain quantity of a certain number of commodities of a quality specified as exactly as possible: wheat, iron, cotton, sugar, tea, etc. The total quantity of these commodities would be the multiple standard, and when, between the time of settling an agreement and its maturity, the price of this total quantity had increased or decreased, the creditor would be entitled to claim a corresponding increase or forced to accept a corresponding decrease in the amount of his credit. In my system, instead of decreeing these increases or decreases – as I mentioned in my [earlier] memoir and again at the beginning of this one – one would act on the quantity of money in circulation 'in such a way that the price of the multiple standard would not vary'. In my opinion, this way of regulating the variation in value of money with the value of the multiple standard seems to be at one and the same time the simplest and most rational. There is nothing impossible about the designation of a certain number of very common consumer **[10]** goods and the establishment of their prices. Moreover, if one gives it a little consideration, one sees that this way of handling the matter consists not in maintaining the stability of the *rareté* and the value of the money commodity, but in providing it with a variation in *rareté* and value equal to the variation in average *rareté* and value of the most important commodities. Now this is just what should happen. The growth of economic production endeavours to bring about greater and greater reduction in the intensities of the last wants satisfied, or the *raretés*, of the products, and this does in fact occur. It will have attained its utmost limits when we all have as much as we want of everything. There is no reason why the money commodity should be an exception to this rule; and since it buys all other commodities, it is only just and in everybody's interest that its purchasing power should always remain the same.

Be that as it may be, and whatever combination one favours, the mode of regulating the value of money is invariably the same: introducing besides the gold money (that is, the actual money) a special silver token. The State will increase or decrease its quantity according to the circumstances. If the *rareté* and, consequently, the value of money tend to climb over the limit assigned to it, the quantity of the special token should be increased. This would allow for the demonetization of a certain quantity of gold, reducing the *rareté* and the value of the money commodity. If the *rareté* and, consequently, the value of money tended to remain below the limit, the quantity of special token should be lowered. This would entail the monetization of a certain quantity of gold and increase the *rareté* and value of the money commodity. In fact, in the absence of any exceptional circumstance provoking a deep crisis raising or lowering prices, the intervention of the State would be reduced to almost zero. Should such a circumstance arise, it would be possible to avert the recession and prevent catastrophe. A very prominent Italian economist and statistician, Professor [Angelo] Messedaglia, **[11]** to whom I explained this system in Rome, on 1 March 1883, summarized it as follows: 'Gold standard with restricted minting of silver'.[viii] In a brochure by Mr Tullio Martello, *L'interregno monetario in Italia dopo l'abolizione del biglietto inconvertibile*,[ix] I found a letter from Mr [Agostino] Magliani, Minister of Finance, dated 17 March 1883, pointing out that he could solve the monetary question, just as universal bimetallism at $15\frac{1}{2}$ does. He writes: 'Monometallismo aureo con larga coniazione d'argento regolata mediante convenzioni internationali' [Gold monometallism with considerable coinage of silver according to internationally established rules]. If, in my turn, I had to express it in a striking way, I should say: 'Gold money with twofold silver token: one fractional currency and one regulating token.'

This system, which invests the State with the task of moderating prices by acting on the quantity of money, is diametrically opposed to the opinion at present prevailing in French economics, that the State should intervene as little as possible. I do not personally share this horror of State intervention and I am patiently awaiting the time when rigorous definitions and scientific demonstrations are called for in this matter rather than facile, rather hackneyed clichés. Every month, for many years, I have received a list of questions proposed for the discussion by the 'Société d'Économie Politique de Paris', just as I did last month. There were among them things that should strike us all of salutary modesty regarding the degree of progression of our science. For example: '8. Does economics differ from ethics, law and politics?' '9. What, in economics, is the limit of what is assigned to the State?'[x] Let the writers who enjoy mocking the State and its intervention in business be kind enough to discuss and settle the second question before the Société d'Economie Politique de Paris. They would render us a considerable service, as in theory they would have encompassed the whole of applied economics. While they are at it, let them also **[12]** tell us 'what is, in politics, the limit of the tasks assigned to the State', and they will have thoroughly studied social science. In the meantime, applied economics and social science will be left in abeyance and everybody will remain free to go by his own impressions and follow his own feelings. In my own opinion, the State in France carries out its task of providing us with money of good alloy at least as well as private industry does in procuring us woollen cloth unmixed with cotton. Should it not succeed, though, it seems to me that this would not be a reason to set up the ineptness of the French State as general incompetence and deprive it of all its tasks. Money is a State responsibility and, moreover, an international concern. The States of the Latin Union would do as well to agree in order to avert monetary crises as they would to protect themselves against cholera, if that were possible. Nevertheless, I am perfectly aware of the impossibility of campaigning against the general current of ideas. If it concerned the entire implementation of my system, I should leave that to my descendants. Fortunately, the system exists and is functioning. We do not need to get it accepted. It suffices to make sure that it will not be renounced. In these conditions success might be easier; anyway, the attempt would be more attractive.

The monetary system that rules the Latin Union is protean. Based on the silver standard, it became bimetallism the very day it was decided to mint gold in coins of fixed weight and of a predetermined value in silver. This bimetallism, however, ceased to exist with the limitation of minting silver écus in 1874 and its complete suspension in 1878.[xi] Since then, irrespective of what the legal text says about it, the monetary unit is no longer silver but gold. Indeed, gold being the only metal which may be coined by the State in unlimited amounts on behalf of private persons, it is also the only commodity that necessarily has the same value as a commodity and as money: it is the only money metal. As for silver, its minting was suspended precisely **[13]** because it was profitable to mint considerable quantities. It has a higher value as money than as a commodity. It is a token that could not provide the monetary unit. The *Journal des économistes* of August 1876 contains a letter from Mr [Alphonse F. M.] Léon entitled: 'La pièce de cinq franc en argent vaut toujours cinq francs' [The silver five-franc coin is still worth five francs], in which he wanted to demonstrate his thesis by reasoning that the coin in question still contained 25 g, that is to say, five times 5 g silver, 9/10 fine, and that, in legal terms, the franc weighed 5 g silver, 9/10 fine. No doubt. However, it is certain that the Germinal year XI law, instituting the gold twenty-franc coin, 155 making 1 kg, created besides the 5 g *silver franc*, a *gold franc* of 10/31, 9/10 fine, and that though these two francs are legally of the same value at present, commercially the second one has a higher value than the first. According to a table I have under my nose, the 1876 price of gold in silver was on average 17.83 g in the precious metal market. So if, at the time when Mr Léon was writing, one could obtain 1 g of gold for 17.83 g of silver, one would have roughly 1.40 g of gold in exchange for 25 g of silver and not 1.60 g, the price of the gold five-franc piece. So it is obvious that the 25 g of silver, which was legally five gold francs, would only have a value of 4.375 F commercially.[xii] However often Mr Léon, and many others too, repeat that the value of money does not depend on the pleasure of the legislator, the evidence overwhelmingly proves the contrary. The legislator is perfectly able to make a token, and does so every day. Will it be contended that the legislator could not attach a conventional value to copper or nickel? Well, what was done for copper or nickel was done for silver the very day it was decided to limit the minting of silver at will just as the minting of copper or nickel is regulated.

Hence, silver is obviously no more than a token, either in its form of alloy 9/10 écus, or in the form of small change of alloy 835/1000. Besides, it is clear that *grosso modo* it is **[14]** a regulating token, i.e. a token whose quantity will be manipulated in order to obtain a certain stability of the value of money with respect to the commodities, or of the value of the commodities with respect to money, in other words, stability of prices. When minting of écus was limited in 1874, and completely suspended in 1878, this was done because it was observed that, because of various circumstances, a considerable quantity of silver bars were going to be transformed into écus, and that, consequently, the money would depreciate and commodities become more expensive. It was well done and will still be well done to act in the same way or the opposite, that is to say, withdraw écus from circulation or add them as the quantity of gold turns out to be superabundant or insufficient. It is only in this way that satisfaction must be given either to monometallists or to bimetallists. It is well known that monometallists affirm *a priori* the abundance of gold. In their opinion, the gradual increase in the quantity of gold, combined with the growth of payments as a counterpart, should suffice to serve the circulation of goods. So the quantity of écus at present existing is useless and it should be demonetized. Let them prove to us the accuracy of this point of view, showing us clearly by means of judicious statistics that prices in general increase daily, and we shall ask the next monetary conference to decide to withdraw silver écus from circulation. The bimetallists use the inductive, historical method. History has taught them that gold and silver have always replaced each other, each being abundant or scarce as the other was scarce or abundant, and induction leads them to conclude that this will always be the case. Therefore, gold and silver should both be money. The écus that the State refuses to mint are sadly lacking and they should quickly be coined. Fine, but if this whole theory has any basis, a decrease in prices should be noticed. Show us these decreases **[15]** and we will put pressure on the conference to put silver écus back into circulation. This is the only prudent and wise way of proceeding. The importance of the interests at stake and the mere facts make this the only choice for statesmen at present and in the future.

Monometallists are interested in creditors; but debtors will not let themselves be thus sacrificed, and they are right. Bimetallists speak in favour of producers; but consumers rightly complain. Why demonetize the remaining écus suddenly, risking a considerable fall in prices, which will ruin entrepreneurs, instead of doing it gradually as and when the abundance of gold allows it? Why suddenly mint silver freely, at the risk of enormous price increases, which will upset landowners, persons of private means, workers and civil servants, instead of doing it progressively and in the proportions required by the development of transactions? If gold is not plentiful and business remains stationary, why not then maintain the *status quo*? So the only necessity is to note the rise, fall or stability of the prices most carefully, and decrease or increase the quantity of silver écus, or leave it untouched. In a nutshell, doing rationally what had always previously been done empirically.[xiii]

This is certainly not easy. First, disentangling the tendency of prices to rise or fall over a long period from their daily movements occurring because of fluctuations in production and consumption is an operation that demands time and attention. Then disentangling from the tendency of prices to rise or fall over long periods those parts that come from the commodities themselves and those inherent in the money, using the procedures I have indicated, is another equally long, delicate operation. Even in combination with the multiple standard, which seems to be the simplest and **[16]** easiest, there is a preliminary operation which might complicate the establishment of the standard. However, none of this is impossible. It is the same with these economic and statistical problems as with astronomic operations which, though simple in theory, are very complicated in practice. Measuring the respective distances of the celestial bodies is an operation that often consists of a triangulation in theory, but in reality can only be calculated more or less approximately and with great effort. Yet it can be done. Estimating the variations in value is much the same thing. When the theory of prices becomes another scientific theory like astronomy, and when the Bureaux of Statistics become, according to another expression of Mr Messedaglia's, 'price observatories', deciding how much regulating silver token needs to be put into or kept in circulation can be done quite rigorously enough – more so than is the case at present anyway, for it should not be forgotten that this is actually already happening. Everything seems to indicate that this moment is approaching. In the last volume of the late W. Stanley Jevons, published by his widow with the aid of his successor at University College, London, Mr H. S. Foxwell, and entitled *Investigations in Currency and Finance*,[xiv] which is a collection of earlier articles concerning variation in prices and the value of money, the most interesting essays dealing with these kinds of questions may be found. I have brought from Rome sheets of unpublished price statistics provided by Mr [Luigi] Bodio, Director, and Mr [Luigi] Perozzo,[xv] Inspector of Statistics of the Kingdom of Italy, which are most remarkable attempts to represent graphically the development of markets. If only economics could shrug off its jargon and reach this mode of precision and analysis, we should be able to rise above the monetary chaos in which we now find ourselves.

Moreover, whether this happens sooner or later, the main thing will be not to **[17]** stray from this path. Therefore the forthcoming monetary conference ought to prolong the Latin Union on the following basis:

> *The monetary unit is the* FRANC, *that is to say,* 10/31 *of one gramme of gold of an alloy of* 9/10 fine.

The MONEY will consist of gold ten-franc and twenty-franc coins. These will be minted by the State at the request of private persons. The minting may be neither suspended nor limited.

Independently of the gold money, there will be double silver token:

1 *A* FRACTIONAL *token consisting of silver coins of* $2\frac{1}{2}$ *g, 5 g and 10 g of silver of an alloy of 835/1000 of a nominal value of half a franc, one franc and two francs.*

2 *A* REGULATING *token consisting of écus, namely silver coins of 25 g in an alloy of 9/10 fine, of a nominal value of five francs.*

> *The silver token should be minted by the State; it will circulate only within its issuing country and will be accepted for payments only up to a certain amount. The quantity of token that may be issued by each of the States forming the Latin Union will be determined by international conventions. This should be done, as far as the fractional token is concerned, for the sake of circulation, for small payments, and, with regard to the regulating token, for assuring a regular variation in the value of money. Every State of the Union will profit from the benefits and bear the losses coupled with the issue or withdrawal of its token.*

I should like to add to these arrangements a final one to which I am most attached. In my *Théorie mathématique de la richesse sociale* there is a memoir devoted to the 'Théorie mathématique du billet de banque'.[2] This theory has demanded much long, hard thought. After formulating it I took it up to study again and I am increasingly convinced that in fact the issue of banknotes **[18]** could not be reimbursed at a moment's notice without social upheaval, nor be reduced without considerable economic difficulty. Here follows a short demonstration of this proposition which will be helpful in this context. Imagine a country where no banknotes are issued and the credit for circulating capital, in the form of commercial paper, is given in current accounts by banks through short-term deposits. If it is decided to issue banknotes in this country freely or as a monopoly, the banks could certainly return the deposits to the depositors in

2 This memoir is to be found in this volume (pp. 273–98).

metal money and the latter could bury the cash in the ground. All transactions would take place in banknotes just as was also the case with metallic money. The banknotes would be assets representing circulating capital and a means of exchange. The takers of the notes would replace capitalists, and the notes would replace money. The only difference would be that the banks kept for themselves the interest on the circulating capital instead of remitting it to the depositors. Now, should the capitalists unearth their metallic money and put it on the market, they could demand new capital for an equal amount. What sort of capital would this be? It would be fixed capital. For a certain period, that I have called the *issuing period*, a certain quantity of productive services would be shifted from producing consumer goods to producing fixed capital. At the same time, the quantity of money in circulation would be increased in proportion. After this issuing period, capital would have been immobilized and an amount of money equal to that of the banknotes would be brought into circulation. With this in mind, I should like it to be explained to me how the issue of banknotes could be wholly or partly liquidated without creating a double crisis: a financial crisis for lack of takers of the assets representing circulating capital and a monetary crisis because of the reduction of the quantity of money as a means of exchange. So if the economists were right in rejecting the socialists' expedient of the mobilization of land or fixed capital in order to avoid fiat money, the only way to escape this **[19]** predicament, they should also reject the mobilization of circulating capital achieved by the issue of banknotes.

When making this choice the economists would cease to be fooled by the bankers, who are perfectly aware that reimbursing their notes is impossible anyway. If we scrutinize the new notes issued by the Banque de France we shall find all sorts of nice things – a careful engraving in blue ink 'La Sagesse fixant la Fortune' and so forth – but one will not find on it those seven words which should be the very essence of a banknote: 'Il sera payé à vue, au porteur...' [We promise to pay the bearer, on demand, the sum of...]. Moreover, what is said to be true of these notes, which do not, however, declare themselves reimbursable on presentation, is even more obviously true of the notes of fiat money, that are plain representations of fixed capital. It is also quite certain that the suppression of supposedly reimbursable banknotes will lead to the suppression of non-reimbursable notes and that the complete suppression of paper money which comes and goes and sometimes comes again, will provide metallic money with much more fixity. For these reasons I should like to add to the foregoing resolutions:

> *The States constituting the Latin Union that would like to suppress every issue of banknotes in their country will be permitted to mint silver écus to an amount equal to the excess of circulating banknotes over the metallic cash in banks.*

I call your attention to the opportunity arising of using the large quantity of silver at present available to rectify a huge economic error.

Notes

i In the version of the present chapter published in the *Revue de droit international et de législation comparée* (Brussels and Leipzig), vol. XVI, no. 6, 1 December 1884, pp. 575–88, Walras inserted a second footnote at this point: 'This paper has been transmitted to the delegates at the conference who had to meet in Paris, last 25 November, and is said to be going to meet in January 1885.' In the reprint that Walras had demanded before the publication of the paper in the *Revue de droit international et de législation comparée* a slightly different version is found: 'This paper has been transmitted to the delegates at the conference who were to meet in Paris, last 25 November.' This international conference for the prolongation of the Latin Union (see below) had initially been convened for 21 October at Paris. Postponed in November and then in January, it was finally held on 20 July 1885. It ended with the signing of the convention of 6 November 1885, extending the Latin Union from 1 January 1886 to 1 January 1891. See, on this subject, the documents collected under the title 'Convention monétaire du 6 novembre 1885', *Journal des économistes*, 4th series, 9th year, vol. 33, January 1896, pp. 96–109; see also Ministère des affaires étrangères, *Conférence monétaire entre la Belgique, la France, la Gréce, l'Italie et la Suisse en 1885. Convention et procès-verbaux*, Paris: Imprimerie Nationale, 1885. At the end of the latter work is to be found an appendix, the 'Acte additiononel à la Convention monétaire du 6 novembre 1885, signé le 12 décembre 1885 entre la France, la Belgique, la Grèce, l'Italie et la Suisse'.

The Latin Union originated from the monetary conference in Paris, 20 November 1865, between France, Belgium, Italy and Switzerland; it was presided over by Félix Esquirou de Parieu, vice-president of the French Conseil d'État. The convention of 6 November 1865 created a monetary union that was soon called the 'Latin Union'. The four signatories committed themselves to:

- Unifying the fineness, the weights and the dimensions of their metallic money.
- Coining freely gold 5 F, 10 F, 20 F, etc., pieces and a silver 5 F coin of 900/1000 fine, in conformity with the circulation at the time.
- Coining fractional silver money (20c, 50c, 1 F and 2 F coins) 835/1000 fine (instead of 900/1000), the issue of these coins to be limited to 6 F per inhabitant.
- Ensuring international circulation of money (with the exception of worn coins and under conditions as far as fractional currency is concerned).

In 1868 Greece was admitted to the Latin Union. The above bimetallic system, that was soon characterized as 'limping', first led to the limitation, then to the suspension, of the coinage of silver pieces as a result of additional conventions and agreements concluded between 1874 and 1877. The new convention of 5 November 1878 prolonged the Latin Union from 1 January 1880 until 1 January 1886. As already indicated above, the conference of 1885 resulted into a further prolongation until 1 January 1891. From the latter date onwards the Latin Union was renewed from year to year until it disappeared because of the First World War. The following works on the history of the Latin Union should be mentioned: E. Broussault, '*Histoire de l'union monétaire latine*', thèse de droit,

Université de Rennes, Rennes: Imprimerie des arts et manufactures, 1903; P. Chausserie Laprée, *L'Union monétaire latine: son passé, sa situation actuelle, ses chances d'avenir et sa liquidation éventuelle*, Thèse de droit, Université de Paris, Paris: Arthur Rousseau, 1911; Paul Fauchille, 'L'Union monétaire latine – son histoire', *Annales de l'École libre des sciences politiques* (Paris), 1st year, 1886, pp. 510–33; Jean-Marie Thivaud, 'L'Union latine: Europe, monnaie, et toile d'araignée', *Revue d'économie financière*, nos. 8–9, March–June 1989, pp. 19–25; Henri Parker Willis, *A History of the Latin Monetary Union: A Study of International Monetary Action*, Chicago: University of Chicago Press, 1901; Eugène van der Rest, 'L'Union latine, son origine et ses phases diverses', *Revue de droit international et de législation comparée* (Brussels), vol. XIII, 1881, no. I, pp. 5–21, and no. III, pp. 268–80.

ii The 'Théorie du bimétallisme' brings together the following three articles: 'Note sur le $15\frac{1}{2}$', *Journal des économistes*, 3rd series, 11th year, vol. 44, no. 132, December 1876, pp. 454–57; 'Théorie mathématique du bimétallisme', *Journal des économistes*, 4th series, 4th year, vol. 14, no. 41, May 1881, pp. 189–99; 'De la fixité de valeur de l'étalon monétaire', *Journal des économistes*, 4th series, 5th year, vol. 20, no. 10, October 1882, pp. 5–13. These articles were inserted with some modifications in *Théorie mathématique de la richesse sociale*, Lausanne: Corbaz/Paris: Guillaumin/Rome: Loescher/Leipzig: Duncker & Humblot, 1883, pp. 119–44 and three plates (vol. XI of the *ŒEC*).

iii The article 'Théorie mathématique du bimétallisme' constitutes lessons' 31 and 32 [of the fourth edition] of the *Eléments d'économie politique pure* [*ŒEC*, vol. VIII, pp. 487–514].

*iv An increase or decrease of utility means that all intensities (marginal utilities) increase or decrease, respectively (*Eléments*, section 103).

v The four first memoirs of the *Théorie mathématique de la richesse sociale* are, respectively, 'Principe d'une théorie mathématique de l'échange' (1873), 'Équations de l'échange' (1875), Équations de la production' 1876), 'Équations de la capitalization et du crédit' (1876).

*vi In the next chapter Walras speaks of the expediency of money as just a means of payment, making circulation possible.

vii In a copy of the *Études d'économie politique appliquée* conserved in the Walras archives of Lausanne Walras added in his handwriting at this point the word 'secular' (F.W. VII b, file 40).

viii During the months of February and March 1883 Walras stayed in Rome with his daughter Aline. There he had the opportunity of meeting fellow economists and statisticians, among them Luigi Bodio (1840–1920), with whom he had been corresponding since 1874, and Allessandro Messedaglia (1820–1901). These two and some other colleagues and friends (Marco Monghetti, 1818–86, Luigi Perozzo, 1856–1916, Ranieri Simonelli, 1830–1911, Bonaldo Stringher, 1854–1930, Achille Sinigaglia, etc.) held a banquet for him in the Café de Rome on 9 March 1883, thanking him for explaining 'the main points of his economic and social doctrine' (see also *Correspondence*, letter 547, Léon Walras to Gustave Maugin, 16 March 1883).

ix Tullio Martello, *L'interregno monetario in Italia dopo l'abolizione del biglietto inconvertibile*, Florence: Tip. di M. Cellini & C., 1884; offprint from *Rassegna nazionale*, vol. XVI, 1884, pp. 679ff. and 699ff.

x Walras is referring to a list of questions raised, in 1884, to stimulate debate among the members of the Société d'économie politique de Paris. Question no. 8, formulated as 'Is political economy as a science different from moral science and law?', was to be discussed at the meeting of 6 September 1886 (*Journal des économistes*, 4th series, 9th year, vol. 35, no. 9, September 1886, pp. 421–31). Question 9, 'What is the limit of duties to be attributed to the State in political economy?', was to be treated at the meetings of 5 February and 5 March 1885 (*Journal des économistes*, 4th series, 8th year, vol. 29, no. 2, February 1885, pp. 294–308, and no. 3, 1885, pp. 450–65). In October 1884 Walras proposed as a subject for discussion 'A system of gold money with regulating silver token'. In April 1885 the president of the society, Léon Say, decided to withdraw this theme from the programme under the pretext 'we do not allow the value of the cash balances of the Banque de France to be a subject of discussion'. Later on Walras decided to resign from the Société d'économie politique. See also the 'Notice autobiographique' in *Correspondence*, I, 8 (also in *ŒEC*, vol. V) and the letters from Walras to Alphonse Courtois of 14 October 1884 and 28 January 1887, and to Charles Gide of 28 October 1887 (*Correspondence*, letters 613, 766 and 816, respectively).

xi The additional convention of 31 January 1874 put a strict maximum on the production of silver 5 F coins in the countries of the Latin Union, except Italy, which obtained special conditions. The new monetary convention of 5 November 1878 confirms the decision of 1877, established via diplomatic channels, to suspend the minting of silver 5 F coins.

*xii The figures 1.40 g and 1.60 g should be 1.43 g and 1.61 g, respectively, from which it follows that 4.375 must be 4.441. This correction does not change the argument, however.

*xiii For the special Walrasian meaning of the word 'empirical' as opposed to 'scientific' see the *Eléments*, for instance (1988: 85, 358).

xiv W. S. Jevons, *Investigations in Currency and Finance*, edited with an introduction by H. S. Foxwell, London: Macmillan, 1884.

xv On the question of the variation in prices and that of the value of money see the letter from Walras to Luigi Perrozzo of 5 December 1884 (*Correspondence*, letter 622; see also note 4 to that letter, by the editor, William Jaffé).

[20]

2 Measuring and regulating variations in the value of money

I Critical examination of Mr Cournot's doctrine on changes in relative and absolute value[1]

Mr Cournot says:

> In the writings of economists the definition of value, and the distinction between absolute and relative value, are rather obscure: a very simple and strikingly exact comparison will serve to throw light on this.
>
> We conceive that a body moves when its situation changes with reference to other bodies which we look upon as fixed. If we observe a system of material points at two different times, and find that the respective situations of these points are not the same at both times, we necessarily conclude that some, if not all, of these points have moved; but if besides this we are unable to refer them to points of the fixity of which we can be sure, it is, in the first instance, impossible to draw any conclusions as to the motion or rest of each of the points in the system.
>
> However, if all of the points in the system, except one, had preserved their relative situation, we should consider it very probable that this single point was the only one that had moved, unless, indeed, all the other points were so connected that the movement of one would involve the movement of all.
>
> We have just pointed out an extreme case, viz. that in which all **[21]** except one had kept their relative positions; but, without entering into details, it is easy to see that among the possible ways of explaining the change in the state of the system there may be some much simpler than others, and which without hesitation we regard as much more probable.

1 Lesson 28 of the first edition of the *Éléments d'économie politique pure* (1874). [Lesson 39 in the second edition; omitted from edition 3 onwards.]

> …Just as we can only assign situation to a point by reference to other points, so we can assign value to a commodity by reference to other commodities. In this sense there are only relative values. But when these relative values change, we perceive plainly that the reason of the variation may lie in the change in one term of the relation or of the other or of both.
>
> …We can therefore readily distinguish the relative changes in value manifested by the changes in relative values from the absolute changes in value of one or another of the commodities between which commerce has established relations.
>
> Just as it is possible to make an indefinite number of hypotheses as to the absolute motion which causes the observed relative motion in a system of points, so it is also possible to multiply indefinitely hypotheses as to absolute variations which cause the relative variations observed in the values of a system of commodities.
>
> However, if all but one of the commodities preserved the same relative values, we should consider by far the most probable hypothesis, the one which would assign the absolute change to this single article; unless there should be manifest such a connection between all the others, that one cannot vary without involving proportional variations in the values of those which depend on it.
>
> **[22]**…Without reference to this extreme case, where the disturbance of the system of relative values is explained by the movement of a single article, it is evident that among all possible hypotheses on absolute variations some explain the relative variations more simply and more probably than others.[i]

Mr Cournot does not restrict himself to a comparison; by means of an ingenious combination he clearly reduces the problem of the determination of absolute changes in the values of a certain number of commodities in a market to that of the determination of absolute changes in the position of the same number of points on a straight line. He proceeds as in Figure 2.1. Let (A), (B), (C), (D)… be these commodities, and let μ, π, ρ… be the prices of (B), (C), (D)… Upon the straight line *XY* [Figure 2.1] let AB $= \log \mu$, AC $= \log \pi$, $-$AD $= \log \rho, \ldots$ Obviously, $-$BA $= -\log \mu = \log(1/\mu)$, BC $=$ AC$-$AB $= \log \pi - \log \mu = \log(\pi/\mu)$, $-$BD $= -$AD$-$AB $= \log \rho - \log \mu = \log(\rho/\pi)$, etc. In this way the system of the positions of the points A, B, C, D… represents the system

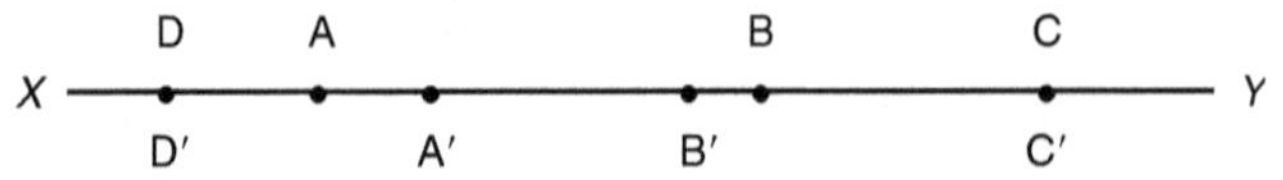

Figure 2.1 Cournot's logarithmic price line.

of the values of the commodities (A), (B), (C), (D) ... According to which of these points is taken as the origin, one of the commodities will be taken as the standard [étalon *numéraire*]. As a result, the prices $\mu, \pi, \rho \ldots$, having changed into $\mu', \pi', \rho' \ldots$, in which case the distances AB, AC, −AD ... have become A′B′, A′C′, −A′D′ ..., the problem of whether the change from π into π', for instance, finds its cause in a change in the value of (A) or in the value of (C) or in the value of both commodities at the same time is reduced to whether the change from AC **[23]** into A′C′ originates from a change in the position of A or in the position of C or in the position of both points at the same time. Generally:

> the calculations for determining the most probable hypothesis as to the absolute movement of a system of points, can be applied, by going from logarithms back to numbers, to the determination of the most probable hypothesis for the absolute variations of a system of values.[ii]

In these data let us suppose that, for instance, C′D′ = CD. One of two things may then be the case: either points C and D did not change position, or both moved backwards or forwards in the same way. But then we also have $\rho'/\pi' = \rho/\pi$ and there are two alternatives: either commodities (C) and (D) did not change in value, or their values both increased or decreased proportionally. The first hypothesis may be the most probable; this probability will become the more certain as the number of points other than C and D with unchanged relative positions increases, that is to say, the greater the number of other commodities than (C) and (D) whose relative values do not change. This settles the problem, for we have not merely one fixed point *XY*, but several; in other words, there is not merely one fixed value in the market, but several. Calculating the absolute change in the position of A relative to the position of C, we find that this point has moved forward over a distance AA′; or, calculating the absolute change in the value of (A) based on the value of (C) we find that [the value of] this commodity has increased in the proportion of π' to π. And that:

> if no article exists having the necessary conditions for perfect fixity, we can and ought to imagine one, which, to be sure, will only have an abstract existence. It will only appear as an auxiliary term of comparison to facilitate conception of the theory, and will disappear in the final applications.[iii]

This is Mr Cournot's theory on the changes in absolute and relative values. It can be criticized only by introducing the notion of *rareté*. Mr Cournot carefully avoids **[24]** speaking about changes in absolute value, speaking only of absolute changes in value. In his book the difference between these two expressions is somewhat obscure, but for us it may become perfectly clear. If π were the price of (C) in (A) and if $r_{c,1}, r_{c,2}, r_{c,3} \ldots r_{a,1}, r_{a,2}, r_{a,3} \ldots$ were the *raretés* of these commodities for those exchanging, the latter being indicated by (1), (2), (3) ..., we would have:

$$\pi = \frac{v_c}{v_a} = \frac{r_{c,1}}{r_{a,1}} = \frac{r_{c,2}}{r_{a,2}} = \frac{r_{c,3}}{r_{a,3}} = \cdots$$

Now these ratios of *raretés* are the only ones where we are permitted to consider their two terms as having both an absolute and a well determined value. Hence, only with respect to these may we wonder: if π becomes π', do (C)'s *raretés* change, or (A)'s, or both commodities' *raretés* at the same time? Only in this sense can we understand assertions about absolute changes in value. That being said, a fundamental distinction presents itself.

Suppose there is equilibrium at prices $\mu, \pi, \rho \ldots$ and that the utility of (A) increases for a certain number of those exchanging.[iv] According to the theorem of maximum satisfaction these exchangers will then improve their situation by demanding (A) while offering (B), (C), (D)... and the prices $\mu, \pi, \rho \ldots$ will decrease. When these prices drop, the other exchangers, for whom the utility of (A) does not change, will consequently find an advantage in demanding (B), (C), (D)... while offering (A). A new equilibrium will thus be established at lower prices $\mu', \pi', \rho' \ldots$[v] Because of this operation all the *raretés* of (A) will change; they will all increase, for the exchangers whose utility of this commodity increased, as well as for those for whom this utility did not vary. But at the same time the *raretés* of the commodities (B), (C), (D)... will change as well. They will all increase for the first category, who will have sold some. They will drop for the second category, who will have bought. **[25]** Therefore we are, in principle, not permitted to imagine, as Mr Cournot proposes, a commodity of fixed value because we are not permitted to imagine a commodity with fixed *rareté*, unless we suppose the *raretés* of the other commodities to be likewise fixed, which we may come across in a case analogous to that which he [Cournot] took care to put aside, viz. that in which there exists such a dependence in the market between (A), (B), (C), (D)... that the value of one of them cannot change without a change in the value of them all; consequently, the points A, B, C, D... of *XY* would all be connected so that the position of one of them cannot change without a change in the position of all the other points.

In principle it is therefore not only impossible to identify a commodity with a constant value, it is even impossible to imagine such a commodity. But, that said, the empirical procedure indicated by Mr Cournot for determining absolute changes in value does nevertheless have real importance. Indeed, it is indubitable that, in the above-mentioned case, *if there are a great number of* [*different*] *commodities in the market, in considerable quantities*, only the changes in the *raretés* of commodity (A) are perceptible, whereas the changes in the *raretés* of (B), (C), (D)..., whose utility does not change, will be imperceptible. The average *rareté* of (A) will increase, whereas the average *raretés* of (B), (C), (D)... will remain roughly the same. Consequently, there is good reason to say, by virtue of a sound application of the *law of large numbers*, that, concerning the change of π in π', it was the value of (A) that increased, the value of (C) remaining the same. In this respect only, one may admit likewise, with Mr Cournot, the possibility of reducing relative variations of value to absolute variations, in particular as far as the *numéraire* and money are concerned. Suppose, indeed, that as a result of changes in quantity of the *numéraire* and money, the prices of the commodities all increased or all decreased considerably, either at once or gradually; would not it be **[26]** of the highest importance if we could measure these effects, either to increase or diminish the civil servants' salaries and the workers' wages, or to modify certain contracts? This question simply must be examined today, and it undoubtedly deserves to be taken up and settled. It should be observed, however, that this theoretical possibility will perhaps only very rarely be a practical possibility; for, in practice, it will most frequently happen that the greatest number of commodities will be subject to price increases or decreases of diverse proportions and there will be no means of discovering and selecting a group of commodities whose prices did not vary or varied proportionally, necessary for applying the method.

II A method of regulating the variation in the value of money[2]

The system of *gold money with regulating silver token* that I expounded in the 1 December 1884 issue of the *Revue du droit international* is based entirely on a theorem of pure economics to which I attach fundamental importance and which I demonstrated mathematically in my preceding work, namely: *the values of the commodities are proportional to the intensities of the last wants satisfied, or to their raretés.* The last want satisfied is the point at which the consumer ceases to consume. His intensity is greatest when his consumption starts. It diminishes steadily as and when consumption increases; it is zero when unlimited consumption has taken place. If the price of corn in gold is 0.20 F, that is to say, one-fifth of a franc per pound, the intensity of the last want for **[27]** corn satisfied for every consumer, after the exchange, is one-fifth of the intensity of the last want for gold satisfied. For the ratios of the intensities of each consumer's last wants satisfied one may substitute the ratio of the averages of the intensities of the last wants satisfied over all consumers. Consequently, in the above example the average intensity of the last wants for corn satisfied will be one-fifth of the average intensity of the last wants for gold satisfied. When I speak merely about *rareté*, it will always concern this average *rareté*.

2 Report read before the Société vaudoise des sciences naturelles, Lausanne (meeting of 6 May 1885).

When the values are proportional to the *raretés*, the elements of variation in the *raretés* are elements of variation in the values. For an ordinary commodity there are two elements: (1) its utility, (2) its quantity. The increase or decrease in the utility leads to the increase or decrease in the *rareté*. The increase or decrease in the quantity leads to the decrease or increase in the *rareté*. When the utility and quantity act simultaneously but in inverse senses, it may happen that they both vary without changing the *rareté*. For a commodity that serves as money, the elements of variation in the *rareté* are threefold: (1) its utility as merchandise, (2) its utility as money, i.e. as the total amount of gold to serve the circulation of goods, (3) its quantity. An increase or decrease in one of the two utilities leads to an increase or decrease in the *rareté*. An increase or decrease in the quantity leads to a decrease or increase in the *rareté*. Here, too, the two utilities, on the one hand, and the quantity on the other, acting simultaneously and in an inverse sense, may vary, all three or two of them, without changing the *rareté*.

This being so, it is easy to show how the State or the legislator may regulate *rareté*, and, accordingly, the value of the money commodity.

Suppose, for convenience's sake, that gold money like ours and a special silver token, that we call a regulating token, exist distinct from the *divisional* currency as our five-franc écus are different from the **[28]** half-, one- and two-franc coins. Gold is *money* because its minting is neither suspended nor limited. The State transforms bullion into coins at the request of private persons and, therefore, gold tends to have the same value both as a commodity and as money. Silver money is a token because the State mints silver coins in a quantity that suits it and to which it attributes a nominal value as money that exceeds its value as a commodity. It is quite clear that in these conditions the State, or legislator, may counterbalance effects of variations, not caused by the State itself, in the two utilities or the quantity of the money commodity, by itself organizing a variation in this commodity that serves as money by means of the regulating token that it has at its disposal. For instance, one of the two utilities of the money commodity increases: it becomes fashonable either to cap one's teeth in gold instead of lead stoppings, or existing paper circulating in the country is withdrawn to replace it by a circulation of coins. The intensities of the last wants for gold satisfied will increase. How will the legislator react? He will introduce some special token into the circulation; a certain quantity of gold money will be transformed into gold as a commodity, and so the *rareté* of gold as a commodity will not increase. Alternatively, the quantity of the money commodity may increase: gold mines have been discovered somewhere. The intensities of the last wants for gold will decrease. What will the legislator do? He will withdraw special token from circulation; a certain quantity of gold in the form of a commodity will be transformed into gold money, and the *rareté* of gold as a commodity will not decrease.

It is obvious that in this system silver pays for gold. The State fixes or varies the *rareté* of gold at its convenience; but at the same time it creates an additional cause for the variation in the *rareté* of money by this systematic use of the special silver token, which sometimes enters circulation and sometimes leaves it. It is much better that silver should vary a little bit more in *rareté* and, consequently, in value, and that gold, with which **[29]** all transactions have to be settled, acquires a *rareté* and, consequently, a fixed or regularly varying value. Moreover, it is not necessary to insist on the advantages of the fixity or regularity in variation in the value of the money-commodity. The normal objection with respect to this fixity or regularity in variation is not that it is of little advantage, but that it is impossible. We have just seen that it is in fact perfectly possible.

But nevertheless, that is not to say that this monetary system, which is rational, is also simple or easy. The intensities of the last wants satisfied, or the *raretés*, cannot be measured directly: they do have a size, but this size cannot directly be estimated. Their tendency to increase or to decrease is revealed only by the tendency of their values, which are proportional to them, to increase or to decrease. But the values themselves are only given by their ratios to other values. How can their real movement be discerned? Let the price of corn increase from 0.20 F to 0.25 F, hence from a fifth to a quarter of a franc per pound. It is sure that the average intensity of the last want for corn satisfied, which was previously one-fifth of the average intensity of the last want for gold satisfied, now will be one-quarter. But was it the average *rareté* of corn that increased? Was it the average *rareté* of gold that decreased? Or have both of them varied? This seems difficult to answer. Several methods for finding the solution have been proposed. In the twenty-eight lesson [of the first edition] of my *Eléments d'économie politique pure* I criticized the method exposed by Cournot in his *Principes mathématiques de la théorie des richesses* (1838). I shall here criticize the one used by Jevons in his famous memoir *A Serious Fall in the Value of Gold Ascertained and its Social Effects set forth* (1863).[3]

Let, a, b, c, d ... be the prices in gold of a number m of commodities (A), (B), (C), (D)... at a given time; a', b', c', **[30]** d'... are the prices in gold of these commodities a certain time later. According to Jevons the geometric average of the ratios a'/a, b'/b, c'/c, d'/d..., or:

$$\sqrt[m]{\frac{a'}{a} \cdot \frac{b'}{b} \cdot \frac{c'}{c} \cdot \frac{d'}{d} \cdots}$$

3 This memoir is the second of those that have been collected in the volume entitled *Investigations in currency and finance*, London [Macmillan], 1884 [pp. 13–118].

represents the average increase or decrease in the prices in gold of the commodities. The inverse ratio, i.e.:

$$1 \Big/ \sqrt[m]{\frac{a'}{a} \cdot \frac{b'}{b} \cdot \frac{c'}{c} \cdot \frac{d'}{d} \cdots}$$

will represent in its turn the decrease or the increase in the price of gold. Cournot looked for commodities that do not vary in value relative to each other. Jevons chooses his commodities arbitrarily, and as many as possible: his method, he said himself says, is not *exclusive*, but *inclusive*. We will examine its principle later on, but first of all it would be sensible to allude to several interesting details of its application.

The elements of the calculations are annual prices that are themselves arithmetic averages. The price a_1 of year 1 is equal to the sum of the prices a_J, a_F, a_M ... of the months January, February, March ..., divided by 12 according to the formula:

$$a_1 = \frac{a_J + a_F + a_M + \cdots}{12}$$

After the prices $a_1, b_1, c_1, d_1 \ldots$ for year 1, the prices $a_2, b_2, c_2, d_2 \ldots$ for year 2 are looked up, the prices $a_3, b_3, c_3, d_3 \ldots$ for year 3, etc., up to the prices $a_{20}, b_{20}, c_{20}, d_{20} \ldots$ of year 20. So Table 2.1 of the *Average annual prices of each of* m *commodities during the period 1–20* is made up as shown: **[31]** That done, we could compute the ratios $a_2/a_1, a_3/a_1 \ldots b_2/b_1, b_3/b_1 \ldots c_2/c_1,$

Table 2.1

a_1	a_2	a_3	...	a_{20}
b_1	b_2	b_3	...	b_{20}
c_1	c_2	c_3	...	c_{20}
d_1	d_2	d_3	...	d_{20}
⋮	⋮	⋮	...	⋮

$c_3/c_1 \ldots d_2/d_1, d_3/d_1 \ldots$ and we would also have the annual variation in the prices of the commodities in gold and the annual variation in the value of gold. But for reasons based on a most ingenious theory Jevons proceeds somewhat differently.

In a country where the population saves and where capital formation takes place, every year a part of the productive services (*rentes*[vi] from the land, labour from the personal faculties, profit[vii] from capital) is used for the production of new capital rather than the production of consumer goods. This production of new capital goods, however, which constitutes the very fact of capitalization, does not take place in a regular way. A country that capitalizes 5 billion in ten years does not capitalize 500 million per year; this [amount of] capitalization will be the result of certain average years; some years it will be higher and may rise to 700 million or 800 million; other years it will be lower and might go down to 200 million or 300 million. This movement is analogous with the sea's: it includes flood tides, high-tides, ebb tides and low-tides. The periods of high-tide, those of substantial capitalization, are characterized by a high discount rate, high prices of iron and building materials and an increase in the price of consumer goods, whose productive services compete for the construction of new capital. The periods of low-tide, those of low capitalization, are characterized by opposite phenomena: a decrease in the discount rate, low prices of iron and building materials, a fall in the prices of consumer goods. The ebb tide takes less time than the flood: in general, it will coincide with a recession. With rare patience and sagacity Jevons collected **[32]** observations and analysed the subject, and he claims that the decade we mentioned as an example, in the nineteenth century, in Europe and in the United States, [the 1850s] was in reality an economic flood and ebb, with high- and low-tides. Perhaps his explanations are more or less questionable; the fact itself seems more[viii] certain. The consequence is that prudence must be observed in calculating price variations, since, if comparisons are made between prices separated by an interval of several years, one would run the risk of comparing non-comparable things. Ideally, high-tide prices should be compared with high-tide prices, or low-tide prices with low-tide prices, or, better still, average flood and ebb prices with other average flood and ebb prices. This latter way of proceeding seems to be highly obvious according to Jevons's theory, although he did not really adhere to it in his memoir. In order to measure the decrease in the value of gold as caused by the discovery of gold in California and Australia, he took the ratio of average prices for 1860–2, a low-tide period, and the average prices of 1845–50, a period of both ebb and flood ending in the phenomenon whose effect he wanted to measure. True, in proceeding in this way he mitigates the effect in question rather than exaggerating it, but why not measure accurately, if one is going to measure at all? In any case, taking the theory of economic tides into account, we suppose that prices $a, b, c, d \ldots a', b', c', d' \ldots$ are the arithmetic averages of the prices of successive periods of ebb and flood, that is to say, arithmetic averages over decennial periods according to the formulas:

$$a = \frac{a_1 + a_2 + a_3 + \cdots}{10}$$

and

$$a' = \frac{a_{11} + a_{12} + a_{13} + \cdots}{10}$$

[33] and these averages $a, b, c, d \ldots a', b', c', d' \ldots$ will be introduced into the formula:

$$\sqrt[m]{\frac{a'}{a} \cdot \frac{b'}{b} \cdot \frac{c'}{c} \cdot \frac{d'}{d} \cdots}$$

to deduct from it the average increase or decrease in the commodities' prices in gold, by means of the formula:

$$\log \sqrt[m]{\frac{a'}{a} \cdot \frac{b'}{b} \cdot \frac{c'}{c} \cdot \frac{d'}{d} \cdots} = \frac{1}{m}(\log a' + \log b' + \log c' + \cdots) - \frac{1}{m}(\log a + \log b + \log c + \cdots)$$

Nevertheless, before calculating this final ratio, Jevons presents a second table accompanied by a very important graphical construction.

$a, b, c, d \ldots$ being the arithmetic averages of the prices of the first decade of ebb and flood, we may make a table of *Ratios of annual prices during period 1–20 with respect to average prices during period 1–10* as in Table 2.2 and construct for every commodity curves representing the table by taking time as the abscissa and the above ratios as the ordinates. In the memoir in consideration Jevons drew curves corresponding not to this second table but to a third one, **[34]** presenting the ratios of annual prices during the whole period to average prices over the

Table 2.2

$\frac{a_1}{a}$	$\frac{a_2}{a}$	$\frac{a_3}{a}$	$\cdots$	$\frac{a_{20}}{a}$
$\frac{b_1}{b}$	$\frac{b_2}{b}$	$\frac{b_3}{b}$	$\cdots$	$\frac{b_{20}}{b}$
$\frac{c_1}{c}$	$\frac{c_2}{c}$	$\frac{c_3}{c}$	$\cdots$	$\frac{c_{20}}{c}$
$\frac{d_1}{d}$	$\frac{d_2}{d}$	$\frac{d_3}{d}$	$\cdots$	$\frac{d_{20}}{d}$
$\vdots$	$\vdots$	$\vdots$	$\cdots$	$\vdots$

first period in the form of geometric averages of ratios *per group of more or less analogous commodities.* Still adopting his point of view, one may imagine that there is good reason here to construct a curve representing the variation in annual prices during the whole period as a ratio of the average price over the first period *for each commodity separately*. It seems to me that only in that way could one recognize and establish that each commodity has undergone a general price variation in common with all the other commodities owing to monetary causes, independently of its special price variations. I shall come back to this point later on.

According to Jevons, the table [Table 2.3] and the curve [Figure 2.2] below will represent this general and common variation. This curve is striking in Jevons's memoir. One sees the average price of about forty commodities, of

Table 2.3

$$\sqrt[m]{\frac{a_1}{a}\cdot\frac{b_1}{b}\cdot\frac{c_1}{c}\cdot\frac{d_1}{d}\cdots} \quad \sqrt[m]{\frac{a_2}{a}\cdot\frac{b_2}{b}\cdot\frac{c_2}{c}\cdot\frac{d_2}{d}\cdots} \quad \sqrt[m]{\frac{a_3}{a}\cdot\frac{b_3}{b}\cdot\frac{c_3}{c}\cdot\frac{d_3}{d}\cdots} \quad \cdots \quad \sqrt[m]{\frac{a_{20}}{a}\cdot\frac{b_{20}}{b}\cdot\frac{c_{20}}{c}\cdot\frac{d_{20}}{d}\cdots}$$

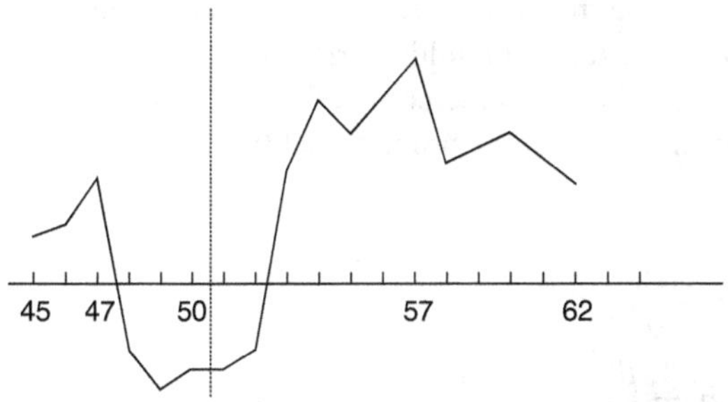

Figure 2.2 Variation in the average price of 40 commodities.

all kinds, rising from the horizontal line representing the average price for the period 1845–50, rising further in 1846, flood time, and remaining high in 1847, at high-tide; then descending till under the horizontal line in 1848, ebb time, remaining low in 1849–52, a period of low-tide, rising again, above the horizontal line, in 1853, flood time, remaining there in 1854–57, a period of high-tide, but at a level that is perceptibly higher than in 1847, descending again in 1858, ebb time, but remaining in 1859–62, a period of low-tide, above the horizontal line and no longer beneath, at a level superior to that of 1849–52.

[35] It seems therefore obvious that, as an effect of the abundance of gold, all the undulations of the curve were raised to a higher level. This is simply the difference of the level of the second period to the first one, expressed by the ratio:

$$\sqrt[m]{\frac{a'}{a}\cdot\frac{b'}{b}\cdot\frac{c'}{c}\cdot\frac{d'}{d}\cdots}$$

and not by the difference of the level of low-tide and the horizontal line, that provides the degree of the average increase in the gold prices of the commodities; and it is simply the inverse difference, expressed by the ratio:

$$1\Big/\sqrt[m]{\frac{a'}{a}\cdot\frac{b'}{b}\cdot\frac{c'}{c}\cdot\frac{d'}{d}\cdots}$$

that provides the degree of depreciation of money, at least if the principle itself of Jevons's method is correct.

This is the principle to be examined now. I shall base this investigation on the observation that values are proportional to *raretés*, which is, as far as money is concerned, the decisive observation in economics and on which my analysis of Cournot's method was based.

Let $\alpha, \beta, \gamma, \delta \ldots o$ be the average *raretés* of the commodities (A), (B), (C), (D) ... and the average *rareté* of gold at prices $a, b, c, d \ldots$;[4] and let α', β', γ', $\delta' \ldots o'$ be the *raretés* of the same commodities at prices a', b', c', $d' \ldots$ By virtue of the **[36]** theorem on the proportionality of prices to *raretés* we have simultaneously:

$$a = \frac{\alpha}{o}, \quad b = \frac{\beta}{o}, \quad c = \frac{\gamma}{o}, \quad d = \frac{\delta}{o} \cdots$$

$$a' = \frac{\alpha'}{o'}, \quad b' = \frac{\beta'}{o'}, \quad c' = \frac{\gamma'}{o'}, \quad d' = \frac{\delta'}{o'} \cdots$$

From this one deduces successively:

$$\frac{o'}{o} \cdot \frac{a'}{a} = \frac{\alpha'}{\alpha}, \quad \frac{o'}{o} \cdot \frac{b'}{b} = \frac{\beta'}{\beta}, \quad \frac{o'}{o} \cdot \frac{c'}{c} = \frac{\gamma'}{\gamma}, \quad \frac{o'}{o} \cdot \frac{d'}{d} = \frac{\delta'}{\delta} \cdots$$

$$\left(\frac{o'}{o}\right)^m \left(\frac{a'}{a} \cdot \frac{b'}{b} \cdot \frac{c'}{c} \cdot \frac{d'}{d} \cdots\right) = \frac{\alpha'}{\alpha} \cdot \frac{\beta'}{\beta} \cdot \frac{\gamma'}{\gamma} \cdot \frac{\delta'}{\delta} \cdots$$

$$\frac{o'}{o} \sqrt[m]{\frac{a'}{a} \cdot \frac{b'}{b} \cdot \frac{c'}{c} \cdot \frac{d'}{d} \cdots} = \sqrt[m]{\frac{\alpha'}{\alpha} \cdot \frac{\beta'}{\beta} \cdot \frac{\gamma'}{\gamma} \cdot \frac{\delta'}{\delta} \cdots}$$

$$\frac{o'}{o} \Big/ \sqrt[m]{\frac{\alpha'}{\alpha} \cdot \frac{\beta'}{\beta} \cdot \frac{\gamma'}{\gamma} \cdot \frac{\delta'}{\delta} \cdots} = 1 \Big/ \sqrt[m]{\frac{a'}{a} \cdot \frac{b'}{b} \cdot \frac{c'}{c} \cdot \frac{d'}{d} \cdots}$$

From this it may immediately be concluded that the inverse of the geometric average of the variations in the prices of commodities (A), (B), (C), (D), ...[ix] does not provide *the variation in the* rareté *of gold, nor that of the value of gold, but rather the ratio of the variation in this* rareté *(and of the value of gold) to the geometric average of the variations of the* raretés *(and of the values) of the commodities (A), (B), (C), (D)* ... For it to give the variation in the *rareté* and in the value of gold, one must be allowed to say:

$$\lim \sqrt[m]{\frac{\alpha'}{\alpha} \cdot \frac{\beta'}{\beta} \cdot \frac{\gamma'}{\gamma} \cdot \frac{\delta'}{\delta} \cdots} = 1$$

4 These $\alpha, \beta, \gamma, \delta \ldots$ are the *raretés* R_a, R_b, R_c, R_d, ... that will appear below in the *Théorie de la monnaie*.

which is not the case. Even if all the commodities other than the money commodity are taken without exception, one would not have:

$$\sqrt[m]{\alpha' \cdot \beta' \cdot \gamma' \cdot \delta' \cdots} = \sqrt[m]{\alpha \cdot \beta \cdot \gamma \cdot \delta \cdots}$$

[37] The geometric average of the *raretés* of these commodities is not constant. On the contrary, science demonstrates that, in a progressive society, that is to say in a society where capital grows more quickly than the population, this average should decrease. In a shrinking society it should increase, and in a static society it could vary because of incidental variations in utility or in the quantities of commodities. In such a society, it is true, it might also remain constant if the utility and quantities of a certain number of commodities remained the same and the effects of the variation in utility and quantities of the other commodities compensated each other exactly. How might one realize that this would be the case? It might be inferred from a comparison of the curve of the general and common variation in prices we discussed above with the curves of the special price variation in each commodity separately. When there were a large number of curves of the latter type with remarkable similarity to the first, it might be supposed that the price variations they represent result from causes inherent to money and not from causes inherent to the commodities. This seems to have taken place with respect to the application Jevons made of his method for measuring the depreciation of gold from 1850 to 1862. We would have seen this even better if, instead of drawing special curves for groups of commodities, he had drawn these special curves for each commodity separately. Only it must be noticed that, proceeding in this way, we actually renounce Jevons's inclusive method and come back to Cournot's exclusive method, which seems definitely preferable, for we want to observe and measure absolute variations in value, either of an arbitrary commodity or of the commodity money.

But a question arises here that can be answered in a way which would again rate Jevons's method superior. Would it be *desirable for money not to change in* rareté *or value*? Or would it rather be desirable *for the* **[38]** *variation in the* rareté *and value of money to be exactly equal to the geometric average of the variations of the* rareté *and value of the other commodities*? Personally, I do not hesitate to posit, as I have already said in the exposition of my *gold money with regulating silver token*, that one should incline towards the latter rather than the former, because there is no reason at all to withdraw the money commodity from the law of the larger and larger reduction of the *raretés* of products resulting from economic progress, and, on the contrary, it is in our interests if its purchasing power remains the same. Now, nothing is simpler than to obtain this double result by using regulating silver token on the basis of the hints found in Jevons's method. Let us suppose that in this way we have succeeded in achieving constancy of the geometric average of prices, in other words:

$$\sqrt[m]{\frac{a''}{a} \cdot \frac{b''}{b} \cdot \frac{c''}{c} \cdot \frac{d''}{d} \cdots} = 1$$

then one would also have:

$$\frac{o'}{o} = \sqrt[m]{\frac{\alpha'}{\alpha} \cdot \frac{\beta'}{\beta} \cdot \frac{\gamma'}{\gamma} \cdot \frac{\delta'}{\delta} \cdots}$$

and the variation in the *rareté* and the value of money would be equal to the geometric average of the variations of the *rareté* and the value of the commodities.

Should the latter be a *geometrical* average? Jevons did not discuss this point theoretically, so I am going to try to elucidate it, still basing the solution on the principle of the proportionality of values to *raretés*.

From the system of equations:

$$a = \frac{\alpha}{o} \quad b = \frac{\beta}{o} \quad c = \frac{\gamma}{o} \quad d = \frac{\delta}{o} \cdots$$

$$a' = \frac{\alpha'}{o'} \quad b' = \frac{\beta'}{o'} \quad c' = \frac{\gamma'}{o'} \quad d' = \frac{\delta'}{o'} \cdots$$

[39] one might also deduce:

$$\frac{o'}{o}\left(\frac{a'}{a} + \frac{b'}{b} + \frac{c'}{c} + \frac{d'}{d} + \cdots\right) = \left(\frac{\alpha'}{\alpha} + \frac{\beta'}{\beta} + \frac{\gamma'}{\gamma} + \frac{\delta'}{\delta} + \cdots\right)$$

and, consequently:

$$\frac{o'}{o} \Big/ \left[\frac{1}{m}\left(\frac{\alpha'}{\alpha} + \frac{\beta'}{\beta} + \frac{\gamma'}{\gamma} + \frac{\delta'}{\delta} + \cdots\right)\right]$$
$$= 1 \Big/ \left[\frac{1}{m}\left(\frac{a'}{a} + \frac{b'}{b} + \frac{c'}{c} + \frac{d'}{d} + \cdots\right)\right]$$

If, by means of the regulating token, one had succeeded in keeping the arithmetic average of the prices constant, i.e.:

$$\frac{1}{m}\left(\frac{a'''}{a} + \frac{b'''}{b} + \frac{c'''}{c} + \frac{d'''}{d} + \cdots\right) = 1$$

one would also have:

$$\frac{o'''}{o} = \frac{1}{m}\left(\frac{\alpha'}{\alpha} + \frac{\beta'}{\beta} + \frac{\gamma'}{\gamma} + \frac{\delta'}{\delta} + \cdots\right)$$

and the variation in the *rareté* and value of money would be equal to the arithmetic average of the variations of the *raretés* and values of the commodities.

What is more, if, by using the regulating token, one had managed to keep the *harmonic* average from changing, i.e.:

$$1\bigg/\left[\frac{1}{m}\left(\frac{a}{a^{iv}} + \frac{b}{b^{iv}} + \frac{c}{c^{iv}} + \frac{d}{d^{iv}} + \cdots\right)\right] = 1$$

one would then also have:

$$\frac{o^{iv}}{o} = 1\bigg/\left[\frac{1}{m}\left(\frac{\alpha}{\alpha'} + \frac{\beta}{\beta'} + \frac{\gamma}{\gamma'} + \frac{\delta}{\delta'} + \cdots\right)\right]$$

as may easily be verified, **[40]** and the variation in the *rareté* and the value of money would be equal to the harmonic average of the variations of the *rareté* and the values of the commodities. Why should one prefer the geometric average to the arithmetic and harmonic averages?[x]

Under the hypotheses of the harmonic average we would successively have, with the same quantity $a + b + c + d + \cdots$ of gold.

$$1 \text{ of (A)} + 1 \text{ of (B)} + 1 \text{ of (C)} + 1 \text{ of (D)} + \cdots = m$$

at prices $a, b, c, d, \ldots$ and:

$$\frac{a}{a^{iv}} \text{ of (A)} + \frac{b}{b^{iv}} \text{ of (B)} + \frac{c}{c^{iv}} \text{ of (C)} + \frac{d}{d^{iv}} \text{ of (D)} + \cdots = m$$

at prices a^{iv}, b^{iv}, c^{iv}, d^{iv}, ... Under the hypothesis of the arithmetic average, with an equal quantity $a''' + b''' + c''' + d''' + \cdots$ of gold, one would have successively:

$$\frac{a'''}{a} \text{ of (A)} + \frac{b'''}{b} \text{ of (B)} + \frac{c'''}{c} \text{ of (C)} + \frac{d'''}{d} \text{ of (D)} + \ldots = m$$

at prices $a, b, c, d, \ldots$ and:

$$1 \text{ of (A)} + 1 \text{ of (B)} + 1 \text{ of (C)} + 1 \text{ of (D)} + \ldots = m$$

at prices a''', b''', c''', d''', ... Hence in these two cases equal quantities of money would always buy the same quantity of social wealth.

Therefore there is no reason to prefer one result to any other; we should do as Jevons did and take the geometric average if it is true – as Jevons asserts without proving it – that it gives an intermediary result. So it needs to be proved here that the geometric average of the variations **[41]** of the *raretés* of the commodities lies between the arithmetic and the harmonic averages, that is to say that we should have:

$$\frac{1}{m}\left(\frac{\alpha'}{\alpha}+\frac{\beta'}{\beta}+\frac{\gamma'}{\gamma}+\frac{\delta'}{\delta}+\cdots\right) > \sqrt[m]{\frac{\alpha'}{\alpha}\cdot\frac{\beta'}{\beta}\cdot\frac{\gamma'}{\gamma}\cdot\frac{\delta'}{\delta}\cdots}$$

and:

$$\sqrt[m]{\frac{\alpha'}{\alpha}\cdot\frac{\beta'}{\beta}\cdot\frac{\gamma'}{\gamma}\cdot\frac{\delta'}{\delta}\cdots} > 1\Big/\left[\frac{1}{m}\left(\frac{\alpha}{\alpha'}+\frac{\beta}{\beta'}+\frac{\gamma}{\gamma'}+\frac{\delta}{\delta'}+\cdots\right)\right]$$

Hence:

$$\left(\frac{\alpha'}{\alpha}+\frac{\beta'}{\beta}+\frac{\gamma'}{\gamma}+\frac{\delta'}{\delta}+\cdots\right)^m > m^m\left(\frac{\alpha'}{\alpha}\cdot\frac{\beta'}{\beta}\cdot\frac{\gamma'}{\gamma}\cdot\frac{\delta'}{\delta}\cdots\right)$$

and:

$$\frac{1}{m^m}\left(\frac{\alpha'}{\alpha}\cdot\frac{\beta'}{\beta}\cdot\frac{\gamma'}{\gamma}\cdot\frac{\delta'}{\delta}\cdots\right) > 1\Big/\left(\frac{\alpha}{\alpha'}+\frac{\beta}{\beta'}+\frac{\gamma}{\gamma'}+\frac{\delta}{\delta'}+\cdots\right)^m$$

Now it would not be difficult to prove that this double inequality, that holds for two or three commodities, will hold good for an arbitrary number of commodities.

Proceeding in the same way, it would be appropriate to investigate how near we are to the scheme of the multiple standard. The principle of this scheme, viz. that equal quantities of money always buy the same well determined quantities of the same commodities, could in general be expressed by the equation:

$$pa+qb+rc+sd+\cdots = pa^v+qb^v+rc^v+sd^v+\cdots$$

Commodities (A), (B), (C), (D) and quantities p, q, r, s have arbitrarily been chosen. If one unity is taken from all commodities, the principle can be expressed by the equation:

$$a+b+c+d+\cdots = a^v+b^v+c^v+d^v+\cdots$$

In this system compensation, takes place if, when the price of some commodity has increased by π, the price of another **[42]** decreases equally. In our system, the principle of which is generally expressed by:

$$a \cdot b \cdot c \cdot d \cdots = a'' \cdot b'' \cdot c'' \cdot d'' \cdots$$

compensation takes place if, when the price of some commodity is multiplied by π, the price of another is divided by the same. Both systems are such that equal quantities of gold will always buy the same value in commodities.

So Jevons's system is possibly[xi] excellent under the condition that instead of being used to measure the variation in the *rareté* and the value of gold, it is used as a device for regulating this variation by keeping it equal to the average variation in the *rareté* and the value of the commodities; it is perfectly simple and rigorous for this purpose. The commodities sold in normal markets, whose prices, resulting from rigorous bargaining, are recorded in public market price lists, are not very numerous. Let them all be examined at certain intervals of time and the geometric average of their price variations calculated. Then all that needs to be done is: add or withdraw regulating token according to whether this average is above or below unity. The problem of regulating the variation in the value of money will thus be settled, and so it will be, completely without any arbitrariness. For instance, let us suppose we have:

$$\sqrt[m]{\frac{a'}{a} \cdot \frac{b'}{b} \cdot \frac{c'}{c} \cdot \frac{d'}{d} \cdots} \lesseqgtr 1$$

and then wonder what quantity of regulating token would need to be added to or withdrawn from the circulation to obtain:

$$\sqrt[m]{\frac{a''}{a} \cdot \frac{b''}{b} \cdot \frac{c''}{c} \cdot \frac{d''}{d} \cdots} = 1$$

Let Q' and Q'' be the total quantities of money corresponding to the two series of prices $a', b', c', d', \ldots a'', b'', c'', d'', \ldots$ According to the **[43]** theory of money, *the money prices are more or less proportional to the quantity of money in circulation*, i.e. we have:

$$\frac{Q''}{Q'} = \frac{a''}{a'} = \frac{b''}{b'} = \frac{c''}{c'} = \frac{d''}{d'} = \cdots$$

from which we easily derive as the value of Q''/Q':

$$\sqrt[m]{\frac{a''}{a'} \cdot \frac{b''}{b'} \cdot \frac{c''}{c'} \cdot \frac{d''}{d'} \cdots} = \sqrt[m]{\frac{a''}{a} \cdot \frac{b''}{b} \cdot \frac{c''}{c} \cdot \frac{d''}{d} \cdots} \Big/ \sqrt[m]{\frac{a'}{a} \cdot \frac{b'}{b} \cdot \frac{c'}{c} \cdot \frac{d'}{d} \cdots}$$

$$= 1 \Big/ \sqrt[m]{\frac{a'}{a} \cdot \frac{b'}{b} \cdot \frac{c'}{c} \cdot \frac{d'}{d} \cdots}$$

Hence in order to ensure that the geometric average of the prices does not vary, or that the variation in the rareté *and value of money be exactly equal to the geometric average of the variations of the* raretés *and values of the commodities, the total amount of money in circulation has to be multiplied by the inverse of the average variation in the prices of the commodities.*

To demonstrate how the system would work, I have made use of the Latin Union gold money and its token of silver écus. What is appealing about my solution of the monetary question is that, to achieve it, we only need use our present monetary system although correcting it by a modification consisting of defining the franc as a certain quantity of gold and no longer as a certain quantity of silver, in conformity with the following principles which I put forward for adoption by the International Monetary Conference:

- *Gold money* of a fineness of 9/10 consisting of ten-franc and twenty-franc coins, viz. of ten and twenty times 10/31 g *of gold*, still minted without restriction by the State at the request of private persons.
- *Divisional silver currency* of [fineness] 835/1000 consisting of coins of $2\frac{1}{2}$g, 5 g and 10 g, with a nominal value of $\frac{1}{2}F$, 1 F and 2 F.
- *Regulating silver token* of [fineness] 9/10 consisting of **[44]** 25 g écus of a nominal value of 5 F; all these silver coins minted by the State in quantities determined by international conventions: for small-change silver coins in proportion to the necessity for circulation, and, for the regulating token, *with a view to providing the value of money with a variation equal to the average variation in the value of the commodities*. Limitation of the circulation of the token to the country of issue; restriction of the legal payments in divisional currency to 50 F and in regulating token to 500 F.

At the same time as prolonging the Latin Union on this basis, an international statistical commission should immediately be instituted to study price variations and calculate every ten years the increase or decrease in the geometric average, noting the superabundance or the deficiency of money in circulation, and to give the authorities the exact figure for the amount of silver écus to be added or withdrawn.

This system, which keeps the balance between creditors and debtors, producers and consumers, should be favoured by both monometallists and bimetallists, for it leaves it to experience to put either in the right or the wrong. If, as the monometallists claim, gold alone would suffice to serve the circulation of goods, the existing quantity of money, including the écus, would be too large. Prices would increase; we should be led to demonetize the remaining écus step by step and gradually be led to gold monometallism. If, as the bimetallists claim, gold and silver are both necessary to serve circulation, the existing quantity of money, including the écus, would be too small. The prices would decrease; we should be induced to mint the remaining silver at our disposal little by little and would thus return smoothly to bimetallism. But probably the adherents of these exclusive systems would insist on recommending what may be called a leap in the dark; and the politicians among them, unsure of the outcome, would continue to trail behind events.

[45] Before concluding I want to answer an objection presented by some economists, not unfavourable to my system, who are only worried about the losses due to the system that the State might incur at one time or another. To begin with, I might observe that this objection ought to be put to the monometallists. The withdrawal of silver écus that I propose if necessary the monometallists proposed as a certainty. If I might possibly inflict a loss on the State, they would inevitably do so. Only the bimetallists, who are calling for the resumption of unrestricted coinage of silver, may boast about saving the State from loss. In reality, they let this loss fall back on the creditors and consumers; and I might ask which loss would distress economic relations less, the one borne by the State or that borne by certain private persons? I prefer, however, to search for ways to preserve the State from loss of any kind.

The possibilities that may arise can be reduced to the following four elementary ones: (1) a decrease in the quantity or an increase in the utility of gold; (2) a decrease in the quantity or an increase in the utility of silver; (3) an increase in the quantity or a decrease in the utility of silver; (4) an increase in the quantity or a decrease in the utility of gold. The first possibility is distinctly advantageous: if the quantity of gold decreases or its utility increases, its value will increase; gold money will be transformed into commodity gold; the State has to raise the quantity of regulating silver token; it makes a profit that it keeps in reserve. The second possibility is favourable: if the quantity of silver decreases or its utility increases, its value will increase; the token is less token. The third possibility is unfavourable: if the quantity of silver increases or its utility decreases, its value will decrease; the token is more token. But just as the second possibility does not yield a profit, the third one does no harm. Hence the fourth possibility remains. This is the only **[46]** detrimental one: if the quantity of gold increases or its utility decreases its value will decrease; gold as a commodity will be transformed into gold money; the State has to decrease the quantity of regulating silver token; it incurs losses that may be considerable if the third possibility appears simultaneously with the fourth, which may be heavy when previous profits have not been set aside for such an eventuality.

The State absolutely must be sheltered from these losses, so the last part of my proposal should be accepted. The banks issuing notes payable to the bearer on presentation should be told to liquidate their issues when their concessions expire and then mint regulating silver token equivalent to the amount of banknotes in circulation. Thus a double result will be obtained: first, by minting écus the State will make a profit that it may capitalize. Furthermore, the value of money will rise, making the token less token. If then, in the relatively near future, there occurs an increase in the quantity or a decrease in the utility of silver, at the same time as an increase in the quantity or a decrease in the utility of gold, it [the State] could withdraw écus from circulation while covering its losses by means of the previous profit capitalized.

Moreover in this way two birds could be killed with one stone, as considerable progress would be made by getting rid of paper money in the shape of banknotes.

The issue of banknotes representing bills of exchange is not the same as what the socialists called the mobilization of land or fixed capital. It is the mobilization of the entrepreneurs' circulating capital in the form of raw materials and manufactured products. When a bill of exchange is created, it is a title deed of property in raw materials; as its maturity approaches it becomes a title deed of a product in the process of manufacture; at its maturity it is a title deed not only to a finished product but one already sold, that is to say, money. So banknotes representing it **[47]** could then be redeemed. But if the operation has not been repeated, the entrepreneur would not be able to obtain raw materials again to manufacture another product. Consequently, if one had to suspend the issue of banknotes, willingly or not, every part of agricultural, industrial or commercial production that borrows its circulating capital from the issue of banknotes would come to a standstill. Under these conditions, I do not hesitate to repeat that issues of banknotes which cannot be liquidated other than by the suspension of economic life must not be liquidated at all.

Title deeds to circulating capital should not be used as money. Just as is the case with fixed capital, these deeds have to be kept in the portfolios of the capitalists who created savings. The discount rate should be determined on the basis of three-month interest-bearing bank deposits. Where bank deposits are fixed owing to issues that have been authorized, new savings must be built up as drawing credit [*crédit à l'escompte*]. But allowing disposable capital to come to rest was not the only effect of the banknote issues; another effect was the increase of the amount money in circulation by adding paper money to metallic money. So if paper that has to disappear is not replaced by an equal sum of metallic money, a recession in the form of a fall in prices will occur. The large amount of silver not at present in use offers a unique, exceptional occasion to avoid this drawback. The State will have to mint écus to an amount equal to the notes in circulation. As a matter of fact, the issue of these écus will take place gradually for new savings to pile up; no recession will occur, monetary or financial.

It is obvious that the State will make a profit by buying silver at its real commodity price and reselling silver-money against its nominal value. A special fund will be assigned with the capitalization of these profits; and, if **[48]** circumstances are favourable, it could provide the means of paying off a considerable part of public debt. The aforementioned special fund could also be merged with the redemption fund. Suppose the State issues 1 billion écus to liquidate 1 billion in banknotes and makes a profit of 10 per cent, i.e. of 100 million. 100 million capitalized at 4 per cent compound interest will make it possible to redeem 5 billion after 100 years. What is needed to obtain this result? That for a century from now a flood of gold should not be produced which would compel the State to demonetize silver. These risks generally have to be taken if prudence is the watchword. Would it not be better, too, if there are profits to be made, to keep them for the State rather than speculators, who will do their utmost to bring back unlimited coinage of silver?

Hence the reform of our monetary system by means of regulating the variation in the value of money, the reform of our credit system by getting rid of fictitious drawing credit, the redemption of part of the public debt – these are the advantages of the plan I have laid before the members of the International Monetary Conference, to consider whether it may be completely executed. We may not hope for such success, the less so because at present the Latin Union seems to be breaking miserably up, disappointing all the hopes of those who saw in it a first step towards a universal monetary union. Therefore I am resigned to seeing our monetary legislation, at the very moment it had reached an almost rational system, without knowing or aspiring to it, fall back into a muddle, just like a blind man who stumbles upon velvety meadows and cool shade in the course of his walk, then leaves them as quickly as possible, returning to marshes and potholes. But I hope that when economists with open and independent minds are kind enough to read attentively the memoirs I have devoted to metallic and fiduciary circulation, and to use it for further study, monetary theory will be more or less **[49]** renovated quite soon, thanks to the use of the mathematical method. Of course, the means of suppressing the movements in the general price level – up or down – which in certain cases constitute the necessary indications of the proper functioning of exchange and production will not be found – nor indeed should they even be sought. However, following the track opened up by Cournot and Jevons, if not by their method then at least by some analogous one, we shall find a way of removing those shifts caused exclusively by special circumstances relating to money which are a source of confusion and perplexity, not an essential element in the pursuit of economic equilibrium.

III A contribution to the study of price variations since the suspension of silver écu minting[5]

To finish down to the last detail the exposition of the monetary system to which I was led by mathematics, in spite of myself in a way, I should have liked to complete my theoretical investigation of Jevons's method by a practical application of that method to the present situation. But as we have seen, the result of my analysis obliged me to modify the objective of this operation slightly.

5 Report read before the Société vaudoise des sciences naturelles, Lausanne (meeting of 3 June 1885).

Jevons used his method to seek the variation in the value of money caused by the discovery of gold in California and Australia in 1850. I should have applied it to determine the quantity of regulating token to put into circulation at present to bring the value of money to the level of the geometric average of the values of the commodities.

But here a first complication appears. By virtue of **[50]** his theory of economic tides, Jevons should have taken two periods for comparison: 1841–50 and 1851–60. For reasons that I shall not discuss here he took the two periods 1845–50 and 1860–2. In my case, I had to take the two periods 1869–78 and 1879–88. Now, on one hand it seems to me difficult to take 1870 into consideration since it was too turbulent because of political events, and, on the other, we are still living in 1885. So the application was necessarily incomplete with respect to the stretch of time it encompasses. The first problem, however, did not appear serious enough to stop me. Reduced to the eight years 1871–8, the first period still constitutes sufficiently exactly a period of ebb and flood, with high-tide in 1873 and low-tide in 1878; and as for the period of the six years 1879–84, it is long enough for us to see at least an outline of the phenomenon of a general decrease or increase in prices.

It would obviously be of interest if this research, even limited as it is to the period 1871–84, could be performed simultaneously in every Latin Union country: France, Belgium, Switzerland, Italy and Greece. I intend to try it in those countries that are best equipped for such an exercise. But first I considered attempting the research in Switzerland. Having found among my students in the first year of Law Mr Alfred Simon, from Bern,[6] a very intelligent and willing young man, I explained to him what to do and I asked him to realize it for those commodities whose price statistics he could procure himself, from the federal bureau or from the cantonal bureau of statistics at Bern. Mr Simon acquitted himself conscientiously of his task and transmitted me the result by means of the following letter, to which he attached Tables [I and II, appendix to this chapter] and graphs [Figures 1–23, appendix] that can be found at the end of the present memoir:

[51] Bern, 24 April 1885

Sir,

The work you were so good as to charge me with is finished, and I hasten to send you the result. It comprises:

1 Table I of the *Average annual prices during the period 1871–1884 and the Averages of the prices during the periods 1871–1878 and 1879–1884* of twenty commodities in the Bern market.

6 Dr Alfred Simon [?–1900] has since become head of the Bureau fédéral de la statistique commerciale in Bern. [Afterwards he was attaché at the Swiss legations in Berlin and Vienna.]

2 TABLE II of the *Ratios of the average annual prices* during the period 1871–1884 with respect to the averages of the prices during the period 1871–1878 and the *Geometric averages of these ratios.*

3 PAGE OF GRAPHS representing the curves of the variation in these ratios and averages and the curves of variation in the discount rates at the Cantonal Bank of Bern and the Bank of France of Paris during the period 1871–1884.

I procured as follows the prices mentioned in the first of my two tables, the elements of all the calculations.

For the years 1871–1877 I found them in the *Statistisches Jahrbuch für den Kanton Bern, herausgegeben vom kantonalen statistische Bureau.* The prices of meat for the year 1873 were not mentioned in the *Jahrbuch*; I replaced them by the arithmetic averages of the prices in 1872 and 1874.

For the years 1878–1883, for which the *Jahrbuch* had not yet appeared, I asked the authorization of Mr de Steiger, Director of Interior Affairs [of the canton of Bern], to consult the manuscript documents in the Cantonal Bureau of Statistics. This authorization was kindly granted and Mr Mühlemann, secretary of the Bureau, was good enough to send me copies of these documents. At this point, I take the liberty of expressing my gratitude to Mr de Steiger and Mr Mühlemann.

[52] Finally, since the Cantonal Bureau had not yet calculated the average prices for 1884, I calculated them myself from the same sources as theirs, viz. from the three Bern newspapers *Intelligenzblatt der Stadt Bern, Berner Stadtblatt, Bernerpost*, in which weekly prices are reported. I likewise thank the editors of these three newspapers for the kindness with which they have put their collections for the year 1884 at my disposal.

The prices of bread are not mentioned in these newspapers. The Cantonal Bureau of Statistics obtains them by taking the averages of the prices provided by a certain number of bakers. For 1884 Mr Mühlemann gave me an approximate indication.

I believe I ought to indicate the units of measurement relating to these prices. They are as follows: for spelt [German wheat] and oats the *maldre* [150 l]; for wheat 200 lb or 100 kg; for barley and rye the *viertel* or quarter (15 l); for bread 2 lb, or 1 kg; for meat, butter, lard and bacon 1 lb or 0.5 kg; for eggs ten units; for potatoes 5 l; for hay and straw 100 lb or 50 kg; for firewood the *moule* or 3 m^3.

Finally, I should note that I found indications for the discount rate in the *Jahresberichte* of the Cantonal Bank of Bern; because of its frequent fluctuations I had to take annual averages.

Please, accept, sir, my respectful and sincere sentiments.

Alfred Simon, stud. jur.

Where, unfortunately, the span of time is incomplete, the number of commodities considered is no less incomplete. Jevons was able to work with thirty-nine commodities in twelve categories: **[53]**

I 1 Silver.
II Metals: 2 Tin, 3 Copper, 4 Lead, 5 Bar iron, 6 Pig Iron, 7 Tin plates.
III Oil: 8 Palm oil, 9 Linseed oil.
IV Leather and skins: 10 Tallow, 11 Hides, 12 Leather.
V 13 Timber.
VI Dyestuffs: 14 Logwood, 15 Indigo.
VII Cotton: 16 Upland cotton, 17 Pernam cotton, 18 Surat cotton.
VIII Textiles: 19 Wool, 20 Silk, 21 Flax, 22 Hemp.
IX Cereals: 23 Wheat, 24 Barley, 25 Oats, 26 Rye, 27 Beans, 28 Peas.
X 29 Hay, 30 Clover, 31 Straw.
XI Meat and butter: 32 Beef, 33 Mutton, 34 Pork, 35 Butter.
XII Groceries: 36 Sugar, 37 Spirits, 38 Tea, 39 Pepper.

As for us, we could only work with twenty commodities divided into eight categories:

I Cereals and bread: 1 Spelt, 2 Wheat, 3 Barley, 4 Rye, 5 Oats, 6 White bread, 7 Brown bread.
II Meat: 8 Beef, 9 Mutton, 10 Veal.
III 11 Butter.
IV 12 Lard, 13 Bacon.
V 14 Eggs.
VI 15 White potatoes, 16 Red potatoes.
VII 17 Hay, 18 Straw.
VIII Firewood: 19 Beech, 20 Pine.

Our two categories I Cereals and bread and VI Potatoes are only the equivalent of Jevons's category IX Cereals. Our two categories II Meat and III Butter are only the equivalent of his category XI Meat and butter. Our category VII Hay and straw is equivalent to his category X Hay, clover and straw. Our category VIII Firewood may make up for his category V Timber. Compared with his commodities, we have in **[54]** addition lard, bacon and eggs; but silver, metals, oils, leather and skins, dyestuffs, cotton, textiles and groceries are lacking in our list. We shall need another twenty or thirty commodities taken from these categories. I take this occasion to beg the Bureaux of Statistics to get down to organizing economic statistics, in addition to population statistics and other statistics that they pursue so ardently; that is to say, the statistics of *prices* and, as far as possible, the *quantities* of commodities corresponding to these prices. These elements are indispensable to attempt rational practical economics.

Where our principal commodities are foodstuffs and constitute not industrial products, but only agricultural products, and where the price and the quantity of these commodities will be influenced considerably by good or bad crops, it is easy to foresee that in our results the effect of social phenomena common to all the commodities will be concealed almost entirely by the effects of their peculiar natural phenomena. This is, indeed, what happens. To begin with, the social phenomenon of the tide does not appear here. Probably, one should not exaggerate the importance of the theory of economic tides and certainly not be excessively strict about it. Obviously, this tide is much more apparent on certain points than others. The recessions that mark the moments of ebb are more or less general; perhaps they do not occur exactly every ten years, any more than the high-tides or the low ones. But it does seem incontestable that there is a succession and alternation of active periods with periods of industrial and commercial stagnation. According to Jevons, the curve of discount rates of the Bank of England indicates two periods of activity or high-tide, in 1847 and in 1857, and two periods of stagnation or low-tide, in 1849–52 and in 1862. His curve of the general variation in prices rises and descends **[55]** at exactly the same periods; and the movements up and down of the general curve can again be found more or less in all the particular curves that are curves of price variations of groups of commodities. In our case, the two curves of the exchange rate at the Cantonal Bank of Bern and the Bank of France indicate two periods of activity or high-tide, in 1871–3 and in 1882, and a period of stagnation or low-tide, in 1878. But no corresponding movements up or down are noticeable with regard to the particular curves of the variations of prices per commodity, or in the general curve. This general curve rises considerably in 1876 and 1877; but the movement is due to the fact that in this period, and in particular in 1877, all prices rose, especially those of barley and rye, meat, lard, bacon and potatoes, probably because of bad crops.

That being said, it is nevertheless impossible not to be struck by the decline of our general curve of the variation in prices during the period 1879–84;[xii] all the more so because this fall can be observed in nearly all the particular curves, alternately rising and falling, with the exception of those concerning meat, which, on the contrary, show a rise. We might therefore be inclined to believe that here we have a social phenomenon and not a natural one. Anyway, we find in the case under consideration that:

$$\sqrt[m]{\frac{a'}{a} \cdot \frac{b'}{b} \cdot \frac{c'}{c} \cdot \frac{d'}{d} \cdots} = 0.9327$$

this means that we note an average decrease from 1 to 0.9327, or 6.73 per cent, of the commodities' prices in gold from the period 1871–8 to the period 1879–84.

Where does this general fall in prices originate? What remedy should be applied to it? According to the bimetallists, the decrease originates exclusively from the growing scarcity of money, and, in order to redress this, **[56]** the unlimited minting of silver écus must be resumed. The monometallists will say that the fall originates from advances in agriculture and industry, from the development of means and routes of transport, from the opening of the Suez Canal, etc., and that there is no reason to redress it by any monetary measure. Remarkable expositions regarding this double thesis can be found in two recently published essays. One of them is entitled 'La crise et la contraction monétaire', by Mr [E. L. V.] de Lavaleye under the rubric 'Correspondance' in the March 1885 issue of the *Journal des économistes*, the other is a brochure by Mr [E.] Nasse, *Währungsfrage in Deutschland*. The more I think about it the more inclined I am personally to join one or other of these points of view without reservation. I really believe, just as the monometallists do, that the general price decrease is not solely due to the growing scarcity of money, and that agricultural, industrial and commercial progress plays quite a large role in it. But these gentlemen will grant me it is rather distressing that this progress was not extended to the money commodity. Such progress would have brought about two advantages: it would have satisfied our wants of that commodity more completely and it would have avoided the general fall in money prices of the other commodities that occurred, to the serious disadvantage of entrepreneurs. The bimetallists, however, might ask if it is not precisely the legislator's action that prevented the extension of economic progress to the money commodity. Anyway, I would say personally that we have the means of procuring ourselves an artificial decrease in the *rareté* and value of gold that will not occur naturally: it is not resuming unlimited minting of silver écus, which would probably change rise into fall – from Charybdis into Scylla – but just put back into circulation the quantity of silver écus that is strictly necessary and sufficient to let the prices rise to their level again.

The quantity of silver écus to be brought into circulation would be given by:

$$\frac{Q''}{Q'} = 1 \bigg/ \sqrt[m]{\frac{a'}{a} \cdot \frac{b'}{b} \cdot \frac{c'}{c} \cdot \frac{d'}{d} \cdots}$$

[57] In this formula the denominator:

$$\sqrt[m]{\frac{a'}{a} \cdot \frac{b'}{b} \cdot \frac{c'}{c} \cdot \frac{d'}{d} \cdots}$$

represents the average decrease in the money prices of the commodities; it is equal to 0.9327. Q' is the total quantity of metallic and fiduciary money at present in circulation in the Latin Union; it is equal to 10 billion. I adopt this number as follows from the data in Mr A. de Malarce's publication *Monnaie, poids et mesures des divers États du monde*,[xiii] which for 1882 seems to be as shown in Table 2.4.

Table 2.4 Money in the Latin Union, 1882

	Metal	*Notes*	*Cash balances (million)*
France	6,000	2,600	1,800
Belgium	904	307	226
Switzerland	492	110	44
Italy		1,600	
Greece		70	
	7,396	4,687	2,070
	+2,617	−2,070	
	10,013	2,617[7]	

There would be reason enough to bring and keep this up to date, which would be possible in a sufficiently approximate manner. In the present case this would give:

$$Q'' = 10 \times \frac{1}{0.9327} = 10 \times 1.0720 = 10.720$$

So let us suppose for a moment that the two periods under comparison, instead of being cut short as they **[58]** both are, had obviously the span of an economic tide, that the commodities under consideration, instead of being most insufficient in number and of a very special nature, were numerous enough and sufficiently varied, and that the calculations, instead of relating to the Bern market, were extended throughout the whole Latin Union. Then the result of the calculations would show that from the total quantity of money at present in circulation, the sum of 720 million silver écus was lacking to be divided among the various States of the Union, for each of them, proportionally to their share in the 10 billion of money. This amount is very largely due to various circumstances, such as the competition of American products arriving at the same time as the

7 In *Théorie de la monnaie* it will be demonstrated that, in contrast to what has been done at this point, the amount of banknotes in circulation should not be taken into consideration.

production of gold was slowing down, while new demands were appearing. Probably, in normal times the quantity of regulating token to inject into or withdraw from circulation would be much smaller.

But I do not want to make the impression of founding, even by hypothesis, a specific conclusion on data which are obviously too limited and uncertain. Far from it, I should not have taken the liberty of communicating our work, that is, Mr Simon's and my own, to the Société vaudoise des sciences naturelles without very special motivation. As I said, my intention is to address some enlightened, experienced economists and statisticians in the Latin Union, asking them to help me complete a system of sufficient and decisive data. I therefore have to provide them, together with the theoretical exposition of Jevons's method, a practical model of its application. Jevons's book *Investigations in Currency and Finance* has not been translated into French and probably will not be in the near future. My latest memoir and the present one may be considered in a sense as such a translation; and that is why I claim hospitality for them in the *Bulletin* [*de la Société vaudoise des sciences naturelles*]. I must urgently suggest that those who would like to should go deeper into the question read Jevons's work with the greatest care, if they can. In the editor's introduction they will find **[59]** references to numerous works devoted to Jevons's method, by Giffen, Ellis, Patterson, Goschen, Gibbs, J-B. Martin, Cork, Sidgwick, Chevassus and Edgeworth. Until recently I could not read all these works, but now I have every reason for being sure that none of these authors possessed the principle of the proportionality of values to *raretés*, on which whole my criticism has been founded. I did not believe it necessary to wait any longer to write and publish it [the present article].

Appendix

Below are the tables and the graphs mentioned in Alfred Simons's letter. Walras's original numbering has been maintained. Figures 1–21 correspond with the twenty-one rows of Table II.

Table I Average annual prices over the period 1871–84, and average prices over the periods 1871–8 and 1879–84

Commodities	*1871*	*1872*	*1873*	*1874*	*1875*	*1876*	*1877*	*1878*	*Av. 71–8*	*1879*	*1880*	*1881*	*1882*	*1883*	*1884*	*Av. 79–84*
1 Spelt	16.77	17.48	16.82	18.10	11.90	13.12	15.65	13.55	15.42	13.41	14.83	14.81	14.12	10.72	10.26	13.02
2 Wheat	33.39	34.33	36.34	34.96	26.92	26.80	32.58	29.76	31.88	27.72	30.76	29.32	29.88	24.33	24.09	27.35
3 Barley	2.15	2.08	2.24	2.49	2.24	2.23	2.54	2.38	2.27	2.20	2.30	2.29	2.26	2.04	2.04	2.19
4 Rye	2.04	2.05	2.30	2.46	2.46	2.06	2.42	2.21	2.20	2.30	2.30	2.29	2.26	2.04	2.00	2.20
5 Oats	16.82	14.24	15.51	18.59	16.50	17.36	16.63	14.87	16.44	14.54	15.64	15.63	15.45	14.76	14.90	15.15
6 White bread	0.47	0.49	0.46	0.50	0.45	0.45	0.48	0.44	0.47	0.44	0.44	0.44	0.46	0.46	0.38	0.43
7 Brown bread	0.42	0.45	0.43	0.46	0.40	0.40	0.43	0.39	0.42	0.39	0.39	0.39	0.41	0.41	0.33	0.38
8 Beef	0.61	0.64	0.59	0.54	0.55	0.66	0.71	0.75	0.63	0.75	0.65	0.64	0.59	0.68	0.72	0.67
9 Mutton	0.55	0.63	0.58	0.54	0.55	0.68	0.73	0.78	0.63	0.77	0.68	0.64	0.62	0.66	0.72	0.68
10 Veal	0.62	0.58	0.56	0.55	0.55	0.70	0.75	0.76	0.63	0.67	0.60	0.66	0.70	0.66	0.65	0.65
11 Butter	1.11	1.15	1.14	1.14	1.27	1.28	1.23	1.15	1.18	1.10	1.16	1.14	1.14	1.19	1.15	1.14
12 Lard	0.97	1.04	1.04	0.91	0.93	1.04	1.08	0.95	0.99	0.95	0.95	0.93	1.01	0.91	0.97	0.95
13 Bacon	0.96	1.04	1.10	0.98	0.91	1.04	1.10	1.02	0.99	0.92	0.93	0.95	0.95	0.96	0.98	0.95
14 Eggs	0.60	0.66	0.75	0.70	0.77	0.75	0.75	0.75	0.72	0.75	0.75	0.75	0.67	0.75	0.76	0.74
15 White potatoes	0.30	0.47	0.52	0.39	0.43	0.52	0.54	0.42	0.45	0.45	0.35	0.34	0.32	0.39	0.30	0.36
16 Red potatoes	0.33	0.52	0.56	0.40	0.47	0.56	0.56	0.45	0.48	0.47	0.38	0.39	0.37	0.44	0.34	0.40
17 Hay	5.84	3.89	3.00	4.19	6.40	5.45	4.56	3.70	4.64	3.25	4.34	4.25	4.63	4.22	3.62	4.05
18 Straw	4.59	3.10	2.76	2.98	3.68	4.16	4.00	3.17	3.56	3.00	3.78	3.51	3.69	3.82	3.29	3.51
19 Firewood, beech	48.36	50.43	49.82	53.22	62.44	62.86	56.08	54.50	54.71	49.85	49.00	48.06	46.42	48.60	48.06	48.33
20 Idem, pine	32.15	35.62	37.13	39.76	41.30	43.83	35.98	35.30	37.63	32.75	37.07	29.16	29.06	30.90	32.64	31.93

Table II Ratios of the average annual prices of the period 1871–84 to the average prices over the period 1871–8, and geometric averages of these ratios

Commodities	*1871*	*1872*	*1873*	*1874*	*1875*	*1876*	*1877*	*1878*	*1879*	*1880*	*1881*	*1882*	*1883*	*1884*
1 Spelt	1.087	1.133	1.090	1.173	0.771	0.850	1.015	0.878	0.869	0.961	0.960	0.915	0.695	0.665
2 Wheat	1.047	1.077	1.140	1.097	0.844	0.840	1.022	0.933	0.869	0.964	0.919	0.937	0.763	0.755
3 Barley	0.947	0.916	0.986	1.096	0.986	0.982	1.118	1.048	0.969	1.013	1.009	0.995	0.898	0.898
4 Rye	0.927	0.931	1.045	1.118	0.927	0.936	1.100	1.004	1.045	1.045	1.041	1.027	0.927	0.909
5 Oats	1.023	0.866	0.943	1.131	1.003	1.056	1.011	0.904	0.884	0.951	0.950	0.939	0.897	0.906
6 White bread	1.000	1.042	0.978	1.063	0.957	0.957	1.021	0.936	0.936	0.936	0.936	0.978	0.978	0.808
7 Brown bread	1.000	1.071	1.023	1.095	0.952	0.952	1.023	0.928	0.928	0.928	0.928	0.976	0.976	0.785
8 Beef	0.968	1.016	0.936	0.857	0.873	1.048	1.127	1.191	1.191	1.031	1.016	0.936	1.079	1.142
9 Mutton	0.873	1.000	0.928	0.857	0.873	1.079	1.158	1.238	1.222	1.079	1.016	0.984	1.048	1.142
10 Veal	0.984	0.920	0.896	0.873	0.873	1.111	1.190	1.206	1.063	0.952	1.048	1.111	1.048	1.032
11 Butter	0.940	0.974	0.966	0.966	1.076	1.085	1.043	0.974	0.932	0.983	0.966	0.966	1.008	0.974
12 Lard	0.979	1.051	1.051	0.919	0.939	1.051	1.090	0.959	0.959	0.959	0.939	1.020	0.919	0.979
13 Bacon	0.969	1.051	1.111	0.989	0.919	1.051	1.111	1.030	0.929	0.939	0.959	0.959	0.969	0.989
14 Eggs	0.833	0.916	1.042	0.972	1.070	1.041	1.042	1.042	1.045	1.042	1.042	0.930	1.042	1.055
15 White potatoes	0.666	1.044	1.155	0.866	0.955	1.155	1.200	0.933	1.000	0.777	0.755	0.711	0.866	0.666
16 Red potatoes	0.625	1.083	1.166	0.833	0.979	1.166	1.166	0.937	0.979	0.791	0.812	0.770	0.916	0.708
17 Hay	1.258	0.838	0.646	0.903	1.379	1.193	0.982	0.797	0.700	0.935	0.915	0.997	0.909	0.780
18 Straw	1.289	0.870	0.775	0.837	1.033	1.168	1.123	0.890	0.842	1.062	0.985	1.036	1.073	0.924
19 Firewood, beech	0.883	0.921	0.910	0.972	1.141	1.148	1.025	0.996	0.911	0.895	0.878	0.848	0.888	0.878
20 Idem, pine	0.854	0.946	0.986	1.056	1.097	1.164	0.956	0.938	0.870	0.985	0.774	0.772	0.821	0.868
Geometric averages	0.945	0.980	0.980	0.977	0.975	1.046	1.074	0.982	0.939	0.958	0.939	0.935	0.931	0.882

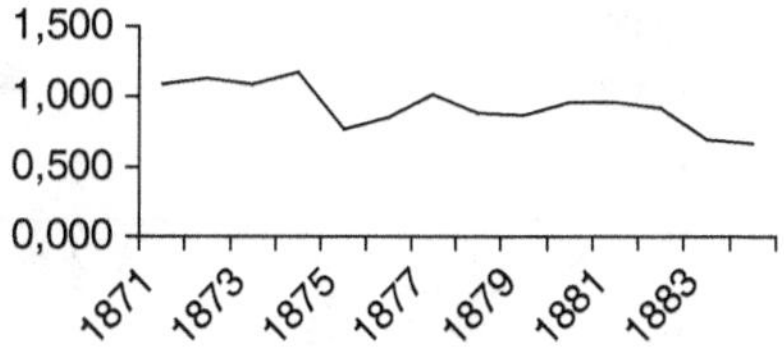

1 Spelt

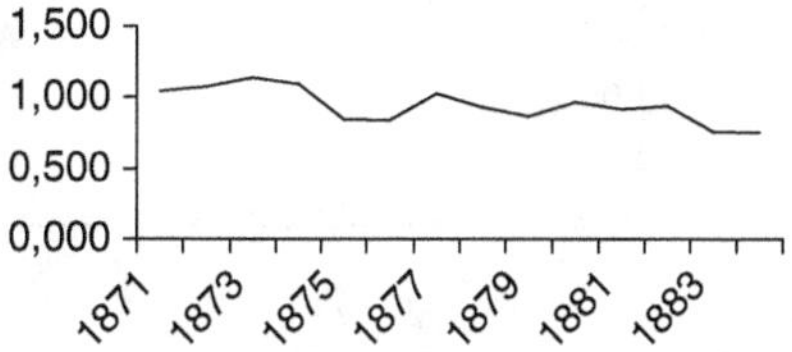

2 Wheat

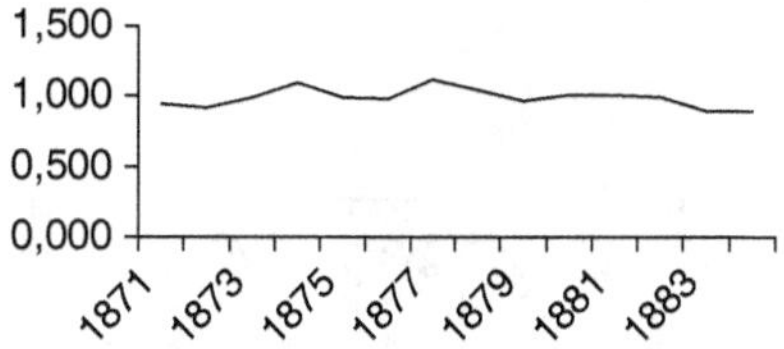

3 Barley

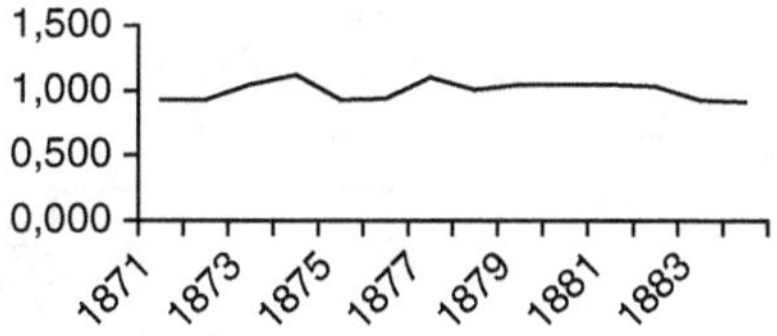

4 Rye

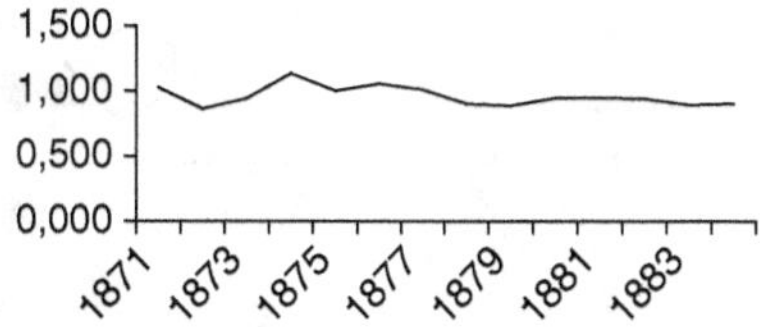

5 Oats

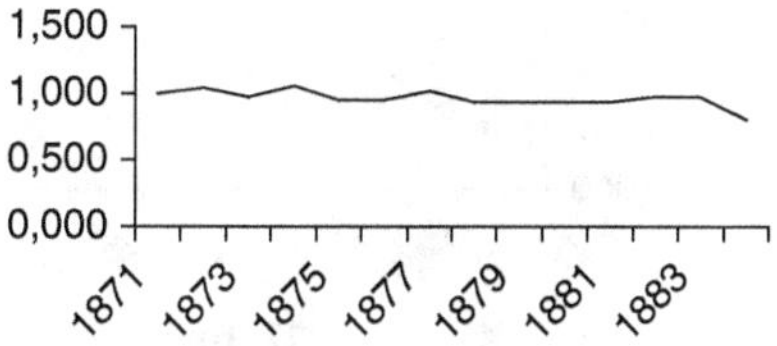

6 White bread

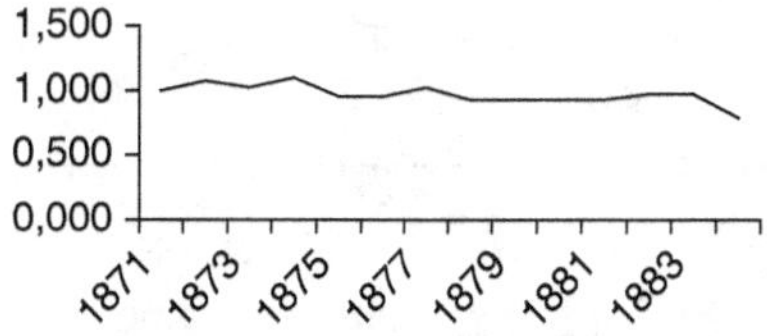

7 Brown bread

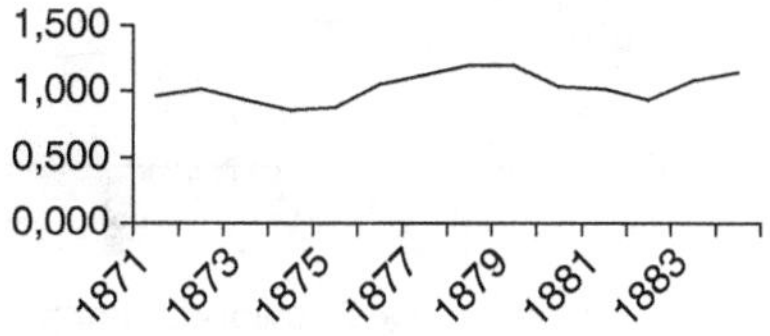

8 Beef

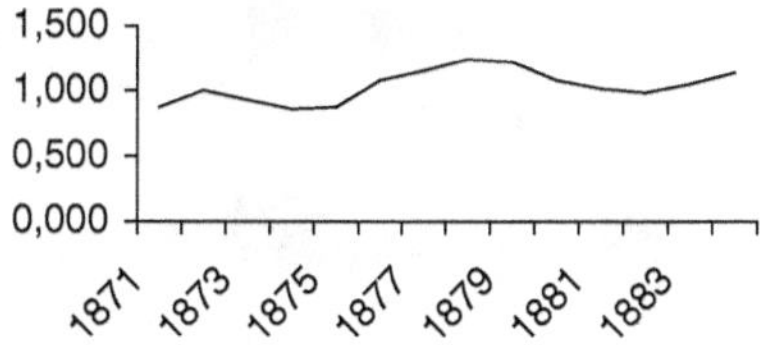

9 Mutton

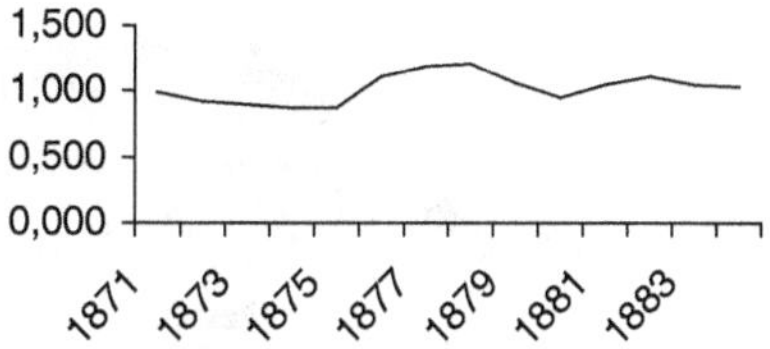

10 Veal

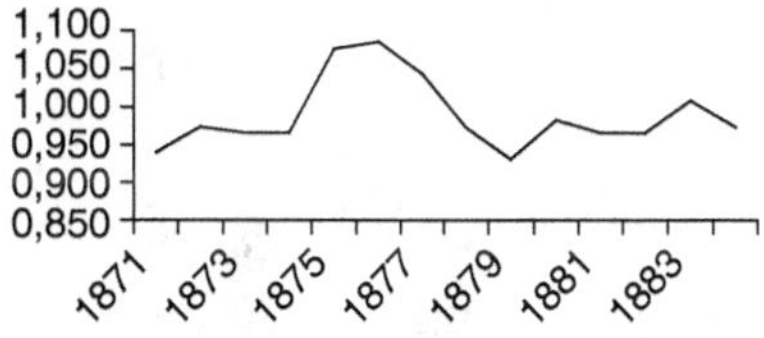

11 Butter

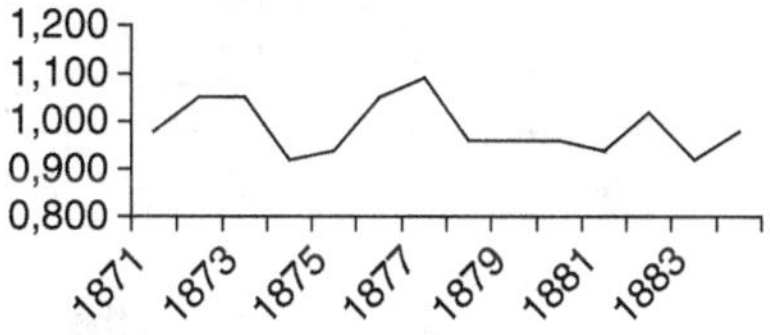

12 Lard

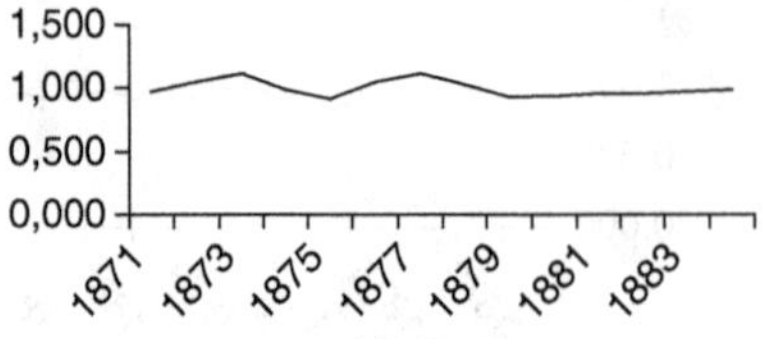

13 Bacon

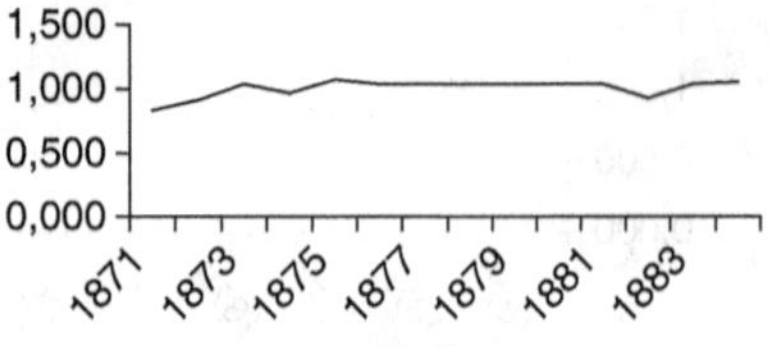

14 Eggs

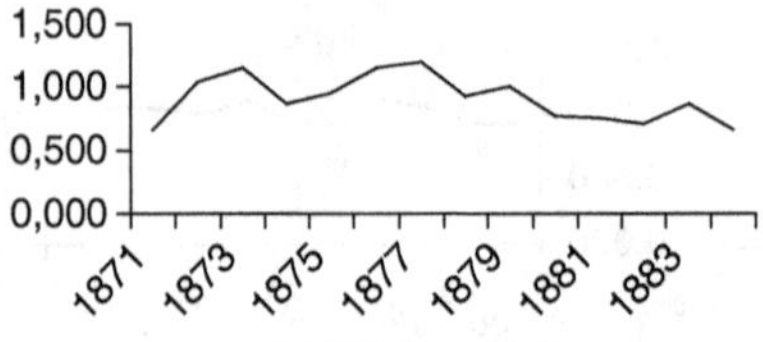

15 White potatoes

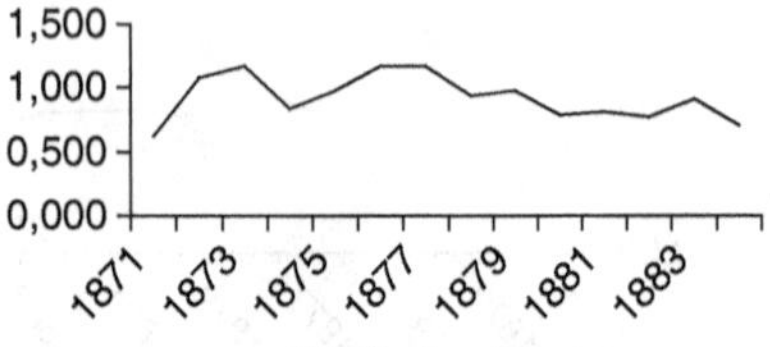

16 Red potatoes

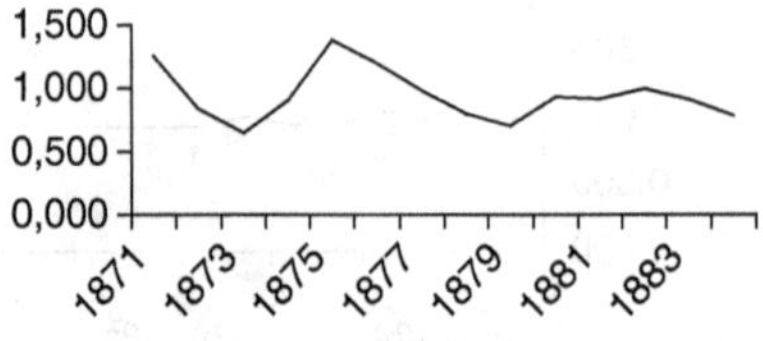

17 Hay

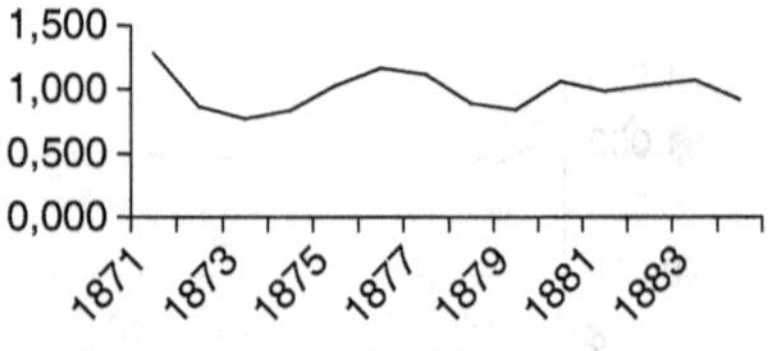

18 Straw

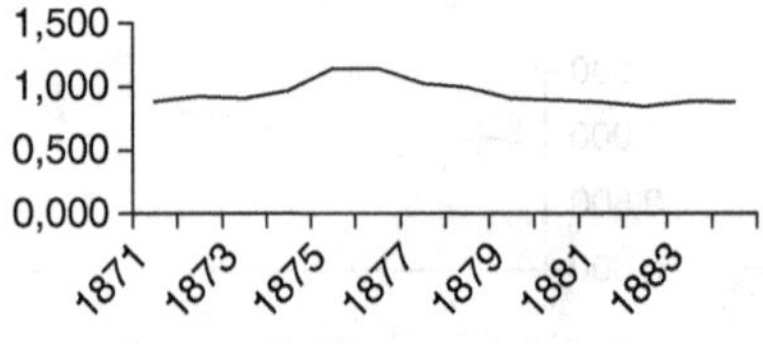

19 Firewood, beech

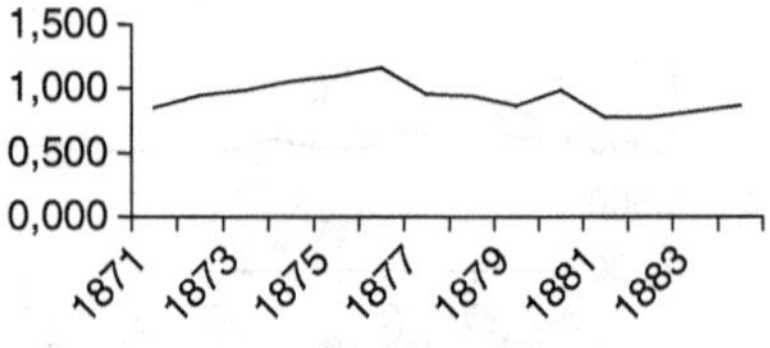

20 Idem, pine

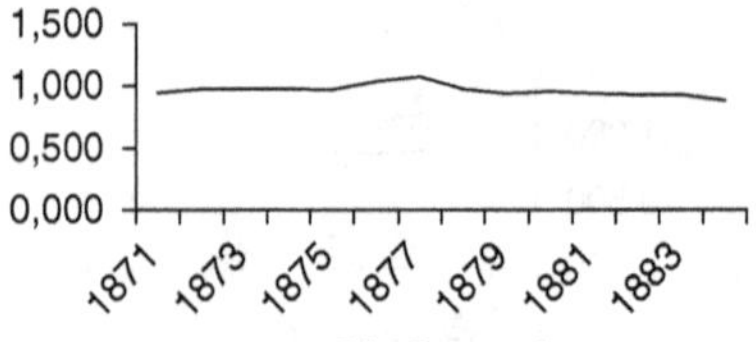

21 General

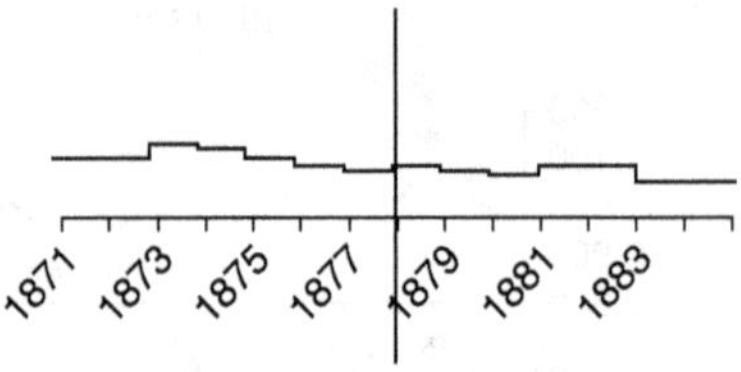

Discount rate at the Banque cantonale de Bern

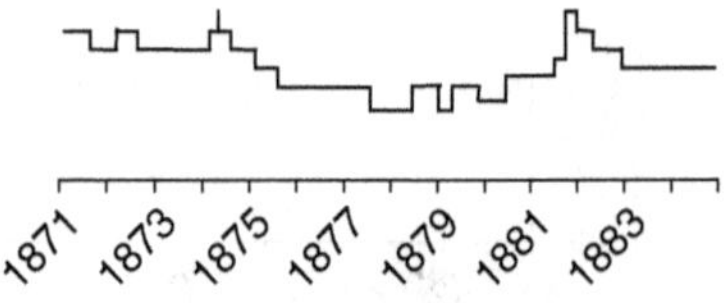

Discount rate at the Banque de France

Notes

i Cournot (1838), pp. 15–21. The English translation is taken from Cournot (1897), pp. 18–22.
ii Cournot (1897), p. 23 (Cournot 1838: 21).
iii Cournot (1897), p. 26 (Cournot 1838: 24).
*iv This means, in modern terms, that these individuals' marginal utility functions expand, i.e. shift in a direction from the origin.
*v Note that the price of (A), the *numéraire*, remains equal to 1.
*vi We leave this word untranslated. Walras did not mean rent from land in the sense of an amount of money but the services that land provides and that are the *raison d'être* of rent in the form of money. A correct but ugly paraphrase would be 'income in kind from land'. I shall also use the somewhat uncommon expression 'land services'; see the appendix to the Introduction (p. liii).
*vii Again, income in kind is meant; from machines, buildings, means of transport, etc.
*viii The word 'more' was absent in the first published version of this text.
*ix I.e. the right-hand side of the last equation above.
*x The following paragraphs seem very obscure.
*xi This word does not figure in the versions preceding *EEPA*.
*xii See also and in particular the last row of Table II.
xiii Paris: Firmin-Didot and Guillaumin (1882).

[63]

3 *Theory of Money*

Preface and introduction

[Chapters 3, 4, 5 and 6 of the *EEPA* together form a revised reprint of Léon Walras's booklet *Théorie de la monnaie*, published in 1886. The introduction, Part I and Part II, in their turn, had already been published, under the title 'Théorie de la monnaie', in the *Revue scientifique (Revue rose)*, 3rd series, 11, no. 15 (10 April 1886), pp. 449–57, and no. 16 (17 April 1886), pp. 493–500. A preface and a third part entitled 'Desiderata statistiques' were written to complete the *Théorie de la monnaie* in the form of a booklet. Afterwards, before inserting it in his *EEPA*, Walras adapted the text of Parts I (considerably), II (slightly) and III (very little); see *ŒEC*, vol. X. The text presented here is a translation of this latter version.]

Preface

[65] The Introduction, below, will explain how I came to draw up the two first parts of this *Theory of Money*, entitled 'Exposition of the principles' and 'Critical discussion of the systems'. I wrote the third part, entitled 'Statistical desiderata', in June and July this year [1886] when I was hoping to be able to attend a meeting of statisticians and economists, among whom could be found some of the most qualified people in the whole world of money matters.[i] It seemed to me that I had to present a specific, definite method of regulating the variation in value of money to these authorities, however imperfect it might be, coming from an economist who is not a statistician. I hoped that the notion of a system immediately ready for application in practice would result from the discussion, criticism and even refutation of this outline. Because I missed this occasion I thought I ought to present my ideas to the public of scholars and professors, whose attention and kindness have encouraged me up to the present. I repeat that in publishing this work I am deliberately downplaying my statistical scheme to pay serious attention only to my economic conclusion, which one of my British correspondents, Mr Aneurin Williams, formulated so cleverly by writing the following lines to me: 'I have been particularly interested in your suggestion of *billon régulateur*. I have no doubt that a vast social improvement will some day be brought about by regulating the standard of value instead of allowing it to vary haphazardly as at present.'[ii] 'Regulating the standard of value, instead of allowing it to vary haphazardly as at present', he has hit the nail on the head! Monometallism surrenders itself entirely to hazard; bimetallism already avoids it a little; the system with gold money and regulating silver token, put into practice under the conditions of my monetary quadriga,[iii] will be far the most freed from it, I believe. If someone can show me a better system, I am ready to be won over.[iv]

A last remark. When completing the printing of my opuscule, I received the first part of an important book in which Mr E. von Böhm **[66]** Bawerk, Professor of Economics at Innsbruck University, expounds the same theory of value as I did in my previous works, which can be found recapitulated in §II of the first part of the present *Theory of Money*. The last lines in this [Böhm-Bawerk's] book touched me greatly, not only because of the flattering way in which I was mentioned, but also because of an observation that I want to make my own because it entirely agrees with my deepest and most intimate convictions as with the true idea that governed the writing of the present study:

> We currently see – Mr Von Böhm-Bawerk[v] says – how the most original minds from widely differing countries, Jevons, Pierson, Walras, each in his own way, are pushing the new principle of *Grenznutzen* [marginal utility] as a foundation for the laws of exchange: would this not provide strong evidence that the theory of subjective value is more than a mental trifle, and that it would be a fertile basis for our science?[1]

Mr von Böhm-Bawerk's *Grenznutzen* is no other than Gossen's *Größe in dem Augenblick in welchem seine Bereitung abgebrochen wird* [magnitude (intensity) at the moment when its enjoyment is broken off], or the *Wert des letzten Atoms* [intensity of pleasure of the last atom],[2,vi] Jevons's *Final degree of utility*[3] and my *intensité du dernier besoin satisfait*, or *rareté*;[4,vii] the latter, irrespective of the fact that it is imagined as a mathematical magnitude, is

1 'Grundzüge der Theorie des wirtschaftlichen Güterwerts.' Reprint from *Jahrbücher für Nationalökonomie und Statistik*, new series, vol. XIII, Jena, 1886 [p. 82].

2 *Entwickelung der Gesetze des menschlichen Verkehrs und der daraus fließenden Regeln für menschliches Handeln*, Brunswick [Druck und Verlag von Friedrich Vieweg & Sohn], 1854 [pp. 12 and 45, respectively; see also pp. 27, 29–33]. Mr von Böhm-Bawerk obviously ignores the existence of Gossen. If he had been informed with respect to this point, he would have acknowledged how much the absence of a reference to the name and the book of this author would have constituted a regrettable lack in his *Theory of value*.

3 *The Theory of Political Economy*, London [Macmillan], 1871 [p. 51].

4 *Eléments d'économie politique pure ou Théorie de la richesse sociale*, Lausanne [Corbaz], 1874–7, §75. *Théorie mathématique de la richesse sociale*, Lausanne [Corbaz], 1883 [§74].

nearly the same as the *rareté* defined by my father A.-A. Walras[5] fifty years ago as a combination of utility and limitation in quantity.

[67] Besides, it is certainly true that *highly original minds, in widely differing countries, are now trying to base the whole system of the laws of value and exchange on this idea.* Among these are, as far as I know, not only Professor Carl Menger,[6] in Vienna, Professor F. von Wieser[7] in Prague and Professor N.-G. Pierson[8] in Amsterdam, followed or quoted by Mr von Böhm-Bawerk, but also Professors Alfred Marshall[9] and Henry Sidgwick[10] in Cambridge, Professor H. S. Foxwell in London, Mr F. Y. Edgeworth M.A.,[11] the Reverend P. H. Wicksteed, Professor J. d'Aulnis de Bourrouill[12] in Utrecht, Professor H.-B. Greven in Leyden, General Francis A. Walker, PhD, LL.D., President of the Massachusetts Institute of Technology,[13] Professor Charles Gide[14] in Montpellier, Professor Wilhelm Launhardt[15] in Hannover and Dr G.-B. Antonelli.[16] As Mr von Böhm-Bawerk says, these economists go on 'each in his own way'. Some of them, like my father and Mr Menger, use ordinary language. Mr von Böhm-Bawerk is among them. Others, like Gossen and Jevons, make use of mathematical language. I count myself among these, but God forbid that I should start a discussion on that subject! In my opinion, when it comes to studying essentially quantitative proportions like the ratios of **[68]** value, mathematical reasoning allows a much more exact analysis, more complete, clearer and quicker than ordinary reasoning, and has the superiority of the railway over the stagecoach when travelling. But I know that many people detest the idea of learning mathematics, as many people once did the idea of taking the train. Being convinced that the day will come when the old means of transport will completely give way to new ones, I cannot sufficiently

5 *De la nature de la richesse et de l'origine de la valeur*, Evreux [Ancelle fils], 1831.

6 *Grundsätze der Volkswirtschaftslehre*, Vienna [Wilhelm Braumüller], 1871–2.

7 *Ueber den Uhrsprung und die Hauptgesetze des wirtschaftlichen Werthes*, Vienna [Adolf Hölder], 1884.

8 *Leerboek der Staathuishoudkunde*, Eerste deel, Haarlem [De Erven F. Bohn], 1884. Grondbeginselen der staathuishoudkunde. Tweede druk [second edition], Haarlem [De Erven F. Bohn], 1886.

9 [*The*] *Economics of Industry*, London [Macmillan], 1881 [second edition].

10 [*The*] *Methods of Ethics*, London [Macmillan], 1874. [*The*] *Principles of Political Economy*, London [Macmillan], 1883.

11 *Mathematical Psychics: An Essay on the Application of Mathematics to the Moral Sciences*, London [Kegan Paul], 1881.

12 *Het Inkomen der Maatschappij: Eene Proeve van Theoretische Staathuishoudkunde*, Leiden [S. C. van Doesburg], 1874.

13 *Political Economy*, New York [Macmillan], 1883.

14 *Principes d'économie politique*, Paris [L. Larose et Forcel], 1884.

15 *Mathematische Begründung der Volkswirtschaftslehre*, Leipzig [W. Engelmann], 1885.

16 *Sulla teoria matematica della economia politica.* Capitolo primo: *Concetto di utilità*, Pisa [Tipografia del Folchetto], 1886.

express my gratitude to fellow economists and my colleagues who take it upon themselves to lead these persons to the new land that has to be explored and colonized in any vehicle at all. I am sure a day will come when the old modes of locomotion give way to the new ones. The most important thing is that a school in the field of our theory of value and exchange will be formed. Now it seems daily more obvious that such a school is emerging, and, indeed, '*we have here considerable evidence that the theory of subjective value is not simply a mental exercise, but the cornerstone of all economics*'. But, this being the case, is the present time not decisive? In social science in fact, just as in natural science, pure theory is the light of applied theory. When we really thoroughly understand the mechanism of free competition in exchange, production and capital formation, still so imperfectly grasped until now, we shall know exactly how far it is self-driving and self-regulating and under what circumstances its running needs to be aided and guided. Then we will be excused from taking part in the endless, tedious struggle of socialists who only know how to get the State to intervene in everything and the economists who only know of *laisser-faire* the individual in any matter, anywhere; and we will be able to side with those theories that, rationally and on principle, trace the line of demarcation between the rights and duties of the individual and the rights and duties of the State in all categories relating to production and distribution of social wealth. That is not all. With respect to social, as well as industrial, progress pure and applied theory is the light for practical application. When we have sketched the outline of normal organization of production and distribution of wealth, we shall clearly see how far present organization is satisfactory and where it is defective, demanding modification. Then, in the twentieth century, our children and grandchildren will be able to avoid **[69]** being shuttled between smug conservatism and muddled progressivism, as we were during the whole of the nineteenth century. One considers everything, from the monopolies in mining, railways and the issue of banknotes to taxation on consumption, wholly admirable; the other turns everything upside down haphazardly. Then they [the grandchildren] will be able to take measures, both bold and prudent, for reforming legal conditions of money, agriculture, industry, commerce, credit, speculation, companies, insurance, property and taxation, successively.

So the notion of *rareté* is the starting point for elaborating pure economics to use in applied economics, then setting out applied economics with a view to economic reform. I cannot affirm that this idea is also Mr von Böhm-Bawerk's or one of the other economists' working on the development of this notion, as he and I are. But I do declare that it is mine, quite contrary as it is to the total absence of philosophy of science and pure science that adorns itself nowadays with the title of 'experimental method', which is only stale and sterile empiricism, in my opinion. From 1870 to 1877 I did my utmost to deduce a general theory of the determination of prices under a regime of free competition from the theory of *rareté*. Since then I have attempted to derive successively from that theory of the determination of prices a rigorous demonstration of the law of the surplus value of rent in a progressive society, with a view to a new theory of property, as well as a rigorous demonstration of the proportionality of prices to the amount of money in circulation, with a view to a new theory of money. I am doubly interested in the question of money, because it is important and topical, and even more perhaps because it is one of the first and most decisive applications of my system of economics. This is what I think:

> When all is said and done, here is a point that appears at the top of the list of economic problems; our men of science and statesmen of the so-called experimental school palpably hesitate and erratically move around it. If we were lucky enough to solve it theoretically and practically through new principles, these principles would then be of use for solving **[70]** all other economic and social problems both theoretically and in practice.

The system of pure economics I was just speaking about was demonstrated in my *Eléments d'économie politique pure* (1874–7); the first edition of that work is nearly exhausted and the second edition has been delayed precisely because of revising my theory of money.[viii] It is also in my *Theory mathématique de la richesse sociale* (1883). I can only suggest my readers look in these works for the demonstration of theorems the *Theory of Money* is based on, and which I present here.

November 1886

[71] Introduction
Reply to some objections

My research has gradually led me to a total change of opinion about money and the issue of banknotes.

In Part III of my *Eléments d'économie politique pure* (1874), entitled 'Du numéraire et de la monnaie', I preached the gold monometallism doctrine.[ix] I had, moreover, professed that same doctrine as regards both metallic circulation and the doctrine of free issue in matters of fiduciary circulation, in various articles published before, particularly in an article on 'Les erreurs du système monétaire français' and another entitled 'Des billets de banque en Suisse'. But in the same Part III of the *Eléments* there is a thirtieth lesson entitled 'Problème de la valeur de la monnaie' in which, by means of the addition of two functions, or the superposition of two curves, I explained how the total value of a money commodity results simultaneously from its use as merchandise and money in a system with a single standard. This analysis was the first step along a new track.[x]

In 'Note sur le $15\frac{1}{2}$ légal', *Journal des économistes*, December 1876, I claimed that one can analogously explain how the constant ratio of value between two money commodities is established and within what limits it will remain in a system with a double joint standard. I gave that explanation in 'Théorie mathématique du bimétallisme', also in the **[72]** *Journal* [*des économistes*], dated May 1881. In an article entitled 'De la fixité de valeur de l'étalon monétaire', appearing in the same journal in October 1882, I demonstrated the steadiness of the value of the bimetallic standard in comparison with the two monometallic standards, showing how one could obtain an even greater stability by means of a system consisting of gold monometallism combined with silver token that one could put into, or withdrawn from, circulation according to the circumstances. Furthermore, this token, analogous to our present five-franc pieces, is quite distinct from divisional currency. These three papers form the memoir entitled 'Théorie mathématique du bimétallisme' that is contained in my *Théorie mathématique de la richesse sociale* (1883). In the period between writing and publishing the first and the second I had improved the memoir 'Théorie mathématique du billet de banque', read to the Société vaudoise des sciences naturelles in November 1879 and inserted it in the same volume as the previous three. I took a formal position against every issue of banknotes.

Still absorbed by these questions in 1884, I was struck more and more deeply by the fact that the system of *gold money with regulating silver token*, to which I was led by reason, was exactly the same as that to which facts had led us. I showed this in the article published under that title in the 1 December 1884 issue of the *Revue de droit international.* I asked that the present state of affairs should become the regular situation by basing the definition of the franc on gold and by raising the special silver token to regulating token.

It was only a question of fixing the price of the gold franc by this regulating silver token, but in what other commodities should this price be measured? I had not yet cleared up this point when, in 1885, while rereading Jevons's volume *Investigations in Currency and Finance*, I came to believe that **[73]** the curve of the average price in gold of the other commodities, the inverse of the average price of gold in the other commodities,[xi] in which Jevons wrongly sought to measure the variations in the value of gold, was precisely the curve that should not be made horizontal but undulating around the horizontal axis. I developed this thesis in the memoir entitled 'D'une méthode de régularization de la variation de la valeur de la monnaie' which I communicated to the Société vaudoise des sciences naturelles in May 1885. Finally, in the memoir entitled 'Contribution à l'étude des variations de prix depuis la suspension de la frappes des écus d'argent', communicated to the same society in June 1885, with the aid of my student Mr Alfred Simon, I tried to draw the curve of the average price of gold in twenty commodities, taken on the Bern market, and calculate the downward tendency of this curve during the period 1879–84 in relation to the period 1871–8.

These are the exact eight stages I went through successively, progressing from gold monometallism and free issue of banknotes to gold money with regulating silver token and the prohibition of all issues of banknotes, in which I now summarize the theory of money circulation. This system has been discussed abroad and been lucky enough not to remain unnoticed in France, thanks to Mr Adolphe Coste and Mr Emile Cheysson. Both have explained and contested it, the former in his work *Les Questions sociales contemporaines*,[xii] the latter in a report presented to the Société de statistique de Paris at its session on 16 December 1885. I wanted the public to be able to form its own judgement and so I gave a broad outline of my system. In the *Theory of Money* below, published in the *Revue scientifique*, on 10 and 17 April of this year, it was connected, as indeed it should be, with the theory of economics it stems from. Moreover, I shall take the opportunity to reply briefly to the objections raised against it, in particular Mr Cheysson's, a mathematician who has read me carefully and understood everything.[xiii] **[74]** In his discussion he touched on the essential points of the problem. I shall point out these objections one by one, the last one first.

> Finally – Mr Cheysson says – even when admitting all these insoluble complications solved, the constancy of the geometric average of prices will only be realized for the rational person buying all the commodities appearing in the calculations of that average precisely in the proportions in which they appear therein. But for all consumers of flesh and blood, with budgets that are not patterned according to a formula, the differences would appear as before, perhaps even magnified.[17,xiv]

This objection should be discussed first of all because it gives evidence of a general point of view of my eminent adversary that seems completely unsuitable for adoption here. Supposing I were an inspector responsible for writing out regulations for food in colleges, the army or prisons and that I prescribed a certain average weight of bread and meat per head daily. Mr Cheysson would obviously object that this would be suitable for the 'rational person', endowed with an average appetite, but that it would be somewhat too little or too much for 'all consumers of flesh and blood' in my institutions. I agree with this, but would it be better to leave my inmates to the discretion of governors or caterers who would let them more or less starve? I shall join to this objection of Mr Cheysson's a similar, but nevertheless slightly different, criticism levelled at me by a writer in the *Revue trimestrielle d'économie politique* in Berlin, who also did me the honour of carefully reading and enthusiastically attacking my system and who, on the subject of my latest memoirs, thought it necessary to point out that, depending on whether Mr A or Mr B were a member of the International

17 I borrowed this synopsis of Mr Cheysson's report from the January 1886 issue of the *Journal de la Société de statistique de Paris* containing the proceedings of the session of 16 December 1885 (pp. 1–5).

Statistical Commission **[75]** responsible for the evaluation of the average price differences of the commodities from one period to another, more or somewhat less regulating token would be added or withdrawn.[18] Quite likely! But if I had a temperature it is also probable that, depending on whether I sent for doctor A or doctor B, I should have to take more or less quinine sulphate. But is that a reason for not taking care of myself at all? The regularity of variation in the value of the money commodity can only be obtained approximately by averages. It is therefore from this point of view that the various procedures forming the method of regulating [the value of money] have to be examined. This is what I intend to do now, returning to the order adopted by Mr Cheysson.

> Nothing is more difficult than ascertaining exactly the price of any commodity at a certain moment. As an example one could mention how the price of bread in Paris varies between one district and another today. How would this be for a large country, and, *a fortiori*, for all countries constituting the Latin Union? Can we be sure beforehand that the variations are parallel? Is their average taken in the final result?[xv]

I am absolutely no statistician; but last year, when I wanted to have records of average prices during the period 1871–84, I found these all ready in the Bern Cantonal Bureau of Statistics. These prices related only to the market of Bern. Would it be very difficult to obtain the same prices from major Swiss markets: Zurich, Basle, Lausanne and Geneva, and thus derive average prices relating to the whole of Switzerland? I really do not think so; for, after writing and bringing my memoir up to date, I received from Paris a publication from the Ministry of Agriculture,[xvi] dated June 1885, containing tables of harvests in France in 1884 together with some statistical agricultural information among which there were: (pp. 74–7) a table (Table VIII) of the 'Average prices per prefecture of cereals, foodstuffs, fodder, **[76]** fuel, etc. in 1884' and (pp. 81–2) a table (Table IX) of 'Average yearly prices for all of France for the last twenty years [1865–84] for cereals, flour, bread, meat, fodder, etc.'. These tables relate to twenty commodities that are almost exactly the same as those I have used. If I had had them earlier, I should have preferred to use them because of their more general character.

> Which will be the commodities raised to the distinction of types and admitted, as such, to the multiple standard? The final variations and, in last instance, the actions of the regulator will depend on this choice. A conclusion fixed beforehand might very well be the result of a cunning choice.[xvii]

18 *Vierteljahrschrift für Volkswirtschaft*, [vol. LXXXVIII], 22nd year, no. IV, [1885], p. 258.

The commodities raised to the distinction of types will be those of which it is easiest to make the statistics and will probably be the most important ones. Care will be taken, for instance, to join a certain number of industrial products and agricultural ones. The choice of these commodities will be fixed at the time of calculation, so there will be no need to take precautions against a 'cunning choice' which would give a 'conclusion fixed beforehand'. What are these insinuations about the incapacity in all economic matters levelled at the State or its representatives and borrowed from the vulgar catalogue of orthodox school jokes? If the engineers of the Ponts et chaussées or the Mines[xviii] were charged with the computations under discussion, would they then tolerate being accused of being bribed by the holders of silver into injecting a considerable amount of regulating silver token into the circulation? Of course they would not. Why then afflict civil servants in general with an injustice that would not be tolerated if it were addressed to one of them in particular? Let us be reasonable. The day it is generally admitted that a professional sense of duty and honour no longer suffices to keep the people responsible for the promotion of State welfare above the temptation to renounce that welfare one **[77]** would have to give up trying to achieve any progress whatsoever. In establishing the average one cannot, as Mr Walras does, give the same weight to commodities of unequal consumption like bread and iron, or indigo and pens. Considerable complication to be overcome in practice![xix]

One could answer that the commodities forming the average are precisely those generally consumed, such as bread and iron, but not indigo and pens. After all, though, what great complication would there be in giving the selected commodities different weights to establish the average by classifying them in three or four categories, each corresponding to some coefficient of consumption?

> Here Mr Cheysson presents the Society with a diagram representing, according to *The Economist*, London, the variations in prices of twenty commodities in England from 1845 to 1884. It is a confusing tangle where it is quite difficult to pick out the 'economic tide' and where the averages have been distorted by sudden shocks caused by perturbing phenomena such as the War of Secession [US Civil War] for the 1866 price of cotton and speculation in 1873 for the price of coffee.[xx]

It is quite certain that the curves of variation in prices of a certain number of commodities, subjected to normal variations in utility and quantity, must form a confusing tangle. But in order to find out whether or not one may emphasize the phenomenon of the economic tide, one has to derive from these specific curves the general, or average, curve by taking precautions, if need be, with respect to the commodities affected by exceptional circumstances. This is what Mr Cheysson has not done, but Jevons did in two cases: in the memoir entitled 'A serious fall in the value of gold ascertained and its social effects set forth'

(1863)[xxi] for the period 1845–62, and again in another memoir entitled 'The variation of prices and the value of the currency since 1782' (1865)[xxii] for the period 1782–1862. In both cases, the phenomenon of the economic **[78]** tide is clearly apparent. I do not know of any French statistician who has made a study of this subject which may be opposed to Jevons's investigations, but on the contrary, I have very recently had the pleasure of noticing that the conclusions of the English economist are confirmed by French observations. According to Jevons, the undulations of the curve of the average price of commodities corresponding to the movements of the economic tide agree with those of the exchange rate at the Bank of England. Mr Jacques Siegfried presented, in *Le Temps* of 1 February last, a graph of the two curves of securities [commercial securities, treasury bills not included] and the amount of cash in the Banque de France [gold and silver], during the period 1847–85, according to which the economic tide distinguishes itself as clearly as possible, high tide and ebb appearing when the curve of the security is at its maximum and beginning to descend whereas the curve of the amount of cash is at its minimum and beginning to rise; low tide and flood appear when the curve of the securities is at its minimum and beginning to rise whereas the curve of the amount of cash is at its maximum and beginning to fall.[xxiii] Since the economic tide really does exist both in France and in England, how can one possibly doubt that it has an effect on prices?

> Another issue concerns monetary circulation, the second element necessary for the regulator's effectiveness. Supposing that one knows exactly the amount of money proper, how does one take account of the growing fiduciary circulation? Is it not generally known that in clearing houses money plays only a secondary role (in 1883, in New York, 192 million out of a total of 244 billion, less than 1 in 1,000)? The future seems to prepare the phenomenon of decaying precious metals on account of improvement in credit.[xxiv]

This is the last of the 'insoluble problems' brought against me by Mr Cheysson. But it so happens that it is solved in a very simple and ingenious way, however, in an article entitled 'La circulation monétaire en France d'après les recensements [censuses] of 1868, 1878 et 1885' which can be found immediately after **[79]** the minutes of the 16 December 1885 session in the January 1886 issue of the *Journal de la Société de statistique de Paris*, representing a communication read by Mr de Foville before that society on 21 October 1885.[xxv] Let the inventory of all kinds of money in all public stocks be determined at a certain time. The ratio of the total amount of the most recent issue of coins (of which a very small part has been melted down or exported) to the amount of coins in this issue present in that inventory furnishes the ratio of the total amount of coins circulating in the country to the amount of coins in the inventory. It is true that, to solve the problem of regulating the variation in the value of money completely, one would have to know both the amount of commodity metal and money metal; but knowing the latter amount provides no less than a minimum of regulating token to add or withdraw. The amount of compensations carried out in the clearing houses does not change this position in any way and is useless to solve the problem in hand. The amount Q of metallic money, the price p in some other commodity of this money, the desired cash balance H expressed in the latter commodity and the amount Qf of paper money are mutually related by the equation:

$$Q(1 + f)p = H$$

After a certain time this becomes:

$$Q'(1 + f')p' = H$$

Whatever the improvement of credit is in the future, it will always take place, and there will always be means of bringing back p' to p by a change of Q' into Q'', according to the formula:

$$Q'' = Q'\frac{p'}{p}$$

which supposes we know only p, p' et Q'.

> **[80]** After these statistical objections, Mr Cheysson, without even going deep into the matter, indicated the economic objections which contest Mr Walras's system even more strongly, viz. the dangers of State intervention, which, should mistakes occur, might unleash appalling disturbance in the business world, and that might upset equilibrium in public finance. The State would then be powerless in its efforts to resist these forces of widespread violence. Finally, the progressive decline of purchasing power is a sort of gradual liquidation of the State's and private persons' commitments, a goad for the idle proprietor, a slow extinction of debts, and, as Mr Léon Say said, takes the place of the agrarian laws or the cruelty of debts in ancient times.[xxvi]

The picture Mr Cheysson sketches of a wrongful application of my system and its disastrous consequences makes us tremble. Fortunately, we can easily be convinced that the picture is greatly exaggerated. State intervention would, 'should mistakes occur, unleash appalling disturbance, etc.'. The State is not encouraged to intervene unless the necessity appears absolutely obvious; and, if there is the slightest doubt, it will abstain, and the *status quo* will simply continue. The same thing will happen, after all possible steps have been taken to avoid it, in case of 'forces of widespread violence'. Should the State insist on intervening (without rhyme or reason), as I am quite willing to suppose for the moment, I beg my scholarly opponent to observe this: had he brought enough regulating silver token into circulation to raise the market price of silver to the legal level of $15\frac{1}{2}$, he would be back with bimetallism and should stop at that point; and if, on the other hand, he had withdrawn all regulating silver token from the circulation, he would end up with gold monometallism and could not go further. The *status quo*, bimetallism and gold monometallism are the three limits between which the State may shuttle in my system, either by remaining stupidly inert or by introducing or withdrawing regulating token in a disorganized way.

Let Mr Cheysson be reassured: my regulating token **[81]** is definitely not the dangerous instrument he thinks it is. What is more, this instrument is the only one allowing Mr Cheysson himself to realize his own monetary ideal. Both Mr Cheysson and Mr Léon Say consider 'the progressive decline of purchasing power' a fortunate and desirable occurrence because it constitutes 'a sort of liquidation of the State's and private persons' commitments' that 'replace the agrarian laws or the cruelty of debts in ancient times'. I personally do not share this viewpoint for the following reason. Small debtors are either consumers or those who borrowed short-term, and they would not find in a progressive decline of purchasing power the relief that they would have found otherwise from merely redeeming their debts at a certain time. The only debtors who would benefit from such a decline would be those who borrowed long-term, the big debtors, viz. the State and big industrial concerns. For a mining or railway company, for instance, the unquestionable result would be that the whole value and ownership of the concern would pass from the holders of bonds into the hands of the shareholders, that is to say, from small capitalists to big capitalists. Favouring the State, this scheme seems to be inspired by the worst form of communism; and as a benefit to certain private persons it constitutes a further advantage added to all those already at the disposal of high finance. This is my opinion, but I admit that I am making a mistake and that in reality the best monetary system is the one which will allow the State and the big enterprises to let their debtors whistle for their money. Which of the present systems will Mr Cheysson choose to reach this goal? It will not be the *status quo* in which one can observe not a decline of the money's purchasing power but an increase; nor gold monometallism, where this increase would be noticeably further emphasized. Would it be bimetallism? Bimetallism would in all probability bring about not a slow progressive decline but **[82]** an instant considerable drop in the purchasing power of money that would ruin small capitalists at a single stroke to the benefit of the State and the big capitalists. I can really imagine the system of gold money only with regulating silver token, from which I continue to request constancy in average prices. This could just as well give Mr Cheysson his regular upswing. Mr Cheysson is, as I am, a man of science who, having stated a principle logically, pursues its application, a professor who owes explanation only to students. I do not lose hope that one day he will say to them, as I did, '*Gentlemen, up till now I have taught a certain doctrine with respect to money. Because of recent extensive research, and for reasons I will have the honour of explaining to you, I shall teach another doctrine from now on*.' He will observe that this statement is very well received.

From the other opinions put forward at the Statistical Society I shall take up only two:

> Mr Clément Juglar . . . loves to demonstrate that all the more or less ingenious means proposed for increasing or decreasing monetary circulation according the population's needs are absolutely pointless. Nowadays big business uses all the instruments of credit, in which money, though still necessary as a guarantee of transactions, is only of minor importance.[xxvii]

There follow figures showing 'how currency played a minor role in the great financial operations of our day and especially for loans'. These figures, which seem to amaze Mr Juglar utterly, certainly justify the principal predicate that 'Many exchanges are settled nowadays by compensation.' But they do produce the lesser one, necessary as a second basis for the conclusion above, that 'The quantity of money in circulation is totally unimportant.' From here to where Mr Juglar has found the lost fragment of his syllogism again, I take the liberty of sticking to my theory of the determination of money prices of commodities, developed in paragraphs 9 and 10 of the present **[83]** *Theory of Money* and on which I base the following thesis. The *rareté* of money and, consequently, its value in proportion to commodities, increase with the utility and decrease with the quantity of this money. The utility of money depends, if you like, on the number of exchanges that are settled by compensation. There remains the quantity, and depending on whether this quantity is greater or lesser, prices will be higher or lower; hence the quantity of money is absolutely not unimportant. Of these two magnitudes upon which, among others, money prices of commodities depend, Mr Juglar thinks it is appropriate to neglect one. He behaves like the man who, when ordering a garment, says to his tailor, 'The retailer will send you a roll of the cloth I chose; because it is very wide, it seems to me that absolutely any length will be adequate.'

> In summarizing the discussion, Mr Léon Say observes that Mr Juglar has perfectly demonstrated that in times of a recession there will be a considerable fall in the amount of cash at the Bank . . .
>
> The result of this deduction is that procedures such as Mr Walras's, consisting of correcting the absence of currency by silver token, maintain the recession just as long by injecting non-exportable money into the amount of

> cash at the Bank. This procedure would result in nothing less than perturbing the position of public wealth and private resources considerably.[xxviii]

Mr Léon Say, who sacrifices creditors to debtors on principle and would like to see 'this *slow modification of the distribution of wealth*, equivalent to a sort of redeeming of debts and replacing the *agrarian laws and the cruelty of debts* of ancient times',[xxix] reproaches me for 'perturbing the position of public wealth and private resources considerably'; Mr Léon Say, who, in 1878 and 1879, by the suppression of the free coinage of silver, made silver écus into token without taking any precautions against the **[84]** invasion of this token into commercial circulation, reproaches me for 'injecting non-exportable money into the amount of cash at the Bank' – that beats everything! But let it be enough to observe that Mr Say judges and condemns me without reading my work. I want to keep the balance between the creditors and the debtors rigorously equal by letting money keep a roughly constant average value. But I do not pretend to avoid recessions by introducing écu token into the stocks of the Bank; for two reasons: (1) because I do not believe that écu token must serve commercial circulation and appear in the Bank's stocks; (2) because I do not at all aspire to suppressing recessions and preventing the decrease of the Bank's stock of cash in cases of recession, but I give all my attention especially to 'maintaining' these recessions and this decrease of cash. If recessions are a regular phenomenon, as would appear to result from Jevons's beautiful work, and, in some sense, normal it is essential to respect the rise and fall of prices that mark the course of the economic tide and one only has to ensure that, from one high tide to the other, the average of the prices does not rise or fall indefinitely. I pursue this result. In other words, if, as I said above, the curve of the average price of commodities is a curve with undulations, one should not make it horizontal, but make it undulate more or less along a horizontal axis. This is the wonderful practical problem of monetary economics which I have put and to which I persist in drawing the attention of economists and statisticians in all countries.

April 1886

Notes

i At the initiative of the Statistical Society, the 'Institut international de statistique' was founded in London, 24 June 1885. The first article of the statutes defines this institute as (*Bulletin de l'Institut international de statistique*, Rome, vol. 1, 1886, p. 17):

> An international association for the promotion of progress of administrative and scientific statistics by means of:
>
> 1 introducing as much uniformity as possible of methods, framework and diffusion of accounts of the bureaux of statistics in order to make the results obtained in various countries comparable;

2 drawing the attention of the governments to problems that may be solved by statistical observations and by asking for information about matters that have not yet been (sufficiently) dealt with by statistics;
3 creating international publications in order to establish permanent relations between the statisticians of all countries;
4 disseminating the notion of statistics through its publication and through public education where it exists and other means, and by interesting governments and public organizations in the exploration of social facts.

The composition of the first board was as follows: president, Rawson William Rawson (1812–99), president of the 'Statistical Society', London; vice-presidents, Émile Levasseur (1818–1911), professor of the Collège de France, Paris, and Franz Xavier Ritter von Neumann-Spallart (1837–88), professor of the university of Vienna; treasurer, John Bidulph Martin (1841–97), banker, London; general secretary, Luigi Bodio (1840–1920), general director of the Statistical Office of the kingdom of Italy. The institute is composed of 'honorary members', 'members' and 'associate members'. The first lists of these were set up on the occasion of the constituent assembly in London. Among the first twenty-three honorary members one finds the following names: Edward Atkinson, Gerolamo Boccardo, Ernst Engel, Francesco Ferrara, H. G. J. Goschen, Paul Leroy-Beaulieu, Angostino Magliani, Wilhelm Roscher and Léon Say. Among the first fifty-six members: Luigi Bodio, Émile Cheysson, Alfred de Foville, Robert Giffen, Georg-Friedrich Knapp, Émille Levasseur, Wilhelm Lexis, Luigi Luzzatti, Angelo Messdaglia, Franz Xavier Ritter von Neumann-Spallart, R. H. Inglis Palgrave, Rawson William Rawson and Francis Walker. Among the first twenty-six associate members: Richard T. Ely, Clément Juglar (who was promoted member in 1886), Étienne Laspeyres, James Laurence Laughlin, Gustave de Molinari, Gustave Schmoller and Adolf Wagner.

At its meeting in Cologne, May 1886, the board decided that the first session of the association would take place in Rome, September 1886. At the same time Léon Walras sent the first two parts of the *Théorie de la monnaie* (offprints from the *Revue scientifique*) to R. W. Rawson. The latter answered that Walras's name would be proposed for the revised list of associate members, on the occasion of the next session; see *Correspondence*, letter 714 (19 May 1886) and Walras's answer, letter 718 (23 May 1886). The latter, 'much honoured and very pleased' by this proposition, envisaged then to participate in the meeting in Rome and, possibly, to present a paper on questions 'related to the determination of a formula for the average price in money of social wealth, the construction of a curve of the variation in this price and how to make use of this curve'. These topics were to be inserted in the third part of the *Théorie de la monnaie* ('Desiderata statistiques'). He brought this possibility to the attention of the general secretary of the institute, Luigi Bodio, who, in first instance saw no objection and invited Walras to send 'twenty pages to print in the next issue of the *Bulletin* [*de l'Institut international de statistique*], scheduled to appear before the Rome conference'. Walras accepted the proposition and promised to send these pages 'within a month from now, or later' (Bodio to Walras, 19 June 1886, and answer by Walras, 22 June 1866, *Correspondence*, letter 726 and letter 728).

However, the president of the Institute, informed about this project, appears to have had reservations concerning Walras's text: he feared that the article and its presentation in public would remain at the level of mathematical economics and would not be based on real statistical data (Bodio to Walras, *Correspondence*, letter 729, 27 June 1886). Walras decided to withdraw his proposition to present a paper and to send the twenty pages. He remarked to his Italian friend that the president's position was obviously in contradistinction with the second point in the first article of the statutes, stipulating that the Institute draws 'the attention of the governments to questions that may be resolved by statistical observations and by asking for information about matters that have not yet been (sufficiently) dealt with by statistics'. He reminded him that his paper would deal with 'theoretical statistics', just as did Émile Cheysson's 'La statistique géométrique' (*Bulletin de l'Institute international de statistique*, vol. 1, 1886, pp. 244–51), published in the proceedings of the meetings on the occasion of the twenty-fifth anniversary of the Société de statistique de Paris (*Correspondence*, letter 730, 29 June 1886).

In a letter dated 2 July 1886 (*Correspondence*, letter 723). Bodio thanks Walras, for his openness and observes that he cannot come to Rome for the presentation of a paper because he is not yet elected an associate member. In the same letter, Bodio wrote: 'The only thing that remains therefore is the publication of your proposition in the *Bulletin*' in a form that is accessible to non-mathematicians and using 'official statistics of money, prices, production, etc.'. Walras considered any publication in the *Bulletin* useless. Nevertheless, he proposed to publish the third part of the *Théorie de la monnaie* in it (*Correspondence*, letter 735, to Bodio, 9 July 1886).

On this question he remained convinced that the French orthodox liberal school, 'more narrow-minded, more intolerant, more tyrannical than the Inquisition', had probably tried to damage him because of the spread of the two first parts of the *Théorie de la monnaie* (Walras to Bodio, 5 July 1886, *Correspondence*, letter 733).

Because of a cholera outbreak that menaced the Italian capital, the first meeting of the Institut international de statistique could not take place on the date convened and had to be postponed to 12–16 April 1887, in Rome. However, the board organized a postal vote in order to have the initial lists from London approved as well as the additional lists. The results were made known on 13 November 1886. Among the new associate members one finds the following names: Lujo Brentano, Arthur T. Hadley, Maffeo Pantaleone and Léon Walras. In between, Walras had sent the third part of the *Théorie de la monnaie* to the *Revue scientifique* (letters to C. Richet, 7 November 1886 and 1 January 1887), and received a negative answer from Richet (undated; *Correspondence*, letters 742, 760, 761). Informed of his election, Walras envisaged in the first instance to go to Rome to present the content of the third part before some colleagues. Later on, he envisaged presenting, in addition, a paper entitled 'Étude de deux courbes réelles de variation du prix moyen d'un certain nombre de marchandises', which deals with a curve proposed in a brochure by H. S. Foxwell (see below, note iv) and a curve in 'Graphische Darstellungen in Bezug auf die Silberfrage', added to the second edition of *Materialen zur Erläuterung und Beurtheilung der Wirtschaftlichen Edelmetallverhältnisse und der Wahrungsfrage. Auf Veranlassung des Vereins zur Wahrung der Wirtschaftlichen Interessen von Handel und Gewerbe*, Berlin: Puttkammer & Mühlbrecht, 1886; see below (notes to the third part, pp. 127ff.), see also the letter from Soetbeer to Léon Walras (26 January 1887) and the latter's answer (31 January 1887), *Correspondence*, letters 764 and 767. On 5 April 1887 Walras departs from Switzerland to Rome, but in Turin he decides to go back because of nervous breakdown.

The paper 'Étude de deux courbes réelles de variation du prix moyen d'un certain nombre de marchandises' remained unpublished during Walras's lifetime. It has been presented in Supplement II of the Potier edition of *EEPA*.

ii *Correspondence*, letter 727.

*iii See below, Part III of *Theory of Money*, §§37–9.

iv In the first version Walras inserted the following note, suppressed in *EPA*:

> While correcting the galley proofs of this preface, a brochure by Mr H. S. Foxwell arrived – *Irregularity of employment and fluctuations of prices* (Claims of Labour lectures, no. 6), Edinburgh, 1886 – where the idea of regulating the value of the monetary standard was plainly accepted and vividly supported.

The brochure was republished in John Burnett *et al.* (eds) *The Claims of Labour: a Course of Lectures*, Edinburgh: Edinburgh Co-operative Printing Co., 1886, pp. 186–275. See also *Correspondence*, letter 750, from H. S. Foxwell, 26 November 1886 and letter 752, to A. Williams, 2 December 1886 about the dispatch of this letter.

v Léon Walras had received an offprint of the first part of Eugen von Böhm-Bawerk's 'Grundzüge der Theorie des wirtschaftlichen Güterwerts', *Jahrbücher für Natianalökonomie und Statistik* (Jena), vol. XIII, 1886, pp. 1–82 (the second part appeared the same year, pp. 477–541). Both parts were reprinted: London School of Economics, 1932. In Walras's library, preserved by Professor P. Bridel in the Centre d'études interdisciplinaires Walras–Pareto of the University of Lausanne, one finds the two parts together forming one volume (bound by Walras himself in blue linen). Walras asked his colleague and friend Charles Secrétan to translate the German text for him. (*Correspondence*, letter 743 and letter 777, to Böhm-Bawerk, 18 November 1886 and 3 February 1887.)

*vi English version, *The Laws of Human Relations and the Rules of Human Action Derived Therefrom*, translated by Rudolph Blitz, with an introductory essay by Nicholas Georgescu-Roegen, Cambridge MA: MIT Press, 1983, pp. 14 and 53, respectively. The two passages to which Walras refers are (in Blitz's translation):

> In order to maximize his total pleasure, an individual free to choose between several pleasures but whose time is not sufficient to enjoy all to satiety must proceed as follows: However different the absolute magnitudes of the various pleasures might be, before enjoying the greatest to satiety he must satisfy first all pleasures in part in such a manner that the magnitude [intensity] of each single pleasure at the moment its enjoyment is broken off shall be the same for all pleasures.
>
> In order to maximize his life-pleasure, man must distribute his time and his energy among various pleasures in such a way that for every pleasure the intensity of pleasure of the last atom produced shall be equal to the magnitude [intensity] of the discomfort experienced by him at the very last moment of his expenditure of effort.

In a letter (*Correspondence*, letter 770) of 2 February 1887 Böhm-Bawerk wrote to Walras: 'Until now I have only known of Gossen's book from hearsay. I have not yet read this book which has become very rare.' Léon Walras sent his note on H. H. Gossen to Böhm-Bawerk (letter 777, 13 February 1887).

vii *EPE*, §75. Walras (1988), p. 109.

viii See on this subject *Correspondence*, letter 834, to Charles Gide, 27 June 1888.

ix Part III of the first edition of the *Éléments d'économie politique pure* consists of the following lessons: (29) Conditions for the *numéraire* and for money, (30) The problem of the value of money, (31) The qualities of the precious metals, (32) A rational system of the *numéraire* and of money, (33) Of fiduciary money, (34) Of change.

x *Eléments*, first edition, pp. 177–82, *ŒEC*, vol. VIII, pp. 438–80.

*xi We think that Walras confused the mean of the inverses with the inverse of the means.

xii *Les Questions sociales contemporaines. Comptes rendus du concours Péreire et études nouvelles sur le pauperisme, la prévoyance, l'impôt, le crédit, les monopoles, l'enseignement* (avec la collaboration d'Auguste Burdeau et Lucien Arréat), Paris: Félix Alcan-Guillaumin, 1861. Appendix VI, pp. 560–8, is entitled 'Note sur un projet de réforme monétaire de M. Léon Walras', consisting of three sections: (1) Le systéme, (2) Critique des formules, (3) Objection de principe. In a letter to the author, who had sent him the above mentioned work, Walras expressed his disagreement with respect to the exposition of his theses and the criticism (letter of 5 November 1885 to A. Coste, *Correspondence*, letter 683, and answer from the latter of 13 November 1885, ibid., letter 686).

xiii In a letter to Léon Walras (*Correspondence*, letter 639) he writes: 'I perused your work not only with the pen in my hand, but also with a pair of compasses and a ruler. I have drawn diagrams and curves to discuss and 'illustrate' your text and to clear up certain obscurities, which resulted here and there in excessive condensation.'

xiv 'Procès-verbal de la séance du 16 décembre 1885', *Journal de la Société statistique de Paris*, 27th year, no. 1, January 1886, p. 4.

xv 'Procès-verbal', p. 3.

xvi Walras obtained this publication through Daniel-Auguste Rosenstiehl.

xvii 'Procès-verbal', p. 3.

*xviii Two departments of the French government with famous schools educating engineers. These schools gave the title 'engineer' great prestige.

xix 'Procès-verbal', p. 3.

xx Ibid.

xxi 'A serious fall in the value of gold ascertained and its social effects set forth' (1863), chapter II of *Investigations in Currency and Finance*, London: Macmillan, 1884, pp. 34ff.

xxii William Stanley Jevons, 'The variation of prices and the value of the currency since 1782' (1865) in ibid., pp. 119–50.

xxiii In the newspaper *Le Temps* (Paris), 26th year, no. 9041, 1 February 1886, last page, under the heading 'Financial week', the following text and diagram [Figure 3.1] appear:

> We ask the attention of our readers to the diagram that we published today. In an attractive way, the author, Mr Jacques Siegfried, summarizes through this diagram all that meticulous observation, considerable experience with respect to the matter and a rare gift for generalizing may suggest to a mind that is at the same time reflective and practical.
>
> For a number of years, the Bourse was nearly dead; speculation, stricken by the crash, had almost disappeared; new issues, so frequent formerly, abandoned our place to seek support abroad. For some weeks an improvement has seemed to loom; the number of transactions is augmenting; the Bourse looks as it has not done for a long time. Would this at last be the revival?

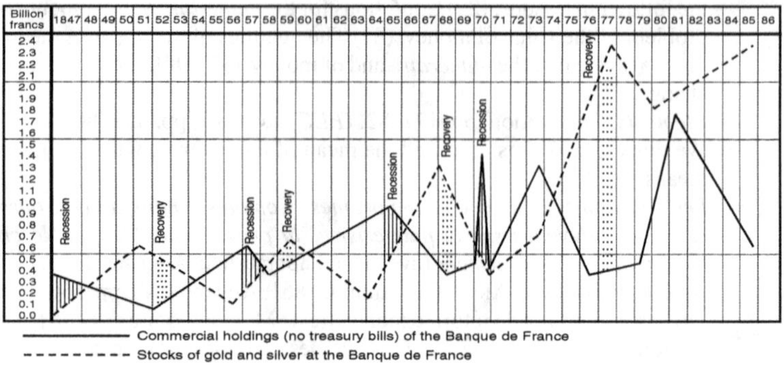

Figure 3.1 Recessions and recoveries in business.

Mr Jacques Siegfried was of the opinion that there should be means of investigation to recognize the real symptoms of an approaching improvement or a probable recession. What does one notice during a normal period? Production is steady, consumption absorbs production without problems, no price perturbations; it is the period of equilibrium.

Inevitably, it is wholly transitory. Producers must benefit from the situation, favourable as it is for selling their commodities quickly – and we use the latter word in its broadest sense. They increase production, aim at new segments of consumers and ask for credit. The portfolios of the banks increase; the monetary and the fiduciary circulation accelerate; a fever seizes the whole country. Shares, in particular those that are most vulnerable to speculation rise to fantastic quotations. It seems that one is then in a situation of exceptional prosperity.

In reality, a recession is approaching. Because of the overexcitement of the producers, obstruction of markets must take place. The excessive call on capital and credit inevitably causes expensive discount rates and carry-overs that cannot be compensated by any rise in the market. At the slightest incident, the overheated machine will explode. We know what will happen then. The example is in everyone's memory. All values fall suddenly. Liquidations increase. Credit will be restricted. Business becomes infrequent. Because of these changes, the banks' portfolios will be increasingly reduced. Capital necessary for transactions becomes superabundant together with a decrease in the latter: that is why the circulation of notes and coins becomes narrower. Simultaneously, while the inclination to overspend has dropped, savings tend, on the contrary, to reconstitute their stocks; the rate of interest diminishes; the carry-overs fall back to nil and even transform into their opposite. We have just had this well known phenomenon under our noses.

What are the characteristics of these alternating movements of rise and fall? This is what Mr Jacques Siegfried perfectly observed and, moreover, made strikingly apparent to everybody.

Let us look at the diagram he drew. Two main lines cross each other, driven by opposite movements. The one line represents the amount of cash in the Banque de France; the other, that institution's credit portfolio. What do these lines say so clearly by their peculiar variations?

This: when a recession approaches, the amount of cash is reduced while the portfolio increases considerably. Look at the year 1856, for instance, when the two lines diverge substantially: there is a maximum of bills of exchange and a minimum of cash. One may safely state that danger threatens business.

And indeed 1857 is a year of mourning. The only thing is that the liquidation soon starts: it is the reparation work that has to take place. Credit, abused thus far, is restricted; the portfolio decreases, while, inversely, cash increases, heralding a resumption of business.

The whole question, from the point of the Bourse, is to know if the line that represents the portfolio has ceased to drop and if that of the amount of cash has ceased to go up. Our diagram evidently cannot pretend to indicate this. It records the facts and displays regularity; asking more of it would certainly be unreasonable. Judging it by the amplitude of the foregoing oscillations, which did not fail to augment, contrary to that of the pendulum, resumption of business was not yet announced: but what one may affirm on the grounds of the indications of the diagram, is that the recession is nearing its end.

Anyway, those who have lost hope in the future of our market are wrong. The ordeals inflicted upon it are essentially temporary. Mr Jacques Siegfried's highly interesting work makes an excellent impression that may be translated into one word: confidence!

Léon Walras showed this diagram 'that would confirm wholly the phenomenon of the economic tide', to his friend Daniel-Auguste Rosenstiehl on 28 February 1886 (*Correspondence*, letter 669). According to Clément Juglar, Jacques Siegfried would have been inspired by his [Juglar's] 'Table of the annual variations (maxima and minima) of the main articles of the schedules of the Banque de France (1851–1885)' published in the study 'Periodical returns of commercial recessions', communicated 18 June 1885 at the ceremony of the twenty-fifth anniversary of the foundation of the Statistical Society of Paris, in 'Vingt-cinquième anniversaire de la Société de statistique de Paris : compte rendu sommaire des réunions', *Bulletin de l'Institut international de statistique* (Rome), vol. 1, no. 2, 1886, p. 255.

xxiv 'Procès-verbal', p. 4.

xxv Alfred de Foville, 'La circulation monétaire en France d'après les recensements [censuses] of 1868, 1878 et 1885', *Journal de la Société de la statistique de Paris*, 27th year, no. 1, January 1886, pp. 6–15. Léon Walras refers in the same wording to this study in his letters to E. Cheysson, 20 January 1886 (*Correspondence*, letter 694), and to D. A. Rosenstiehl, 22 January 1886 (*Correspondence*, letter 695).

xxvi 'Procès-verbal'. In these years Mr Say was Minister of Finance of France.

xxvii Ibid., pp. 4–5.

xxviii Ibid.

xxix The meeting of 7 September 1885 of the Société d'économie politique de Paris discussed the following question: 'Is price increase proof of public prosperity?' At the end of the discussion Léon Say declared:

It is an unquestionable fact that for some years the French *numéraire* has not increased one kilogram. If such a situation continued for a century, it would be a great misfortune. Business could take place, go on and liquidate all the same, but, to the benefit of the poorest classes, there would not be that slow modification of the distribution of wealth equivalent to a sort of liquidation of debts, which replaces the agrarian laws and the cruelty of debts of ancient times.

(*Journal des économistes*,
[44th year, 4th series, 8th year, vol. 31]
September 1885, pp. 440–1)

[85]

4 *Theory of Money*

Part I Exposition of the principles

I Exchange and production

Mechanism

1. The elements of our astronomic system are the planets. Under the influence of universal gravitation, they draw *elliptical orbits* round the sun according to three laws, known in science as *Kepler's laws*.[i] The elements of the economic system are the *services* that, under the regime of free competition, tend to combine themselves naturally into *products* of a nature and in quantities appropriate *to giving the greatest possible satisfaction of the needs* within the limits of the double condition *that each service as well as each product has only one price in the market and that the selling price of each product be equal to its cost price in services.*

These services are of three kinds: services of the *land*, called *land services*,[ii] services of personal faculties, called *labour*, and services of capital, called *profit*.[iii] The holders of these services, with all reservations concerning legality or illegality of the conditions of appropriation, are *landowners*, *workers* and *capitalists*. In addition to these characters, there exists a fourth type, *entrepreneurs* in agriculture, industry or commerce, whose typical function is to transform services into products. Executed under the regime of free competition in exchange and production, this transformation occurs as follows. In a first market, we shall call the *services market*, the landowners, workers and capitalists on one hand meet the entrepreneurs on the other; the former as suppliers and the latter as demanders of services. **[86]** A price in the *numéraire* is announced for each type of land service, labour or profit. If the quantity effectively demanded at this price is higher than the quantity effectively offered, entrepreneurs raise their bid. If the quantity effectively offered is higher than the quantity effectively demanded the landowners, workers underbid each other and lower prices will result. The current price of land services is called *rent*; the current price of labour, *wages*; the current price of capital services, *interest.*

While selling land services and selling labour take place in the form of renting land or hiring workers as such, selling profit takes place by hiring capital in the form of money. Consequently, there is a certain current price for renting money capital, the *rate of interest.* In a second market, which we call the *products market,* the entrepreneurs on one hand meet the landowners, workers and capitalists on the other; the former as suppliers and the latter as demanders of products. A price in the *numéraire* is called for every kind of product. If the quantity effectively demanded at this price is higher than the quantity effectively offered, landowners, workers and capitalists raise their bids. If the quantity effectively offered is higher than the quantity effectively demanded the entrepreneurs underbid. The current price is always where effective supply and effective demand are equal.

Equilibrium

2. Equality of effective demand and supply for each product or service, which provides the current price, gives rise to equilibrium in exchange. This equilibrium may set itself off, under the regime of free competition, because of the price rise that starts when demand exceeds supply and the decline that starts when supply exceeds demand. As far as equilibrium of production is concerned, this is the result **[87]** of equality of the products' *selling price* with their *cost price* in services. This, too, tends to set itself going under the regime of free competition. Indeed, if in certain enterprises the products' selling price is higher than their cost price in services there will be a *profit* for the entrepreneurs; the latter therefore increase their production and so cause a rise in the price of services and a decline in the price of products; if in certain enterprises the products' cost price in services is higher than their selling price the entrepreneurs will make a *loss*; so they then decrease their production, thus causing a decline in price of the services and a rise in price of products. Such is the equilibrium of exchange and production around which economic life invariably oscillates without ever reaching it, as a lake swings back and forth from its horizontal level. Studying the conditions of this equilibrium is the object of pure economics, which will be one of the most beautiful physico-mathematical sciences if it is finished, when I may say so. One of the most remarkable of these conditions follows.

II Proportionality of values to *raretés*

Utility curves or want curves

3. Entrepreneurs try to buy services and sell their products so that they will make a profit and not a loss. Landowners, workers and capitalists try to sell their services and buy products so that they satisfy their needs as far as possible, which means that when there is equilibrium of exchange and production the price of

services is determined by the price of the products (and not the price of products by the price of the services), and that the price of the products is determined by the condition of maximum satisfaction of the needs, which is therefore the basic condition of economic equilibrium. The scientific beauty of this condition of maximum effective utility **[88]** is characterized at one and the same time by enormous range and utter simplicity. To explain it I shall trace the utility, or want curve. This is the mathematical expression of the wants of a person (1) exchanging a commodity (A), or, in other words, the utility of this commodity to this person. To show this let us take (Figure 4.1) two perpendicular axes crossing at zero point O: a vertical axis Oq and a horizontal axis Or. On the first axis we measure out, from the zero point, various lengths representing the various *quantities* of (A) that person (1) could possess *to consume* effectively during a certain period, the interval between two markets, for example. Let O$q_{a,1}$ be one of these lengths. Then, through the ends of the above mentioned lengths, draw parallels to the horizontal axis, measuring from the vertical axis onwards lengths that represent the *intensities of the last wants satisfied*, or the *raretés* corresponding to the various quantities of the commodity consumed. Let $q_{a,1}r_{a,1}$ be one of these lengths, corresponding to the quantity O$q_{a,1}$. This intensity of the last want satisfied by an amount of the commodity consumed, or this *rareté*, is not directly measurable; but that does not matter for the theory, which needs only to conceptualize and not to measure it. Its extent diminishes as the amount consumed grows, moreover. If person (1) were to consume an infinitesimally small quantity of (A), the intensity of his first and last want, or

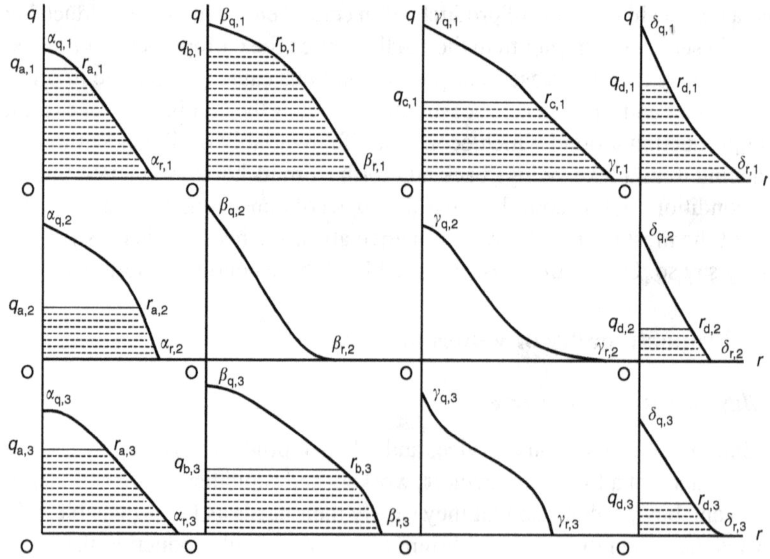

Figure 4.1 Intensities of (last) wants.

rareté, would be $O\alpha_{r,1}$; if he were to consume $O\alpha_{q,1}$ of it the intensity of his last want, or *rareté*, would be zero: he would have consumed as much as he wanted and reached satiation. The ends of the horizontal lengths of *rareté* yield a curve $\alpha_{r,1}\alpha_{q,1}$. This is the want curve or utility curve of the commodity (A) for person (1). If the commodity were consumed by units, as is the case with clothes or furniture, the utility or want curve would be discontinuous. **[89]** For convenience's sake I shall take it here that all commodities may be consumed in infinitely small quantities, as in the case of food, for instance; from this it follows that all utility or want curves are continuous. The utility curve that represents by its abscissae the *rareté* as a function of the quantity consumed, provides the sum of the wants satisfied or the *effective utility*, too, as function of the same quantities, by its areas. For a quantity $Oq_{a,1}$ consumed, the sum of the wants satisfied, or the effective utility, will be represented by the shaded area $Oq_{a,1}r_{a,1}\alpha_{a,1}$. I belong to the group who admit that these utility or want curves depend partly on man's free will; but it should also be granted me that this does not at all prevent them from belonging to the province of mathematics, once they are established.[1]

Equality of [ratios of] prices to ratios of values

4. Having stated this, let (A), (B), (C), (D) ... be *m* commodities, either products or services, that may be consumed directly as products and consequently having their own utility or want curves. Let $p_b, p_c, p_d \ldots$ be the prices of (B), (C), (D) ... in (A), that is to say, the respective quantities of (A) needed for obtaining 1 of (B), 1 of (C), 1 of (D) ... The fact that p_b of (A), for example, can be readily exchanged for 1 of (B), or that p_b times the value in exchange of (A) equals once the value in exchange of one unit of (B) may be expressed by:

$$p_b v_a = 1\, v_b$$

designating by v_a and v_b the value in exchange of one unit of (A) and the value in exchange of one unit of (B). From this we may conclude:

[90] $$p_b = \frac{v_b}{v_a}$$

and similarly:

$$p_c = \frac{v_c}{v_a} \quad p_d = \frac{v_d}{v_a} \ldots$$

1 This mathematical expression was 'invented' successively by Gossen, Jevons and myself, without any knowledge of work preceding ours.

designating by v_c and v_d the value in exchange of one unit of (C) and the value in exchange of one of (D). The prices are equal to the ratios of the values in exchange.

Condition for the maximum satisfaction of wants: equality of [ratios of] prices to ratios of individual raretés

5. Let (Figure 4.1) $\alpha_{r,1}\alpha_{q,1}$, $\beta_{r,1}\beta_{q,1}$, $\gamma_{r,1}\gamma_{q,1}$, $\delta_{r,1}\delta_{q,1}$ ... be utility or want curves of the commodities (A), (B), (C), (D)... for person (1), $\alpha_{r,2}\alpha_{q,2}$, $\beta_{r,2}\beta_{q,2}$, $\gamma_{r,2}\gamma_{q,2}$, $\delta_{r,2}\delta_{q,2}$ ..., $\alpha_{r,3}\alpha_{q,3}$, $\beta_{r,3}\beta_{q,3}$, $\gamma_{r,3}\gamma_{q,3}$, $\delta_{r,3}\delta_{q,3}$ ... utility or want curves of the same commodities for persons (2), (3)... One can prove that when person (1) has distributed his wealth over his wants in a way that procures the greatest possible amount of effective utility, that is to say, when he has kept or acquired (A), (B), (C), (D)... in quantities $q_{a,1}, q_{b,1}, q_{c,1}, q_{d,1}$ ... and achieved *raretés* $r_{a,1}, r_{b,1}, r_{c,1}, r_{d,1}$ ... so that the sum of the shaded surfaces $Oq_{a,1}r_{a,1}\alpha_{a,1}, Oq_{b,1}r_{b,1}\beta_{b,1}, Oq_{c,1}r_{c,1}\gamma_{c,1}, Oq_{d,1}r_{d,1}\delta_{d,1}$ ... be maximum, the *raretés* $r_{a,1}, r_{b,1}, r_{c,1}, r_{d,1}$ ... and the prices obey these equations:

$$\frac{r_{b,1}}{r_{a,1}} = p_b \quad \frac{r_{c,1}}{r_{a,1}} = p_c, \quad \frac{r_{d,1}}{r_{a,1}} = p_d \cdots$$

Similarly, between the *raretés* $r_{a,2}, r_{b,2}, r_{c,2}, r_{d,2} \ldots r_{a,3}, r_{b,3}, r_{c,3}, r_{d,3} \ldots$ and the prices we should then have the equations:

$$\frac{r_{b,2}}{r_{a,2}} = p_b \quad \frac{r_{c,2}}{r_{a,2}} = p_c \quad \frac{r_{d,2}}{r_{a,2}} = p_d \cdots$$

$$\frac{r_{b,3}}{r_{a,3}} = p_b \quad \frac{r_{c,3}}{r_{a,3}} = p_c \quad \frac{r_{d,3}}{r_{a,3}} = p_d \cdots$$

$$\cdots$$

which may also be expressed as follows:

$$[91] \quad \begin{array}{llllllllll} & 1 & : & p_b & : & p_c & : & p_d & : & \cdots \\ :: & r_{a,1} & : & r_{b,1} & : & r_{c,1} & : & r_{d,1} & : & \cdots \\ :: & r_{a,2} & : & r_{b,2} & : & r_{c,2} & : & r_{d,2} & : & \cdots \\ :: & r_{a,3} & : & r_{b,3} & : & r_{c,3} & : & r_{d,3} & : & \cdots \\ . & . & . & . & . & . & . & . & . & \cdots \end{array}$$

Therefore: *in equilibrium of exchange and production the [ratios of the] prices are equal to the ratios of the* raretés; that is to say that in economic reality the commodities have values in direct proportion (or are exchanged against each other in inverse proportion) to the intensities of the last wants satisfied, or the *raretés*; exactly as in the astronomic world, if we make abstraction of the distances, the celestial bodies attract each other in direct proportion to the quantities of substance or the masses.[2]

Reservation about the case of non-consumption

6. An important reservation has to be made regarding the case where an individual does not consume a certain commodity at all. In that case the number that should be written with respect to this commodity in the series of *raretés* exceeds the intensity of the first want to be satisfied. For instance, in the example of our figure person (1) is a rich man who consumes quantities 7, 8, 7 and 6 of commodities (A), (B), (C) and (D) and has little *raretés*, 2, 4, 5 and 1, procuring for himself a very considerable total effective utility represented by the sum of shaded surfaces $Oq_{a,1}r_{a,1}\alpha_{a,1}$, $Oq_{b,1}r_{b,1}\beta_{b,1}$, $Oq_{c,1}r_{c,1}\gamma_{c,1}$, $Oq_{d,1}r_{d,1}\delta_{d,1}$. Person 2 is a poor man who consumes quantities 3 and 2 of (A) and (D) and attains strong *raretés* 6 and 3, procuring for himself a very restricted total of effective utility represented by the sum of shaded surfaces $Oq_{a,2}r_{a,2}\alpha_{a,2}$ and **[92]** $Oq_{d,2}r_{d,2}\delta_{d,2}$. He denies himself, however, commodities (B) and (C) because the numbers 12 and 15, which had to be written in the series of his *raretés*, exceed the intensities 8 and 11 of the first want of these commodities to be satisfied. Person (3) is simply well enough off to consume (A), (B) and (D) in quantities 5, 4 and 3 and obtains satisfactory *raretés* 4, 8 and 2, procuring a total of effective utility of a normal importance represented by the sum of shaded surfaces $Oq_{a,3}r_{a,3}\alpha_{a,3}$, $Oq_{b,3}r_{b,3}\beta_{b,3}$ and $Oq_{d,3}r_{d,3}\delta_{d,3}$, but he denies himself the consumption of (C) because the number 10 that has to be written in the series of his *raretés* exceeds the intensity 8 of the first want of this commodity to be satisfied. Bracketing these proportional numbers corresponding to the virtual and non-effective *raretés*, one gets the following table of equilibrium [the first row indicates the prices]:

	1	:	2	:	2.5	:	0.5	...
::	2	:	4	:	5	:	1	...
::	6	:	(12)	:	(15)	:	3	...
::	4	:	8	:	(10)	:	2	...
...								

2 For the demonstration of the principle of the proportionality of the values to the *raretés* see *Eléments d'économie politique pure*, lessons 8, 9, 10, 22. [*ŒEC*, from the second edition onwards, vol. VIII, pp. 103–51 and 333–42.]

Equality of [ratios of] prices to ratios of average **raretés**

7. We know that the ratios of the average *raretés* will be the same as those of individual *raretés*. In establishing these averages, we should take into account only the numbers corresponding to virtual and non-effective *raretés*, which means that we may define *rareté* as the intensity of the last want that is or *should be* satisfied. Under this condition and designating by R_a, R_b, R_c, R_d... the average *raretés* of (A), (B), (C), (D)... we could substitute for the equations:

$$p_b = \frac{R_b}{R_a} \quad p_c = \frac{R_c}{R_a} \quad p_d = \frac{R_d}{R_a} \cdots$$

the following:

$$p_b = \frac{v_b}{v_a} \quad p_c = \frac{v_c}{v_a} \quad p_d = \frac{v_d}{v_a} \cdots$$

[93] This substitution of the *raretés*, whether individual or average, for values is of capital importance: it is the key to all problems of economics. To begin with, value in exchange is a relative phenomenon, whereas *rareté*, whether individual or average, is an absolute one. When the price of one commodity in some other has varied it cannot be said that it was the value of one or other of the commodities that varied, for the value of a thing does not exist otherwise than in proportion to the value of another thing. *Rareté*, on the contrary, exists by itself; and when a price has varied it makes perfect sense to investigate which of the *raretés* of which the price is the ratio has increased or decreased. There is more to come, however. In our figure we can immediately see that the *rareté* increases, or decreases, depending on whether the utility or want curve moves away from, or closer to, the origin, that is to say, depending on whether the utility increases or decreases, or [alternatively] depending on whether the parallel to the horizontal axis moves closer to or away from that axis, that is to say, depending on whether the quantity consumed decreases or increases. Hence the causes of variations in prices from variations in *utility* and *quantity* may be understood: these prices will increase when the utility increases or the quantity decreases and they will decrease when the utility decreases or the quantity increases. It is this possibility of leaving the variations of the prices and going back to their primary causes which allows us to solve the main problems of economics, and in particular those of money.

III Establishing the value of the money commodity

The role of the numéraire*; the role of money*

8. The free competition mechanism working in exchange and production supposes the operation:

1 Of a *numéraire*, that is to say, a commodity in which the prices of the other commodities are called, or to the value of which the values of the other commodities are converted, **[94]** either in the services market, or in the products market, in order to achieve general equilibrium, then to raise or lower these prices according to whether there is excess demand or excess supply.
2 Of *money in circulation*, that is to say, a commodity against which landowners, workers and capitalists sell services of land, persons and capital to entrepreneurs in the services market, and with which they buy the products of these same entrepreneurs in the products market.
3 Of *money for saving*, that is to say, a commodity to which capitalists convert their excess of revenue over consumption and which they lend as fixed or circulating capital to entrepreneurs.

The role of the *numéraire* and that of money are different. We may suppose that one commodity is chosen as *numéraire* and another as money, or even that money is not merchandise. For the time being, and in order to study the effect of choosing a commodity as money on its value, we shall suppose this commodity both *numéraire* and money at the same time.

Monetary stocks; proportionality of prices to the quantity of the money commodity

9. As soon as a commodity – gold, silver, wine or tobacco – has been designated to serve as money its quantity has to be split in two: the merchandise part, which is just for consumption, and a money part that plays the role of a means of exchange or an instrument of savings and credit. When the merchandise part decreases, its *rareté* increases accordingly and its value with respect to other commodities increases proportionally, which means that the values of the other commodities decrease in proportion. This phenomenon should be examined.

When a landowner, worker, capitalist or entrepreneur wants to have in his possession **[95]** a certain provision of gold, silver, wine or tobacco as money at a certain time, it is obvious that he is not in the least interested in the quantity of that money but only in the quantity of commodities, products or services that he can buy with it. In other terms, the want for money is nothing more than the want for the commodities that one may buy with this money. This want is a want for stocks; its satisfaction is paid at the price of an interest, and that is why the effective demand for money is a decreasing function of the rate of interest.

Let the general equilibrium be established therefore on the basis of the prices $1, p_b, p_c, p_d \ldots$ of (A), (B), (C), (D)... in (A) that is already a *numéraire* and is to become money. Let at a certain time i be the rate of interest, and let $\alpha, \beta, \gamma, \delta \ldots$ be the respective quantities of (A), (B), (C), (D)... that the consumers and the producers wish to buy at that rate to conserve their fixed and circulating capital. The quantity of money:

$$H_a = \alpha + \beta p_b + \gamma p_c + \delta p_d + \cdots$$

will be the *desired cash balance*, and if this quantity H_a of (A) as money could fall from the blue at this moment and be added to the quantity Q_a of (A) as merchandise, in order to form a total quantity of (A), merchandise and money:

$$Q_a + H_a = Q_a + \alpha + \beta p_b + \gamma p_c + \delta p_d + \cdots$$

the equilibrium of circulation would exist together with that of exchange and production without any change in prices. But it cannot happen like this; the necessary amount of money has to be taken from the existing quantity of commodity (A). Let us therefore suppose, taking n, by hypothesis, as the ratio of $Q_a + H_a$ and Q_a, according to the equation:

$$Q_a + H_a = n Q_a$$

that, in order to constitute the monetary cash balance, we proceed by decreasing the quantity of (A) as merchandise for each consumer by making the *rareté* n times larger. **[96]** Suppose then that at the same time the prices $p_b, p_c, p_d \ldots$ drop to n times less. To these two hypotheses, add another two that are more gratuitous, but which do not breach the limits of quite a narrow approximation of reality, however: first, for making the consumers' *rareté* of (A) n times higher the quantity has to be made n times smaller; second, under these new conditions the consumers of (A) do not want to have in their cash balance the equivalent in money of more than the nth part of this commodity. Now, the existing quantity Q_a of (A) splits into a quantity Q'_a of (A) as merchandise equal to Q_a/n and a quantity Q''_a of (A) as money equal to H_a/n, or:

$$\frac{\alpha}{n} + \beta\frac{p_b}{n} + \gamma\frac{p_c}{n} + \delta\frac{p_d}{n} + \cdots$$

such that for the total quantity of the money commodity one has:

$$Q_{\mathrm{a}} = Q'_{\mathrm{a}} + Q''_{\mathrm{a}} = \frac{Q_{\mathrm{a}}}{n} + \frac{H_{\mathrm{a}}}{n}$$
$$= \frac{Q_{\mathrm{a}}}{n} + \frac{\alpha}{n} + \beta\frac{p_{\mathrm{b}}}{n} + \gamma\frac{p_{\mathrm{c}}}{n} + \delta\frac{p_{\mathrm{d}}}{n} + \cdots$$

We must now first make sure that the same equilibrium will exist under those conditions as in the preceding ones, and then that this equilibrium will be realized automatically under the system of free competition.

Now, the equilibrium of exchange will then continue to exist, since, [the ratios of] the prices still being equal to the ratios of the *raretés* in conformity with the equations:

$$\frac{p_{\mathrm{b}}}{n} = \frac{R_{\mathrm{b}}}{nR_{\mathrm{a}}} \quad \frac{p_{\mathrm{c}}}{n} = \frac{R_{\mathrm{c}}}{nR_{\mathrm{a}}} \quad \frac{p_{\mathrm{d}}}{n} = \frac{R_{\mathrm{d}}}{nR_{\mathrm{a}}} \cdots$$

the consumers will still attain maximum satisfaction of their wants. The equilibrium of production will continue to exist, since, the prices of the services and of the products all being increased in proportion, the selling prices of the products will still be **[97]** equal to their cost prices in services, with the result that the entrepreneur will still make neither benefit nor loss; and, finally, the equilibrium of circulation will exist, since the value of (A) as merchandise and that of (A) as money will be equal at the time the exchangers have their desired cash balance at the interest rate i.

Moreover, the supposed operation will take place automatically, under the system of free competition. Let a certain, randomly determined quantity $q > (<) Q''_{\mathrm{a}}$ of (A) be put in the form of money and lent to the exchangers as circulating capital, at a certain rate of interest i', to represent a desired cash balance $H_{\mathrm{a}}/\nu > (<) H_{\mathrm{a}}/n$, according to the equation:

$$\alpha' + \beta' p_{\mathrm{b}} + \gamma' p_{\mathrm{c}} + \delta' p_{\mathrm{d}} + \cdots = \frac{H_{\mathrm{a}}}{\nu} = q$$

Then, on one hand, a certain value of (A) as money would establish itself in the market by virtue of the equivalence of the quantity of money that would buy the commodities and the quantity of the commodities that could be bought with the money according to the equation:

$$q = \frac{H_{\mathrm{a}}}{\nu} = \frac{\alpha}{\nu} + \beta\frac{p_{\mathrm{b}}}{\nu} + \gamma\frac{p_{\mathrm{c}}}{\nu} + \delta\frac{p_{\mathrm{d}}}{\nu} + \cdots$$

On the other, a certain value of (A) as money being thus established, (A) money could be transformed into (A) merchandise, in so far as the amount of money was superior to the desired cash balance, if (A) had a greater value as merchandise than as money, or (A) merchandise could be transformed into (A) money, as far as the quantity of money being inferior to the desired cash balance, if (A) had a greater value as money than as merchandise. We should then end up with the equation:

$$Q''_{\mathrm{a}} = \frac{H_{\mathrm{a}}}{n} = \frac{\alpha}{n} + \beta\frac{p_{\mathrm{b}}}{n} + \gamma\frac{p_{\mathrm{c}}}{n} + \delta\frac{p_{\mathrm{d}}}{n} + \cdots$$

[98] We had only to make all prices n times lower to restore equilibrium with an amount of commodity-money n times smaller. It would even have been sufficient to make all prices n times larger with an n times larger quantity of money commodity. Hence it is unquestionable that: *each increase or decrease in the quantity of the money commodity has as a consequence a proportional increase or decrease in prices.*

Paper money and compensations

10. The following two complications should be taken into account:

1. The idea arose of representing a part of the entrepreneurs's capital by deeds of property, bills of exchange or banknotes, namely that part which consists of raw materials and products in stock, and to use these titles instead and in place of money. This is *paper money* as opposed to *metallic money*.
2. Furthermore, there arose the idea of settling a certain number of daily exchanges by means of the following procedure. People who have a credit account at a bank buy and sell commodities all day long to or from each other, just paying by means of receipts on their bank called *cheques*. Between 5.00 p.m. and 6.00 p.m. the bankers meet and *compensate* their clients' debts and credits and each of them supplies in money only the surplus of cheques written over those he received, or obtains in money only the excess of the cheques he received over those he wrote.

Purchases and sales are also made by credit, that is to say, settling them only later on in paper or metallic money. We shall not deal with this type of exchange. We only notice that the ensuing request for money will be carried out when maturity is reached, whatever the case may be.

As for settlements by compensation let us notice that: (1) to pay by cheque one must have provision in the **[99]** bank arising from a credit account and represented by metallic money or banknotes or by bills of exchange rediscountable in the portfolio; (2) the compensation of cheques between banks, in *clearing houses*, has as a result that things take place as if all exchangers had the same bank, in the sense that, where a cheque is brought to the credit of one client and at the same time to the debit of another, its handing over does not bring any transfer of money with it; (3) in these conditions the banks may have the representation of their clients' credit balances partly in bills of exchange in portfolio, bearing interest, partly in metallic money and in banknotes in a proportion known from experience as necessary to render the service of withdrawals of deposits and in particular of payments of cheques, generally speaking; and, in keeping this fraction of cash in portfolio by a rise or a decline of the rate of interest depending on whether payments exceed withdrawals or withdrawals payments; (4) in the same conditions, where banks pay their clients interest on their credit balance against the current interest rate in proportion to the fraction of the balance of bills of exchange to the total balance, these clients have, in fact, reduced their desired cash balance in the same proportion as the total balance to the balance of metallic money, say, in the proportion of 1 to $1/\nu$, for example.

Now, in the circulation equation, we must obviously take the paper money in banknotes into account by inserting, in addition to a term $Q_{\mathrm{a}}^{\mathrm{IV}}$ representing the amount of metallic money if paper money actually exists, a term F representing the amount of this paper money. F expresses the amount of the specific fraction of social wealth allowed to provide the mass of paper money by means of this wealth's titles to property, and these are represented by the banknotes. Because it has been demonstrated that the prices of commodities are proportional to the quantity of metallic money irrespective of the role of paper money, it is likewise demonstrated that the **[100]** term F is naturally proportional to $Q_{\mathrm{a}}^{\mathrm{IV}}$, or takes the form

$$F = fQ_{\mathrm{a}}^{\mathrm{IV}}$$

The equation expressing the equality of supply and demand of money at a certain time, which is the equilibrium equation of circulation, taking account of compensations and paper money, thus becomes:

$$Q_{\mathrm{a}}^{\mathrm{IV}}(1+f) = \frac{1}{\nu}\left(\frac{\alpha}{n'} + \beta\frac{p_{\mathrm{b}}}{n'} + \gamma\frac{p_{\mathrm{c}}}{n'} + \delta\frac{p_{\mathrm{d}}}{n'} + \cdots\right)^{\mathrm{iv}}$$

But the fact that $Q_{\mathrm{a}}^{\mathrm{IV}}$ is less than Q_{a}'' because of the simultaneous introduction of factor $1/\nu$ in the second member of the equation and the introduction of F in the first does not preclude it still being proportional to $p_{\mathrm{b}}/n', p_{\mathrm{c}}/n', p_{\mathrm{d}}/n' \ldots^{\mathrm{v}}$ that is to say: with or without paper money or compensation, and all other things remaining unchanged, *prices are proportional to the quantity of metallic money.*[3]

3 See the final note ['Note on the "Theory of the quantity"', which ends the *Theory of money*; pp. 122–6 below].

By substituting prices in one of the commodities (B), (C), (D) . . . for the prices in (A), neglecting the first term of the second member, which is insignificant, and adding the other terms, we will reach the equation of monetary and fiduciary circulation in the form:

$$Q(1 + f)p = H$$

expressing that: *the price of money in some other commodity is inversely proportional to its quantity*.[4]

[101] IV Variation in the value of the *numéraire* and money

11. After defining the double role as *numéraire* and money [of the money commodity] and formulating the *laws* concerning the effect the institution of money has on the value of the money commodity, as well as concerning the effect of the variation in the quantity of the money commodity on prices, it seems that the *pure theory* of money has been completed and this is the moment to ask various questions whose answers would form *rules* constituting the entirety of the *applied theory* of money. Among these rules, there are two that one is tempted to express straight away. The first is that: *there should be only one numéraire*. Indeed, two or three *numéraires* would mean calling two or three series of prices for all commodities, which would be a complication as enormous and awkward as two or three series of lengths, surfaces, volumes, weights evaluated in two or three different units of measurement! The second rule is: *the numéraire must be money*. Indeed, when prices in the *numéraire* commodity are called in the services and products markets, it would be especially convenient for the entrepreneurs who buy services and the landowners, workers and capitalists who buy products to have the same commodity as money in their pockets to pay with. Yet these two rules should be set out only with all due reservations. The *numéraire*'s role and that of money being distinct, we should keep the possibility of having one or several *numéraires* or one or more sorts of money if that were advantageous from the point of view of the conditions to be fulfilled by the *numéraire* and by money. Let us then consider what these conditions are.

I shall first indicate four conditions, one of which is common to the *numéraire* and money. The other three are specific to **[102]** money; it happens that these can be satisfied in two ways, rather than one. [1] The *numéraire* commodity and the Money commodity should both be of *one and the same constitution* so that no uncertainty may occur nor any dispute about their nature, whether deciding

4 In this form the equation of circulation has been presented in the *Eléments d'économie politique pure*, lesson 33, no. [section] 304 [second edition, *Œ EC*, vol. VIII, p. 523].

on a transaction or paying for it. [2] The Money commodity should be *very rare*, valuable enough to avoid bulk. [3] It should be *easy to divide* to become proportional to the importance of purchases and sales. [4] It should be *easy to keep* and should not get debased in the hands of exchangers between the time they receive it while selling until they spend it by buying. Now there are two commodities, *gold* and *silver*, or the *precious metals*, that fulfil these four conditions admirably. From this it follows that the problem of whether either gold or silver only should be *numéraire* and money, or whether both should figure as such, depends only on a last condition also common to both *numéraire* and money, i.e. with a view to the greatest possible stability of prices, the commodity that is *numéraire* and money must have *a* rareté *and, consequently, a value as little variable, or at least as regularly variable, as possible.* The detailed explanation of the free competition mechanism in exchange and production that we have presented will allow us to grasp better than previously the nature and significance of this condition.[vi]

Disadvantages of the variation in the value of the numéraire *and money*

12. Let (A) be the *numéraire* and money and let

$$\pi_b = \frac{\rho_b}{\rho_a} \quad \pi_c = \frac{\rho_c}{\rho_a} \quad \pi_d = \frac{\rho_d}{\rho_a} \ldots$$

be the prices, equal to the ratios of the *raretés*, of (B), (C), (D) . . . in (A) at a certain given time. These prices are current prices of equilibrium, hence they are the result, at our given time, of **[103]** the immense *tâtonnement* that consisted of first announcing prices at random, then raising those whose demand was superior to supply and lowering those whose supply was superior to demand; then increasing the quantity of the products whose selling price exceeded their cost price in services and decreasing the quantity of the products whose cost price was higher than the selling price; then, finally transforming (A) as a commodity into (A) as money or (A) money into (A) commodity, depending on whether the value of (A) was greater as money than as a commodity or greater as a commodity than as money. This triple series of operations took place simultaneously, while reacting to each other. Equilibrium is finally achieved. There is a current price in (A) for each sort of service, a rent for each sort of land service, a wage for every sort of labour, a rate of interest for ever sort of capital service; these rents, wages and interest are often fixed by contract for a certain period. There is also a current price in (A) for each sort of product, equal to the cost price in rent, wages and interest. The value of the Money commodity is the same in the form of money as in the form of merchandise. In the last analysis, on what does the maintenance of this equilibrium depend? The maintenance of its initial conditions, which are the utilities and quantities, and, more precisely, the *raretés* of the commodities (A), (B), (C), (D) . . . Notice the difference! If (B)'s *rareté* varies, the price π_b varies too. If (B) is a service, the prices of all products will vary where the service is implicated. If (B) is a product, the prices of all the services that enter its production will vary. But, after all, this is only an isolated phenomenon, like a lake's slight movement at a particular point. On the other hand if (A)'s *rareté* varies, then all prices π_b, π_c, π_d . . . will have to vary. Now, how is this variation carried out? If (A)'s *rareté* increases, the selling prices of all products will first decrease and fall below their cost price in services. Landowners, workers and capitalists all benefit from this; but the **[104]** entrepreneurs will suffer losses until, their contracts expired, they may manage a decrease in rents, wages and interest with a view to establishing a new equilibrium. If (A)'s *rareté* decreases, the selling price of all products will first increase and rise above the cost price in services. Entrepreneurs will benefit from it, but landowners, workers and capitalists will lose until, at the end of their contracts, they may manage to raise their rents, wages and interest and re-establish a new equilibrium. This means a complete change in the level of the lake. This general disorder of the economic equilibrium is called a *crisis*. Theoreticians of the orthodox school strive in vain to convince us that 'money is a commodity like any other'; it is not a commodity like any other when each variation in either its utility or its price provokes a crisis. The question arose as to which crisis is preferable: the answer varied depending on whether those who asked belonged to the category of consumers or producers. Without bothering to discuss this kind of theory, I limit myself to noting that actually every crisis, whether from a fall in prices or a rise in prices, is detrimental and should be avoided; and that is what I mean to convey when I vaunt the advantages of price stability.

Principle of the constancy of the price of social wealth in **numéraire** *and money*

13. What should we do to establish this? Make sure the *rareté* of commodity (A) is constant? Certainly, if the *raretés* of the other commodities (B), (C), (D) . . . were constant as well. But suppose that the latter *raretés* were all expanding; would not it be preferable for the *rareté* of (A) then to be the same, so that prices would not increase? Suppose that these same *raretés* were all decreasing; would not it be preferable that the *rareté* of (A) should then be the same, so that prices would not decrease? Finally, since it is well known that **[105]** in a progressive society there are some commodities among (B), (C), (D) . . . whose *raretés* are continually more or less rising, like agricultural products for instance, and other commodities, industrial products, for instance, whose *raretés* are constantly more or less falling, would it not be obvious, all things considered, that the ideal of interest and justice should be that the *rareté* of the numéraire *and money commodity should vary in such a way that a certain*

average price of social wealth in this commodity should remain stable? Let us here pass by the question of how the price in (A) of social wealth should establish itself. Should it be pure and simply the *geometric, arithmetic or harmonic average of the prices* of (B), (C), (D) ... in (A), or should it rather be the price in (A) of some *multiple standard* composed of a quantity b of (B), c of (C), d of (D)... so that the quantities of these commodities retailed will be taken into account? Whichever of these four combinations is adopted, it is certain that, depending on whether the relation between the new prices $p_b, p_c, p_d \ldots$ and the old ones $\pi_b, \pi_c, \pi_d \ldots$ were

$$\sqrt[m-1]{\frac{p_b}{\pi_b} \cdot \frac{p_c}{\pi_c} \cdot \frac{p_d}{\pi_d} \cdots} = 1$$

or

$$\frac{1}{m-1}\left(\frac{p_b}{\pi_b} + \frac{p_c}{\pi_c} + \frac{p_d}{\pi_d} + \cdots\right) = 1$$

or

$$1 \Big/ \left[\frac{1}{m-1}\left(\frac{\pi_b}{p_b} + \frac{\pi_c}{p_c} + \frac{\pi_d}{p_d} + \cdots\right)\right] = 1$$

or

$$\frac{bp_b + cp_c + dp_d + \cdots}{b\pi_b + c\pi_c + d\pi_d + \cdots} = 1$$

there would always be, between the new *raretés* $R_a, R_b, R_c, R_d \ldots$ **[106]** and the old ones $\rho_a, \rho_b, \rho_c, \rho_d \ldots$, the relation:

$$\frac{R_a}{\rho_a} = \sqrt[m-1]{\frac{R_b}{\rho_b} \cdot \frac{R_c}{\rho_c} \cdot \frac{R_d}{\rho_d} \cdots}$$

or

$$\frac{R_a}{\rho_a} = \frac{1}{m-1}\left(\frac{R_b}{\rho_b} + \frac{R_c}{\rho_c} + \frac{R_d}{\rho_d} + \cdots\right)$$

or

$$\frac{R_a}{\rho_a} = 1 \Big/ \left[\frac{1}{m-1}\left(\frac{R_b}{\rho_b} + \frac{R_c}{\rho_c} + \frac{R_d}{\rho_d} + \cdots\right)\right]$$

or

$$\frac{R_a}{\rho_a} = \frac{bR_b + cR_c + dR_d + \cdots}{b\rho_b + c\rho_c + d\rho_d + \cdots}$$

and, consequently, in other words, it would be desirable *that the* rareté *of the* numéraire *and money commodity varied according to the average* rareté *of social wealth.*

Notes

i Kepler's three laws on the movement of planets round the sun are: (1) Each planet draws an ellipse in the same direction; the sun is one of the focuses. (2) The surfaces drawn by the radius from the centre of the sun to the centre of the planet is proportional to the time needed to draw it. (3) The squares of the sidereal revolutions of the planets are proportional to the cubes of the grand axes of their orbits.

*ii We use this translation for Walras's *rente*, and not the word *rent*, because the service as such is what Walras meant and not an amount of money. See the Introduction.

*iii Again the service as such, in kind, is meant and not an amount of money.

*iv Walras never explains why he wrote n' instead of n.

*v Here Walras made a slight mistake. He should have said 'proportional to $1/n', p_b/n', p_c/n', p_d/n' \ldots$' The mistake is not serious if the number of goods is large. This is, apparently, Walras's idea, as follows from the fact that in the next paragraph he neglects the first term of the circulation equation's second member.

vi Sections 12 and 13 that follow can be found in sections 361 and 362 of the second edition of the *Eléments d'économie politique pure* (1889), pp. 429–32, *ŒEC*, vol. VIII, pp. 546–9. They do not figure in any of the other editions of the *Eléments*.

[107]

5 *Theory of Money*

Part II Critical discussion of the systems

I Systems with a single standard or with two independent standards

Single gold standard

14.[i] Now we have a well defined monetary ideal, we shall investigate how far it has been put into practice by the many varied systems already existing or proposed.

The first is the system of the *single gold standard*, or *gold monometallism*. In this system, only gold is both the *numéraire* and money. The utility of gold as merchandise increases incessantly with the development of the population. Note, moreover, that, among all wants that form this utility, some can be satisfied only by the consumption of the commodity itself and not its service alone. The utility of gold as money also increases with the development of business. Does the quantity of gold increase in proportion, however? Far from it! The only gold ore that may quite advantageously be exploited is that which nature took the trouble to grind and can be found in the sand of alluvial terrains. We may certainly hope to find still more goldfields with this gold-bearing sand like those in California and Australia; but it is quite obvious that, as and when the surface of the earth becomes more and more familiar and inhabited, the lodes will be more difficult to find. Hence there will be an ever-growing increase in the *rareté* of gold, with some accidental, sudden falls. Consequently, there will be an ever-growing decrease in prices, with a few accidental, sudden rises in price: this is the monetary future that gold monometallism holds in stock for us. There will be a permanent industrial crisis. **[108]** No matter! The monomania for this system is rampant nearly everywhere, just as was the case earlier of monomania for the mercantile system. England clings to it; Germany was heading in that direction but had to stop half-way when it observed that it was selling its silver cheap to buy gold at higher and higher prices. The proceedings of the last monetary conference on the prolongation of the Latin Union[ii] confirm that

Belgium and Switzerland were imagining the gold standard and strove for it *per fas et nefas* [whether right or wrong]: Belgium, speculating on the absence of a clause concerning liquidation [of the Union], coined until suspension an excessive quantity of écus, intending to transfer them to the other States, collect gold in exchange and then leave the Union to fall to pieces while trying to claim that it was not obliged to reimburse its token. Switzerland, on the contrary, speculated on the introduction of such a liquidation clause, did not coin any money, letting itself be flooded with écus from other States to leave the Union at the first opportunity while getting these écus reimbursed in gold. All this was aimed at the splendid result of having very expensive money and therefore getting all merchandise at a ridiculously low price! It is true that scholars and statesmen in all these countries profess, with that kind of enthusiasm that is specific to gratuitous assertions, that payment by compensation would be more than sufficient to mitigate the exigencies of the monetary circulation. I leave this consoling hypothesis for what it is worth to agricultural, industrial and commercial entrepreneurs.

Single silver standard

15. The *single silver standard*, or *silver monometallism*, would be infinitely less foolish. Silver exists in nature in much larger quantities than gold, and ore of mediocre quality may be profitably treated thanks to improvements in metal working techniques. It would therefore be perfectly acceptable to hope that the quantity of silver might be at least maintained at an adequate level to keep its double utility as a commodity and as money in the sense that not only would its *rareté* **[109]** not increase, but that it would, rather, decrease with time just like most other commodities and so prices of commodities would be fairly stable. But it should still be said that this stability is not certain and that in any case it would be interrupted by alternating rises and falls corresponding to extreme activity or slowing down in the production of the metal.

Double independent standard

16. Close behind the systems with a single standard are those with a multiple standard; in particular, that with the *double independent standard*, recommended by some economists, but I believe it has never worked anywhere sufficiently to be considered an experiment carried out. In this system gold and silver are, if not both *numéraire*, at least both money. The State coins gold or silver in precise weights for anyone who asks. Those who exchange in cash make use of one or the other of the two kinds of coins, basing their exchange upon the variable ratio of the value of gold to the value of silver. Those who buy or sell at a contract stipulate that they prefer payment in gold or in silver, but when due the metal may be substituted for the other at the rate of the day.

Judging *a priori* a system not yet tried out is not completely impossible if some sound principles are at our disposal and if just reasoning is applied: it is merely a little difficult and delicate. I draw the attention of the supporters of this system to a point that they have neglected to clarify, failing to take into consideration all the elements for determining the value of the money commodity. Nothing in the combination in question seems to indicate that a certain given category of business, whether settled in cash, or on contract, will fall to the circulation of gold money and that certain other categories will fall to the silver circulation. Sheer free will of the contracting parties will mean fancy, hazard; that is to say that the limits of both circulations will be completely undetermined and variable, each in turn encroaching on **[110]** the other. Today silver circulation is extending; the value of silver money rises above the value of the silver commodity; silver commodity is transformed into silver money and the price of silver as a commodity increases. At the same time the circulation of gold is reduced; the value of gold money falls below that of gold as a commodity; gold money is transformed into gold commodity and the value of gold as merchandise decreases. Tomorrow it may be the opposite. In this way the values of the two metals and their ratio will be in perpetual, excessive unbearable movement. This is a most awkward circumstance that, added to the very serious inconvenience of the calculations to convert one standard into another, must make the system seem unworkable.

II The system with a double interdependent standard, or bimetallism

The parachute theory

17. As for the following system, we need have no regrets that practical evidence does not join hands with rational indications. The French system of the *double interdependent standard* or *bimetallism* has become the Latin Union's also. It should be attentively studied. Although some economists who have not examined it sufficiently closely maintain the contrary, bimetallism is definitely not a system founded purely and simply on the crude violation of economic laws which consists in decreeing a fixed ratio between the values of two commodities; or anyway, even if it stems from this error it is nonetheless such a most ingenious system and highly efficient within certain limits, so it is well worth understanding it before all else. In this system, gold and silver are both merchandise for a certain fraction of their total quantities and also both money for the rest. The legislator certainly does not fix the ratio of the value of **[111]** gold as a commodity to the value of silver as a commodity; this ratio remains free and continues to vary in the market according to the variations in the utility and the quantity of the two metals. He [the legislator] merely fixes the value

of gold money to the value of silver money at a certain ratio ω. In order to control the laws of economics he obeys them, acting indirectly on the respective quantities of gold and silver as merchandise and money and on the ratio of the value of gold as a commodity to that of silver as a commodity, and this how: if the ratio of the value of gold as merchandise to that of silver as merchandise is higher than ω in the market, gold, being more valuable as a commodity than money, will be demonetized and silver, being more valuable as money than commodity, will be minted. From this double phenomenon, the resulting ratio of the value of gold as merchandise to that of silver as merchandise will decrease, drawing nearer to ω in the market. However, if the ratio of the value of gold as merchandise to that of silver as merchandise is inferior to ω in the market, on the contrary, gold, being more valuable as money than as merchandise, will be minted, while silver, being more valuable as merchandise than as money, will be demonetized. The result of this double phenomenon is that the ratio of the value of gold as merchandise to that of silver as merchandise will rise, drawing nearer to ω in the market. In a nutshell, metal that abounds will enter monetary circulation, moderating its loss of value; metal becoming rarer quits monetary circulation, moderating its increase in value. Such is the substance of Wolowski's so-called *parachute theory*;[iii] put forward in this way this theory is unimpeachable, but unfortunately the bimetallists themselves did not know it very well, so they exaggerated and slanted it at one and the same time. An illustration follows that will make both its scope and its limitations obvious.

[112] *Position of the price curve of the bimetallic standard in relation to the price curves of monometallic standards*

18. Once the ratio of the value of gold money to the value of silver money is fixed, at $\omega = 10$ for instance, the amounts of the two metals may be expressed in *francs*: 5 g silver francs, 9/10 fine and gold francs of $5/10 = 0.5$ g, 9/10 fine. All other things being unchanged, let these amounts vary and take a horizontal axis O–45 (Figure 5.1) to measure time on, and a vertical axis qOq' on which (or on the parallels of which) to measure *quantities* corresponding to each period: the quantities of silver francs above the horizontal axis, following curve AA_{45}, and the quantities of gold francs below, curve BB_{45}.

After that let us take another horizontal axis O–45 on which to measure time again and another vertical axis Op on which (or upon the parallels of which) to measure the *prices* of the silver and the gold franc expressed either in another commodity (B) according to the formula:

$$p = \frac{1}{p_b}$$

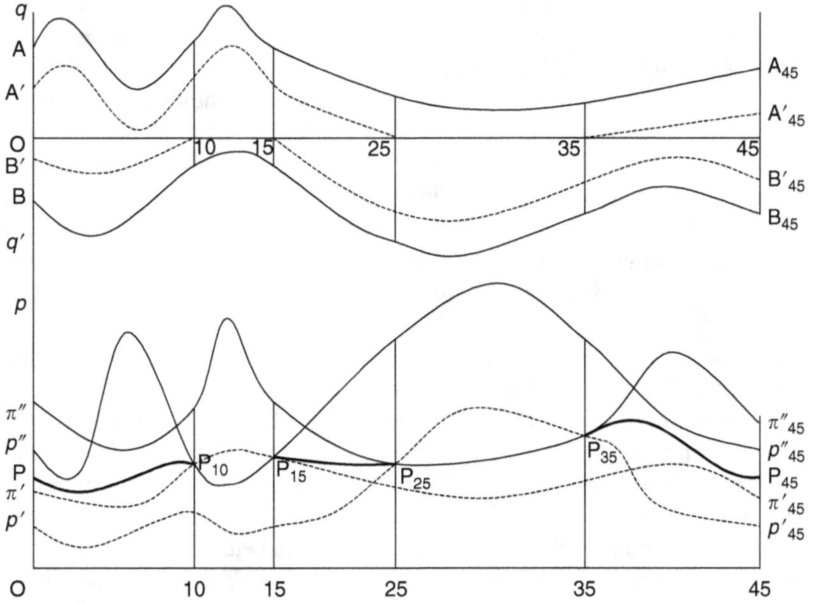

Figure 5.1 Prices of the gold and silver franc measured in some commodity ($\omega = 10$).

or in all other commodities, according to the formula:

$$p = \frac{1}{\sqrt[m-1]{p_b \cdot p_c \cdot p_d \cdots}}$$

or according to the formula:

$$p = \frac{1}{bp_b + cp_c + dp_d + \cdots}$$

corresponding to the quantities indicated in the upper part of Figure 5.1. The various price lines correspond to the three hypotheses: gold monometallism, silver monometallism and bimetallism.

In the first hypothesis, gold is at the same time a commodity and money, its price curve is $\pi''\pi''_{45}$; silver is only merchandise and its price curve is $p'p'_{45}$. In the second hypothesis, silver is a commodity and money at the same time and its price curve is $p''p''_{45}$; gold is only merchandise and its price curve is $\pi'\pi'_{45}$. In the third hypothesis, three cases may appear. Curve π'' of the price of gold, both as merchandise and as money, is necessarily always above **[113]** curve π' of gold as a commodity only; but it is not necessarily always above curve p' of the price of silver as merchandise only. Similarly, curve p'' of the price of silver both as merchandise and as money is necessarily always above curve p' of silver as merchandise only; but it is not necessarily always above the curve π' of gold as merchandise only. If [first] both curve π'' and curve p'' are above both curve π' and curve p' then bimetallism will be effective, since the two metals are both in monetary circulation, and their common price is inferior to both prices of the two metals as money and merchandise at one and the same time [separately] and superior to the two prices of the two metals as merchandise only. Curve P of the price of the gold or silver franc is found below both curves π'' and p'' and above both curves π' and p'. This takes place during periods 0–10, 15–25 and 35–45. If [second] curve π' rises above p'', which means that the gold franc as merchandise only has a higher value than a franc of silver, money as well as merchandise, bimetallism passes into silver monometallism. Curve P yields its place to π' and p''. This is what takes place during period 10–15. If [third] curve p' happens to rise above curve π'', which means that the silver franc as merchandise only has a higher value than the gold franc as merchandise and money, bimetallism passes into gold monometallism. Curve P yields its place to p' and π''. This is what takes place during the period 25–35. Thus eventually in the condition of the quantities supposed in our figure the price curve of the money commodity in the system of bimetallism is curve PP_{45}, supplied by curve p'' from P_{10} to P_{15} and by curve π'' from P_{25} to P_{35}. This curve is remarkably horizontal, which finds its explanation in our supposition that the quantities of gold and silver generally vary in opposite directions; meanwhile, as it stands, **[114]** the curve shows the limits of the compensatory effect of bimetallism perfectly.[1]

Limits of the compensatory effect of bimetallism

19. Let us continue by completing the first part of Figure 5.1 by means of two curves $A'A'_{45}$ and $B'B'_{45}$ of the bimetallic system: the first one separates the total quantity of silver into silver francs as merchandise (superior part, between the curves A and A′) and silver francs as money (between curve A′ and the horizontal axis), the second one separates the total quantity of gold in gold francs as merchandise (lower part, between the curves B and B′) and gold francs as money (between curve B′ and the horizontal axis). Now, all other things being unchanged, it may happen that, while the quantity of one of the two metals increases or decreases, the quantity of the other metal decreases or

1 For the construction of the price curve of the bimetallic standard, see lesson 32 [of the second edition] of the *Eléments d'économie politique pure*. [*OEC*, vol. VIII, pp. 501–14.]

increases so that the total quantity of francs in gold or silver remains the same and that, moreover, the quantity of gold francs as merchandise, the quantity of silver francs as merchandise and the quantity of gold or silver francs as money also remain the same; therefore only the proportion of gold to silver francs as money changes, as during period 15–25, for example. In this case, bimetallism is always effective and, consequently, the ratio of the value of gold as a commodity to the value of silver as a commodity stays the same at 10 in the market. Moreover, the quantity of money neither increases nor decreases and, consequently the money prices of commodities neither increase nor decrease. Nevertheless, in the event that one of the two metals becomes abundant or rare while the other becomes **[115]** rare or abundant, it is possible that the abundant metal will drive the rare one out of monetary circulation and provide on its own more or fewer francs than were before provided by both metals together. This happens during periods 10–15 and 25–35. In this case, bimetallism passes into monometallism and consequently the ratio of the value of gold as merchandise to the value of silver as merchandise rises above 10 or falls below it in the market. Moreover, the quantity of money increases or decreases, so the money prices of commodities rise or fall also. Consequently, it may also happen that, while the quantity of one of the metals increases or decreases, the quantity of the other metal does the same at the same time so that both gold and silver are still in monetary circulation but jointly provide more or fewer francs than they provided previously, as occurs at the beginning of period 0–10 and at the end of period 35–45. In this case bimetallism is still effective and consequently the ratio of the value of gold as a commodity to the value of silver as a commodity is maintained at 10 in the market; but the quantity of money increases or decreases and, consequently, the money prices of commodities increase or decrease also.

These are the effects of the possible variations in the quantities of the precious metals; it should be noticed that the effects of the possible variations in their utility are precisely the opposite to the effects of the variations in quantities. The limits of the compensatory effect of bimetallism should also be noticed. However, this is just what the supporters of the system have neglected. They thought it more expeditious (and, indeed, it was) to deny the possibility of all these variations *a priori*.

> The production of gold is highly irregular [said Mr. Cernuschi in the third preamble to his *Projet de convention internationale bimetallique*, proposed at the monetary conference **[116]** of 1881] highly irregular that of silver, too, while the joint production of gold and silver evaluated at the legal ratio is quite sufficiently regular.[2,iv]

2 [Ministère des Affaires Etrangères,] *Conférence monétaire internationale*, [vol. II,] June–July 1881. Procès-verbaux, [Paris: Imprimerie nationale, 1881, annexe II, pièce C,] p. 154.

That the total production of two metals should be less irregular than that of only one, that the total production of three should be more regular than that of two, that of four more than that of three . . . and so forth, would conform to the theory of probability; but since the production of gold is very unpredictable, and that of silver too, the total production of these two metals evaluated at the proportion $\omega = 15\frac{1}{2}$ would be quite satisfactorily predictable, that would really be extraordinary and verging on the miraculous! In addition, certain particularly convinced and enthusiastic bimetallists do not hesitate to guarantee the good intentions of Providence. Unfortunately, the facts that are provided us by history and statistics neither require nor justify such a supernatural intervention in any way. On the contrary, they confirm our theory and at the same time they are irresistibly illuminated by it. At least three times since its institution, that is to say since the beginning of the century (Providence being apparently too absorbed by other problems), bimetallism has been ruled out by variations in the utility and the quantity of gold and silver that went far beyond the limits of its compensatory effect, and eventually perished, as we shall see, in the test.

III Transformation of bimetallism into a gold money system with a regulating silver token

The 1810–50 slump

20.[v] From 1810 to 1850 there was a simultaneous slowing down of the production of gold and silver due to the **[117]** disorganization of American mines. In conformity with the theory explained above, the money prices of the commodities fell. In March 1882 Mr de Laveleye himself acknowledged this drop in the *Bibliothèque universelle*,[3] and in March 1885 in the *Journal des économistes*.[4] The recession was long and severe, but because bimetallism remained effective nonetheless, the legislator was not forced to take any measures. In any case, the parachute did not break the fall.

The 1850–70 recession: creation of a divisional token; rise in prices

21. Towards 1850 gold became highly abundant owing to the discoveries in California and Australia, and tended to drive silver completely out of monetary circulation. Bimetallism passed into gold monometallism, and the ratio of the value of gold as a commodity to the value of silver as a commodity fell to

3 [Emile de Laveleye,] 'Des fonctions de la monnaie', [First part, *Bibliothèque universelle et revue suisse*, 83rd year, third period, vol. 13, no. 39, March 1882] p. 400.

4 [Emile de Laveleye,] 'La crise de la contraction monétaire', [*Journal des économistes*, 44th year, 4th series, 8th year, vol. 29, no. 3, March 1885] p. 415.

below $15\frac{1}{2}$ in the market. Moreover, the quantity of money increased and the money prices of commodities expanded. The first consequence – the disappearance of silver – forced the legislator to intervene. In order to keep silver in circulation as small change it was transformed into a token by decreasing its alloy from 9/10 to 835/1000. This was the first blow to hit bimetallism; bimetallists, too, bitterly deplored this modification in the alloy of the silver small change. They would have done better to tell us how small payments could have been made without silver small change. In what concerns the second consequence, that of the price rises, this was considered as a sign of prosperity thanks to the excellent governments, and the producers and debtors were allowed to benefit from it, while the consumers and creditors had to suffer. It is this price rise that Jevons measured and found to be about 10.25 per cent, remaining **[118]** considerably below the true value, as I have explained elsewhere.

The recent recession: creation of **special** *or* **complementary** *token; fall in prices*

22. After 1870, because of the discovery of silver in Nevada and the substitution of silver coin for gold in Germany, silver became very abundant and tended to drive gold completely out of monetary circulation in France, in its turn, and in [the rest of] the Latin Union. Bimetallism was transformed into silver monometallism and the ratio of the value of gold as merchandise to the value of silver as merchandise rose to above $15\frac{1}{2}$ in the market. Moreover, the quantity of money increased and so did the prices. Now government was under the influence of the monometallic doctrine and intervened accordingly. First, in 1874 it restricted the coinage of silver; second, in 1878–9 it suspended all coinage of silver. This is where we are now, a situation to be precisely assessed.

The suspension of silver coinage has certainly stopped the complete substitution of silver for gold in the monetary circulation of the Latin Union and has prevented bimetallism from resigning itself to becoming silver monometallism; but is has no less certainly accelerated and accented the increase to above $15\frac{1}{2}$ the value of gold as a commodity to silver as a commodity. Furthermore, it has suppressed silver money and killed bimetallism. Mr Cernuschi speaks about *metallic banknotes* and *hunchbacked monometallism* all the time;[vi] these expressions are neither sufficiently scientific, nor sufficiently exact. From the very moment when coining silver écus is no longer free, the value of silver money will always be 1/15.5 of the value of gold money, while the value of silver as a commodity will be no more than 1/19 or 1/20 of the value of gold **[119]** as a commodity; in other words, silver écus have a legal and conventional value as money that is superior to the real commercial value they would have as merchandise: they are not *metallic banknotes* but *token*. Moreover, from the very moment that silver becomes token and gold the only money, we are, in fact, ruled by the gold standard; this would also be the case formally if, as should be done, the franc was no longer defined as '5 g silver, 9/10 fine' but as '5/15.5 = 10/31 g gold, 9/10 fine'. We have only to admit that we follow a regime of *gold money with special, or complementary, silver token* and not a regime of hunchbacked monometallism. This monetary system is the fifth to appear in this study, and, as I will demonstrate in a moment, it happens to be the right one.

So this is the relation between the values of gold and silver. As far as price movements are concerned, the suspension of silver minting has completely missed its goal: it has substituted a decrease for an increase in the amount of money and a fall for a rise in commodities' money prices. Silver issue has been brought to a halt, but not the demonetization of gold. Nobody has brought gold to the mint to be transformed into money for two or three years and it seems that, on the contrary, gold money is transformed into gold as a commodity. The production of gold is lower than its consumption. So the quantity of money is diminishing; consequently, the money prices of commodities are on the decrease. Perhaps they are falling for still other reasons; but they certainly do for the former reason. On this point the bimetallists are absolutely right against the monometallists' prejudices. However, they should not have limited themselves, as they did, to affirming the drop in prices; they should make sure and measure it.

[120] *The one thing that remains to be done: make special, or complementary, token: a* regulating *token*

23. I shall summarize the process as follows: if the legal ratio of $15\frac{1}{2}$ had been left to produce its consequences freely, as the bimetallists had wished, all silver demonetized in Germany together with that of the Nevada mines would have come to be coined in the Latin Union; all our gold would have been transferred to Germany; we should have had money consisting exclusively of silver, a lot of it, too, and a considerable rise in prices to the cost of landowners, workers and capitalists alike. The monometallists intervened and succeeded first in restricting, then in suppressing écu minting; the silver from Germany and from America, rejected as metallic money everywhere, accumulated in the metal market as a commodity and caused a price decrease of 20 per cent there. A good deal of our gold remained; but nevertheless, money is very scarce and a considerable price fall has occurred, to the cost of the entrepreneurs. I wonder: 'Why stop minting écus altogether instead of simply issuing them within limits, ensuring that there will be no more slumps with a price fall nor crises with rising prices?' But the answer will be a question: 'What is your regulating principle?'

I already have told you. The goal to pursue is not the absolute fixation of the *rareté* and value of the money commodity. Among ordinary commodities there are those, like certain agrarian products, which tend to increase regularly in *rareté* and value, independently of weekly, monthly or annual fluctuations. There are other commodities, like most industrial products, that tend to decrease regularly in *rareté* and value, independently of the fluctuations due to varied causes. Everything would be fine if *the* rareté *of the money and* numéraire *commodity varied in the same way as the average* rareté *of social wealth.* No more than any other commodity **[121]** would gold naturally undergo such a variation in *rareté* and value; but this may be imposed artificially by adding or deducting silver écus from monetary circulation as may be necessary. I have demonstrated that exactly this result will be obtained by these additions or subtractions *so that the average price in* numéraire *and money commodity of social wealth would not vary.* It is certainly obvious that one cannot add silver écus to money circulation or withdraw them in such a way as to avoid any variation in the average price in gold of social wealth; but it seems that it might be arranged so that this price would periodically be brought back to the constant average price by adding écus when it tended to fall and taking them out of circulation when it tended to increase.

This is what I call the system of *gold money with regulating silver token*, and I stress the point that it is in fact our present system; the logic of facts has brought us this system, rather than the bimetallists' logic. Gold alone is *money* today and should provide the definition of the franc, which should be defined as '5/15.5 = 10/31 g of gold, 9/10 fine'. Silver is a *token*: it must be fractional currency for the half-franc, one-franc and two-franc coins, that is to say 2.5 g, 5 g and 10 g of 835/100 alloy, and it must be *regulating* token for the five-franc coins, that is, 25 g of 900/1000 alloy. Creditors are not bound to accept more than 50 F in fractional currency, or more than 500 F regulating token. A mathematical calculation, the details of which have yet to be fixed, will teach us whether we add or remove the regulating token little by little. In the first case we lean towards bimetallism, to which we should return entirely if we took enough silver from the commodity metal market to make its price rise from 1/19 or 1/20 to 1/15.5. In the second case, we would lean towards **[122]** gold monometallism, where we should finally arrive at the day when silver écus are no longer in circulation. In this way we could avoid plunging blindly into one or the other of these systems, or hesitating paralysed and irresolute between the two; but we settle in a half-way position with space to move in either one or the other direction according to the scarcity or abundance of gold to protect prices from any general, persistent contraction or inflation.

IV Problems of realization

Constructing the curve of the price in numéraire *and money of social wealth: The necessity of an international treaty*

24. Much has yet to be done in order to grasp the monetary question from all angles. I still have to give the details and explain by means of an example borrowed from history, how, when and in what proportions the introduction or the withdrawal of regulating token would have to be managed to keep the

money-price curve of social wealth as level as possible. It is here that problems are to be found. Some of them have already been pointed out, but I do not know whether the most serious of all has been omitted. Is it possible to predict the movement of the curve in question, at least up to a certain point, by means of straight, indubitable indices like the variation in quantities and utilities of precious metals? If not, who can guarantee that we will not introduce token into circulation the day before a price increase or withdraw token the day before a decrease, thus magnifying instead of limiting the fluctuations of the market? I shall also have to explain that a system like mine should not be put into practice by one isolated country only, nor even a limited union of nations such as the Latin Union; to **[123]** a certain degree, it should be universal. This is another serious problem. Germany and the United States are already in fact, like the Latin Union, under a regime of gold money with complementary silver token: the old silver one-thaler coin is still circulating, as well as the new silver five-mark piece and the silver dollar; the minting of all these has been suspended or limited, but they are token just as the silver five-franc piece is. If we were to restrict ourselves to the idea of adopting one universal money, or even to the less complicated and more pressing idea of adopting a universal ratio between the value of gold money and that of silver money, England would necessarily have to consent to begin minting the silver crown or five-shilling piece as special token again, and England, Germany and the United States would have to agree with the Latin Union to make all this special, complementary silver token into regulating token that could be coined in amounts determined for each country according to international conventions. Otherwise, if the Latin Union alone resumed coining écus, the first result would be that all its gold flew abroad, leaving it devoid of money. That is not all: the principal monetary powers would have to agree to make regulations for the issue of paper money and especially banknotes as fiat money. If not, any regulation of the variation in the value of money would be illusory. I shall not go into details on this point of the question, because not only there is no room within the framework I have set today, but because, I must frankly confess, I have not studied the matter sufficiently. I cannot allow myself the temptation of affirming things about which I am still hesitant. Quite the contrary, I should like to stick to points I am certain of. I do not know what is possible; I only know what is desirable. In other words, I do not flatter myself that I have solved the problem, I claim only to have voiced it and here are the exact terms.

[124] *In any case, monetary optimism must be renounced*

25. The optimism that has prevailed until now and still does in official economic circles should be eschewed. This is really hard, for nothing is easier and pleasanter than such a point of view, celebrated by all pure science as the providential harmony of social wealth, where all applied science was reduced, consequently,

to the formula *Ne rien faire!* [Do nothing!] Unfortunately, this conception is overwhelmingly contradicted by reality every day and under our very noses. Probably, the system of economic phenomena tends towards equilibrium by itself, under the regime of free competition, as the system of astronomical phenomena does under the influence of universal attraction; but, whereas serenely celestial bodies gravitate along their trajectories, services and products undergo abrupt, violent price changes the causes of which we must know considerably better than we do in order to foresee, and possibly prevent, them. Let us leave aside production disturbances to concentrate on those of money circulation. The monometallists never consent to admit them.

> Nothing – they say – leads us to imagine a decline in the quantity of gold, but if, contrary to all expectations, this quantity were to diminish, the development of compensations would more than make up for the absence of metallic money, etc.

The bimetallists have definitely studied the monetary problem more seriously; they get the State to intervene to fix a ratio between the value of gold and silver money. They are heterodox but how much more steeped in optimism! Mr Cernuschi has been heard to say:

> The production of gold is highly irregular, highly irregular also is that of silver, whereas the joint production of gold and silver evaluated at the legal ratio is quite sufficiently regular.[vii]

So this is supposed to be a scientific analysis of the effects of variations in the quantity of **[125]** money on prices; this is the frail basis of the whole system! Alas no! It is not true! The production of gold is very irregular, as is the production of silver, and the joint production of the two metals evaluated at a ratio of $15\frac{1}{2}$ is irregular too. Moreover, their naive applied economics is based on the succinct evaluation of pure economics. 'Money, Mr Cernuschi says, should be self-operating.'[viii] Is this the rule? Of course not! Money should have a real value equal to its nominal value; it should, moreover, have a value that varies as regularly as possible. That is how it should be. If the State has to intervene a little more than you [Cernuschi] have permitted to achieve this end, money should not, and will not, be automatic.

Action must be according to the nature of things in both the social and the industrial order

26. Facing the variations in the quantity of the precious metals that feed monetary circulation, we are like the inhabitants of a valley faced with variations

in the amount of water in the rivers that irrigate the valley. Our Bernardin de Saint-Pierres were in ecstasies at the beauty and grandeur of the huge river that always returns to its bed in the end, sooner or later, after it has chanced to overflow its banks. They entreat us not to touch the work of nature, not to substitute (one of their favourite phrases) for the admirable scheme of Providence the conceptions of our feeble brains. But, rhetoric apart, if we examine the facts carefully, we will observe the ravages inflicted by the river in flood, and the disadvantages of the total drought that follows; and, detachedly but firm, we wonder whether it would not be possible to transform a devastating torrent into an irrigating, fertilizing canal by means of a system of basins and reservoirs which would collect water when there was far too much and give it back in times of shortage. Objections might be raised that **[126]** this operation would be difficult and costly, that if ill informed about a great number of physical and meteorological phenomena we would be at risk of filling our reservoirs and emptying them inopportunely; and it would be possible only if those living upstream agreed with those living downstream. So be it! We always have an advantage over those who close their eyes for fear of seeing. Impossible at present, this work might become possible some time from now. But is it really impossible anyway? What huge, prolific projects have been accomplished in the domain of physical and natural sciences and their application in civil engineering that would still remain to be launched if as much ignorance and weakness had been shown in this field as there is in the domain of moral sciences and political science and their application to social progress? Once and for all, let us bring to this domain of enquiry and exertion the method that consists in first carefully developing pure science and then energetically move on to applied science. It may be that with a little more light on the subject we shall also be a little braver. Perhaps we shall cease to present the lamentable spectacle of the utmost powerlessness to carry the most urgent economic and social reforms through to a successful conclusion, first and foremost the reform of our monetary system.

Notes

i Sections 14, up to '. . . the permanent industrial recession', 15, 16 and the first lines of 17, up to '. . . that of the Latin Union' can also be found in the sections 373, 374, 375 and the first lines of 376 of lesson 38 of the second edition of the *Eléments d'économie politique pure* (1889), pp. 439–45. See also *OEC*, vol. VIII, pp. 559–62.

ii See Ministère des affaires étrangères, *Conférence monétaire entre la Belgique, la France, la Grèce, l'Italie et la Suisse en 1885. Convention et procès-verbaux*, Paris: Imprimerie Nationale, 1885.

iii The parachute theory, summarized by Walras, was explained by Louis Wolowski in his answer to the *Enquête sur la question monétaire*, 8 April 1870, in which he indicates with regard to bimetallism:

Experience, with which reasoning appears to be in accordance, shows that when one may choose between two metals to accomplish the same task, from the very moment that by a more abundant supply of the one the other would decline, the entire demand will move to that side and equilibrium will restore itself. We have watched this spectacle produced on the largest scale when the increased demand for gold served as a parachute allowing the billions [of gold] from Australia and California to find their place in circulation without provoking serious oscillation (Conseil général du commerce, *Enquête sur la question monétaire. Déposition de M. Wolowski*, Paris: Guillaumin, 1870, p. 72; reprinted with the same pagination as an appendix to the book by Léon Wolowski, *L'Or et l'argent*, Paris: Guillaumin, 1870).

The same theory has been explained by the same author elsewhere, while using the analogy with the pendulum:

To measure the march of time, science resorted to the oscillations of the pendulum; if the latter had been formed only by a single metal bar, the influence of the temperature would accelerate or delay the movements, thus incessantly modifying the regular observation of the time elapsed. Technology has grappled with this difficulty and overcome it by putting together two metal strips, acting in opposite directions, in the *swinging* pendulum, adjusted in such a way as to count the moments that pass with great precision. With respect to the measurement of value, it is the same as the measurement of time: it would be too sensitive, it would deviate too frequently if one could utilize only one single metal in the world as money metal: in making use of gold and silver, one gets at each relative increase in the supply of either of these metals an increase in the demand [for the other metal] that restores equilibrium, which maintains considerable fixity in the monetary equipment. As we hope to demonstrate, such has been the beneficial result of the law of Germinal, year XI [March–April 1804] ('L'or et l'argent. Question monétaire', memoir presented 7 October 1868, *Séances et travaux de l'Académie des sciences morales et politiques*, 28th year, 5th series, vol. 19 (89th volume of the collection), 3rd trimester 1869, p. 360).

In fact, this analogy with the pendulum was previously suggested by Adam Müller in his *Theorie des Geldes* (Berlin, 1809) and by Sismonde de Sismondi in his *Nouveaux principes d'économie politique* (Paris, 1827 ([1819]), as was remarked by Emile de Laveleye in his *La Monnaie et le bimétallisme international*, second edition, Paris: Félix Alcan, 1891, p. 30. Identical arguments are to be found in Evert Seyd, *Token and Foreign Exchanges Theoretically and Practically Considered, followed by a Defence of the Double Valuation*, London, 1868. William Stanley Jevons, though criticizing bimetallism while referring to Gresham's law, presents Wolowski's argument with approval in chapter 12 of his *Money and the Mechanism of Exchange*, London: King, 1875. About the analogy of the reservoirs see below, section 26; see also 'Gold and silver' (1868), letter from Jevons to Wolowski, published in *Investigations in Currency and Finance*, edited and introduced by H. S. Foxwell, London: Macmillan, 1884, pp. 303–4.

iv There exists an English translation: *Proceedings of the International Monetary Conference held in Paris 1881*, printed by the Hon. Secretary of State, Cincinatti, OH 1881.

v Sections 20–2 and 23, with the exception of the paragraph 'I said it. The goal to pursuit... when it tended to rise,' can be found in the sections 377–9 of lesson 38 of the second edition of the *Eléments d'économie politique pure* (1889), pp. 446–50. (*OEC*, vol. VIII, 563–7.)

vi See the three brochures by Henri Cernuschi collecting articles published in *Le Siècle* (Paris): *Les Assignats métalliques, faisant suite au 'Grand procès de l'Union Latine'*, Paris: Guillaumin, 1885; *Le Monométallisme bossu, faisant suite aux 'Assignats métalliques'*, Paris: Guillaumin, 1885; *La Danse des assignats métalliques, faisant suite au 'Monométallisme bossu'*, Paris, Guillaumin 1885.

vii 'Projet de convention internationale bimétallique préparée par M. Cernuschi', in Ministère des Affaires Etrangères, *Conférence monétaire internationale*, vol. II, June–July 1881, Procès-verbaux, Paris: Imprimerie nationale, 1881, annexe II, pièce C, p. 154.

viii Henri Cernuschi: 'Metallic money should be issued automatically: the limit of issue should not be restricted by anybody. Paper money will be issued by government, who will fix its limit of issue' ('Propositions présentées à la Commission par M. Henri Cernuschi', annexe A, proposition no. v, p. 48). The complete text just mentioned is also reproduced in 'Conférence internationale des monnaies', *Journal des économistes,* 4th series, vol. 14, no. 41, May 1881, p. 253. In the Walras Lausanne archives a handwritten report of a conference held by Henri Cernuschi is preserved: 'La question monétaire et la crise économique', 10 March 1886 (F.W. Vb carton 28; we did not manage to identify the occasion when this manuscript was presented). On this occasion Cernuschi declared: 'Good money is automatic money, that is to say, everybody is free to have it minted by bringing metal to the State institutions that transform it into coins' (p. 1).

6 *Theory of Money*

Part III Statistical desiderata

I Determination of the price of social wealth in money

Stating the problem of price stability

27. The last problems to be solved with a view to completion of a rational theory of money are of a statistical nature. After some reflection, I believe it would be better to present them to statisticians than attempt to solve them myself. The first problem I shall raise concerns the determination of the money price of social wealth. It is presented as follows.

(A), (B), (C), (D)... are a certain number of commodities; (A) is the *numéraire* and money, π_b, π_c, π_d ... are the prices of (B), (C), (D)... in (A) at a certain time, p'_b, p'_c, p'_d ... are the prices at another time, Q and Q' are the total quantities of (A), merchandise and money, at the two times in question; we assume it already demonstrated that, if wished, all prices p'_b, p'_c, p'_d ... could be proportionally augmented or diminished by a proportional increase or decrease of Q' [to Q''] according to equation:

$$\frac{p''_b}{p'_b} = \frac{p''_c}{p'_c} = \frac{p''_d}{p'_d} = \cdots = \frac{Q''}{Q'}$$

This possibility results from the double fact that (1) *the* [*ratios of the*] *prices are equal to the ratios of the* raretés, and that (2) *all other things being equal, the* rareté *of the money commodity is approximately inversely proportional to its quantity*. The rigorous demonstration of these two facts implies pure economics that is completely new and wholly mathematical. But in the first two parts of the present *Theory of money* I have summarized this form of pure economics and the demonstration **[128]** to which it leads; this allows me to make the assumption already spoken of. Now under this assumption, the problem presented is the following.

What should the ratio be between Q'' and Q', in other words what should the ratio between p''_b, p''_c, $p''_d \ldots$ and p'_b, p'_c, $p'_d \ldots$ be so that prices remain as stable as possible, that is to say, so that the inconvenience caused by substituting economic equilibrium on the footing of prices p''_b, p''_c, $p''_d \ldots$ for economic equilibrium on the basis of prices π_b, π_c, $\pi_d \ldots$ is the least possible, both from the point of view of entrepreneurs, who buy services at the most recent prices and who sell products at the former prices, and from the point of view of landowners, workers and capitalists, buyers of products at the former prices and sellers of services at the most recent prices?

The special case of a proportional rise or fall in all prices

28. The answer in this case is obvious. If it happened that:

$$\frac{\pi_b}{p'_b} = \frac{\pi_c}{p'_c} = \frac{\pi_d}{p'_d} = \cdots = \mu$$

it is quite clear that one should take care that:

$$\frac{Q''}{Q'} = \mu$$

and so:

$$p''_b = \pi_b, \quad p''_c = \pi_c, \quad p''_d = \pi_d \cdots$$

because in this way the first equilibrium is simply maintained.

This is the case in which, all other things being equal, the original quantity Q of the money commodity becomes $Q' = Q/\mu$ and so, making $Q'' = \mu Q' = Q$, **[129]** the sole reason for the modification of the prices would be redressed. The same case could occur, though less probably, not by a rise or fall in the quantity of (A) but rather by a fall or a rise, under certain conditions, in quantities of (B), (C), (D) . . . ; even then the old equilibrium could be re-established at a stroke by means of a change of Q' to $Q'' = \mu Q' = Q$ instead of leaving it to find its own level by means of a rise or fall in the prices of services.

We must dwell on this point for a moment, since it relates directly to our present circumstances.

A more or less proportional decrease in the prices of a large number of commodities, if not all, may be noticed just now, and a controversy between scholars has arisen on the subject. The bimetallists, on one hand, assert that the drop is caused by a proportional decrease in the amount of money, which should be remedied by supplying silver as an auxiliary to the gold in circulation. The monometallists, on the other hand, maintain that the drop is due to an increase in the quantity of commodities resulting from a certain progress in industry and commerce and that, consequently, there is absolutely no reason to remedy it. Allow me to point out that this controversy is not very interesting. If the bimetallists were right and managed to demonstrate that the amount of money had decreased while the quantities of other commodities had not varied, an increase in the amount of money would obviously have been enough to raise prices again. But if the monometallists were right and managed to put beyond any doubt that the quantity of commodities had increased while the amount of money had not varied, it seems to me that it would be equally suitable to augment, if possible, the amount of money to keep the price level up and thus maintain equilibrium. For, in the end, whether the **[130]** amount of the money commodity diminishes, the quantities of other commodities remaining the same, or whether the amount of money remains the same while the quantities of other commodities increase, in both cases there will not be enough of the money commodity in relation to the quantities of other commodities. This reasoning would be the same in the case of a price rise.

The general case: a system with a multiple standard; a system of the geometric average of the prices

29. However, these simple cases hardly ever occur in reality. Generally there will always be, from one minute to the next, variations in utility together with variations in the quantities of all commodities, among them the money commodity;[i] hence, in the general theory as well as in present circumstances, a solution has to be found to the problem of how to stabilize prices by means of modifications to be brought about on the quantity of money by supposing that variations in the utility and quantity of the money commodity, as well as variations in the utilities and quantities of other commodities, take place at the same time.

In my memoir entitled 'Théorie mathématique du bimétallisme' [1881] I pointed out the stability of the price of a *multiple standard* as a solution to the problem. This standard was to consist of a quantity *b* of (B), a quantity *c* of (C), a quantity *d* of (D) . . .; the money price of social wealth would then be:

$$bp_{\mathrm{b}} + cp_{\mathrm{c}} + dp_{\mathrm{d}} + \cdots$$

Later on, in my memoir entitled 'D'une méthode de régularisation de la variation de la valeur de la monnaie' [1885], I believed it was to be found in the stability of the geometric average of the prices of (B), (C), (D) . . . The price of social wealth would then be:

$$\sqrt[m-1]{p_{\mathrm{b}} \cdot p_{\mathrm{c}} \cdot p_{\mathrm{d}} \cdots}$$

These two formulae are equally suitable in the **[131]** special case of a proportional increase or decrease in all prices. Several people have pointed out that the second one did not take an essential circumstance into account, that is, the differences in production and consumption of the commodities; it seems to me that this observation is well founded and now I am inclined to return to the first formula.

Let (A) still be *numéraire* and money. But now, in conformity with the notations of my *Éléments d'économie politique pure*,[1] let (B), (C), (D)... be products and (T), (P), (K)... productive services; let π_b, π_c, π_d... be equilibrium prices of (B), (C), (D)... and π_t, π_c, π_d... equilibrium prices of (T), (P), (K)..., all measured in (A); finally, let b_t, b_p, b_k... c_t, c_p, c_k... d_t, d_p, d_k... be the *production coefficients* of products (B), (C), (D) ... in services (T), (P), (K) ..., that is to say, the respective quantities of (T), (P), (K)... that are needed for the production of one unit of (B), (C), (D)... On one hand, we should have, in virtue of the original equilibrium:

$$\pi_b = b_t\pi_t + b_p\pi_p + b_k\pi_k + \cdots$$
$$\pi_c = c_t\pi_t + c_p\pi_p + c_k\pi_k + \cdots$$
$$\pi_d = d_t\pi_t + d_p\pi_p + d_k\pi_k + \cdots$$
$$\cdots$$

While, on the other, we should have:

$$p''_b \gtreqless b_t\pi_t + b_p\pi_p + b_k\pi_k + \cdots$$
$$p''_c \gtreqless c_t\pi_t + c_p\pi_p + c_k\pi_k + \cdots$$
$$p''_d \gtreqless d_t\pi_t + d_p\pi_p + d_k\pi_k + \cdots$$
$$\cdots$$

But let us suppose that Q_b, Q_c, Q_d... were the respective quantities of (B), (C), (D)... that entrepreneurs were to put at the **[132]** disposal of landowners, workers and capitalists at prices p''_b, p''_c, p''_d... while obtaining from the latter productive services at the old prices π_t, π_c, π_d... If one had the equation:

$$Q_b p''_b + Q_c p''_c + Q_d p''_d + \cdots = Q_b\pi_b + Q_c\pi_c + Q_d\pi_d + \cdots$$

it is certain that neither the entrepreneurs on one hand, taken as a group, nor the aggregate of landowners, workers and capitalists would gain or lose anything

1 Lesson 20, no. 203 [Second edition, *ŒEC*, vol. VIII, pp. 304–5].

because of the substitution of prices $p''_b, p''_c, p''_d \ldots$ for prices $\pi_b, \pi_c, \pi_d \ldots$, even before the prices of services became in equilibrium with those of the products. In fact, what the consumers taken as a group would lose by the rise in the prices of certain commodities they would gain precisely because of the fall in prices of certain other commodities. They would only have to consume more of the commodities whose prices had decreased and less of the commodities that had increased in price. Similarly, the producers in their totality would lose because of the fall in the prices of some commodities just what they would gain by the rise in the prices of other commodities. It is true that the compensation would apply only from one producer to another; that is to say, what some producers would lose because of the drop in the prices of their products others would gain precisely because of the rise in the price of theirs. The former would have to restrict their production and the latter would have to expand theirs, in order to restore equilibrium. In all cases hazard would have been reduced and the redress of equilibrium made as easy as possible.

In practice there is some reason for making $b, c, d \ldots$ reasonably proportional to $Q_b, Q_c, Q_d \ldots$ hence to compose the multiple standard by inserting a suitable number of commodities to which one must assign an equally suitable set of coefficients more or less proportional to the quantities produced and consumed.

[133] II The construction of the curve of variation in the price of social wealth in money

Unspecified formula of the price in money of social wealth. The equation of constancy

30. Meanwhile I am forgetting that I wanted to set, not solve, the problem of the determination of the price of social wealth in money, which is a question of averages and therefore statistical. This is the reason I now go on to study the most appropriate practical means to ensure its constancy, denoting this price by the unspecified formula

$$\mathrm{F}(p_b, p_c, p_d \ldots)$$

If $\pi_b, \pi_c, \pi_d \ldots$ were the prices of the commodities (B), (C), (D) ... in the money commodity (A) at a certain initial moment and if $p_b, p_c, p_d \ldots$ were the prices at some later time, the ideal to pursue from the point of view of greatest possible stability would then be that we had $\mathrm{F}(p_b, p_c, p_d \ldots) = F(\pi_b, \pi_c, \pi_d \ldots)$. Hence:

$$\frac{\mathrm{F}(p_b, p_c, p_d \ldots)}{\mathrm{F}(\pi_b, \pi_c, \pi_d \ldots)} = 1$$

So the first thing to do is construct the curve with the times $t_1, t_2, t_3 \ldots$ elapsed since the initial moment as abscissae and with the corresponding values:

$$\frac{F(p_{b,1}, p_{c,1}, p_{d,1} \ldots)}{F(\pi_b, \pi_c, \pi_d \ldots)}$$

$$\frac{F(p_{b,2}, p_{c,2}, p_{d,2} \ldots)}{F(\pi_b, \pi_c, \pi_d \ldots)}$$

[134] $$\frac{F(p_{b,3}, p_{c,3}, p_{d,3} \ldots)}{F(\pi_b, \pi_c, \pi_d \ldots)}$$

$$\ldots$$

as ordinates, and see, should this curve not naturally be a horizontal line, how far it could be artificially straightened to horizontal, at least approximately.

The curve of the variation in the geometric average of prices. Jevons's construction

31. As far as I know, the curve in question has not been constructed for the formula:

$$\frac{bp_b + cp_c + dp_d \cdots}{b\pi_b + c\pi_c + d\pi_d \cdots}$$

corresponding to the system of the multiple standard. But it has been done for the formula:

$$\frac{\sqrt[m-1]{p_b \cdot p_c \cdot p_d \cdots}}{\sqrt[m-1]{\pi_b \cdot \pi_c \cdot \pi_d \cdots}}$$

corresponding to the system of the [geometric] average of prices. This same circumstance led me to prefer the system of the average to that of the multiple standard. As a matter of fact, in this form it appeared to obey an important law that must obviously govern under any form, the *economic tide*.

Jevons was the first to perform this construction; he even did it twice: first, for thirty-eight English commodities for the period 1845–62, where π_b, π_c, $\pi_d \ldots$ were calculated as the arithmetic averages of the prices during the period 1845–50;[2, ii] second, for forty English commodities **[135]** for the period 1782–1865, π_b, π_c, $\pi_d \ldots$ being the 1782 prices.[3, iii] On both occasions the

2 'A serious fall in the value of gold ascertained, and its social effect set forth', 1863.
3 'The variation of prices and the value of the currency since 1782', 1865.

curve appears to be subjected to a twofold movement: (1) an undulating movement caused by temporary fluctuations that reproduces itself roughly every ten years, and (2) a movement of rise or fall caused by incessant fluctuations that reproduces itself irregularly, like the rise from 1782 to 1810, the fall from 1810 to 1850 and the rise from 1850 to 1865. It seems to me that Jevons committed a theoretical error concerning the second movement in believing that the incessant fluctuations arise from variations in the absolute value of money and by presenting a way of measuring them. In fact I am inclined to believe, like him, that the rise from 1782 to 1810, the fall from 1810 to 1850 and the rise from 1850 to 1865 are mainly the result of variations in the quantity of money; but, in principle, I must insist that they might as well have been, or be, the result of variations in the quantities and utilities of the commodities. On the other hand, it seems that Jevons definitely has provided us with the theory of movements brought about by temporary fluctuations. He has indicated that their genuine causes are to be found in the alternation of growth and shrinkage of capital formation ('variations of permanent investment'),[iv] thus indicating the real symptoms, namely the increase in prices of construction materials and the discount rate for a period of rise and the decrease in these prices and this rate for a period of fall; finally, he has given the phenomenon its name of 'commercial tide' [*marée économique* in French]. Subsequent observations not have only confirmed the reality and regularity of the phenomenon in question but have moreover established that it is not nationwide but international or universal.

[136] *Construction of the Hamburg commercial statistics*

32. The curve of the variation in the price of social wealth in money has also been constructed, recently, according to the formula corresponding to the system of the average price by [the Bureau of] Commercial Statistics of Hamburg. The operation concerned 114 commodities for the period 1847–84, where π_b, π_c, π_d . . . were taken as the arithmetic averages of prices during the period 1847–50. A summary of this work can be found at the end of Mr A. Soetbeer's publication, entitled *Materialen zur Erläuterung und Beurtheilung der wirtschaftlichen Edelmetalverhältnisse und der Währungsfrage* (October 1885).[v] If the ordinates had been calculated according to the formula corresponding to the system of the multiple standard, and if, in particular, they had been reported from year to year, this construction would have been extremely important and perhaps decisive in the question of money because of the large number of commodities, the markets from which they were taken, the conditions under which the prices were noted and, finally, because of the period to which it relates. As it is now, we could split up the period 1850–84 into four sections each of which, going from low tide to low tide, comprises exactly one economic tide, take the averages of these four periods and distinguish, in the movement of these averages, the essential movement of rise and fall in the price of social wealth in *numéraire* and money.

But neither the Hamburg statisticians nor Mr Soetbeer believed that they had to take the phenomenon of the economic tide into account; they have split the period 1850–84 into the five sections 1851–60, 1861–70, 1871–75, 1876–80 and 1881–84, which are not equally interesting. Nevertheless, the construction as such is expressive. During the period 1851–60, when gold arrived in great quantities, the average of the prices is 15.61 per cent above that of period 1847–50; during the period 1861–70, when the production of **[137]** silver was at a high rate after the high output of gold, it was 23.41 per cent more; during the period 1871–5, when the silver rush continued and was combined with free coinage of silver in the Latin Union, it was 32.90 per cent more; during the period 1876–80, with limited coinage of silver écus, it was no more than 22.61 more; and, finally, during the period 1881–4, with the suspension of écu minting, it was 19.49 more. It would seem that this is enough to demonstrate that, if the growing scarcity of money is not the only cause of the present fall in prices, it has a large share in it.[4]

III Correcting the curve of variation in price of social wealth in money

The unspecified curve submitted to the economic tide, the variation in the average level of the tide has to be corrected [vi]

33. Proceeding as one usually does in mathematical sciences, viz. building theory on the general, abstract and hypothetical data before moving on to the practice concerning specific, concrete and real data, I shall represent the various values of the function:

$$\frac{F(p_b, p_c, p_d \ldots)}{F(\pi_b, \pi_c, \pi_d \ldots)}$$

at forty different times, viz. during forty consecutive years, by a curve ABCDE (Figure 6.1), arbitrarily drawn and submitted only to a twofold movement: (1) of temporary undulation, (2) of permanent descent; second, **[138]** I represent them by a curve GHIKL (Figure 6.2) arbitrarily drawn and submitted only to the twofold movement of (1) temporary undulation, (2) permanent rise.

4 In the second edition of [Soetbeer's] *Materialen* (1886) the values of the ordinates of the curve of variation in the average price of the 114 commodities are presented from year to year, and this very curve is represented graphically. Since then numerous other statistical studies of price variations have been undertaken in succession to those by Jevons: in England, under the name of *index numbers*, by Messrs Newmarch, Bourne, Palgrave, Ellis, Giffe, Sauerbaeck, Mulhall; in Germany by Messrs Laspeyres, Paasche and Von der Borght; in the United States by Messrs Burchard and Grosvenor.

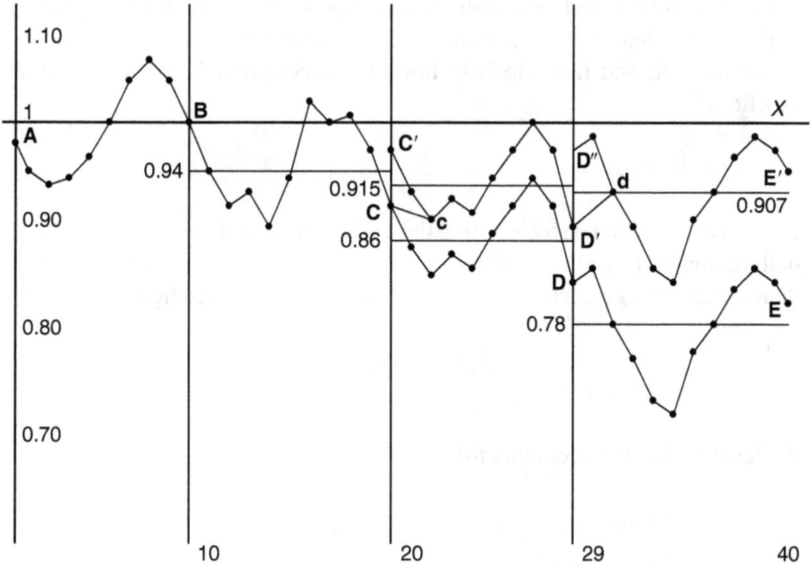

Figure 6.1 Decreasing price change curve (Table 6.1).

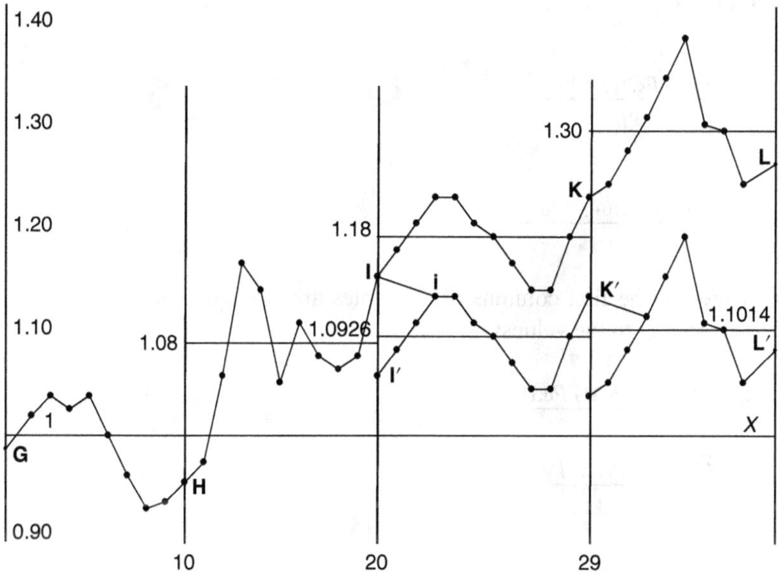

Figure 6.2 Increasing price change curve (Table 6.2).

The values of the ordinates of these two curves (see the four columns of Tables 6.1 and 6.2, just next to the years) are obtained in the following way.

During the ten first years, being by hypothesis years from ebb to ebb for curve ABCDE and from flood to flood for curve GHIKL, the values of the function:

$$F(p_b, p_c, p_d \ldots)$$

are consecutively taken by inserting the arithmetic annual averages of the prices of the commodities (B), (C), (D) . . . for the values of the variables p_b, p_c, $p_d \ldots$; then we take the geometric average of these ten values yielding as value of the function:

$$F(\pi_b, \pi_c, \pi_d \ldots)$$

the level of the first economic tide:

$$\nu_1 = \tfrac{1}{10}F((p_{b,1}, p_{c,1}, p_{d,1} \ldots) + F(p_{b,2}, p_{c,2}, p_{d,2} \ldots) + \cdots$$
$$+ F(p_{b,10}, p_{c,10}, p_{d,10} \ldots))$$

Then above and under the line $1 - x$ the points corresponding to the values:

$$\frac{F(p_{b,1}, p_{c,1}, p_{d,1} \ldots)}{\nu_1}$$
$$\frac{F(p_{b,2}, p_{c,2}, p_{d,2} \ldots)}{\nu_1}$$
$$\ldots$$
$$\frac{F(p_{b,10}, p_{c,10}, p_{d,10} \ldots)}{\nu_1}$$

presented in the first columns of the tables are marked. Similarly the points corresponding to the values:

[139]

$$\frac{F(p_{b,11}, p_{c,11}, p_{d,11} \ldots)}{\nu_1}$$
$$\frac{F(p_{b,12}, p_{c,12}, p_{d,12} \ldots)}{\nu_1}$$
$$\ldots$$
$$\frac{F(p_{b,20}, p_{c,20}, p_{d,20} \ldots)}{\nu_1}$$

presented in the second columns of the tables are marked; the same for the other forty points of the curve.

This done, the problem to solve is simple: it consists of leaving curves ABCDE and GHIKL their undulating movement while stopping for one the falling movement and for the other the rising movement. Below we present an indication of how to proceed in either case.

Fall in the average level of the economic tide; introduction of regulating token

34. Taking the arithmetic average of the values in the second column in Table 6.1, we have the ratio ν_2/ν_1 of the level of the second tide compared with the first. Since this ratio is, by hypothesis, less than 1, we increase the total quantity of the money commodity in the proportion ν_1/ν_2, by the introduction of regulating token; consequently, the amount of money in circulation is increased. Hence, the function values:

$$\frac{F(p_{b,21}, p_{c,21}, p_{d,21} \ldots)}{\nu_1}$$

$$\frac{F(p_{b,22}, p_{c,22}, p_{d,22} \ldots)}{\nu_1}$$

$$\ldots$$

$$\frac{F(p_{b,29}, p_{c,29}, p_{d,29} \ldots)}{\nu_1}$$

Table 6.1 Falling average price level

(1)		*(2)*		*(3)*			*(4)*		
1	0.99	11	0.94	20	0.90/0.94 =	0.9550	29	0.82/0.86 =	0.9533
2	0.96	12	0.88	21	0.85	0.9042	30	0.83	0.9652
3	0.95	13	0.90	22	0.82	0.8723	31	0.78	0.9070
4	0.96	14	0.85	23	0.85	0.9042	32	0.75	0.8721
5	0.97	15	0.93	24	0.84	0.8936	33	0.71	0.8256
6	1.00	16	1.03	25	0.86	0.9150	34	0.70	0.8140
7	1.04	17	1.00	26	0.89	0.9476	35	0.76	0.8838
8	1.07	18	1.01	27	0.92	0.9787	36	0.78	0.9070
9	1.05	19	0.96	28	0.89	0.9467	37	0.82	0.9535
10	1.01	20	0.90	29	0.82	0.8723	38	0.83	0.9652
							39	0.82	0.9535
							40	0.80	0.9303
$\nu_1/\nu_1 = 1$		$\nu_2/\nu_1 = 0.94$		$\nu_3/\nu_1 = 0.86$		$\nu_3/\nu_2 = 0.9150$	$\nu_4/\nu_1 = 0.78$		$\nu_4/\nu_3 = 0.9070$

[140] take on, for reason of this first addition of regulating token, values:

$$\frac{F(p_{b,21}, p_{c,21}, p_{d,21} \ldots)}{\nu_2}$$

$$\frac{F(p_{b,22}, p_{c,22}, p_{d,22} \ldots)}{\nu_2}$$

$$\ldots$$

$$\frac{F(p_{b,29}, p_{c,29}, p_{d,29} \ldots)}{\nu_2}$$

presented on the right-hand side of the third column of the table; this means that section CD of the curve has been replaced by C′D′. Taking the arithmetic average of the values in question, we get the ratio ν_3/ν_2 of the level of the third tide to that of the second. Since this ratio is again, by hypothesis, less than 1, the total quantity of the money commodity is increased once more, now in the proportion ν_2/ν_3, by introducing regulating token; thus the amount of money in circulation, already augmented in the ratio ν_1 to ν_2, increases further. Hence the functions:

$$\frac{F(p_{b,30}, p_{c,30}, p_{d,30} \ldots)}{\nu_1}$$

$$\frac{F(p_{b,31}, p_{c,31}, p_{d,31} \ldots)}{\nu_1}$$

$$\ldots$$

$$\frac{F(p_{b,40}, p_{c,40}, p_{d,40} \ldots)}{\nu_1}$$

take on, for reason of this second addition of regulating token, values:

$$\frac{F(p_{b,30}, p_{c,30}, p_{d,30} \ldots)}{\nu_3}$$

[141]
$$\frac{F(p_{b,31}, p_{c,31}, p_{d,31} \ldots)}{\nu_3}$$

$$\ldots$$

$$\frac{F(p_{b,40}, p_{c,40}, p_{d,40} \ldots)}{\nu_3}$$

presented on the right-hand side of the fourth column of the table; this means that section DE of the curve has been replaced by D″ E′, and so forth. We have supposed that the augmentation in the quantity of money in circulation took place suddenly and that its effect was instantaneous. If we now suppose that the increase is spread over two years, or that its effect will be fully felt only after two years, lines Cc, D′d will be substituted for lines CC′c, D′D″d, so that finally curve ABCDE will be replaced by curve ABCcD′dE′.

[142] *Rise in the average level of the tide; withdrawal of regulating token*

35. Proceeding exactly analogously, that is to say similarly, with the exception that, instead of increasing the amount of money in circulation at the time of reflux by introducing regulating token, it is decreased at the time of flux by withdrawing regulating token, and instead of supposing that the operation will be accomplished within two years, or its effect felt only after two years have passed, we suppose it spread over three years or its effect felt only after three years have gone by; curve GHIKL [of Figure 6.2, derived from Table 6.2] can then be replaced by curve GHIiK′kL′.

Rules to observe

36. The success of this regularization of the value of money by the introduction and withdrawal of regulating token supposes two conditions that should be confirmed by experimental statistics: (1) the undulating movement (temporary fluctuation) of the curve of the **[143]** variation in the money price of social wealth must be sufficiently regular in order to distinguish flood, high tide, ebb and low tide; (2) the movement of rise or fall (permanent fluctuation) of the curve should be sufficiently long, in general, to distinguish several consecutive tides. Under these conditions it is obvious that the rise and fall in the tide level are roughly counterbalanced by the correction relating to the rise or fall in the preceding tide level and that the value of money will be sufficiently stationary during the whole course of permanent fluctuation, only increasing

Table 6.2 Increasing average price level

(1)		*(2)*		*(3)*			*(4)*		
1	0.99	11	0.98	20	1.15/1.08 =	1.0649	31	1.22/1.18 =	1.0337
2	1.02	12	1.05	21	1.17	1.0834	32	1.23	1.0421
3	1.06	13	1.18	22	1.19	1.1019	33	1.26	1.0675
4	1.05	14	1.14	23	1.22	1.1297	34	1.31	1.1099
5	1.06	15	1.03	24	1.22	1.1297	35	1.36	1.1523
6	1.00	16	1.10	25	1.19	1.1019	36	1.41	1.1946
7	0.97	17	1.06	26	1.18	1.0926	37	1.31	1.1099
8	0.94	18	1.04	27	1.15	1.0649	38	1.30	1.1014
9	0.95	19	1.07	28	1.13	1.0463	39	1.25	1.0591
10	0.96	20	1.15	29	1.13	1.0463	40	1.27	1.0760
				30	1.18	1.0926			
				31	1.22	1.1297			
$v_1/v_1 = 1$		$v_2/v_1 = 1.08$		$v_3/v_1 = 1.18$		$v_3/v_2 = 1.0926$	$v_4/v_1 = 1.30$		$v_4/v_3 = 1.1014$

or decreasing during the course of the first temporary fluctuation. That is why in our Figure 6.1 the descent of the curve will be felt only from B to C and its horizontality will be assured from C to E′; and in our Figure 6.2 the rise of the curve will be felt only from H to I and its horizontality will be assured from I to L′. Presently the system will certainly seem just as primitive as the first spinning jenny or the first sewing machine seemed, but practice will introduce all kinds of improvements into the system (if feasible). Under the reservation of these future improvements, I venture to formulate the following rules that should be observed.

The system should be inaugurated [i.e. put into practice for the first time] *during a permanent movement of descent and not of ascent, that is to say, by introducing regulating token and not by withdrawing it.* This enables the State to make a profit by means of which it may conveniently cover later losses, instead of suffering losses that are difficult to cover by future profits.

Let the introduction of regulating token take place at the time of ebb, i.e. of recession, when prices fall and money is in great demand for settlements and liquidations, in short, at the time when the Bank of England requested and obtained the suspension of the 1844 Act[vii] and issued **[144]** paper money to remedy the momentary lack of metallic money. On the other hand, *let the withdrawal of regulating token take place at a time of flood*, that is to say, of recovery in business, when prices increase, and let credit compensate amply for money.

The introduction or withdrawal of regulating token should be brought about in exactly inverse proportion to the rise or fall of the last tide's level compared with the level of the preceding tide, so that during the course of any tide prices will not be higher or lower, in relation to the initial prices, than because of circumstances relating to this tide, correction made for the circumstances relating to all preceding tides.

Regulating silver token should be introduced only if there is reason to believe that the fall in prices will continue, and withdrawn only if there is reason to believe that the rise in prices will continue; if in doubt, wait for the flood that will follow the ebb tide; this is to avoid magnifying, instead of restricting, the rising or falling movement of the curve by introducing regulating token on the eve of a price rise or withdrawing it on the eve of a fall in prices.

IV The monetary quadriga

Change in the legal bimetallic ratio

37. It is quite obvious that continual withdrawing of regulating token will lead to gold monometallism and that the continual addition of regulating token will lead to bimetallism and silver monometallism. Could we nowadays return from gold monometallism, from bimetallism or from silver monometallism to the system

of the regulating token? To answer this question, we should first determine how far the legal ratio of the value of gold and silver affects bimetallism.

Monometallists often put an argument to bimetallists **[145]** that they grace with the name 'reduction to absurdity':

> Your ratio of $15\frac{1}{2}$ is arbitrary; instead of $15\frac{1}{2}$, the legislator might have said 20, or $36\frac{1}{4}$, or 10, or $3\frac{3}{4}$ ... Now it is absurd to maintain that the legislator may establish any ratio of value at all between gold and silver.

This argument can only be rather strong against those bimetallists who, indeed, seem too eager to believe that this arbitrary legal ratio, once announced, will be established immediately and maintained in perpetuity. However, it suffices to know that bimetallism may fade sometimes into gold monometallism, sometimes silver monometallism, to refute the monometallists' argument in the following terms:

> The legislator may undoubtedly announce an arbitrary ratio of value between gold and silver; but what he cannot do is ensure that this ratio is kept up, or even that it will become established if it deviates too for from a certain value in line with the actual circumstances. If this legal value were too high, i.e. too much to the advantage of gold, then all silver would remain in the form of merchandise and, in fact, the legislator would decree gold monometallism; if it were too low, i.e. too much to the advantage of silver, then gold would remain in the form of merchandise and, in fact, the legislator would have decreed silver monometallism.

It will be instructive to demonstrate this graphically.

Figure 5.1 [p. 91 above] was constructed in the following way. *Time*, i.e. the years, is counted along horizontal axis O–45. The *quantities* of silver corresponding to each time, and evaluated in 5 g 9/10 francs, are counted along vertical axis Oq and the parallels to that axis; they vary according to curve AA_{45}. The *quantities* of gold corresponding to each time, and calculated in $5/10 = 0.5$ g 9/10 francs, are counted along the vertical axis Oq' and the parallels to that axis; they vary according to the curve BB_{45}. Finally, curve $A'A'_{45}$ divides the quantities of silver into silver francs as a commodity and silver francs as money, and curve $B'B'_{45}$ divides the quantities **[146]** of gold into gold francs as money and gold francs as a commodity, so that the quantities of money are represented by the lengths contained between the two curves $A'A'_{45}$ and $B'B'_{45}$. Figure 6.3 was constructed the same way, but under the hypotheses of a legal ratio $\omega = 5$, that is to say that here the quantities of gold, calculated in $5/5 = 1$ g of 9/10 francs, are 50 per cent weaker than in the preceding figure. The respective quantities of silver and gold as merchandise and as money are indicated [i.e. divided] by curves $A'A'_{45}$ and 18–40.

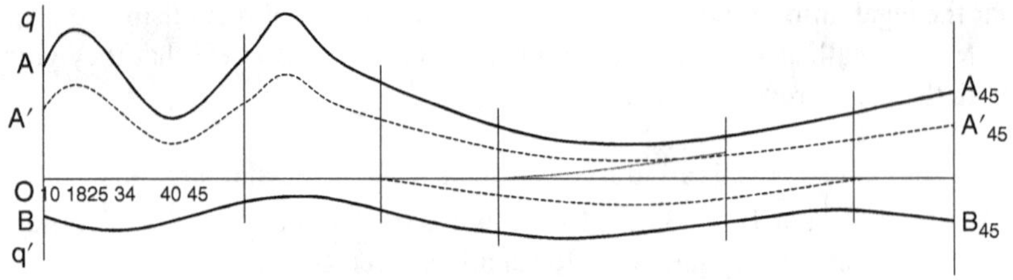

Figure 6.3 Prices of the gold and silver franc measured in some commodity ($\omega = 5$).

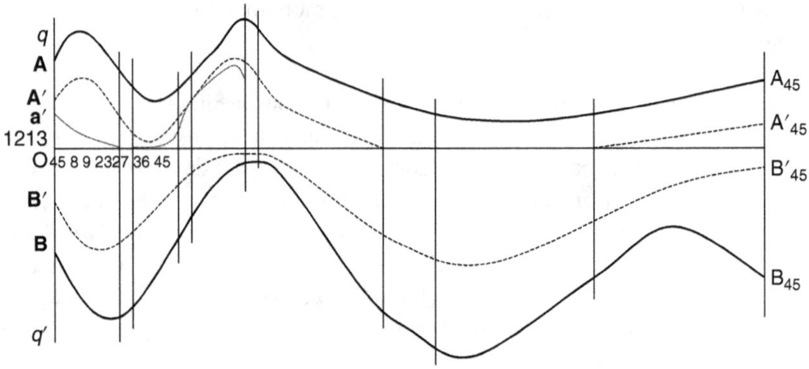

Figure 6.4 Prices of the gold and silver franc measured in some commodity ($\omega = 15$).

Figure 6.4 was also constructed the same way as Figure 5.1, but under the hypotheses of a legal ratio of $\omega = 15$, that is to say that now the amounts of gold, calculated in $5/15 = \frac{1}{3}$ g of 9/10 francs, are 50 per cent higher than in Figure 5.1. The respective quantities of silver and gold as merchandise and as money are indicated by curves $A'A'_{45}$ and $B'B'_{45}$. It can immediately be seen that, just as it should be, appreciated metal tends more and more to take the form of money, and depreciated metal tends to keep the form of a commodity. In Figure 5.1 both metals played more or less the same role in monetary circulation; in Figure 6.3 silver does not go out of circulation, while gold appears only during years 19–40; in Figure 6.4 it is gold that does not go out of circulation, whereas silver appears only during years 1–23 and 37–45. No doubt a ratio lower than 5 would have driven gold out completely and a ratio higher than 15 would have driven silver out just as completely.

Return from monometallism to bimetallism
Return from gold monometallism and bimetallism to regulating token

38. From this it follows that, when bimetallism has turned into gold monometallism, it may be taken up again either after a certain time without changing the legal ratio, if the quantity of gold happens to fall and that of silver to rise, or immediately by means of a lower legal ratio. That, for example, is how **[147]** bimetallism was restored during years 24–36 by substituting the ratio 5 for 15. From this it follows that, when bimetallism is transformed into silver monometallism, it may be restored either after a certain time without changing the legal ratio, if the quantity of silver happens to fall and that of gold to rise, or immediately by means of a lower legal ratio, and that, for example, is how bimetallism would be restored during years 1–12 by substituting the ratio 15 for 5. From this it also follows that, when the system of the regulating token is transformed into gold monometallism, it may similarly be restored either after a certain time without changing the legal ratio, if the quantity of gold happens to fall without changing that of silver, or immediately by means of a lower legal ratio, and that, for example, is how in year 28 [Figure 6.4] the system of the regulating token could be restored by limited minting of silver money by the State at the rate of 5, instead of substituting the [legal] ratio of 5 for 15, and leaving it to the private individuals to coin silver at that rate as much they liked.

It is possible to return from bimetallism to the regulating token when the quantity of gold increases without a decrease in the quantity of silver, while limiting the coinage of silver. This may likewise happen when the quantity of gold decreases but the quantity of silver increases in a more considerable proportion. Care should only be taken in this case not to fall abruptly into silver monometallism; it would be better to end up there smoothly, via bimetallism. It is obviously impossible to go directly back from silver monometallism to regulating token: the path should be through bimetallism, with the result that bimetallism should in the first place be considered as an intermediate system between regulating token and silver monometallism (abstraction being made from the exceptional case where the variations in the quantities of both metals exactly compensate).

[148] ***All four systems should be used***

39. The final result of all this study is that the greatest possible stability of prices cannot be obtained by seeking it in any one of these four systems – gold monometallism, silver monometallism, bimetallism, regulating token, or any other – but only by making alternating use of all four. The four systems may be imagined as ranked in the following order, from high to low in our figures: silver monometallism → bimetallism → regulating token → gold monometallism.

While starting from one of the two middle systems, care should be taken to be guided by circumstances in one or the other direction to one of the two extremes, with or without changing the legal ratio of the value of the two metals, acting like the driver of a coach and four, or, even better, like one of those bareback circus riders straddling four horses at a time and leaping from the one to the other. I will elucidate this by means of Figures 6.3 and 6.4, setting aside variations in the utility of the precious metals, the variation of their quantities only being taken into account; what is more, I am now going to suppose that the horizontal units represent the decades of the economic tide, instead of years.

At the beginning of period 1, we are under the regime of regulating token. The amount of gold francs as money is represented by OB′ (Figure 6.4); the amount of silver francs as money is limited to Oα'; it would have been represented by OA′ if coining were free on the basis of a ratio of 15. At the end of period 4 the system of the regulating token fades into gold monometallism because of the increase in the quantity of gold. During period 5 gold monometallism rules the roost. Because of the fall in the quantity of gold at the beginning of period 6, regulating token may be preferred to gold monometallism, without changing the legal ratio. **[149]** At the end of period 8 regulating token turns into bimetallism, because the rise in the quantity of silver is greater than the fall in the quantity of gold. During period 9 bimetallism rules. At the beginning of period 10, due to an increase in the quantity of silver more significant than the decrease in the quantity of gold, it would be possible to return from bimetallism to regulating token, but beware of falling abruptly into it instead of smoothly arriving as was the case at the end of period 12. During period 13 silver monometallism is the regime. At the beginning of period 14 it is possible to return from silver monometallism to bimetallism without changing the legal ratio because of the decrease in the quantity of silver and the increase in the quantity of gold. At the end of period 23 bimetallism fades into gold monometallism because of the continual decrease in the quantity of silver and the continual increase in the quantity of gold. From the beginning of period 24 until the end of period 27 gold monometallism reigns. Because of the decrease in the quantity of gold at the beginning of period 28, it would be possible to go back from gold monometallism to bimetallism by reducing the legal ratio from 15 to 5. Regulating token might then be reached by resuming, at a rate of 5, the restricted coining of silver (Figure 6.3). From the beginning of period 28 up to the end of period 34 regulating token again reigns but then fades into bimetallism because of the decrease in the quantity of gold and the increase in the quantity of silver. The same causes make bimetallism fade into silver monometallism at the end of period 40, which lasts from the beginning of period 41 up to the end of period 45.

In this way all variations in the quantities of both precious metals would have been remedied, except the increase in the quantity of gold in the case of gold monometallism or the increase in the quantity of silver in the case of **[150]** silver monometallism or, finally, the simultaneous decrease in the quantity of gold and silver in the case of bimetallism. On reflection, already, it must be admitted that it is impossible to guard against the first two contingencies by maintaining the condition that the value of money must be no higher than its value as merchandise. Whichever of these contingencies presents itself, increases in the prices of the products must therefore be accepted while allowing equilibrium to be re-established by increases in the prices of the productive services. The State could encourage this re-establishment of equilibrium by raising the salaries of all its civil servants and employees in a proportion that would serve as a basis for raising all wages, rents and profits. As far as the third contingency is concerned, that of a simultaneous fall in the quantity of silver and the quantity of gold in the case of bimetallism, it would not be difficult to fend it off by an issue of a certain quantity of paper money made by the State under the same conditions as those of the regulating token.[5] It is understood that in this combination, as well as under regulating token, issuing banknotes would be either prohibited or limited. Thus the management of the monetary quadriga, although not achieving absolute stability in money prices, would realize the greatest possible stability.

At present the regulating token must be kept, while inclining to bimetallism

40. Let us return to the present state of affairs. I hope that for all readers who have followed me thus far the present monetary question will be as clear as it is to **[151]** me. Nowadays the quantity of gold tends to diminish and the quantity of silver to increase. So the most favourable situation we could wish for would be under the regime of the regulating token with the possibility of putting more of the token into circulation. Now this situation is exactly the case of the Latin Union, Germany and the United States. England is opening its eyes and finally understands that the growing appreciation of gold, together with the growing depreciation of silver, will ruin its industry and throw its economic relations with India off balance. Consequently, England and India will have to adopt the system of regulating token, and then all the great monetary powers will have to head towards bimetallism as long as necessary to maintain the prices. In heaven's name, however, let them not commit the enormous stupidity of rushing blindly in it, making prices increase abruptly, followed by an equally sudden price drop. This would put them completely at the mercy of a decrease in the quantity of silver replacing its increase. The only result would be to put

5 One could also react upon these contingencies in having the mines controlled by the various States, which would suspend or resume their operation according to international agreements depending on whether the money is going to become abundant or to become scarce. In justification of this measure it would suffice to establish that the use of the precious metals as merchandise should be to subordinate their use as money, which would be easy enough.

some speculators in the way of making profits that could easily be reserved for the State. True, to make the system of the monetary quadruple function more or less universally, an international ratio between the values of the two metals should undoubtedly be set up. In conclusion I return to the domain of statistics, from which I have distanced myself somewhat in this section, to note that it is up to that science to set the ratio at the most suitable figure and modify it when necessary.

[153] Note
On the 'theory of quantity'[viii]

The prevailing idea developed in my *Théorie de monnaie*, i.e. regulating price variations by regulating the quantity of money, has not been accepted any more favourably in France than the idea of applying mathematics to economics; but, just as the latter did, it has had the good fortune to find an immediate response abroad, in particular in America, where Messrs Benjamin Andrews,[ix] E. A. Ross,[x] John R. Commons,[xi] L. S. Merriam,[xii] J. B. Clark,[xiii] J. A. Smith[xiv] and others have studied the question of a 'standard of deferred payments', of an 'elastic currency', of a 'multiple money standard' in numerous memoirs and articles published in the *Publications of the American Economic Association*, in the *Annals of the American Academy of Political and Social Science* and in various other journals, just as I did.

These publications have not yet yielded positive results, which is not surprising, since America has more urgent things to do concerning money than introduce 'regulating money': it has to get rid of its 'unorganized money'. For both operations a rigorous theory of money is needed and it is gratifying to note that leading American economists,[xv] who already know the theory of the 'final degree of utility', know the 'quantity theory', too; they disagree only about some nuances regarding presentation. I am convinced that these slight differences of opinion can be bridged only by the mathematical method, which I am going to use once more in order to connect the theory of quantity with that of *rareté* so that the latter would have to be overthrown before the former is allowed to be denied.[xvi] We therefore have to emphasize the notion of *final degree of utility, intensity of the last want satisfied* or *rareté* of money. This permits us to develop the notion of desired cash balance straightforwardly.

[154] Let Q_a be the quantity of (A) at a certain time; (A) is already *numéraire*, but not yet money. Let i be the rate of interest and let $\alpha, \beta, \gamma, \delta \ldots$ be quantities of (A), (B), (C), (D) ... producers and consumers wish to buy, at the rate of interest i, with a view to maintaining their fixed and circulating capital; let $p_b, p_c, p_d \ldots$ be the current equilibrium prices of (B), (C), (D) ... in (A). Consequently, $\alpha + \beta p_b + \gamma p_c + \delta p_d$ is then the *desired cash balance*, or the quantity of (A) as money that has to be added to the quantity Q_a of (A) as merchandise to combine equilibrium of circulation and exchange.

Let n be the ratio of that total quantity of (A) as merchandise and as money to the existing quantity Q_a, in conformity with the formula:

$$Q_a + \alpha + \beta p_b + \gamma p_c + \delta p_d + \cdots = nQ_a$$

It has been proved[xvii] that, theoretically and in practice, equilibrium of circulation can be established by a division of prices p_b, p_c, p_d ... by n and by splitting up Q_a into a quantity:

$$Q'_a = \frac{Q_a}{n}$$

of (A) as merchandise and a quantity:

$$Q''_a = \frac{\alpha}{n} + \beta\frac{p_b}{n} + \gamma\frac{p_c}{n} + \delta\frac{p_d}{n} + \cdots \tag{1}$$

as money. Equation [1] expresses then equality of supply and demand of money, that is to say, equality of its quantity to the desired cash balance.

By virtue of the theory of the *rareté* this equation can be put into the form:[xviii]

$$Q''_a = \frac{\alpha}{n} + \beta\frac{R_b}{nR_a} + \gamma\frac{R_c}{nR_a} + \delta\frac{R_d}{nR_a} + \cdots$$
$$= \frac{(\alpha/n)nR_a + \beta R_b + \gamma R_c + \delta R_d + \cdots}{nR_a}$$

From this we derive:

$$nR_a = \frac{\alpha R_a + \beta R_b + \gamma R_c + \delta R_d + \cdots}{Q''_a}$$

[155] α, β, γ, δ ... are decreasing functions of the rate of interest i. If we suppose i to be given at a certain time, we may suppose α, β, γ, δ ... as given and consider $\alpha R_a + \beta R_b + \gamma R_c + \delta R_d + \cdots$ as a constant ν_a. We have then:

$$nR_a = \frac{\nu_a}{Q''_a} \tag{2}$$

nR_a is the *rareté* of (A) as merchandise; thus in general we may consider ν_a/Q''_a as the '*rareté* of (A) as money', in equilibrium necessarily equal to the former. Simple inspection of equation [2], which expresses this equality, suffices to show that: *the* rareté *and, consequently, the value of money are inversely proportional to its quantity.*

For (A) as merchandise we have approximately:[xix]

$$nR_a = \frac{u_a}{Q'_a} \tag{3}$$

Regarding (A) both as merchandise and money, we then have:

$$nR_a(Q'_a + Q''_a) = u_a + v_a$$

Hence:

$$nR_a = \frac{u_a + v_a}{Q_a} \tag{4}$$

which shows that: *the* rareté *and, consequently, the value of the money commodity is roughly in inverse proportion to its quantity*. This is, strictly speaking, the exact formulation of what is known as the law of quantity.

Equation [1] proves adequately that: *the money prices of the commodities are proportional to the quantity of money*. From this it follows that: *the amount of all or a part of social wealth evaluated in money is proportional to the quantity of money*. From this proposition we can derive an interesting and useful corollary.

When there is already metallic money but not yet paper money, let:

[156] $$s = \frac{a}{n} + b\frac{p_b}{n} + c\frac{p_c}{n} + d\frac{p_d}{n} + \cdots$$

be the well defined part of social wealth evaluated in money and represented by receipts, and let this become the amount of paper money. Q_a will then, instead of being divided into Q'_a and Q''_a, be divided into Q'''_a and Q^{iv}_a.

The prices p_b, p_c, $p_d \ldots$, instead of becoming p_b/n, p_c/n, $p_d/n \ldots$, will become p_b/n', p_c/n', $p_d/n' \ldots$ and the amount of paper money will be:

$$s' = \frac{a}{n'} + b\frac{p_b}{n'} + c\frac{p_c}{n'} + d\frac{p_d}{n'} + \cdots \tag{5}$$

By virtue of the theory of *rareté* one can easily find:

$$s' = \frac{a}{n'} + b\frac{R_b}{n'R_a} + c\frac{R_c}{n'R_a} + d\frac{R_d}{n'R_a} + \cdots$$
$$= \frac{aR_a + bR_b + cR_c + dR_d + \cdots}{n'R_a}$$

Considering $aR_a + bR_b + cR_c + dR_d + \cdots$ as a constant v'_a, we have:

$$s'n'R_a = v'_a$$

Moreover, we have by virtue of equation [2]:

$$n'R_a(Q_a^{iv} + s') = v_a$$

Hence:

$$n'R_a Q_a^{iv} + n'R_a s' = v_a$$

Consequently, we have:

$$n'R_a Q_a^{iv} = v_a - v'_a$$

and:

$$s' = \frac{v'_a}{v_a - v'_a} Q_a^{iv} \tag{6}$$

This shows explicitly that: *the amount of paper money spontaneously becomes proportional to the quantity of metallic money.*

[157] We know[xx] that the effect of compensations is a conversion of the desired cash balance in metallic money and paper money in a certain proportion. If we had taken account of this, we would have had, by virtue of equation [2]:

$$n'R_a(Q_a^{iv} + s') = \frac{v_a}{v}$$

and:

$$n'R_a Q_a^{iv} = \frac{v_a}{v} - v'_a$$

Moreover, we have approximately:

$$n'R_a Q_a''' = u_a$$

Hence:

$$n'R_a(Q_a^{iv} + Q_a''') = u_a + \frac{v_a}{v} - v'_a$$

or:

$$n'R_a = \frac{u_a + v_a/v - v'_a}{Q_a} \tag{7}$$

Comparing equations [4] and [7] we get:

$$\frac{n'}{n} = \frac{u_a + v_a/v - v'_a}{u_a + v_a} \tag{8}$$

From this we may conclude that $n > n'$, and that, consequently, $nR_a > n'R_a$. Further, we can conclude $p_b/n' > p_b/n, p_c/n' > p_c/n, p_d/n' > p_d/n \cdots$ Hence: *the intervention of paper money and compensations decreases the* rareté *of the money commodity and increases the prices of commodities*. But it will suffice to affirm that mathematically it follows from the inspection of equations [4] and [7] that: *both before and after intervention of paper money and compensations the* rareté *and, consequently, the value of the money merchandise is always roughly in inverse proportion to its quantity*.

[158] Economists and statisticians who have some notion of algebra[xxi] may now provide an exact account of the effect of compensations and money paper from the point of view of the 'theory of the quantity'.

The coefficient g in the formula:

$$e = \frac{gt^2}{2}$$

of the law of gravity diminishes from pole to equator and, consequently, the distance e covered diminishes. But e is always proportional to t^2, the square of time. Now in formula [4] of the law of the quantity:

$$nR_a = \frac{u_a + v_a}{Q_a}$$

which is the law of the *rareté* or of the value of money, we see likewise that compensations reduce the term v_a by dividing it by v and that paper money reduces it further by subtracting v'_a from this quotient. Consequently, nR_a, the *rareté* and the value of money, diminish but are always inversely proportional to Q_a, the quantity of money. So, when the *αγεωμετρητοι*[xxii] invoked facts stemming from the imposition of paper money and compensations for demonstrating that the value of money is not inversely proportional to its quantity, they would have done the same as if they had alleged from facts relating to the intensity of gravitation that the distance covered by a falling body is not proportional to the square of time. And when, as they do often enough, they go so far as to say that 'as far as compensation and paper money are concerned, there is no correlation at all between price and quantity of the money commodity', they still do exactly the same as amateur physicists who say that 'at the equator there is no correlation at all between the distance covered by falling bodies and the time they take to fall'.

Notes

i At this place in the manuscript of the *Theory of money* Walras crossed out the following passage:

> It will perhaps be allowed to disregard, more or less, variations in utility. Utility is a relation between the personality of man and the nature of things that are permanent elements in spite of accidental changes. The quantities of the money commodity or other commodities on the contrary, form an element that is essentially variable, which should always be taken into account.
>
> (Walras Archives, Lausanne, F. W. Vb, file 24, p. 3)

ii See above, footnotes to the introduction of the *Theory of money.*

iii Ibid.

iv In Jevons's own terms.

v Adolf Georg S. Soetbeer, *Materialen zur Erläuterung und Beurtheilung der wirtschaftlichen Edelmetalverhältnisse und der Währungsfrage*, Verein zur Wahrung der wirtschaftlichen Interessen von Handel und Gewerbe, no. 9, Berlin: Puttkammer & Mühlbrecht, October 1885. In the *Théorie de la monnaie* Walras makes use of this first edition. In the Walras Archives of Lausanne the following note by Walras can be found:

> At the end of the recent publication of Mr Ad. Soetbeer, *Materialen zur Erläuterung und Beurtheilung der wirtschaftlichen Edelmetalverhältnisse und der Währungsfrage*, a statistic of the variation of the average price of 100 commodities in the market of Hamburg during the period 1851–84 established according to the method of Jevons can be found that seems really interesting in view of the statistics in the same volume of the variation in the quantities of metallic and paper money, both as an experimental confirmation and as an indication of the practical application of my rational theories, if it had presented the average annual prices so that they take account of the economic tide. Unfortunately, this statistic only gives the average prices for the periods 1851–60, 1861–70, 1871–5, 1876–80 and 1881–4 as compared with those of the period 1847–59 as a basis. As it stands, however, this statistic gives some striking indications that should be mentioned.
>
> (F. W. Vb, file 21)

In 1886 a second edition of Soetbeer's book appeared: *Materialen zur Erläuterung und Beurtheilung der wirtschaftlichen Edelmetalverhältnisse und der Währungsfrage. Auf Veranlassung des Vereins zur Wahrung der wirtschaftlichen Interessen von Handel und Gewerbe*, Berlin: Puttkammer & Mühlbrecht, October 1886. To this book a fold-out page has been added: 'Graphische Darstellungen in Bezug auf die Silberfrage.' Walras, undoubtedly with the aid of his friend Charles Secrétin, translated chapter 7 of the second edition of the book (pp. 81–117), 'Variations de prix des merchandises en général et du pouvoir d'achat de l'or', which can be found in a notebook in the Lausanne Walras Archives (F. W. Vb, file 26, 28 pages). A French version of Soetbeer's book appeared in 1889: *Matériaux pour faciliter l'intelligence et l'examen des rapports économiques des métaux précieux et de la question monétaite. Réunis sur la demande de l'Association pour la protection des intérêts économiques du commerce et de l'industrie* (translated by F. P. S. P. Ringeisen), Paris and Nancy: Berger-Levrault, 1889.

vi Sections 33–40 can also be found in sections 395 to 402 of lesson 40 of the second edition of the *Éléments d'économie politique pure* (1889) (*OEC*, vol. VIII, pp. 472–85).

vii The 'Bank Charter Act' or 'Peel's Act', voted 19 June 1844 at the initiative of Sir Robert Peel, marks the triumph of the 'currency principle'. The Bank of England consisted of two departments, the Issue Department and the Bank Department. The Issue Department would remit an amount of notes to the Bank Department fixed at £14 million (guaranteed in principle by State certificates). It would issue notes above this amount against recompense in gold or silver (covered for 100 per cent). The Bank Department operates as a normal bank (loans, bills of exchange, etc.) but in cases of a general demand for reimbursement the other banks apply to it. Peel's Act gradually instituted the monopoly of the Bank of England of the issue of banknotes. Only these notes would have a legal rate of exchange and the volume of the notes of the joint stock banks and the country banks would be strictly limited to £8 million. Later on, during the recessions of 1847, 1857 and 1866, the British government authorized the Bank of England to exceed the provisions of the Peel Act and issue as many notes as necessary. In 1890 (the Baring recession) and in 1908 another procedure was applied: the Bank of England borrowed gold from the Banque de France, guaranteed by English bills of exchange. The Peel Act disappeared officially with the Currency and Banknotes Act of 28 February 1939.

viii On 25 October 1897 Léon Walras sent the Note sur la 'théorie de la quantité' to Henri Carter Adams (1851–1921), president of the American Economic Association, for presentation at the tenth annual meeting of the Association. On the same day also he asked Irving Fisher to have it translated into English (*Correspondence*, letter 1328). Frank William Taussig (1859–1940), the officer responsible for the Association's publications, took it upon himself to present Walras's text orally, but he found it too short for publication in the *Economic Studies* or in the Monographs (I. Fisher to L. Walras, 23 December 1897, *Correspondence*, letter 1331). The text therefore did not figure in the proceedings of the meeting, published in February 1898 in the *Economic Studies* of the AEA, nor was it published later. Walras was much irritated by this incident and he noted in his *Notes d'humeur* (*ŒEC*, p. 551):

> Consider American economists as not having understood anything of the 'Note sur la théorie de la quantité' and as incapable of understanding anything about mathematical economics because of their narrow, utilitarian minds and their deficient scientific culture.

ix E. Benjamin Andrews, 'An honest dollar', *Publications of the American Economic Association*, vol. IV, no. 6, November 1889, pp. 7–70 [401–40]. The author claims in particular (pp. 8, 36–40):

> Were money merely a medium of exchange, something to be spoken into being for each act of traffic and then annihilated, permanence in its worth could be dispensed with. However, money, besides furnishing our system of value denominations, also measures value, serves as a reservoir of value, and as a standard for deferred payments. To fulfil ideally any one of the last-named offices it must preserve its general purchasing power unchanged.
>
> . . .
>
> Are we then to despair of stability in general prices? I believe not. I am impressed with the practicability of preserving prices permanently at whatever level they

have at any time assumed, by swelling or contracting the volume of money in circulation, on some such plan as has been outlined by Professor Walras, of Lausanne. The method would involve (1) the critical, official ascertainment of the course of prices; (2) the use of some form of subsidiary full legal tender money; and (3) the injection of a portion of this into circulation or the withdrawal of a portion therefrom, according as prices had fallen or risen.

There is, of course, much labour and care involved in determining the course of prices; but the task can be accomplished, with all sufficient exactness, without excessive difficulty. Plans for a compound standard of value have been numerous. The articles composing them, it is always and justly urged, must be staples, and must be the same in kind, quality and amount at all the successive listings. There are five conditions besides these, on which stress should be laid. One is that the commodities must be taken from each of the two great classes, those subject and those not subject to the law of diminishing return, as far as possible in the proportion which each bears to the total consumption. The second is that those articles must be chosen which are the least subject to accidental and artificial fluctuations, as by customs regulations, peculiarity of seasons, weather, and the like. Thus Soetbeer is doubtless right in thinking prices in Hamburg, which till lately has been a wholly free market, somewhat more normal than those of London, even. The third is that the greater the number of staples the better, provided the just indicated requirements be adhered to. The fourth is that, as a rule, prices are to be registered in all the major markets of the country or countries whose prices are in question. In not a few cases, as wheat and standard silver, London prices would serve as well for other countries as for Great Britain. For many staples trustworthy price-records are now kept, as by the London *Economist*, and *Gazette*. For others, new or more accurate records would have to be instituted. The first special condition is that of quantity-coefficients – an arrangement by which the figures for each commodity are made to enter into the grand total a number of times in proportion to the quantity of it consumed.

At intervals, now, whether directly or index-number wise, as may be found intrinsically the more correct as well as the less subject to mistakes of calculation, the entire price-list of the articles determined on is to be added up. The geometrical, the arithmetical, or the harmonic mean may be sought. If the amount at any addition is greater than at the last, general prices have risen: money has grown cheaper, has lost in purchasing power: too much of it is in circulation: some must be withdrawn.

If, on the contrary, the amount is less than at the last summation, prices have fallen: money has grown dearer, has gained in value: too little of it is in circulation, and more must be set free or coined, to redress the balance. In a word, inflate or contract, rarefy or condense, so as to keep the footing of your great price list perpetually the same. The universally conceded equity of a composite value-standard would in this way be incorporated in the monetary system itself, and would spread to all the exchange transactions of the nation. The very knowledge of an existing purpose thus to regulate would do much to regulate.

Walras's project differs from this as follows: He would work *a priori*. He judges that the volume of commerce, the volume of money, and the relation between the two can all be so closely figured out and followed that threatened changes in general prices may be forecast and prevented. I would be less presumptuous, and apply the needed corrective in an *a posteriori* way, as I have indicated.

There is another point of some moment which Walras does not touch. It is the problem how a government would go to work to effect now the increase, now the depletion of the money in circulation. It could, manifestly, accomplish the increase by the purchase of silver and the coining of it into tokens, securing its funds for the purchase as for other outlays. The tokens would take the form of certificates and find vent in ordinary government expenditure. But how recover these certificates should there come a rise in prices? The simplest way would be by selling call bonds redeemable in silver certificates, after which the replenishing process could at any time be set in play by simply calling more or fewer of those bonds.

Léon Walras commented on a bibliographical list, preserved in the Lausanne Walras Archives (F. W. Vb, file 20), upon the reference to him by E. B. Andrews: 'citation p. 39 not exact.

x Edward Alsworth Ross, 'The standard of deferred payments', *Annals of the American Academy of Political and Social Science*, vol. III, no. 3, November 1892, pp. 37–49 [293–305]; 'The total utility standard of deferred payments', *Annals of the American Academy of Political and Social Science*, vol. IV, no. 3, November 1893, pp. 89–105 [425–41].

xi John R. Commons, 'Bullion notes and an elastic currency', *Annals of the American Academy of Political and Social Science*, vol. IV, no. 2, September 1893, pp. 99–101 [299–301]. The author states in particular:

> If these principles be true, may not the United States go further and adopt a scientific elastic system of currency, based on bullion notes? . . .
>
> The distinguished Swiss professor of political economy, Léon Walras of Lausanne, some years ago proposed a plan for an elastic currency, and substantially the same plan has been advocated by President E. Benjamin Andrews, of Brown University, one of the American delegates to the recent Brussels Conference.
>
> (Pages 99–100 [299–300])

He refers to the International Monetary Conference called on the initiative of the United States in Brussels, 22 November 1892, adjourned to 30 May 1893. In the bibliographical list mentioned above concerning E. B. Andrews Walras indicates another study by John R. Commons, 'Economic reform', published in the newspaper *The Voice* of 14 September 1893.

xii Lucius S. Merriam, 'The theory of final utility in its relation to money and the standard of deferred payments', *Annals of the American Academy of Political and Social Science*, vol. III, no. 4, January 1893, pp. 91–109 [483–501]; 'Money as a measure of value', *Annals of the American Academy of Political and Social Science*, vol. IV, no. 6, May 1894, pp. 110–13 [966–9].

xiii John Bates Clark, 'An unfinished study by Dr Merriam', *Annals of the American Academy of Political and Social Science*, vol. IV, no. 6, May 1894, pp. 113–16 [969–72]; 'The gold standard of currency in the light of recent theory', *Political Science Quarterly*, vol. X, September 1895, pp. 389–403.

xiv J. Allen Smith, 'The multiple money standard', *Annals of the American Academy of Political and Social Science*, vol. VII, no. 5, March 1895, pp. 1–60 [173–232].

xv Walras wrote in the first manuscript of the 'Note sur la "théorie de la quantité" ':

> Anyway, a theory of money that is as rigorous as possible is needed for both operations, and while reading the proceedings of the ninth annual meeting of the

American Economic Association, at Baltimore, 28–31 December 1896, I have concluded with great satisfaction that the leading American economists . . .'

(Walras Archives, Lausanne, F. W. Vb, file 20, p. 1)

xvi In the first manuscript Walras wrote:

I am convinced that only the mathematical method can make these last, slight differences of opinion cease and definitely establish the theory of quantity; and that is why I am going to make a supreme effort in the present Note to put this theory above any dispute, if possible, by: (1) founding it on the static notion of the *desired cash balance* rather than on the dynamic notion of the *circulation of goods served by money*, and (2) identifying it with the theory of *rareté* so that one would have to overthrow the latter before being allowed to deny the former.

(Walras Archives, Lausanne, F. W. Vb, file 20, p. 1)

xvii On galley proofs conserved in the Lausanne Walras Archives are to be found the following four notes: '*Note* 1. In the *Théorie de la monnaie*, 9.' '*Note* 2. Because of the relations $p_b = R_b/R_a$, $p_c = R_c/R_a$, $p_d = R_d/R_a$ . . .expressing the proportionality of the values to the *raretés* (*Théorie de la monnaie*, 7).' '*Note* 3. Supposing that the utility curve be an orthogonal hyperbole (*Théorie de la monnaie*, 9).' '*Note* 4. By the *Théorie de la monnaie*, 10.' These notes may possibly have been added with a view to publication in the United States. At this point, Walras inserted *Note* 1.

xviii At this point Walras placed *Note* 2.

xix *Note* 3.

xx *Note* 4.

xxi In the original manuscript Walras wrote in the first instance:

The only attention to pay to economists non-mathematicians is to reply to them *αγεωμτρητοι μηδειζ εισιτω* [Whoever is ignorant of geometry should not enter]; but people who have some notion of algebra may now . . .'

(Walras Archives, Lausanne, F. W. Vb, file 20, p. 6)

Plato had an inscription on the wall of his academy: 'Let nobody enter here who is not a geometer.' One may also refer to Aristotle, *Organon*, vol. IV.

xxii Person who is ignorant of geometry.

[159]

7 The monetary problem

I A note on the solution of the Anglo-Indian monetary problem[1]

The problem of organizing monetary relations between England and India on a rational basis could be solved by the system of *gold money with regulating silver token* as follows. Disregarding fractional currency for reasons of simplicity, let Q_o be the quantity of money existing in England, Q_a the quantity of money existing in India, w the present ratio of the value of gold to silver. Let us imagine that after first suspending free coinage of silver in India, a quantity x of silver from India is taken to England to play the role of regulating token as an addition to gold money, at the legal ratio of w' of the value of gold to silver, and on the other hand, a quantity y of gold from England is taken to India to play the role of money together with the remaining silver, changed into regulating token on the basis of a legal ratio w'' of the value of gold to silver. So that the value of money may be the same in England as in India, the new quantities of money and token evaluated in gold must have the same ratio as the old quantities similarly evaluated; that is to say, we must have:

$$Q_o - y + \frac{x}{w'} : \frac{Q_a - x}{w''} + y :: Q_o : \frac{Q_a}{w}$$

[160] from which we can obtain:[i]

$$x = \frac{(w - w'')Q_o Q_a + w''(wQ_o + Q_a)y}{wQ_o + (w''/w')Q_a}$$

1 Communicated to the Economics section of the British Association for the Advancement of Science (meeting in Manchester, 1887). Published in French in the *Revue d'économie politique*, November–December 1887.

It may be seen that w', w'', x and y are not quite determined and three of these four quantities may be chosen arbitrarily. Let us now suppose, just to fix our ideas, that the quantity Q_o of gold in England be 750,000 kg and that one-third of this quantity (hence y equals 250,000 kg) is to be transferred to India, where the quantity Q_a of silver is supposed to be 25 million kg. Suppose that the present ratio w of the value of gold to silver be 20. Let us further suppose that it is thought reasonable to let the regulating token in India coexist with the present rupee – ten rupees to one sovereign – so that Indian habits are not disrupted. This would bring w'' to a level of about 14.60. Finally, let us suppose that it is thought reasonable, for whatever motive, to let the regulating token in England coexist with the four-shilling coin, which has the same weight and fineness as the five-franc écu in the Latin Union. This would bring w' to about 15.36. Under these conditions, the quantity of silver to be transferred from India to England would be 6,378,500 kg.

This quantity should be broken down into two parts: one part of 2,728,500 kg transferred without compensation, and another part of 3,650,000 kg exchanged for 250,000 kg gold. The first operation could be performed through a loan taken in India by the English State, materialized in English Consols. The second operation could be performed by the issue of banknotes by the Bank of England; so gold could be obtained in India in exchange for silver. If these suppositions are accepted, and because $w' = 15.36$ is greater than $w'' = 14.60$, a heavy loss would be incurred by these two operations **[161]** since the State and the Bank would have to give 1 [kg] of gold or its equivalent for 14.60 [kg] of silver in India and 15.35 [kg] of silver for 1 [kg] of gold or its equivalent in England.

In this way the value of the rupee would rise to 2*s*. It is clear that the disadvantages of the operation would be reduced merely by raising this value to a lower level. If it were decided, for instance on a ratio of twelve rupees to a sovereign, the value of the rupee would rise to only 1*s* and 8*d*; by bringing w'' to about 17.50, x would be equal to 5,102,568 kg of which only 727,568 kg should be transferred without compensation and 4,375,000 kg in exchange for 250,000 kg of gold. These two operations would then yield a profit.

If it is considered impossible or inappropriate to transfer disposable capital from India to England, a new condition should be introduced that the value of silver imported from India to England should exactly balance the quantity of gold imported from England to India. Hence:

$$x = yw''$$

Combined with the preceding equation this yields the equation:

$$y = \frac{w'(w - w'')}{w''(w'' - w')} Q_o$$

in which there are only two quantities to be arbitrarily fixed. It may immediately be observed that w' has to be as small as possible and w'' as large as possible so that y is not too large a fraction of Q_0.[2]

[162] II The Anglo-Indian monetary problem[3]

To the editor of the *Gazette de Lausanne*

La Bugnonne, July 1893

Dear sir,

The *Gazette de Lausanne* has been kind enough to mention my name[ii] in its issue of the 10th of this month in relation to the recently published solution of the Anglo-Indian monetary problem. Therefore I am taking the liberty of sending you the following observations on a subject which I believe liable to throw light on the question of money in general and on the particular position I have taken.

Ten years ago, I completed the pure theory of money. I explained mathematically how the value of the money commodity in proportion to other commodities is established, in other words, how the money prices of commodities are determined, either in the case of a single money commodity (monometallism), or in case of two money commodities with a legal ratio of their mutual values (bimetallism). I was mathematically convinced that, *all other things being equal, an increase or a decrease in the quantity of money will give rise to a proportional increase or decrease in commodities' money prices*. I was not the first person to formulate this law. My only claim is that I have presented its scientific demonstration; and especially I have rigorously pursued its consequences in applied monetary theory and monetary politics.

At the level of applied theory it follows from the law of quantity that neither under monometallism nor under bimetallism would there be money that satisfies the essential condition as a means of exchange, namely procuring the greatest **[163]** possible price stability, or at least not complicating natural variations in the values of other commodities by variation in its own value. In fact, an increase in quantity of money metal, or the two money metals, would raise the selling prices of products above their cost prices in terms of rent, wages and interest

2 [Footnote added from the first edition of the *EPA* onwards.] I realized when drafting this *Note* that I had passed from the idea of *halting the fall* in the value of the rupee to that of *raising* this value in relation to the value of the pound sterling, augmenting the quantity of money in England and in India. I think it would have been better if I had kept to the first idea in supposing w'' as close as possible to w (for instance, by fixing the value of the rupee at 1*s* 6*d*, which means $w' = 19.50$) and, in addition, making $w' = w''$ and $x = yw''$. The operation could then be executed without capital transfer and without either benefit or loss.

3 *Gazette de Lausanne*, 24 July 1887.

and entrepreneurs/producers would make a profit, while landowners, workers and capitalists/consumers would incur losses. If this quantity decreased, selling prices of products would fall below their cost prices, to the detriment of entrepreneurs and the advantage of landowners, workers and capitalists. In both cases economic equilibrium would be upset; there would be a crisis until a new equilibrium was established. To avoid these disadvantages gold should be taken as money to settle international exchange and big national exchanges that can freely be coined; and silver should be used as a token, coined in limited quantities: *regulating* token for interior payments on a moderate scale and fractional currency for small payments. If the quantity of gold increased or decreased the quantity of regulating token would be decreased or increased in order to avoid any recession caused by a rise or a fall of prices.

From the practical point of view it follows from the law of quantity that the gold monometallists, while decreasing the quantity of money by pursuing the demonetization of silver, are preparing a crisis of falling prices for us. The bimetallists, claiming free coinage of silver until its value in gold has again attained the ratio of 1 to $15\frac{1}{2}$, which will increase the quantity of money, are exposing us to a crisis caused by rising prices. What must be done in every country is keep or adopt gold money and limit coinage of silver money with a view to using it as complementary token until it can play the role of regulating token.

These were the principles that I submitted to the international monetary conference **[164]** meeting in Paris for the prolongation of the Latin Union and published in December 1884 in the *Revue de droit international* in an article entitled 'Monnaie d'or avec billon d'argent régulateur', summarized in another article in the *Gazette de Lausanne* of 12 January 1885 under the title 'Un système rationnel de monnaie'.[iii] First, I asked for things to be called by their name, declaring gold to be the only *money*, with the franc defined as 10/31 g of gold, and declaring silver to be *token*, with coins forming fractional currency of $2\frac{1}{2}$ g, 5 g and 10 g of 835/1000 fine, of a nominal value of half a franc, one franc and two francs, and coins of 25 g of 900/1000 fine and a nominal value of five francs forming *regulating* token. Further I proposed that token should circulate only in the country of issue and should be used only as payment up to a certain amount and that the quantity of token to be issued by each Latin Union State should be determined by international conventions, fractional currency in proportion to the needs of circulation and regulating token to assure the normal variation in the value of money. The article in the *Gazette* ended as follows:

> This system, that maintains the balance between creditors and debtors, producers and consumers, should be favoured by both monometallists and bimetallists, because experience will show which is right or wrong. If, as monometallists say, gold alone suffices to serve circulation, the present amount of money, including écus, will be too great, prices will rise and the

> remaining silver écus will have to be demonetized gradually, moving gently towards gold monometallism. If, as bimetallists claim, gold and silver were both needed to serve circulation, the present amount of money, including écus, would be too small, prices would fall, the rest of the available silver would have to be coined gradually and so we should return to bimetallism. But probably the supporters of these mutually exclusive systems will insist on advising what might be called a leap in the dark; and between them the hesitant politicians will continue to trail along in the wake of circumstances.

[165] Indeed, events did occur according to these predictions. The Latin Union could not consider its silver écus as token without immediately wondering, 'Should token be admitted into international circulation?' In other words, 'Should the Latin Union States take measures from now on concerning mutual reimbursement in gold of their silver écus?' The answer to this question was too obvious to discuss. At least for the case of the dissolution of the Latin Union a clause was adopted about a limited reimbursement of écus in gold. I personally continued my studies, particularly driven by the consideration summarized as follows at the end to the preface of my *Theory of Money*:

> I am doubly interested in the question of money, because it is important and topical, and even more perhaps because it is one of the first and most decisive applications of my system of economics. This is what I think. When all is said and done, here is a point that appears at the top of the list of economic problems; our men of science and statesmen of the so-called experimental school palpably hesitate and erratically move around it. If we were lucky enough to solve it theoretically and practically through new principles, these principles would then be of use for solving all other economic and social problems both theoretically and in practice.

In this *Theory of Money*, published in 1886 and 1887, I exposed once more the principles of my system of gold money with regulating silver token, I presented an in-depth critique of the mutually opposed systems of monometallism and bimetallism and I added a detailed description of the statistical desiderata necessary to the regularization of the variation in the value of money. I concluded:

> Nowadays the quantity of gold tends to diminish and the quantity of silver to increase. So the most favourable situation we could wish would be under the regime of the regulating token with the possibility of putting more of this token into circulation. Now this situation is exactly the case of the Latin Union, Germany and the United States. England is opening its **[166]** eyes and finally understands that the growing appreciation of gold, together with the growing depreciation of silver, will ruin its industry and throw

> its economic relations with India off balance. Consequently, England and India will have to adopt the system of regulating token, and then all the great monetary powers will have to head towards bimetallism as long as necessary to maintain the prices.

Subsequently, in the summer of 1887, I was invited to participate in the conference of the British Association for the Advancement of Science in Manchester. Unable to accept the invitation, I drafted a 'Note sur la solution du problème monétaire anglo-indien' that was translated into English by my colleague Professor Foxwell for presentation to the conference in September, and which was included in the proceedings.[iv] In that note I proposed, first, to suspend the coinage of silver in India and then to make a token of all silver money in India by attributing to the rupee a nominal value in sovereigns and shillings and, subsequently, to transport on one hand part of the silver from India to England to make it regulating token in addition to gold money. On the other hand, I proposed to transport a certain quantity of gold from England to India to play the role of money in addition to the silver transformed into regulating token. I provided a formula for the respective quantities of gold and silver to exchange between England and India so that the value of money in both countries would remain the same as before the operation and applied this formula to two assumptions: a ratio of ten rupees to a sovereign, which would increase the value of the rupee to 2*s* or 24*d*, and a ratio of twelve rupees to a sovereign, which would raise the value of the rupee to 1*s* and 8*d*, or 20*d*. Now what is happening today? Free coinage of silver in India has been suspended and silver money in India has been made a token with a nominal value in sovereigns and shillings. The ratio of twelve rupees to a sovereign has been considered, which would have fixed the value of the rupee **[167]** at 1*s* and 8*d*, or 20*d*, but it was eventually fixed at fifteen rupees to a sovereign, which keeps the value of the rupee down at 1*s* and 4*d*, or 16*d*. The creation of effective gold money in India has been postponed although that would permit it to pay other countries the excess of its imports over its exports if necessary.

Apart from the fact that providing India with real money has been postponed, the conformity of the measures taken with my propositions is obvious. It also seems to me that from now on the monetary regime all over the world has been fixed according to our views. Absolute monometallism and unconditional bimetallism are out. Demonetization of the present stock of silver money will not be immediate, nor will free access be given to the Mints for silver on the universal base of $15\frac{1}{2}$ as the ratio of the value of gold money to that of silver money. But if the quantity of gold should increase, as it seems to be doing at present because of [South] African production, nothing will prevent nations willing to bear the expense of the operation from shifting gradually to a gold standard by demonetizing silver token; and, on the other hand, should this quantity of gold diminish because of a slow-down in production, the real value of silver would have to be closer to its nominal value by minting growing quantities of regulating token all over the place. Are these not exactly the terms of the article in the *Gazette* dated 12 January 1885? I shall not insist on this point for the time being, but will restrict myself to noting that because of my method and the principles of pure economics I have been able to indicate, from 1884–5 onwards, the monetary ideal to be pursued and expose the exact points of action conductive to the direction indicated by the theory in 1887.

Yours faithfully, Léon Walras

[168] III The monetary problem in Europe and the United States[4]

Recently I received a volume published in the normal way of official documents of the American administration, containing an English translation of the well known book *L'Avenir de l'argent* by Edouard Suess. Mr Suess is Professor of Geology at the University of Vienna, Vice-president of the Academy of Science in Vienna, Member of the Austrian Parliament, etc. The Financial Committee of the US Senate has published this translation of his book with his authorization.[v] It is preceded by a preface specially written for the occasion, case and I think it worth while to translate it as literally as possible.[vi]

Preface to the American edition

> Seven years after the introduction of the gold standard in Germany, which gave rise to so important movements, I published, in 1877, a small work *The Future of Gold*,[5] wherein I tried to show that from geologic indications we must expect in the future a scarcity of gold and an abundance of silver and that the extension of the gold standard to all civilized states is impossible.
>
> The work *The Future of Silver*,[6] which now earns the distinction of being published in the English language through the Finance Committee of the United States Senate, appeared in the spring of 1892, when the deliberations concerning the introduction of the gold standard in Austria-Hungary began. In the meantime many of the statements I had made in 1877 had been verified. The production of gold, owing to the exhaustion of rich fields, had fallen for several years; afterward, indeed, owing to the discovery of the Transvaal fields, it had once more risen, but in the same time an extraordinary increase of the consumption of gold by industry

4 *Gazette de Lausanne*, 27 February 1894.

5 [Eduard Suess] *Die Zukunft des Goldes*, Vienna und Leipzig [Wilhelm Braumüller, 1877]

6 [Eduard Suess] *Die Zukunft des Silbers*, Vienna and Leipzig [Wilhelm Braumüller, 1892].

had occurred. Simultaneously there was noted an increase in the silver production, **[169]** despite the falling price of silver, an increase which was mainly due to improvements in metallurgic processes. Argentina, Brazil, Portugal, Spain, Italy, Greece, amid vicissitudes of diverse nature, had lost their metallic circulation wholly or in part; nay even, in 1890, a time came when the strength of the Bank of England was not by itself equal to the emergency.

Under these circumstances many of my friends and myself were of opinion that Austria-Hungary, in order to guard herself against all contingencies, ought indeed gradually to acquire a moderate amount of gold, but ought neither to proclaim a gold standard nor establish a definitive ratio between the silver florin and the gold coin.

Our government[vii] went further than we deemed advisable.

Meantime, in the beginning of 1992, the last great work of Ad, Soetbeer on this subject (*Literaturnachweis über Geld- und Münzwesen*)[viii] had appeared, in which (for example, pp. 285, 291) some of the arguments advanced against the exclusive gold standard are conceded. Mr Soetbeer also honoured me with letters in which he expressed his misgivings at the course of affairs and at the appreciation of gold. He regarded the endeavours of the bimetallists as impracticable because of England's attitude, if for no other reason; but he was convinced that some measure must be adopted to check the fall of silver. On July 30 and 31, 1892, I had the pleasure of spending two memorable days at his house at Göttingen. On August 5 he sent out a memorandum containing his propositions. In their essential features these propositions required indeed the recognition of gold as the sole standard, but no state was to keep in circulation gold coins of less than twenty francs, twenty marks, one sovereign, or $10, nor any credit note below that value. The principal silver coins were to be produced at a higher ratio than $15\frac{1}{2}$; every government was to receive its own principal silver coins in payment to any amount, while the legal tender quality of these coins for private payments was to extend three times the amount of the gold coin (for example, to sixty francs). Fully covered certificates were to be issued on silver, but no credit notes.

As regards thee ratio at which the principal silver coins were to be recoined, Dr Soetbeer's views were not settled. In his last letter to me, dated October 7, 1892, he mentioned 22 : 1; Shortly after, on **[170]** October 23, this excellent man, with his wealth of experience, departed from among us, in the seventy-eighth year of his life.

How the international congress rejected all propositions; how, in the year 1893, events developed with overwhelming rapidity, it is not now my purpose to relate. Soetbeer indicated that the effect of his propositions would be but transient, yet he saw no possibility of more radical measures. For a number of years, on the basis of geologic experience, the world has

> been warned that its entire monetary system is drifting toward an abyss. During the past years we have approached close to its edge.
>
> E. Suess, Vienna, Austria, 1 October 1893

I have long entirely agreed with Professor Suess's vision of the future of silver and gold. Already, in 1886, I had expressed this as follows in the second part of my *Theory of Money*, entitled 'Critical discussion of the systems':

> The first is the system of the *single gold standard*, or *gold monometallism*. In this system, only gold is both the *numéraire* and money. The utility of gold as merchandise increases incessantly with the development of the population. Note, moreover, that, among all wants that form this utility, some can be satisfied only by the consumption of the commodity itself and not its service alone. The utility of gold as money also increases with the development of business. Does the quantity of gold increase in proportion, however? Far from it! The only gold ore that may quite advantageously be exploited is that which nature took the trouble to grind and can be found in the sand of alluvial terrains. One may certainly hope to find still more goldfields with this gold-bearing sand like those in California and Australia; but it is quite obvious that, as and when the surface of the earth becomes more and more familiar and inhabited, the lodes will be more difficult to find. Hence there will be an ever-growing increase in the *rareté* of gold, with some accidental, sudden falls. Consequently, there will be an ever-growing decrease in prices, with a few accidental, sudden rises in price: this is the monetary future that gold monometallism holds in stock for us. There will be a permanent industrial crisis.
>
> ... The *single silver standard*, or *silver monometallism*, would be infinitely less foolish. Silver exists in nature in much larger quantities than gold, and, thanks to improvements in metalworking techniques, ore of mediocre quality may be profitably treated. It would therefore be perfectly acceptable **[171]** to hope that the quantity of silver might be at least maintained at an adequate level to keep its double utility as a commodity and as money in the sense that not only would its *rareté* not increase, but that it would rather decrease with time just like most other commodities and so the prices of commodities would be fairly stable. But it should still be said that this stability is not certain and that anyway it would be interrupted by alternating rises and falls corresponding to extreme activity or slowing down in the production of the metal.

I sent all my publications on money to Dr Soetbeer, and in January 1887 I sent him the *Theory of money*. His acknowledgement of receipt, which I have here in front of me, is of such a nature as to make us believe that his monometallic convictions are not yet weakened. I congratulate Mr Suess that he was on the right track and I congratulate myself that Soetbeer, in renouncing pure monometallism, did not throw himself, as so many others did, into radical bimetallism, but finally came to the system of gold money with complementary, regulating token. Indeed, I am sure that all my readers will also have recognized in his propositions, carefully worked out on 5 August 1892, a precise, formal application to which his overwhelming knowledge of statistics and monetary literature lend considerable weight.

This was the first fact I was anxious to point out. The second, no less important nor less fortunate, is the fact that Mr Suess's views and Soetbeer's propositions to which these led have been taken into consideration by the Financial Committee of the US Senate. As the circumstance influencing the system I reached in 1886 by mathematical deduction from the theory of quantity of money is the same as the one Soetbeer was led to in 1892 by the study of facts, this qualifies me to defend his plan, and I should say that the United States could do no better than call all silver in from circulation, except **[172]** for fractional currency, in which silver dollars at 16 could be included. I mean the *Silver Certificates* and the *Treasury Notes*, issued by virtue of the Bland Act and the Sherman Act,[ix] uniquely as *elastic token* at 22 circulating in the form of *deposit certificates at full coverage*: 'A deposit of… silver dollars with a ratio of twenty-two silver for a gold one will be set aside at the disposition of the bearer.' It would not be necessary for silver in deposit, though rigorously corresponding to the number of certificates in circulation, to be entirely monetized; this should only be done as needed. What a remarkable coincidence! The measure by which the free coinage of silver in India was suspended, in June 1893,[x] and a rate established of fifteen rupees a sovereign, made the silver token exactly worth twenty-two Indian rupees. If therefore England could decide to provide its colony with gold money instead of silver money made into token, by lending it a certain amount in sovereigns guaranteed by the remission of the same amount in rupees and putting this sum into its own circulation in the form of deposit certificates of full coverage as indicated above, England, along with India, and the United States, that is to say, the most influential part of the English-speaking world, would find itself under the regime of gold money with an elastic silver token at 22 from now on.

Personally, I do not see the absolute necessity of recoining French écus and German thalers at a rate superior to the present ones of $15\frac{1}{2}$ and 14, whatever Soetbeer may have thought about it. Suppose they were left as they are and under the sole condition that France had liquidated its wretched Latin Union, should money be lacking, well demonstrated by the fall in prices, nothing would prevent England, the United States, France and Germany by common consent managing the coinage of an elastic silver token determined by **[173]** a calculation so that each of these countries kept the stock of gold previously acquired. When because of this coinage the ratio of the value of gold to that of silver approached the value of 22 in the market it could be discussed whether there would be reasons for proclaiming bimetallism at 22, asking France and Germany to take the necessary losses on their écus and thalers. Otherwise, England and the United States could transform their elastic token at 22 into elastic token at $15\frac{1}{2}$, an easy and profitable operation. Were this token circulating in the form of certificates of full coverage this would be an easy operation because it could be achieved by simply substituting silver-pound and silver-dollar certificates at $15\frac{1}{2}$ for the silver-pound and silver-dollar ones at 22. A persisting lack of money could be handled by further coinage of elastic silver token. If, as a result of this coinage, the ratio of the value of gold to silver approached $15\frac{1}{2}$ in the market, bimetallism at $15\frac{1}{2}$ could be proclaimed, if necessary. It should be observed that if gold abruptly became abundant during the first period instead of remaining scarce, the adoption of the figure 22 as the rate of the English and American elastic silver token would result in gold, in a perfectly natural way, taking the place of silver in the monetary circulation of England and the United States, but not of France or Germany if these countries had not considered it expedient to recoin their écus and thalers. So the adoption of elastic silver token at 22 by the United States would constitute for them at the same time a first step towards bimetallism, under the hypothesis of scarcity of gold, and a protective measure for any chance of gold monometallism in the event of an abundance of gold.

I am not altogether sure that I agree with Mr Suess about the monetary abyss towards which he says we are being pushed. In my opinion the world monetary system is between two abysses **[174]** that geology should undoubtedly tell us about, but it is up to any economics worthy of the name to help us avoid them. The first abyss is that of an unceasing, persistent fall in the prices of products because of the growing scarcity of money under gold monometallism, to the detriment of entrepreneurs in agriculture, industry and commerce. This is what I called in 1886 a 'permanent industrial crisis'. The other is the abyss of rising prices, at first certainly sudden, and possibly later on constant and persistent because of the superabundance of money in radical bimetallism, to the detriment of landowners, workers and capitalists. Now the first of these two dangers, which preoccupies Mr Suess, is no longer to be feared. Gold monometallism is now more impossible than ever. Twenty years ago Germany, with 5 billion in stock, was not able to introduce a gold standard on its own; it had to stop because of the enormous losses incurred in purchasing continuously appreciating gold and selling continuously depreciating silver. Every nation that would nowadays like to make the same effort would fail in the same way, according to its most illustrious scientists. On the other hand, the second danger seems to me still serious. Radical bimetallism is supported by American mine owners. For several years English manufacturers have been perfectly aware of the formidable increase in prices which would be the result of a flood of silver in monetary circulation and a single stroke of the pen would suffice to make this reality. Consumers – proprietors, wage earners and persons with private means, who would be impoverished for a long time or for ever – do not recognize their own interests and would not be able to defend themselves. This is the precipice that always yawns at our feet, but a decision by the American government in the style of Soetbeer's monetary testament would prevent us from falling into it.

[175] IV The bimetallist danger[7]

> How did it happen? Bureaucrats probably! Official bodies! Established reputations, the Establishment, well placed people, important people, mighty fools!
>
> (J.-J. Weiss, *A propos de Théâtre*)[xi]

As a consequence of the recent discovery of gold on the frontier between Brazil and French Guyana, in Western Australia, and above all in [South] Africa, in the Transvaal, the monetary problem has entered a new phase: depreciation of gold soon will follow appreciation. Indeed, the annual production of gold, fallen from 700 million F (1856–60) to 500 million F in value, that is, 150,000 kg in quantity (1881–5), increased to 800 million F in 1893, to 900 million F in 1894, will probably go up to 1 billion F in 1895, that is, a quantity of 300,000 kg, and will be maintained at that level for a certain number of years. Those competent have evaluated the quantity of gold that can be found in just one part of the Transvaal (Witwatersrand) at 14 [billion F] or 15 billion F. The principle that 'all else being equal, prices will increase or decrease in proportion to the increase or decrease in the quantity of money', which provides the solution to all monetary problems, is open to very rigorous scientific demonstration nowadays. Money is offered daily in the money market. It is demanded by entrepreneurs, who wish to buy fixed and circulating capital for production (machines, instruments, tools, raw materials, products to place in the shops) and by landowners, **[176]** workers and capitalists, who wish to buy fixed and circulating capital for consumption (furniture, clothing, *objets d'art*, articles of luxury, consumer goods). If their [the capital goods'] quantity supplied increases or decreases, their hiring price, the rate of interest, will decrease or increase and the quantity demanded will increase or decrease. But because the quantity supplied of fixed and circulating capital, the whole of which constitutes all social wealth, will remain the same during the increase or decrease in the quantity demanded, it is beyond doubt that their prices will rise or fall in a common proportion. This will re-establish equilibrium.

Deducting from the 14 [billion] or 15 billion that should then arrive from the Witwatersrand alone, the quantity of gold used for industrial purposes and

7 *Revue socialiste*, 15 July 1895.

luxury goods, the price increase that will occur from now until about ten years hence as a result of the increase in the production of gold was safely estimated at 12 per cent or 15 per cent. All those who benefit from the surplus in the selling price over the cost price, entrepreneurs in agriculture, industry and commerce, and capitalists/shareholders, who will sell their products at high prices for a long time before the prices of productive services begin to increase, will be rolling in money. On the other hand, people living on a fixed income, on contract, landowners, workers and capitalists/bondholders, will find themselves in trouble. Landowners who are cultivating [the land] themselves are also entrepreneurs. Other landowners hope to be able to increase rents quickly. But workers will be obliged to have recourse to the costly and dangerous method of striking to get their wages increased; senior employees and civil servants will have an even greater problem in getting their salaries increased. Finally, small capitalists/bondholders have no means at all of getting their interest increased, since these are definitively fixed, and they can be sure that their capital will be reimbursed in depreciated money.

[177] A day will certainly come when it is possible to take measures to prevent such disruption of the whole economic and social mechanism; we have been led to hope that it will be in the second half of the twentieth century. Taking into consideration that the role of precious metals as money is much more important than their role as merchandise, and that the public interest should take priority over private interests, the mines will perhaps have been put into the hands of the State to exploit them so that production will be in accordance with needs. In the case of an insufficiency of money for natural causes, it would be possible to use complementary, regulating silver token. Should there be a natural surplus of that quantity, the price increases of the products could perhaps be remedied by ordering well calculated increases in the prices of productive services. However, for the time being, at the end of the nineteenth century, such ideas would mean bandying words like 'State socialism'. As a remedy for superabundance of money we shall probably get bimetallism, that is to say, an even greater superabundance.

At present gold is the only metal that really and truly is *money*, since it is the only metal that may be freely coined at the Mints at the request of private persons and of necessity always has the same value as both merchandise and money. As far as silver is concerned, whose free coinage has been suspended everywhere except in Mexico and possibly in a few other places, it is not money but a *token*, because its conventional value as money is about 50 per cent superior to its real value as merchandise. Now, at a conference held last March in Washington the US silver-mine owners (sixteen states were represented) claimed free coinage of silver the same as gold, based on a value ratio of 16 to 1. In February, in the German Reichstag, the agrarians had a **[178]** proposition passed leading to the convocation of an international conference to push Europe into bimetallism, and it is said that the State Council will certainly support this proposition. A national bimetallic league was constituted on 23 March in Paris to demand bimetallism at $15\frac{1}{2}$; protectionists support it; the former governor, the present governor and the cashier of the Bank of France fulfil all functions in it; legal Bills have been tabled. Finally, the English Bimetallic League held its annual meeting at the Mansion House, on 3 April, and Mr Balfour asked for the substitution of bimetallism for 'the absurd monometallic system under which we have the misfortune to live'. Moreover, the production of silver consisted recently of 4 [million kg] to 5 million kg per year, that is to say, fifteen or sixteen times as much as gold. Besides, the production of silver is still much more likely to expand than that of gold. Under the regime of bimetallism at 15 or 16, it [silver] would therefore be equal or even higher in value. This means that, to remedy the disadvantages foisted on us by an enormous mass of gold money, it is intended to inundate us with an even larger mass of money in the shape of silver, or to console us for a price rise of 12 per cent or 15 per cent this rise will be increased to 30 per cent or 40 per cent. The price of things being thus increased by one-third, hence brought to four-thirds of what it is now, our income will be reduced to three-quarters of what it is at present, thus lowered by a quarter.

In the present state of morals it is not surprising that American *silver men*, supported by German agrarians, English manufacturers and French protectionists, have no scruples at all in taking one-quarter of our income away to share a few billion among themselves; and to that end make great efforts and huge sacrifices. Insufficient notice has been taken of the fact that this iniquity has been made probable by the incompetence of governments and **[179]** public ignorance, especiallly that of so-called intellectuals; this gives us a subject of most instructive study.

Credit where credit is due. In this run-up to monetary, financial and economic disorganization the United States is in the lead. In this country the State has the bad habit of borrowing by issuing notes, payable on sight to the bearer, that form the major part of its paper money. The sorry effects of this paper money have already occurred and threaten to happen again. It is easy to fulminate against these effects but it would be more interesting to make them comprehensible.

Because the issue of every sort of paper money increases the quantity of money in circulation, it entails price rises, encourages imports and discourages exports; so it prompts an outflow of exportable metallic money, for which it is ultimately the substitute. The *Journal des débats* dated 30 March 1895 published a series of articles against bimetallism, that do not seem to be written to sadden bimetallists unduly, in which mention is twice made of the 'undeniable and generally admitted fact' that depreciation of money entails export of *numéraire as well as* depreciation and export of merchandise.[xii] I humbly confess that for me this 'undeniable fact' is an incomprehensible one. In relation to what else but merchandise did the money depreciate? How could a country have an excess of outflow over the inflow of *numéraire* and surplus in exports over imports of goods *at the same time*? If it sold a surplus of merchandise, it must have received *numéraire* in exchange and if it had given a surplus of *numéraire* then obviously it would have bought merchandise for an equal sum. The truth is that depreciation of money is translated into a rise in the price of the goods, and, these prices once risen, there is a profit in domestic buyers' purchasing abroad and **[180]** foreigners' selling in the country [in question]; hence there will be incentives to import, discouragement of exports and an outflow of money.

This situation may immediately be recognized by two facts: the rate of exchange will not only be unfavourable but may remain so at the maximum loss of its transport costs plus the costs of recoining into foreign money; and the metallic reserves for paying on sight the notes in circulation will decrease. Indeed, the debtors *vis-à-vis* foreign countries possess the funds to make their payments to them, but either in paper or in metal. In the latter case they will buy [with their metal] exchange bills abroad and add the maximum loss in this change to their costs; in the former case they will, if necessary, change their paper for metal at a public cash desk and add the transport costs plus the cost of recoining the metal into foreign money to their costs. This is how *numéraire* leaves the country. When metallic money has become scarce in the country, and the reserves are too low, fiat money is imposed and deviation from normal conditions is the inevitable result. There is no more parity between metallic and paper money: metallic money benefits from an *agio* [premium] that exactly represents the depreciation of paper. Imports are no longer encouraged nor are exports discouraged. What is more, there is no limit to the losses or gains of change over the rate of exchange because there will be no exportable metallic money left in circulation. The claims on foreign countries are added to the small amount of metal existing in the country to form the supply of this metal; the debts *vis-à-vis* foreign countries are added to the needs of metal to form the demand, and the rate of the *agio* is the result of these circumstances. So then comes an *agio* of 10 per cent, 50 per cent or 100 per cent! Those who are able to procure metal at this rate honour their signature; those who cannot – private persons who have to settle debts or States which have to pay interest – go bankrupt.

These are the consequences of paper money consisting of State certificates. However, the United States have **[181]** made particularly bad use of this dangerous procedure. The single gold standard was established there in 1873. Nevertheless, for fifteen years State certificates (*silver certificates* and *Treasury notes*) have been issued to the amount of 400 [million] to 500 million by virtue of the Bland Act (1878) and the Sherman Act (1890), in order to buy from the mine owners 400 [million oz] or 500 million oz of silver to be kept in cellars. Why does the State not do the same with the supply of furniture, clothing, toys or musical boxes? Simply because the producers of these articles do not have the skill to interest legislators in the prosperity of their industries as money producers do. At present we are confronted with paper circulation of about 6 billion francs, 2 billion of which are State certificates issued during the Civil War and payable in gold; 3 billion State certificates have been issued to buy silver from the *silver men*, legally payable in silver but paid for in gold to keep the certificates in commercial circulation. Furthermore, 1 billion consists of banknotes. Gold from the United States, driven out by paper money, has been added to the money stocks in European banks. The reserves of the Treasury [of the United States] are weak, notwithstanding several successive loans. The exchange rate is unfavourable. They have not yet come to fiat money or the *agio* of the glorious past, but there is nothing to prevent it.

At this juncture our uncompromising monometallists have recommended the United States to abandon silver as a monetary standard for good, which is, indeed, essential, and (1) to sell silver by weight, and (2) to borrow 3 [billion F] or 4 billion F in gold to replace the same sum in paper money. This advice was crazy and impossible at the time of scarcity and appreciation of gold. Nowadays it is not so silly. However, it can be done more cheaply. The silver bought from the *silver men* may serve as complementary token provided it is kept out of commercial circulation and confined to daily circulation, by a simple legal disposition to the effect that *each commercial paper* **[182]** (if it is not in odd money) *should be payable in gold so that it can be discounted by the issuing bank.* By virtue of this law, the banks will always have enough gold in stock for remittance to other countries. The banks only should take due care to decrease or increase the discount rate in proportion to the increase or decrease in their money stocks. The silver certificates and Treasury notes issued for the purchase of silver according to the repealed Bland Act and Sherman Act, legally reimbursable in silver, would be transformed into deposit certificates of silver token, wholly covered, circulating for daily payments instead of the silver dollars. A dead loss of about 2 billion on the sale of silver and annual payments of interest on loans, that might go over 100 million, would be avoided. Gold would return to circulation in the United States because of its abundance in the market and because of the natural interplay of exchanges. But *silver men* do not want to hear this. Their intention, by getting the silver bought by the State, was to drive the State back to bimetallism, and they will insist upon a solution that will set the State free from any loss by attributing to the silver a legal value of 1/16 in proportion to gold; they know quite well how to fulfil such an intention and have already made exceptionally good use of this skill. The 2 [billion] or 3 billion of silver buried in cellars will then be sent to the Mint; all the silver extracted or awaiting extraction from the mines will follow on. The State will escape, the *silver men* will be enriched and the consumers alone will be ruined.

A sequence of errors and mistakes not identical in character, but similar, has brought France to the point of considering bimetallism as an unavoidable choice, just as it seems for the United States. In 1878–9, when bimetallism was the regime, silver flowed into the Latin Union because of the **[183]** adoption of the gold standard in Germany and the output of American mines, and since it threatened to substitute itself entirely for gold, its free coinage was suspended. However, this operation took place recklessly and with a lack of foresight perfectly explicable in a country where the free study and discussion of this kind of question are considered nothing short of scandalous and carefully hidden from view.[xiii] Nobody could have imagined that suspending the free coinage of silver would transform silver money into token of a nominal value superior to its real value, so that, consequently, two urgent measures were to be imposed on the Latin Union: first, the repatriation of the silver écus to their respective countries of origin, and then the restriction in each country of the use of these écus to daily transactions of a non-commercial character. As I said before in relation to the United States, to bring about this restriction it was enough to decide payment in gold of the commercial paper accepted in the portfolio of the Bank of France. Indeed, from that time entrepreneurs should have had two compartments in their moneyboxes. One in which to put gold coins received from other entrepreneurs after the sale of their products or from bankers after discounting commercial paper, and from which they could take gold to pay off other entrepreneurs after purchasing primary goods, or banks to meet their own bonds; and another where silver écus could be put received from consumers as payment for products and with which landowners, workers and capitalists could be paid for productive services. The bankers would have to do the same, distinguishing between gold as a result of rediscounting or cashing portfolio holdings, and due to serve for discounting other papers, and silver coming from deposits of rent, wages and interest serving to cover withdrawals for purchasing consumer goods. If necessary, there could have been two different interest and discount rates. Because of its role and the nature of its receipts and **[184]** spending, the State could have received and spent a lot of silver. The Bank of France, on the other hand, would have received and spent only gold, and its money stock, composed exclusively of gold money, would really have been at the country's disposal for remittances abroad. All these precautions have been neglected. How could the leading lights of economics, finance and the Institut de France, who prepared and constituted the Latin Union, have dreamt up the idea of making the false principle of international token circulation an essential part of it? The principle was introduced for fractional currency and so it seemed obvious that it would also work for token consisting of écus. Today the result is obvious enough: half a billion Italian écus in the form of paper money added to $3\frac{1}{2}$ billion écus from other countries of the Latin Union; to these 4 billion, $1\frac{1}{2}$ billion is stocked in issuing banks at their nominal value of 1,500 million while their real value is only 750 million. Banks no longer pay their notes back in gold for fear of losing it, and commerce in the countries of the Latin Union, even where there is no fiat money, is deprived of real money.

Here, as in the United States, hard-line monometallists know and recommend only one solution: the sale by weight of 4 billion silver écus, with a dead loss of 3 billion or more, and taking out loans of at least 3 billion to buy gold money. Heaven grant that the States of the Latin Union and all States with spoiled money will be successful enough in their business to afford this! The 14 [billion] or 15 billion from the Witwatersrand would there find a use and would not lean with all their weight on the value of the money. Unfortunately, such this is not the case! These countries are heavily encumbered and have not got 3 billion to spend on the luxury of gold money. Well, let them be clever enough to bring in the 4 billion in silver to serve daily circulation, leaving their 5 billion of gold to serve commercial circulation only, **[185]** as I explained before. The State takes $1\frac{1}{2}$ billion écus from the banks' money stocks and withdraws $1\frac{1}{2}$ billion in banknotes from circulation to be transformed, just as the silver certificates and Treasury notes in America were, into silver token deposit certificates of full coverage to circulate instead of the écus. But do you think infallible people will admit to making a mistake? Moreover, protectionists, not considering sufficiently the consumers sacrificed to protect producers, have eagerly seized on a new opportunity to raise prices and enrich their existence, so they have become bimetallists. One of those international monetary conferences will be held where awards glitter upon gold embroidery and green palms, whose minutes we should like illustrated by Caran d'Ache.[xiv] The day when the United States proposes universal bimetallism at that conference, France, too, will see the way to give its écus back their former value in relation to gold and restore the money character of the stocks in the Bank of France in this desperate and extravagant solution; and provided this bimetallism is just bimetallism at $15\frac{1}{2}$, that is to say, as much of a disaster as possible, the country will hasten to accept it to blot out all its blunders.

The English like to keep things simple. They need automatic money, that is to say, money where the State does not have to intervene except to mint the chosen metal in the chosen weights and fineness. Recently they recognized that their gold monometallism was automatic money of growing value, giving rise to low prices, whereas universal bimetallism, after fixing the legal ratio of the value of gold and silver once and for all, would be automatic money of decreasing value, leading to high prices. All people interested in price increases joined it. The Conservative Party **[186]** saw there a trump card to put into its game and seized the bimetallist platform. But there again, the incompetence of those in power has put the opposition in a superior position, missing out on the opportunity of solving the Anglo-Indian monetary question.

This was a matter of the exchange rate or, better expressed, of a sharp *agio*, not so much one of metal over paper, but of gold over silver. Strictly speaking, the exchange rate is the price of credit in a country where a debt has to be paid. This price varies according to the ratio of the respective debts and credits of the two countries, which is also the ratio of the supply of and demand for bills of exchange. The variations, in the sense of a premium or a loss, of the rate of exchange between two countries with the same money, or at least with money of the same metal, have transport costs as upper limit, or at most the costs of transport of metal from the one country to the other and reminting, because when the loss attains that limit the debtor will send metal instead of buying credit. It is precisely for this reason that it would be highly desirable for all countries in the world to use only gold as money, at least for commerce. However, between two countries with money of different metals the rate of exchange results from two factors that can operate either in the same direction or in opposite directions. One, equal to the inverse ratio of the remittances to be made, which is the actual rate of *exchange*, is limited by the transport cost of domestic metal; the other factor, the price of foreign metal in terms of the domestic one, the *agio*, may be limitless. England is under the regime of gold monometallism, India under silver monometallism. In England gold constantly increases in value because of its *rareté*, and in India silver constantly decreases because of its abundance; the loss of the change of English credits *vis-à-vis* India, or, more precisely, the loss because of the *agio*, has constantly risen. The rupee, which **[187]** used to be worth about one-tenth of a pound sterling, was worth no more than one-fifteenth or one-sixteenth. The Indian State lost to London on the collection of taxes; retired civil servants living in England lost on their pensions; merchandise dispatched from England to India at profitable prices at the time of signing the contract appeared to have been sold at a loss because of the fall in the rate of exchange in between.

The Liberal Party, at present in power, is opposed to bimetallism. In 1893 they decided on the suspension of free coinage of silver in India, and certainly they might have solved the problem by the system of gold money with complementary and regulating silver token; but they did not know how to do that. By declaring Indian silver to be gold by convention, first a great quantity of such gold should not have been made and, second, this gold by convention should have had an addition of real gold to permit either exports of gold from India to England or imports from England to India according to whether the remittances to be made were higher or lower with regard to payments from one country to the other. In this way the values of the two types of money could have come into equilibrium and the exchange rate would have oscillated around parity. This could have been managed if England had lent India a certain amount of sovereigns, which would have provided it with gold money, and if, as a guarantee of this loan, India had remitted to England an equal amount of rupees to be used as silver token in England. The present abundance of gold would have enabled India to repay this loan within a relatively short period. Regulating the exchange rate and the *agio* by decreeing, on paper, that fifteen rupees were the equivalent of one sovereign, without knowing whether the nominal rate corresponded to the real one and without giving India gold money, was a presumptuous and infantile claim that reality was forced to humble. Nevertheless, this is all they did, **[188]** except for some loans in gold of a temporary character agreed upon at difficult times. The truth was that Indian money was worth less than it seemed, and the exchange rate for India in London remained below official parity. The rupee in London is at present worth one-eighteenth of a sovereign and not one-fifteenth. The government seems to have lost its head and the Chancellor of the Exchequer was heard to say, on 18 December 1893, in the House of Commons, that the experience that has been gained must be judged by its result and that, if this result proved unfavourable, another measure should be tried.[XV] That 'other measure' is bimetallism. Some days ago, in answer to an application from London merchants and bankers, the same Chancellor expressed 'his intention to adhere firmly to the single gold standard'. However, these phrases do not compensate for the deeds. The genuine way to adhere to the single gold standard would be applying it to solve the Anglo-Indian monetary question; if this is not done we shall have to suffer the bimetallist solution, either at the hands of the Whigs or of the Tories.

Germany alone remains. The Germans harbour no pretensions of applying simple solutions to complex questions. They are patient and ingenious. German science is not dictated to and exploited by the henchmen of high finance; and in German government the representatives of private interest have not, up to now, completely replaced the representatives of public interest. Germany is keen on its monetary regime, which was expensive but has rendered only good service. There, as in the United States and France, gold is money and silver is token; but no more than in America or France was it possible to use gold for commercial circulation and silver for daily circulation. The Bank of Germany does not only give and **[189]** take gold. It offers facilities to the public to change silver for gold and, thanks to circumstances up to now, has set aside enough in stock for remittances abroad. It may be hoped, as I personally do, that Germany, sticking to Moritz Lévy and Soetbeer's indications,[8] will use its veto against bimetallism and then coerce the United States, France and England to renounce their fantasies. Then we would all be set on our way towards the monetary unification of the world by sharing gold money out among the various countries of the globe to settle international and large national payments and by assigning silver token to moderate or small national payments. Token should be put in circulation or withdrawn according to the insufficiency or overabundance of gold. However,

8 See, at the end of the proceedings of the ninth session (30 June) of the International Monetary Conference of 1881 [Paris: Imprimerie nationale, vol. II, June–July 1881, pp. 17–22], appendix II: "Letter from Mr Moritz Lévy [delegate of Denmark] to the [Minister of Finance of France] president of the [monetary] conference". It was this letter that inspired Soetbeer to write his memorandum of 5 August 1892.

in Germany those in power seem to apply sharp practice to abuse some parties in order to attain their own aims. Bimetallism has been promised in exchange for the agrarians' support in voting for construction of armour-plated cruisers and strong measures against socialism. When the Reichstag, as we are told, at the instigation of Mr von Mirbach, lately asked the government to convene an international conference to establish universal bimetallism, the official orators declared themselves bimetallists. According to what is wired from Berlin to the *Standard*, Kaiser Wilhelm II has personally set himself to studying bimetallism; he wishes to preside over a monetary conference. Woe betide us!

Thus bimetallism will take over. It will make itself apparent by the price of subsistence, already pushed too high because of customs duties, through an **[190]** increase of 20 per cent, 25 per cent or 33 per cent, which means a reduction of one-sixth, one-fifth or a quarter in of the revenues, to the detriment of everyone living on rents, wages or contractual interest, and to the benefit of those who speculate on the chance of a gap between the price of products and of productive services. In their turn, these entrepreneurs will doubtless be overburdened, by charges laid upon them by assistance funds, pension funds and progressive taxes, all extra-judicial solutions to problems of justice, all plasters of a kind to make the diseases they are supposed to cure fester. For such is the way affairs progress: depriving some to enrich others; the conservatives excel in this. Then dive into the pockets of the rich to rescue the poor; radicals excel at that. This is how bimetallism will play its part in leading today's world to its destruction. It is time now for economics to become a positive science, establishing its authority by rational practices and favourable results, as medicine is doing at present. Society's body is being treated by Molière's doctors and passing away. Anarchists may keep quiet; the 'bourgeois and capitalist' society is dissolving quite well enough on its own, and their prisons perform less efficiently than the combination of scientific and political empiricism, militarism, protectionism, bimetallism and, above all, legal support of all forms, to try to put those who have gained all in charge of those they have ruined, thus destroying any motivation of will or energy. This is the surest sign of social decay.

Notes

i The corresponding equation in the second edition of the *Etudes d'économie politique appliquée* (1936) is incorrect, and badly printed. We have taken the equation from the first edition (1898), just as it is on the proof of p. 160 destined for the second edition, prepared in 1902 (Walras Archives, Lausanne, F. W. Vb, file 26). The formula is written in Walras's dated notation. We would nowadays write:

$$\left(Q_o - y + \frac{x}{w'}\right) : \left(\frac{Q_a - x}{w''} + y\right) = Q_o : \frac{Q_a}{w}$$

ii In a non-signed article 'La question de l'argent' (The silver question), *Gazette de Lausanne*, 94th year, no. 160, 10 July 1893, p. 1. The author first presents the following long excerpt from the article 'La question de l'argent. Les décisions du gouvernement des Indes et leurs conséquences probables dans le monde', by Paul Leroy-Beaulieu, published in *L'Économiste français* (Paris), 21st year, 2nd vol., no. 26, 1 July 1893, pp. 2–3:

It is well known that the English have a first-rate virtue: they can make decisions. When they saw that all artificial means for maintaining the value of silver were manifestly superfluous, they did not hesitate to give up taking this metal as the basis of the monetary regime of India.

We do not yet know the monetary plan adopted by the Indian government in all its details, and it is even possible that some of the points of application are liable to modification or moderation. The arrangements decided upon may be resumed as follows, however. The Mints of India will practically be closed for coining silver metal from now on, as the Mints in the Latin Union have been for the last twenty years.

The gold standard will not be officially established in India, but from now on gold will be the norm of Indian circulation. The value of the rupee has been fixed at 1*s* and 4*d*. Where the rupee contains sixteen annas, an anna will be equivalent to a penny. On the other hand, fifteen rupees will be equivalent to a pound sterling. In fact, the Mints being practically closed for silver, it is rather the pound sterling that will become the real standard in India.

It is unnecessary to try to substitute gold circulation for silver circulation. This would be very difficult, and a big mistake. By the nature of things, silver becomes a sort of fiduciary money. Undoubtedly, a certain quantity of gold will be needed for some time in India, but it will not be strictly necessary to bring a considerable stream of it into the country. A metal may serve perfectly as a norm and as the basis of the circulation in some country without being available in great quantities if its debts *vis-à-vis* other countries are not serious and if exports considerably exceed imports.

Without saying that India would not have to absorb a certain quantity of gold from now on, it does not seem that this would be a source of serious metallic perturbation in Europe.

India will derive an incontestable benefit from the recently taken measure: it will enjoy stable money instead of uncertain, incessantly depreciating money. English capital can much more easily move into it to be used for various works of civilization. We do not doubt that the new situation will be highly profitable for both India and England. Based on a monetary instrument of some stability, the relations between the two countries will develop favourably.

At a time when Australia is in a deep crisis and will be less interesting for a number of years to Great Britain, it is a masterstroke of this empire's government to assure, by monetary stability, a vast outlet for British capital to Hindustan. England will find here a compensation for the temporary decline of its economic activities in Australia.

Hence no decision could be more useful for both England and India itself. However, what will be the effects of this measure on the rest of the world?

What will become of silver, the poor metal that became a victim of its recent ease of production? Unfortunately, the prospects for silver are cheerless. The very news of the measures decided by the Indian government has driven it to the rate of 31*d* per ounce, never seen up till now. One month previously it was still worth 38*d*, and, as is well known, its normal value, according to our monetary tariffs, is 62*d*. Hence it lost about 50 per cent of its official value and its real value twenty-five years ago.

Had the United States persisted in buying 4,500,000 oz of silver per month, in compliance with the Sherman Act, the fall of the metal would have been blocked. But if the United States had committed the stupidity of working hard on the augmentation of its stock of silver, it would have lost all its gold within a few months: it would have fallen to the ranks of countries with a depreciated standard and be immersed in a deep crisis.

It may be considered as nearly certain that the United States will repeal the Sherman Act in the short term, that is to say, renounce its purchases of silver. It is well known that President Cleveland has long been an advocate of this measure. The quicker the American government does so, the better it will be for itself and for the rest of us.

To what rate must we expect silver to fall in this case? For monetary use, only Mexico and China remain (as far as it may be said that China has money). Industrial use of silver is known to have been at rather low level. A fall of the metal to below 31*d* is therefore conceivable. Certain people go so far as to predict a rate of 20*d* for the reason, they say, that at that price production of silver is still advantageous for many mines. Silver would then have a value of at most one-third of its primitive value, that is to say, of 68–72 F, instead of 218.89 F per kilogram.

This pessimistic evaluation may perhaps be exaggerated. Anyway, it is impossible to make assertions with any certitude. The scale of the fall [in the value] of silver will depend on the reduction of output, which, as we have seen, has not failed to grow every year, and on new industrial applications that may perhaps be found for a metal of such appreciable qualities. Anyway, it is not improbable that, should the Unites States abolish the Sherman Act, silver will fall to between 25*d* and 30*d* per ounce, sooner the first than the latter amount, and will be worth no more than 95–105 F per kilogram.

The industrial use of silver must develop considerably. Such use is rather limited; it is difficult to get an insight into its importance. Some American statistics evaluate industrial uses of silver in the United States at about $8 million, after deducting the recasting of old metal.* This is only some 40 million F. If this sum increased fivefold, or even tenfold (the last figure is highly exaggerated), it would still be unimportant to the rest of the world in view of the annual output, which exceeds 1 billion F. This production, however, would be considerably reduced by the fall in the metal's price.

For silver to find more use in the arts, two conditions should be fulfilled. First, silversmiths, jewellers, producers of silver plates, etc., should begin by no longer counting the gram of silver according to the old tariff, which is nearly twice as much as its present value and three times tomorrow's value. It would also be helpful if the government reduced its fees for marking and guaranteeing silver; in France, these fees are 20 F per kilogram and amounted to 1,700,000 F in 1889. Representing at present 19 per cent of the value, they are excessive and should be decreased by two-thirds. Under these conditions the industrial use of silver could be extended. Possibly its value could be kept between 25*d* and 30*d* per ounce, or between 85 F and 105 F per kilogram so that it would only lose 60–55 per cent.

What will be the consequences of the measure recently resolved upon by the Indian government, and similar measures to be expected from the side of the United States, for the whole world? We believe that the consequences will be favourable. The measures will put an end to a discouraging regime of a means of exchange

* *Report of the Director of the Mint*, 1890, p. 81.

constantly varying and always inclined to depreciate once more. Commerce with the Far East has become very difficult because of the slow but persistent fall in the price of silver. The price of silk in Japan at the time of purchase has sometimes already decreased by 2 per cent, 3 per cent or 4 per cent on arrival in Europe. Trade with the Far East has therefore become a highly hazardous operation.

From now on [the price of] silver will fall rapidly; it will be fixed at one-third of its primitive value, or, at most, at two-fifths. However, this value once attained, its variations will undoubtedly be less frequent than before and not always in the same direction. We believe that this new situation will be much more favourable for commercial operations than the present situation. This is what we have repeatedly asserted for the last twenty years.

Concerning the alleged scarcity of gold, we have often stated that there is no reason for alarm. Without mentioning of other regions, southern Africa will provide us with growing quantities of gold. The production of this metal, which dropped to 494 million [F] in 1883 increased gradually to 677 million in 1892. It is probable that within three or four years it will attain 800 million, a figure that will be equivalent to the annual average of 797,209,400 F of the period 1853–7 when gold production was at a peak.†

It is possible that gold transfers from Europe to the United States and India will be re-established if the first of these countries abandons its absurd monetary policy; there will then result only some restricted, short-lived difficulties, but not a serious crisis, because the stocks of gold in European banks are enormous.

In conclusion, the initiative taken by the Council of India seems to be a good one, not only from the point of view of England and Hindustan, but also from the point of view of general commerce. If the United States followed it then it would solve the monetary question that, since 1873, has been the cause of so many debates, so much trouble and so many financial problems. Leaving out of consideration the countries that blindly dashed into paper money, and seem to persist, we will have a relatively firm basis for international exchanges. All nations will benefit. It will be an honour for England, always so prudent and so determined, to have put an end to the powerless and upsetting efforts to uphold a metal that is condemned to depreciation because of the immense scale of its production. So the monetary regime of the civilized nations will become more regular.

After this long citation the author of the article in the *Gazette de Lausanne* declares:

On this occasion it will be appreciated that from 1887 onwards Mr Léon Walras, who taught political economy at our university, proposed a system of gold money with silver token in a note on the solution of the Anglo-Indian monetary problem communicated to the Economics Section of the British Association for the Advancement of Science. This is, in short, just what has been adopted recently.

iii *ŒEC*, vol. XIII, pp. 391–5.

iv J. E. C. Munro, Jevons's successor at Owens College, invited Walras. However, for reasons of health he could not come to Manchester. Instead Walras sent in the 'Note

† *Documents relatifs à la question monétaire*, 1874, 6th fasc., p. 6.

sur la solution du problème monétaire anglo-indien', which was published under the title 'On the solution of the Anglo-Indian monetary problem' in *Report of the fifty-seventh Meeting of the British Association for the Advancement of Science held at Manchester in August and September 1887*, London: John Murray, *Transaction of Section F*, Tuesday, 6 September, pp. 849–51. On the role of H. S. Foxwell on this occasion see the letters from Léon Walras of 26 August and 18 September 1887 to Foxwell (*Correspondence*, letters 809 and 811) and the latter's answer of 15 September (ibid., letter 810).

v Eduard Suess, *The Future of Silver*. In *Miscellaneous Documents of the Senate of the United States for the First Session of the Fifty-third Congress*, vol. I, doc. no. 95, 1893, Washington DC: Government Printing Office.

*vi Ibid., pp. 3–4. Of course, I did not translate Walras's translation (which seems quite correct) but inserted the original American text.

vii That is, the Austrian government.

viii A. Georg Soetbeer, *Literaturnachweiss über Geld- und Münzwesen, insbesondere über den Wahrungsstreit 1871–1891. Mit geschichtlichen und statistischen Erläuterungen*, Berlin: Puttkammer & Mühlbrecht, 1892.

ix By virtue of the Coinage Act (12 February 1873) the United States renounced unrestricted coinage of silver; kept only as fractional currency. Hence, in practice, the gold standard was adopted. (A dollar contained 23.22 grains of pure gold or 25.8 grains, 9/10 fine. A grain is 0.0647 g.) The resumption of payments in metallic cash, however, was fixed on 1 January 1879 by the Resumption Act of 14 January 1875. Meanwhile the exposed 'silver men' campaigned against the 'crime of 1873' and demanded the resumption of the coinage of silver. The Bland–Allison Act (28 February 1878) re-established free coinage of the silver dollar at the 1837 rate of 16 : 1, but the Treasury had to buy bullion for a monthly amount between \$2 million and \$4 million. This bullion was to be minted in dollars of 371.25 grains of pure silver or 412.5 grains of silver, 9/10 fine. By virtue of the Bland–Allison Act, effective from 1879 onwards, the Treasury could keep silver in its cellars and issue instead 'silver certificates' of \$10 and more. An amendment of 1886 introduced the possibility of issuing \$1, \$2 and \$5 certificates. The public preferred these less cumbersome silver certificates to silver dollars. The Bland–Allison Act remained in effect for twelve years. It could not check the fall in the value of silver, nor that of prices. The pressure of the bimetallists led the Republican Party to put to the vote the Sherman Silver Purchase Act (14 July 1890). This law obliged the Treasury to buy each month 4.5 million oz of silver at the market price, nearly the whole production of the American silver mines and twice the amount required by the Bland–Allison Act. In return, the Treasury issued 'Treasury notes' (called 'Treasury notes of 1890'), being legal money. These notes were reimbursable either in silver or in gold, to the pleasure of the Secretary of the Treasury. This clause, however, was interpreted as a promise to reimburse in gold. In 1893 the bank crisis and the industrial crises caused President Cleveland to convene Congress for an extraordinary session to repeal the Sherman Silver Purchase Act. The House of Representatives voted for repeal of the Act from August 1893 onwards, but the Senate delayed until October. However, the conflict between supporters and adversaries of the gold standard was growing. In March 1895, at a conference in Washington, the silver mine owners claimed free and unrestricted minting of silver (16 : 1). Next year the Democrats adopted the viewpoint of the Populist Party (founded in 1892) in presenting the bimetallist candidate William Jennings Bryan for the presidency, thereby deserting their sitting President. Jennings Bryan pronounced at the Convention of Chicago of 1896 the famous phrase: 'We will answer their demand for a gold standard by saying to them: You shall not press down upon the brow of labor this crown of thorns, you shall not crucify mankind upon a cross of gold.' Bryan was defeated at the elections and the winner; the Republican William McKinley, put the Currency Act (14 March 1900) to the vote, which officially established the gold standard in the United States.

x According to the propositions of the Committee on Indian Currency (1892), chaired by Farrer Herschell, the Indian government suspended from 26 June 1893 onwards the free minting of the silver rupee. The rupee was then linked to gold at a rate of one rupee to 1*s* and 4*d* (fifteen rupees to £1). In reality, only in 1898 was this parity arrived at.

xi The exact citation is as follows:

Hate slipped between the emperor and the poet: and *Punishment* has immortalized the rupture. How did it happen? Bureaucrats probably! Official bodies! Established reputations, the Establishment, well placed people, important people, mighty fools! We have to admit that here we have one of the most astonishing misunderstandings of our contemporaneous history.

(Jean-Jacques Weiss, *Trois années de théâtre, 1883–1885*, vol. 2, *A propos de théâtre*, Paris: Calman-Lévy, 1893, chapter 15, on Victor Hugo, p. 344)

xii Walras refers to the following passage in Léon Say's article 'Le bimétallisme' in the *Journal des débats politiques et littéraires* (Paris), 107th year, 30 March 1895, morning edition, p. 1:

> In countries where metallic money is depreciating at present, which is immediately indicated by the exchange rate, the interior metallic money shows, by the very fact of its depreciation, a tendency to be exported to those countries where it has preserved its earlier value. The export of the depreciated money furnishes the elements of natural speculation. This speculation always takes place under the same circumstances. It is an undeniable and universally admitted fact that the fall in the exchange rate has as a consequence on exports of *numéraire*. It is no less accurate to say that exports of merchandise will also result, and these exports will continue as long as one can get the same profit from them as if one exported money or bullion.

This article and the two published on the 22nd and 26th under the same title in the *Journal des débats* have been republished in Léon Say's brochure *Le Bimétallisme*, Sancerre: M. Pigelet, 1895. In a letter to Pareto of 30 June 1895 (*Correspondence*, letter 1208) Walras says,

> If you want to laugh I encourage you to read an article by Say (*Débats* of 30 March) and a discussion of the Société d'économie politique (*Journal des économistes*, May) where you can learn how *depreciation of money* promotes *exports of merchandise and of money at the same time*. My most recent studies have led me to examine these two items and I was stunned! This is the point political economy has reached!

xiii In the original manuscript Walras added the following passage: 'in such a way that the only discussions on government or big societies of credit and industry are those of the voice of official foolishness or revolutionary stupidity' (Walras Archives, Lausanne, F. W. Vb, file 20, p. 6).

xiv Emmanuel Poiré, named Caran d'Ache (1859–1909), was a famous caricaturist of the day.

xv At that time William George Granville Venables Vernon Harcourt (1827–1904) was Chancellor of the Exchequer, in the fourth Liberal Cabinet (1892–9) of William Ewart Gladstone (1809–98).

Part II

Monopolies

[193]

8 The State and the railways[1]

To certain economists it appears clear that the science of political and social economy is completely contained in these four words: *laisser-faire, laisser-passer*. Whatever the questions asked, whether it concerns children's and women's labour in factories or the regime in the colonies, the corn trade or transport activities, they never see more than a single, unique solution: individual initiative operating in complete freedom. On browsing through the article 'Chemins de fer' [Railways] by Mr Michel Chevalier, in the *Dictionnaire de l'économie politique*,[iii] written about twenty-five years ago and still remarkable in many respects, one finds successively discussed all the problems relating to this means of communication, with one exception only: should construction and operation be the business of the State? The author does not seem to doubt for a single moment that these are tasks for private companies. When talking of the organization of railways in England around 1843, he tells us that some people considered private ownership 'hardly at all in the public interest' and asked for the English railways 'to be bought and exploited by **[194]** the State'[iv] Then he adds:

> This was a far-fetched conclusion. The English government would have been wrong to acquire the railways by compulsory purchase. That would have meant a very serious attack on the spirit of [industrial] association,

1 This memoir was written in 1875, when the question of the acquisition [by the State] of the railways, again actual in Switzerland at present, had been raised in the Vaud canton by two members of the Vaud State Council. One of them, Mr Delarageaz, acted on its authority in writing a series of articles published in the *Nouvelliste Vaudois* in October 1875.[i] I myself have made use of the memoir since as a text for my courses in applied economics, successively extending it by matters supplied by various works published later by authors whose point of view agreed more or less with mine. I leave the piece as it was written and restrict myself to analysing the works concerned in a final 'Note'.[ii] [Published in] *Revue du droit public et de la science politique*, May–June and July–August 1897.

> which is one of the driving forces in English society; it would also have meant an attack on *freedom of trade*, one of the indispensable attributes of modern civilization. Up till now the railway administrators were mistaken and *freedom of trade* had skidded off the straight and narrow. This was no reason for treating the companies with violence, or for systematically impeding *freedom of trade* as far as railways were concerned. The associations would have listened to reason. *Freedom of trade* bears the seeds to remedy its own excesses, with the help of time.[2]

At the end of a long controversial letter on the subject of freedom for issuing banks this same author suggests that Mr Wolowski takes lessons in philosophy from Mr Jourdain:

> You presented a not very convincing work, my respected colleague, because you entered this affair while repudiating the principle of *freedom of labour*; you behaved like the sailor who, as he set sail, throws the compass into the sea. The debate about banks, like every political [economic] debate, has no way out for a person turning his back on *freedom of labour*. Let us observe the good habit of respecting this principle, which is our force and value. Let us not be bashful and return when we have the misfortune to be separated from it.[3,v]

It is clear: constructing and operating railways by private companies and freedom to issue banknotes are applications of the principles of freedom of trade and labour, and everybody who is not an advocate of these systems is an **[195]** adversary of the principle of freedom of trade or freedom of labour, an enemy of economics, or, to speak plainly, a socialist. However, we do not need to go deep into the matter to observe that, for different but equally decisive reasons, the issue of banknotes has just as little to do with freedom of labour as building and running railways has with freedom of trade.

It is well known that the expression *laisser-faire, laisser-passer*, translated as *Free competition and free trade*, is adopted and applied by the Manchester School to its furthest extremes. However, it is equally well known that a powerful reaction against excessive individualism is taking place in Germany, under the name of 'Socialism of the Chair'. A considerable proportion, if not even the majority, of the professors of political and social economy of this country have acknowledged being advocates of State intervention in industry to a certain extent. These reformers declared themselves as taking up a position between

2 *Dictionnaire de l'économie politique*, vol. I, p. 353 [emphasis added by Walras].

3 L. Wolowski, *La Banque d'Angleterre et les banques d'Écosse*, [Paris: Guillaumin, 1867] p. 248 [emphasis added by Walras].

socialism, allowing too much State intervention, and Manchesterism, which does not allow enough. Socialism of the chair has already spread from Germany to Italy, where many distinguished people, and even several eminent economists have adhered to it. It is needless to say that railways and banknotes belong to manifestations of industry and credit where the option of State intervention should be left open. However, until now, regarding the way in which they drew their conclusions, it is not clear whether economists of the new school are much superior to those of the old. The old economists proclaim *laisser-faire, laisser-passer*; the new proclaim State interventionism; but none of them demonstrates anything at all. Now we are thoroughly tired of gratuitous assertions and, above all, we demand rigorous demonstrations. In spite of everything, we blame Mr Chevalier not so much for concluding in favour of **[196]** freedom of trade and labour in matters of railways and banknotes as for not establishing it on any particular basis, whether rational or experimental. It would not suffice, either, to hear socialists of the chair assuring us that they would let the State intervene in railway matters somewhat more than the economists do, without, however, allowing it to the same degree as real socialists. By what right may or must the State intervene in the railway sector? That is what we should like to know. Then we should know exactly in which cases and to what degree it might and must intervene. Then we should at least leave the field of systems to enter that of science.

I Public services and economic monopolies

Pure economics teaches us that production and exchange under the regime of competition[vi] among landowners, labourers and capitalists/consumers, and entrepreneurs/producers in the services and products market is an operation where services are combined into products of a nature and in quantities sufficient to procure the greatest possible satisfaction of needs, under a double reservation: (1) the price of each service and product should be unique in the market and make supply and demand equal; (2) the selling price of products should be equal to their cost price in services.[4]

The two conditions that *services and products have a single price in the market, namely that at which supply and demand are equal, and that the selling price of products is equal to their cost price in services*, can be combined into one: *services are exchanged* **[197]** *for each other in common ratios, as a result of free disposal of property*. This latter condition is one of justice, which should be established in social economics.[5]

4 See *Eléments d'économie politique pure*, lessons 20, 21 and 22. [*ŒEC*, vol. VIII, pp. 301–42.]
5 See *Etudes d'économie sociale*, 'Théorie de la propriété'. [*ŒEC*, vol. IX, pp. 177–206.]

That *products are of a nature and in quantities sufficient to procure the greatest possible satisfaction of needs*, in other words, that the best use has been made of services, is a condition whose utility[vii] is self-evident. Once stated by pure economics, it is up to applied economics to research the cases carefully where it is possible to trust competition and those where this is not possible and recourse to another expedient must be sought.

Competition is frequently possible in the production of services and goods of private interest. These services and goods are those that concern people as individuals free in the choice of their personal positions; in other words, these services and goods satisfy the individuals' varied, unequal needs. Each individual calculates the numbers of units of services, food, clothing, housing, etc., he might consume if need be. He compares intensities of utility of units of both the same and different commodities. The prices once called or posted up, he knows how to distribute his income over the varied commodities to obtain the greatest possible effective utility. Then he demands a certain amount of such-and-such products or services. Generally, there is a crowd of consumers/demanders; and therefore there are many producers/suppliers, confident of being able to sell to one what they cannot sell to another. This is how competition operates. When demand for certain products is superior to supply, consumers **[198]** make a higher bid; the selling price rises above cost price and production will expand. When, on the other hand, the supply of certain products is superior to the demand, producers reduce their prices; the selling prices fall below cost price and production decreases. In equilibrium normal order will be established automatically.

This is not the case with services and products of public interest. Theoretically, these are of interest to people as members of a municipality or the State, charged with the establishment of social conditions; in other words, these services and products satisfy needs that are the same and equal to all people. One may quite well conceive the State as a consumer calculating the amount of services or products of exterior and interior security, justice, education, communication, etc., that it could consume if need be; comparing intensities of utility of units of both the same and different commodities; deciding how to spend its income to obtain the greatest possible effective utility, after evaluating the costs; and, finally, demanding a certain amount of services and products. Here ends the similarity, however. In general, there will only be a single consumer/demander for each service or product of public interest, the State. Therefore, there will be no producers/suppliers at all, because each of them probably says that what he cannot sell to the State could not be sold to anybody else.

In possession of an imperfectly demonstrated and even imperfect but not totally unfounded principle, and eager to apply it in the largest possible number of cases, economists have always endeavoured to put services **[199]** and products of public interest into the same category as those of private interest.

This is an error: there is a fundamental difference between the two. Individuals feel the need for services or products of private interest; the need for services or products of public interest is felt in all its aspects only by local or central government. Just as individuals do not always correctly perceive their needs, the State does not always correctly perceive its own needs if the people representing it have been badly chosen. In both cases, this misfortune is serious and should be set right. However, it does not mean that in the second case we must leave it to individuals to demand services and products of public interest, for it is certain that most often these services and products will not be demanded, supplied, produced or consumed. Consequently economists, when claiming to submit the production of public services to the principle of free competition, make a mistake that is only increased by their confident, scornful tone. They have compromised both social and economic science and caused total confusion in social science.

Only in exceptional cases, therefore, may the State hope for services or goods of public interest which result from competition; generally speaking it has to produce them itself. If there are reasons to want them consumed under certain conditions, the State may quite well determine to produce them all by itself. In technical terms, it may preserve the *monopoly* of these services and goods for itself. On the other hand, in exceptional cases only does an individual himself have to produce services and products of private interest to him. Generally, competition may be expected to produce them. This is where the 'principle of free competition' should be proclaimed. Apart from State monopolies relating to services and goods of public interest based on law, which may be called *moral monopolies*, there is scope for State monopolies based on social interest, regarding services and goods of private interest; these monopolies might be called *economic monopolies*. Where they are not outside industry, as the former are, they are at least outside the realm of the principle of freedom of trade, just as the former are.

[200] Indeed, competition supposes a multiplicity of both entrepreneurs and consumers. Accordingly, the principle of free competition stands or falls entirely by the hypothesis that, in the case of loss the quantity of products will diminish because some entrepreneurs go elsewhere, which will suppress the surplus of cost price over selling price, and that in the case of profits the quantity of products will increase because entrepreneurs will be attracted, which will eliminate the excess of selling price over cost price, making the two prices equal. An inflow of entrepreneurs will not take place when, for any reason, there is only a single enterprise, that is to say, when there is monopoly. Hence in the case of profits the excess of selling price over cost price will not be eliminated because increases in quantity and reductions in the prices of the products take place as long as they bring about a rise in the entrepreneur's profits and not until profits are reduced to zero. From this it follows that the principle of freedom of trade is not necessarily applicable to the production of services and goods of private interest only producible under monopoly.

The difference is well known. Application of *laisser-faire* in an industry open to indefinite competition results in maximum satisfaction for all consumers, on the condition that selling prices be equal to cost prices and entrepreneurs make neither profit nor loss. If, however, this same rule were applied in a monopoly industry, consumers would obtain maximum satisfaction in a situation in which the selling price was higher than the cost price, the monopolist making the greatest possible profit.[6] In the first case, the entrepreneur is an intermediary, of whom abstraction can be made, and landowners, labourers and capitalists exchange **[201]** services for services. In the second case, the entrepreneur steps in to take a certain portion of the wealth exchanged, his profit.

To avoid such an onerous levy, *laisser-faire* should no longer be allowed in certain cases, but the State, on the contrary, should intervene to exercise the monopoly itself, or so organize it that it is exercised without profit or loss. In this way economic monopolies, based on social interests, will arise side by side with moral monopolies, based on natural rights. The former are private monopolies transformed into State monopolies or monopolies conceded by the State. They should be well distinguished from moral monopolies. Their *raison d'être* differs. Moreover, in the case of a moral monopoly, exercised to the benefit of the community, the products, i.e. the public services, may, and often must, be gratuitous, while in the case of an economic monopoly, exercised to the profit of individuals, the products are supplied at cost prices instead of maximum profit prices.

Would this mean that the principle of freedom of trade has to be rejected and that the State should always intervene in every industry open to monopoly? This is far from our conclusion. Our analysis shows monopoly as averse to social interests but State intervention as founded on them. However, interests have to bow before the law,[viii] and furthermore, inferior interests have to bow before superior ones. Such a case appears where a private monopoly is based on [natural] law. For example, let the entrepreneur of a product be its inventor, in exclusive control of the secret, and suppose he does not for ask for co-operation or support from the State in any way. Would it then not be his right to exercise his monopoly? Just as the municipality and the State have rights individuals are not allowed to infringe, the individual has rights the State may not disregard. One might say that in this case the entrepreneur has a right to ownership of his invention; he sells the **[202]** invention when he sells the product in which it has been substantiated; he has the right to produce a quantity that suits him to sell at a price convenient to him. Hence the interests of consumption would give way to the rights of property. One may also conceive of cases of private monopoly

6 See *Eléments d'économie politique pure*, lesson 41. [*ŒEC*, vol. VIII, pp. 655–71.]

based on [social] interests. Suppose, for instance, that an entrepreneur, unlike the former, were not entirely sole owner of his invention and asked for State protection to exercise his monopoly during a certain period on the condition of bringing it into the public domain after that period. It could be in the interests of society to decide on such an arrangement, since it is probably more advantageous to consumers to have the product at their disposal immediately, while recompensing the inventor by some years of monopoly, than to wait indefinitely for the invention of the product by a stroke of luck. In this case, less considerable interests should defer to a more considerable one. Finally, there are cases of private monopoly not based on law or [public] interests; here State intervention will become useful and legitimate.

Suppose that the product in question is water or gas; let the entrepreneur be an individual or a company that brings this water or gas to the houses of private persons. There is no secret to be kept and no invention to be encouraged. However, the entrepreneur needs authorization from the municipality to lay his pipes beneath the streets. Monopoly is inevitable. The municipality cannot authorize an indefinite number of entrepreneurs to lay pipes in the streets; only two or three, at most. Those two or three would soon form a coalition in order to share monopoly profit rather than compete with each other. Competition among few entrepreneurs is logically only a short-lived phenomenon, followed by the more lasting one of monopoly of one individual after the ruin of others or monopoly of all or some by coalition. If therefore, under the pretext of freedom of trade, **[203]** the permission in question were conceded unconditionally to some entrepreneur, or to two or three, the final result would be certain: consumers would be delivered 1,000 m^3 of water or gas per day, at a selling price of 5 F per cubic metre and at a cost price of 2 F per cubic metre, at a profit of 3,000 F per day.[7] What reason of justice or utility may there be for this? None. Hence the town itself should supply 5,000 m^3 of water or gas per day to the consumers at a price of 2 F, without making either profit or a loss. Alternatively, the town might concede the supply, by public 'sale', to the entrepreneur who 'offers'[ix] the lowest selling price; the result will be the same. This is how in matters of economic monopoly the authorities intervene to exercise it themselves at cost price or to get it exercised by a concessionaire.[x,xi]

Moreover, we know also that monopoly undermines not only the condition of equality of selling price and cost price, but also that of uniformity of price.[8] Hence, in our example, the final, permanent result will be that there will be

7 This is why. Suppose prices are, successively, 100 F, 50 F, 20 F, 5 F, 3 F and 2 F; suppose further that at these prices the following quantities could be sold: 0, 10, 50, 1,000, 2,500, 5,000 units. After the deduction of 2 F of costs per unit, profit will be, successively, 0 F, 480 F, 900 F, 3,000 F, 2,500 F and 0 F. Profit will therefore be maximal at a price of 5 F. Fixed costs, to be added to proportional costs, would reduce profit but would not change the price.

8 See *Eléments d'économie politique pure*, lesson 41. [*ŒEC*, vol. VIII, pp. 655–71.]

2,500 m^3 of water or gas delivered to consumers: 10 m^3 at 50 F, 40 m^3 at 20 F, 950 m^3 at 5 F and 1,500 m^3 at 3 F. The individual entrepreneur, or the entrepreneurs in coalition, will thus make a profit of 5,550 F per day.[9] The fact that monopoly so pursues and generates an extra profit by means of multiple prices is quite simple and natural, according to certain authors. At the end of his article 'De l'influence des péages sur l'utilité des voies de communication'[10,xii] **[204]** Dupuit speaks of the solution to all sorts of questions related to the exploitation of a monopoly:

> This solution is based on the general principle that the price asked for a service should not be the amount it costs the person who renders it, but a sum in proportion to the importance attached to it by the person to whom it will be rendered.[xiii]

This so-called principle cannot be accepted unreservedly. Putting it so absolutely would be disastrous to any form of justice. There is no doubt that a multiplicity of prices equal to the greatest sacrifices consumers can agree upon would be most profitable to the monopolist, and not a selling price equal to the cost price or even a single price of maximum profit. Whether he should have the right to do so is another matter altogether.

As far as this is concerned, let us return to the distinction drawn above. We have no objections if it concerns an industry or commerce open to free competition, or a monopoly based on law or the general interest. In these conditions, manufacturers and the tradesmen have the right to sell the same product at different prices, but, on the other hand, it is likewise the client's right to buy the product if it so pleases him. I say the same product, even if it is perfectly identical. The more so if there were some difference regarding nature, quality or appearance. A chocolate maker may use different wrappings and labels, a bookseller different formats and sorts of paper, in order to sell the same chocolate or the same book at different prices, both carefully avoiding potential misinformation about the quality of the goods. You may appraise the price differences as not justified by the difference in the form of the products. However, do not complain if it pleases you to pay for the satisfaction of a whim instead of a real product.

Now, when it concerns an actual monopoly, it is permissible to ask why, in addition to the power to elevate the selling price from the level of cost price to that of maximum profit, the monopolist should **[205]** have the power to maintain several prices in the market, corresponding to the maximum sacrifices

9 The figures presented above may explain the latter calculation.

10 *Annales des Ponts et Chaussées* [vol. XVII, 2nd series, no. 207], nos. of March and April [pp. 170–248].

of consumers. Let us take the example of the supply of water or gas. Why should it not be enough for the concessionaire to make a monopoly profit of 3,000 F per day, at a consumption of 1,000 m^3 at 5 F instead of 5,000 m^3 at 2 F, and why should it be possible for him to further augment his profit from 3,000 F to 5,550 F by maintaining in addition to the price of 5 F two higher prices of 20 F and 50 F and one lower one of 3 F by such arrangements as giving some customers priority at special times? Personally, we think that if there were reason to prevent the first of these two consequences of monopoly, there would be even more reason to prevent the second. Though we have to tolerate multiplicity of prices in cases of monopolies based on law or the general interest, we declare openly that in such multiplicity outside these cases there is one more reason for transforming actual monopolies into economic State monopolies.

II Railways as public services and economic monopolies

Railway tracks are subject to certain conditions of gradient, curvature and quality of the rails along which passenger and goods trains are hauled by locomotives. Together with roads and canals they are among the means of communication, but because they use rails they are distinguished from the latter two by the interdependence of their three elements: the track on one hand, and the train and the engine on the other. It was at first thought that freedom to use the tracks for the various entrepreneurs in the transport sector would be feasible, just as on roads and canals. It was soon realized, however, that on one hand entrepreneurs specializing in railway transport should license **[206]** the track and therefore receive *toll* or rent. On the other hand, at the same time they should be receivers of *freight*, payment for the use of their engines and rolling stock. Nevertheless, where the proper role of science is to distinguish by abstraction what is confused in reality, we first consider the railway as such, independent of the locomotives, passenger carriages and goods wagons running on it, with the sole intention of returning to their association later on.

Do the means of communication constitute a public service? Adam Smith says:

> It does not seem necessary that the expence of those publick works should be defrayed from that publick revenue, as it is commonly called, of which the collection and application is in most countries assigned to the executive power. The greater part of such publick works may easily be so managed, as to afford a particular revenue sufficient for defraying their own expence, without bringing any burden upon the general revenue of the society.

> A highway, a bridge, a navigable canal, for example, may in most cases be both made and maintained by a small toll upon the carriages that make use of them. . . .
>
> This tax or toll, too, though the carrier advances it, is finally paid by the consumer, to whom it must always be charged in the price of the goods. As the expence of carriage, however, is very much reduced by means of such publick works, the goods, notwithstanding the toll, come cheaper to the consumer than they could otherwise have done: their prices not being so much raised by the toll, as lowered by the cheapness of the carriage. . . .
>
> When the high roads, bridges, canals, &c. are in this manner made and supported by the commerce which is carried on by means of them, they can be made only where that commerce requires them, and consequently where it is proper to make them. Their expence too, their grandeur and magnificence must be suited to what that commerce can afford to pay. **[207]** Consequently, they must be made as it is proper to make them.[11,xiv]

In his *Cours* J.-B. Say mentions this opinion of Adam Smith, but only to give himself the opportunity to take the opposite point of view:

> Adam Smith believes that the cost of a road should be paid by those who make use of it, in proportion to this use. The consumer may benefit from a decrease in the costs of production, but he has to pay the necessary costs. But do not we have, in most cases, to classify the means of communication among those institutions of which Smith himself says, elsewhere, that, though highly useful to society in general, nobody feels himself enough interested in their existence to be willing to pay their costs himself? . . .
>
> I believe that, when judiciously conceived, means of communication definitely may be placed among the most evident of social expenditures. They create a decrease of costs of production in general, a reduction in price of all products, from which society benefits.[12]

Insisting upon his opinion, and applying it to an example, he said in a later passage:

> The costs of digging a canal, even the indispensable costs, may be such that the toll to navigate on it is not enough for the payment of the interest on

11 V, section 3, article 1.

12 Jean-Baptiste Say, *Cours* [*complet*] *d'économie politique* [*pratique*, Paris: Guillaumin, 1840], Part 7, chapter XXIII [note 1].

> the loan, although the advantage the nation obtains from it may be highly superior to the amount of this interest. Hence the nation should then bear gratuitously its excavation costs if it wants those benefits.[13]

It is clear that the 'masters of our science' disagree on this point, as on others. Say's thesis seems to be justified to a certain degree, but, at the same time, his example does not appear very well chosen and his arguments seem remarkably unfortunate. If **[208]** communications are to be classed, partly, at least, as public services, then one should not try to obtain motives from the transport of merchandise. Therefore, one should not base oneself on canals, exclusively destined for this type of transport. The carriage of merchandise is part of their nature and, consequently, since they allow or facilitate the movement of goods, means of communication form productive capital and are subject to the rules of the production and formation of capital. Under a regime of competition, savings are transformed into capital goods of such a nature and quantity as to provide the greatest possible effective utility, just as productive services are combined into products of such a nature and quantity as to provide the greatest possible satisfaction of wants. Hence free competition is of social interest in production as well as in capital formation. Every attempt to steer savings into less remunerative investment than is possible results in loss of utility for society. Hence, as far as the context in which the question is placed, Smith was right. Say was beside the (economic) point. However, are the means of communication, and in particular railways, only useful for merchandise transport and the movement of services and products? This was the question to examine. With Adam Smith, who classifies the national defence and administration of justice as functions of the community or the State, we make first the observation that if the means of communication are essential for providing these public services, they are therefore a public service themselves. We need roads and railways for mobilizing armies and getting them to the frontiers. It was with good reason that the French parliament when discussing railways in 1838 attached substantial importance to this strategic aspect.[xv] This importance is real, as appears from the American Civil War and from wars in Europe which have taken place since. **[209]** Roads and railways are necessary to the police in the pursuit of criminals, and it is for lack of adequate means of communication that banditry still persists in countries such as Greece and Sicily.

This first consideration would alone suffice to justify State intervention in setting up communication routes and for the State's share in motivation and subsidy. However, there is more that justifies State intervention. If one subtracts from the number of travellers those who are travelling on roads and railways for pleasure and pay for the service as an item of consumption, if one deducts further

13 Ibid., Part 7, chapter XXIV [p. 316].

those who are travelling on business and whose travel costs can be found back in the price of certain products, and if finally one allows for military personnel and the police, a certain number of travellers remain who are not travelling at their own cost, or at the cost of consumers or of the State. Nevertheless, they are travelling in the interests of society. I mention, for example, those who are going to the various scientific conferences or industrial and art exhibitions, all having become very frequent thanks to the railways. This observation applies similarly to certain commodities whose transport is in the interests not only of the consumer who pays for them but also, in some sense, of society itself; for example, newspapers bringing daily news and political news from one end of the country to the other during the night, thanks to the railways. Indeed, one must be doubly blindfolded by the narrowest individualism and utilitarianism to deny that, irrespective of services rendered by the transport of goods, communication also serves another purpose, namely national unity. Just as a town without streets is reduced to an accumulation of isolated dwellings, a country without communication routes could become an agglomeration of mutually foreign districts. Thanks to communication routes, **[210]** the population will distribute itself over countryside and cities, and some of these cities will become centres of science, industry, literature, art, from which ideas, not always paid for by the production costs of products, will be diffused over the whole country. Therefore these routes are essential for civilization and progress in the widest sense.

The service of communication routes, in particular those of the railways has, to a certain degree, the character of a public service. Moreover, it has the character of a monopoly where particularly the State's co-operation is indispensable for its exploitation. There is a perfect analogy between the entrepreneur we met before, who wanted to deliver water or gas to the inhabitants of a town, and the entrepreneur who wants to undertake the transport of passengers and merchandise from one town to another. The former needs permission to lay his pipes under the streets and the latter needs authorization to acquire the necessary land by means of expropriation. Just as a municipality cannot authorize an indefinite number of entrepreneurs to lay pipes under the streets, the State cannot authorize an indefinite number of entrepreneurs to acquire land between two towns by expropriation.

None of this, however, amounts to the most decisive reason. In both cases there is another one, derived from the industry's nature itself, namely that one and the same amount of initial costs and, to a certain degree, operating costs may be spread over a quite considerable number of products. The workshops of ten carpenters or ten constructors need in total nearly the same space, the same number of workers and machines as a single workshop that can produce the ten workshops' total product. True, in the latter case some small savings might be made in power supplies. However, a single **[211]** network of pipes will provide a population with water or gas just as well as ten such networks.

A single road suffices for the same volume of goods and passenger traffic as ten. Once it is built, the construction costs of the network or the road may be spread over a distribution or amount of traffic that is, say, either ten times larger or ten times smaller. If this distribution or traffic volume were ten times larger or smaller, these costs would not be lower. As J. S. Mill rightly remarked, we have here a situation that puts the industries concerned beyond the principle of free competition because that can work only by multiplying initial costs, which is here absolutely useless.[14] Laying a second system of pipes for water or gas in a town where there is already one that can alone meet all needs, constructing a second network of routes in a country where there is already one sufficient for all communication would be an absurd way of trying to make things cheaper. Even if free competition so introduced brought about relative cheapness, it would not bring about absolute cheapness, because it would always be worth while obtaining products at a cost price into which double or triple initial costs do not enter.

This observation is especially important in the case of very considerable initial costs. Then, indeed, two obstacles will prevent competition from having its normal result, cheapness; they may even prevent competition from occurring altogether. The first is the problem of finding capital, the second is the remuneration of that capital. This is now the case with roads, canals and, particularly, railways. In his article 'Péage' [Toll], Dupuit has made it clear by means of a well chosen example, which now follows:

> Indeed, **[212]** let us imagine that a company, concessionaire of a canal or a railway, increases its tariffs so that its profits will noticeably exceed the normal rate of revenue on industrial capital. Let the latter be 6 per cent or 7 per cent and our company obtain a profit of 12 per cent or 15 per cent, or even 20 per cent. For instance, the rails have cost 100 million. The gross receipts are 30 million. The maintenance, administrative and operating costs come to 15 million: there is 15 million left to distribute among the shareholders, that is to say, 15 F for a share of 100 F. Such a return would certainly tempt competitors and, if it involved any other industry, it is certain that one or more rival entrepreneurs would come to take a share in it, reducing the first one's profit. However, this will not occur in the case of a communication route. First, the enormous mass of capital necessary for the construction of a new track would considerably limit the number of persons able to undertake it. Second, the first company being unique, a new one can exist only at the cost of the former; profit sufficient for one may not be sufficient for two. When a hundred spinning mills

14 [John Stuart Mill] *Principles of Political Economy, with some of their Applications to Social Philosophy*, Book I, chapter IX, §3 [Conditions necessary for the large system of production].

> prosper, the hundred-and-first may prosper as well because it would only need a slight increase in consumption, or a very small fraction of the other mills' clients to obtain the same results. This is not the case, however, with an enterprise that is unique, like a communication route. Let us continue the example above and suppose that bold capitalists put 100 million into the construction of a railway parallel to the first one. First, it may be observed that it is highly probable that the first enterprise, which had the first choice, will have chosen the best route. They followed the right-hand bank and you will have no option but the left-hand bank; or they took the valley and you can only have the plateau. So your line will necessarily be inferior to theirs with respect to the nature of the terrain, wealth, population, etc. Then, starting when **[213]** habits and relations have already been formed, you cannot expect to take half the clients away from the first enterprise. It would therefore be very optimistic to suppose that you might take 12 million from their gross receipts and that you might add 2 million or 3 million of new products to this because new localities are crossed in your track. Altogether 15 million is all you might hope to receive. From this deduct the costs of maintenance and exploitation, which could mount to 12 million because an important part of these costs are independent of the number of passengers and the amount of freight. Thus there would be no more than 3 million to share, that is to say, 3 per cent. The first enterprise, having no more than 18 million in gross receipts and 12 million or 13 million in costs, will yield no more than 5 per cent or 6 per cent instead of 15 per cent. Consequently, the new enterprise would have done a lot of harm to the old one while ruining its own shareholders. Instead of one good business, there would be two inferior ones.[xvi]

It could not be better expressed, but, in his article 'Voies de communication', in the same *Dictionnaire d'économie politique*, the same Dupuit contradicts himself in vain by stressing the similarity between the railway industry and other industries in order to claim the possibility of applying the principle of freedom of trade to railways. This self-refutation does not appear very convincing. It may be remarked, indeed, that the two rival enterprises agree upon one point, namely that it is in their interest to maintain monopoly tariffs and that before or after their so-called competition the consumers pay for their transport at the price of maximum profit and not at cost price. Sooner or later this is what will always occur in reality. Dupuit pays no attention to this fact because he considers it as natural and legitimate. However, we do not agree at all with this opinion and therefore we have to deal with it.

By their nature, the construction and operation of railways escape **[214]** competition, just as roads or canals do. However, there is more. Roads and canals themselves are natural monopolies, but traffic on them is subject to conditions of competition, since an indefinite number of vehicles and boats can use the road or canal. The toll, if there were any, is paid to a monopolist, but the freight costs are paid to competing entrepreneurs. On the other hand, where railways are concerned, both track and traffic are natural monopolies, essentially bound to each other because, as we have said, it is impossible for the passenger and freight trains of an indefinite number of companies to use the same rails. The rent of the track and the rolling stock and locomotives, toll and costs, must all be paid to a monopolist. For all these reasons, it would be an anomaly to appeal to freedom of trade as far as railways are concerned. Since, as we shall see by analysing the question of tariffs, railways constitute the most powerful and most overwhelming monopoly, it is the more important to insist on its cheapness by applying the rules relevant to a monopoly.

III Railway rates

The products of the railway industry are the carriage of travellers and merchandise. The unit of product is the transport of one passenger or one tonne of merchandise over a distance of one kilometre; we call this a *passenger-kilometre* or *tonne-kilometre*. The tariffs are indicated by the price of these units. Studying the problem of tariffs in the railway industry therefore means studying these prices.

This industry being a monopoly, two prices must be considered: a price corresponding to the cost price of a passenger-kilometre **[215]** or a tonne-kilometre and the price of the maximum net product. The consumer wants to pay the first one, the monopolistic entrepreneur prefers the second. It is quite certain that railway companies want to get the highest net product possible, but it is also obvious that, out of ignorance of a rational theory and practice of monopoly, they will only partly achieve this. This really is a strange truth and it appears that Mr Gustave Marqfoy has already substantiated it for the French companies in his remarkable work *De l'abaissement des tarifs de chemins de fer en France* (1863).[xvii] Unlike most economists writing on railways, Mr Marqfoy shows both clear understanding of the fact that the railway industry is a monopoly and profound knowledge of the nature and conditions of a monopoly. He knows that there is a cost price and a price of maximum net product; moreover, he knows that the price of the maximum net product is independent of fixed, or general, costs and depends only on proportional, or specific, costs. He makes the best possible use of these facts.

General costs of a railway company are those relating to the organization of the services necessary for operation: buildings, central services and staff. These are added to interest and redemption of capital. They have to be paid whatever the quantity of passengers or goods transported may be, in other words, irrespective of the traffic load; they are more or less fixed.

Specific costs are those relating to the very fact of transport, that is to say, everything that a passenger train or a freight train consumes when running: coal, train crew wages, wear and tear of materials and rails, etc. They are approximately proportional to the traffic load.

In these conditions, the course of the companies' action in the determination of tariffs is obvious. They must, **[216]** in their own interests, from their own point of view, determine the specific-costs price per passenger-kilometre or tonne-kilometre and regard it as the lower limit when reducing rates as long as such reduction will increase net product, ceasing this reduction as soon as it results in a decrease of net product. This is exactly the same thing as the owner of Mr Cournot's mineral spring and the supplier of water or gas in our example were supposed to do; the postal services acted similarly in trying to find an increase of their revenue in the reduction of postage on letters and printed matter. That said, some facts and data concerning French railway companies, borrowed from Mr Marqfoy, will demonstrate how little companies in general are aware of the problem that they have to solve.

According to the specifications of the French companies, the maximum passenger fares are as follows: first-class 10c, second-class 7.5c, third class 5.5c per head and per kilometre.[xviii] Average 7.66c.

On the other hand, after long calculations based on the 1860 results of the Compagnie du Midi, and perfectly applicable to other companies, Mr Marqfoy has determined the specific-costs prices of a passenger-kilometre as follows: first-class 1.12c, second-class 0.56c, third-class 0.24c.[xix] Average 0.64c. To keep matters simple, we shall only deal with local trains and not with express trains, nor with composite ones.

Hence, between 7.66c and 0.64c the companies had a range of 702 hundredths of a centime to experiment with by trial and error to find the price of the maximum product. They never took a single step in that direction. Since the foundation of French railways, passenger fares have remained fixed at the maximum in their tariffs. The only price reductions the companies ever tried were related to special **[217]** excursion trains, season tickets and return tickets, which we shall discuss later.

For merchandise the tariffs give the following maximum prices: first-class 16c, second-class 14c, third-class 10c per tonne-kilometre.[xx] Average 13.33c.

Moreover, Mr Marqfoy calculated the following specific-costs prices per tonne-kilometre: 1c for a train with fully laden wagons, 2c for one with half-empty wagons.[xxi] Average 1.5c.

Hence from the price of 13.33c to the price of 1.5c the companies had an interval of 1,183 hundredths of a centime to find the tariff of the maximum product. Here they did something interesting. They reduced their rates to an average of 6c or 7c. Rates below 4c are very unusual; there are none below 3c.

Does this mean that the companies acted on good grounds and stopped just when the reductions in rates started to produce a decrease in the net result? It is difficult to believe. During the decade 1852–61 receipts per kilometre increased as follows: 7 per cent for passengers, whose fares remained fixed, and 142 per cent for freight, where rates were reduced. The reduction in rates certainly played a role in the latter result. We may wonder whether a reduction in passenger fares would not have raised receipts per kilometre, which remained nearly the same, but we may even wonder whether a more daring reduction in freight rates would not have raised even more the already increased receipts per kilometre. Browsing through the various documents, among which were the reports submitted by the companies to the shareholders' meetings, we are inclined to think so.

In none of the reports is a distinction drawn between general costs and specific costs and nor is there any suggestion that the tariff of maximum product is independent **[218]** of general costs. The Compagnie de Lyon (Report, 1860) mentions managers, offices, maintenance of buildings, heating, lighting, charges on fixed capital, etc., as elements of the cost price of transport. In particular they invoke the construction costs of their Rhône-et-Loire network (more than 1,200,000 F per kilometre) to justify their tariff of 10c for conveying coal, whereas 7c or 8c, 5c or 6c, probably would have yielded more. All these companies are astonished that a reduction in rates is invariably followed by an immediate increase in yields. In the early days of the railways, passenger traffic was thought to be the more profitable. The predictions were erroneous: price reductions and increases in the speed of trains especially have stimulated the carriage of merchandise. The Compagnie du Nord (Reports, 1853 and 1855), the Compagnie de l'Est (1853), the Compagnie de l'Ouest (1859), the Compagnie du Midi (1855, 1856, 1861 and 1862) cannot get over their amazement at this development, although several years' experience could have taught them better. In 1847, because of exceptional circumstances, the Compagnie du Nord reduced its rate for the carriage of corn, with the intention of doing so for six months only. They made such a profit that several years later this tariff still applied. The same company (1860 report) congratulated itself for having 'adopted the practice of reduced prices, particularly for heavy goods and for goods satisfying the first necessities of life'. However, the idea of extending this practice in a more general and systematic way did not enter their heads. The same goes for other companies: they cling to high tariffs, detrimental not only to the public interest but also to their own. They do not try to find the cost price, but they do not even think of trying to proceed in the direction of the maximum product price either.

[219] In addition to the fact that monopoly permits the establishment of prices of maximum net product higher than the cost price, it makes several different prices for the same product easy to maintain, as we have seen. We have just noted that railway companies take advantage of the first fact (more or less cleverly). They benefit likewise from the second.

In the first instance, this observation does not seem to apply to passenger tariffs. French companies ask 10c from first-class passengers, 7.5c from second-class passengers and 5.5c from third-class passengers, but they seat twenty-four first-class passengers, thirty second-class passengers and forty third-class passengers per carriage. The seating is progressively less comfortable, etc. The services are therefore not identical with regard to space or comfort. The prices seem to be proportional to the difference. This would be exactly the case if they were not far from cost prices: 1.12c, 0.56c and 0.24c. However, they are noticeably higher and, therefore, quite independent of the standard of service, and so we have to reason differently. Rightly or wrongly, the companies in fact consider the average price of 7.66c as the price of maximum profit, roughly the second-class price. However, they do not want to overlook passengers who are willing to pay more, nor do they wish to refuse passengers who cannot pay as much. This explains the three classes and the considerable efforts to emphasize the advantages of the first class and the disadvantages of the third. Those who insisted some years ago on glazed windows in the third class, as stipulated in the specifications of 1857–8, those who now demand heating in winter-time and those who complain of the companies' insensitivity do not understand these companies' real motives. If the third-class carriages were comfortable enough many second-class passengers, and some of the first-class, would use them and the total net product would be reduced, as described by the theory of monopoly. That is the reason! The **[220]** companies have their third-class carriages only to prevent the loss of a large number of less prosperous travellers who would have continued travelling by stagecoach rather than pay first or second-class fares. Similarly, the companies have special rates for season tickets whose holders would not commute if they had to pay the normal fares. There are also reduced rates for excursion trains or for day trips, to attract people who would otherwise not travel at all. All these rates are still considerably above cost price, of course.

However, this observation may in particular be applied to goods rates, where multiple prices for one and the same service are sustained by classification. Transporting a ton of one commodity and a ton of another between two well determined points are two identical services, apart from a few differences in respect of the space that bulky goods may take. Special care required by the nature and value of the merchandise justifies only insignificant price differences. Let us browse through the list of goods of each specific class: *spirits*, *timber*, *chemical products*, *game*, *sugar*, *coffee*, *cloth*, *manufactured goods* in first class; *wheat*, *seeds*, *flour*, *firewood*, *large timber*, *cotton*, *wool*, *beverages*, *metal* in the second; *coal*, *manure and fertilizers*, *stone*, *minerals*, *gravel*, *sand*, *clay*, *bricks*, *slate* in the third. Obviously, the classification is based only on the price of the goods, in other words on the pecuniary sacrifices consumers are willing to make for having them delivered. In a report dealing with tariff reform, Mr de Ruolz said, 'Diversity of prices is the indispensable condition for an average tariff high enough to attain the amount [of the interest] of the capital involved.'[xxii] Mr Lamé-Fleury, who quotes this passage, adds: 'Why not say plainly that railway companies **[221]** are only concerned with maximizing receipts by any legal means?'[15]

This is Dupuit's doctrine of monopoly without conditions or reservations. Let it be said that the classification of travellers and goods established by the tariffs puts a limit on the multiplicity of prices; probably it is in the companies' interests to stretch this multiplicity even more.

As we have already said, the maximum rates for goods in the tariff have never been considered by French companies as those yielding maximum profit. At least, they behaved as if they believed these rates could be found at a somewhat lower level. That is why they substituted lower rates for them in certain cases. These rates were either *general* or *specific*: general when they were applicable to all consignors without further conditions than those specified in the tariff, special when valid for certain customers only, under conditions different from the tariff. These conditions might be a longer delivery than normal, the company not being liable for loss or damage during the journey, lower limits for the weight of goods to be carried. Special rates were usually lower than general ones. The reduction depended on the conditions. At one time in France a clause stipulating that the shipper must agree to send all his consignments by the one railway company appeared among the requirements for special rates. This same condition appeared in conventions of a more particular character. In 1890 the General Councils of the different departments prohibited it, in either form, in order to support the canals. Apart from this special case, the principle of special rates has developed considerably: at present these tariffs cover half to three-quarters of all lower-speed transport.

[222] Be it general or specific, a rate is *proportional* if it is based on a constant kilometre price, for instance 5c per kilometre irrespective of the distance covered. A rate is *differential*, on the other hand, if it is based on a kilometre price that decreases as the distance covered increases. For instance, one pays 5c per kilometre for distances less than 100 km, 4c for distances between 100 km and 200 km, and so on. It is obvious that, in the latter case, the company sells the service of transport per kilometre at different prices according to whether more or fewer units are required. They do so on a much more extensive, complicated and serious scale than does the shopkeeper who gives a baker's dozen. Two examples suffice to convey an idea of how flexible and far-reaching this device is. According to the report presented by Mr Moussette to the 1862 committee of inquiry, the average prices in 1860 for the carriage of coal per tonne per kilometre, excluding the costs of loading and unloading, over the five companies Nord, Ouest, Est, Orléans and Lyon, came to 9c, 8.10c, 7.60c, 6.90c,

15 [E. de Lamé-Fleury, 'Des réglementaires du transit et de l'exportation par chemins de fer'], *Journal des économistes*, 2nd series [9th year], vol. XXXV [no. 29, July 1862], p. 57.

6.20c, 4.90c, 4.70c and 4.20c for distances respectively of 6 km, 19 km, 32 km, 58 km, 80 km, 120 km, 161 km and 241 km. In England the Great Northern Railway's prices for the transport of minerals in 1862 were 31c, 13c, 9c, 6.5c, 5.6c, 5.5c 5.2c for distances of 6 km, 20 km, 50 km, 100 km, 161 km, 200 km and 300 km respectively.

These differential tariffs and those for *transit*, which have analogous effects, are a subject of lively debate. They have been energetically accused of the embarrassment caused to the position of industrial and commercial towns, bringing them nearer to or further from centres of production, raw materials or manufactured goods in an arbitrary way. The companies' right to modify the cities' natural conditions of industry and commerce was a point at issue, as was the question of whether the State should intervene to maintain those **[223]** conditions. Another point against these rates, in the interest of the canals, was whether the companies have the right to kill the canals and whether the State should intervene to keep them alive. Confused questions like these will become immeasurably clearer in the light of principles. Changes in the industrial and commercial positions of cities or threats to canals by the simple fact of railway transport at cost price are obviously very normal effects of technical and economic progress, which alter situations in this way all the time. If these results were produced by running railways under local or central government monopoly, serving some well defined purpose, then there would only be some sacrifice of private interests to the general interest. This happens daily. But if they were the consequences of operation at monopoly prices by private companies, for the greater profit of their shareholders, then it would, indeed, be rather curious and must seem so from a commonsense point of view as well as it really is to the eye of science.

IV State intervention in railways

The conclusion to be drawn from the preceding considerations is obvious enough. For two reasons the State can and must intervene in the activities of railways: (1) railway services are a public service in so far as transport of services and products of public interest are concerned; (2) railway services form a natural and necessary monopoly in so far as transport services and products of private interest are concerned. As a private monopoly, it should be founded neither on law nor on [public] interest and, consequently, should be made an economic State monopoly. If the **[224]** latter case prevailed, railway monopoly should simply be exercised by the State, or on its behalf, at cost price. However, this stipulation should be understood in a broader sense than would seem at first sight, given the special character of railway activities mentioned in the first point above.

Let us leave transport of public interest aside for a while, and consider railways as capital goods used for the production of services and goods of private interest. The revenue of these capital goods may be observed in the same way as the revenue of certain other agricultural or industrial capital goods: it depends on the time and place. Reclamation of marshland unprofitable in a certain district or at a certain time could be useful elsewhere or later, near a large city or after a measure of growth in population or wealth. In the same way, a railway that would not cover its costs (either specific or general) at a certain time or in a certain place could do so in another place, between two industrial or commercial centres, or at another time, thanks to a certain degree of economic progress. For instance, in a given country there could be four of five railway lines initially just covering their specific and general costs, in other words their operation under monopoly would, in fact, be operation at cost. Some years later those same lines could earn more than their costs, since their sales or consumption curve is not fixed for ever; this curve, decreasing in prices, is the basis of the whole theory of monopoly.[xxiii] Hence, as population and wealth increase, the cost price decreases because general costs are divided up between a larger quantity of services or products. From that time onwards, passengers and merchandise rates will become profitable rates, when they were cost-price rates at the beginning. What is more, when **[225]** the lines first built begin to earn more than enough to cover their costs, other lines will appear, as if able to cover theirs. Under these conditions, the State could manage its monopoly in two quite distinct ways. It could regard the various lines as mutually independent and not intervene in their construction or working before they appeared ready to cover their costs. When a line began to yield regular profits it could then reduce its rates. Alternatively, the state could consider all the lines together as a single network, and rather than reducing the rates of the lines first built, it might build and run other lines at first unprofitable. Profits made by the former lines might serve to cover losses suffered by the latter; it would be enough for profits and losses to balance. The State would then be in the same position as farmers who suffer losses in cattle breeding but make money from arable. Mr Demongeot put it as follows: 'How many iron and steel works have benefited on casting and lost on smelting, or the other way round, or have lost on forging and benefited on construction?'[16] Anyway, operation will take place at cost price in some sense, both in the second and in the first mode.

In the first mode, transport would be somewhat lower in price and completion of the railway network would be rather slower in the country in question. In the second mode, transport would be more expensive but completion of the network much quicker. If railways are considered only as industrial capital goods offering a way of transporting merchandise, perhaps the first mode should

16 [Alfred Demongeot] 'Les clauses financières des conventions passées entre l'État et les six grandes compagnies de chemins de fer,' *Journal des actuaires* [*français*], vol. III [December 1874], p. 386[–7].

be preferred. If, on the other hand, the point of view of public service is to be considered, the second mode would certainly be more suitable. Note, moreover, that railways are a powerful means **[226]** of stimulating growth and by this very fact a strong incentive to advantageous production. On their own they hasten the progress that turns them from unprofitable into profitable or from already profitable into even more so. Note too, that on all lines the price of maximum profit would decrease constantly thanks to the growth of sales, i.e. consumption.

Low transport prices and quick completion of the network are the two advantageous alternatives to choose from if the railway monopoly is handed over to the State. What will happen if, on the contrary, this monopoly is left in the hands of private companies? The companies will be happy to construct and exploit lines that reimburse costs. However, from the very moment that they yield more than their costs they will take good care not to reduce the tariffs or construct and operate other lines that would not earn enough to cover costs, while compensating for these losses with profits drawn from the first lines. The country will pay a high price for transport and will see the network completed only slowly. This is what happens in France.

The preceding reasoning has been founded on the hypothesis, generally accepted in matters of economic questions, that private interests are at the same time selfish and clear-sighted. However, as we have observed, this hypothesis is not quite consistent with reality. Selfish, private interests certainly always are, but clear-sighted is another matter. Here is a second proof, taken from the history of railways. In certain countries, like England and Switzerland, for instance, the success of the first lines happened to encourage capital to be poured into the industry in huge amounts without much thought. Companies whose shares yielded two or three times the normal interest rates (and had therefore double or triple value) incessantly overloaded themselves with endless branch lines and assisted others to do the same thing by means of subscriptions and guaranteed interest payments. So they reduced their own revenue to **[227]** 2 per cent or 3 per cent and lowered the value of their shares to below par. It seems therefore that rash impetuosity of individual initiative has had the same result as rational progress within the system of State intervention would have had. However, only petty, cynical minds would consider achievement of a purpose by normal means the same thing as achieving it by irregular means. In a country where the State had proceeded as we have explained, there would have been neither profit nor loss for anybody, no unrest, no crisis. The development of railways would continue from day to day. In the countries just discussed, there were profit and loss: profits for those who created the first lines, losses for those who created the latest ones; profits for those who sold their shares when above par and losses for those who bought them then and who saw them descend below par. In addition to speculation, *agiotage* [misuse at the Bourse[xxiv]] was manifested, and that is not all. Minor disturbances accompanied these main disturbances: money spent, corruption used to obtain concessions, a species of blackmail, too, by holders of concessions of parallel lines to force those of existing lines to buy them back, the desperate and crippling struggle of those lines where the merger could not take place. These crises and scandals brought railways into disrepute for a time. So they stopped these practices; taking them up again would only entail the same consequences.

Questions of science should be treated scientifically. Scientific method in applied economics means supposing private interest is clear-sighted and if this is not so at first, it will learn from experience. In speculating on the blindness of private interest, one would be exposed to definite drawbacks while hoping for advantages with strings attached. According to this **[228]** scientific point of view, it should be agreed that railway enterprises will be built up when they are remunerative but not when they are a burden, if they are simply left to private initiative. Hence the construction of railways by the State and their operation on behalf of the State under a monopoly has this immense superiority over construction and operation by private companies under the same conditions, that progressive success of the lines already constructed will assure the construction of later lines, while in the other case success will only serve to enrich a parasitic class of speculators whose gains will have no relation to the risks incurred.

Today's school of economists, for whom *laisser-faire, laisser-passer* sums up economic and social science completely, will not fail to make the eternal objection against State construction and operation of railways: that the State is incapable of running a business. The State, they say, represented by uninterested, negligent civil servants, cannot obtain the same profits as shareholders do from their monopoly when represented by alert and attentive administrators. In the hands of the State, railway offices will become well paid sinecures distributed by political nepotism and favouritism. Constructed and run by such staff, railway lines will prove costly and yield nothing. Instead of profits spent on developing the network, the State will incur losses falling heavily on taxpayers.

Personally, we cannot accept a prejudice which endows the individual with every virtue and the State with every vice. This is abuse of the principles of economics. If it were true that private initiative, stimulated by free competition, better accomplished services of private interest than anything else, then collective initiative, controlled by **[229]** discussion and publicity, would better accomplish services of public interest. There where political minds are well formed, the press free and critical, public functions appropriately performed, magistrates incorruptible and officials honest, well informed administrators and skilful chief engineers[xxv] often do very important and extensive work for very modest remuneration. It should be admitted that respect and honour are natural motivations for a man, just as much as the wish to earn a great deal of money. The State has its role just as the individual has, and must be trusted in fulfilling it, just as the individual should be, within the limits of his role. It would be unseemly if the State substituted itself for private initiative in industrial enterprises. However, the individual taking the place of the community's initiative in public functions is no less wrong. Strictly speaking, there is a *raison d'être* not only for developing applied theory of the functions of the State, but also for managing the concrete organization of the State, ensuring that the staff of civil servants be made up of university graduates, who have had professional training and passed examinations, and not the sort of people who are essentially novelists or vaudeville script-writers.

If the railways were exclusively a public service then their construction and operation should be put unhesitatingly in the hands of the State, but the service is also private. Well, this could possibly be a reason for leaving them to the intervention of private companies if competition were possible in that branch, but this is not the case when there is a natural and necessary monopoly. This fact alone, and *a priori*, means that the economists' partiality for individual initiative is no longer feasible. Indeed, who are we trying to persuade that privileged railway companies are a type of intelligent activity and not 'wicked little States', as Dupuit called them in private? Who could be cajoled into believing that nepotism and favouritism are unknown here? Who is unaware that their administration and **[230]** operation is mediocre and mean-spirited? They underpay their employees, treat the public as an exploitable resource, stick to the highest rates even when it would certainly be in their interests to reduce them – in short, stingy and indifferent, they merely cream off a fruitful monopoly. At least they make a profit, it may be said! Who would stop the State doing exactly the same? Everybody knows that the railway companies' shareholders are nobody, that most of the administrators do not have much influence and that management of these enterprises is concentrated in the hands of a few directors and chief executives who are interested because of circumstances that have nothing to do with the companies' success. Who would forbid the State from using the same people, in the same conditions and to the same ends? Supposing the shareholders to be apathetic, the administrators dismissed, the directors and chief executives only maintained and the State claiming the dividends, then nothing would be changed, except the use of these dividends. Even if the State did nothing to increase the receipts, and did not use them any better, there would still be an advantage for society. Fares would not be what they should, either in the interests of the consumer or in those of the railways, but, on the other hand, the pointsmen would no longer be responsible for a task far above human strength for ridiculous wages. Nor would the employees' and passengers' lives be endangered any longer. In that sense, the public would still benefit from gains received by the shareholders at present.

What is more, a solution to this problem does exist. Let it be admitted that in railway matters the aspect of private services outweighs that of public ones and that therefore their exploitation requires imperatively that spirit of mercantile acuity which is the motive of agricultural, industrial, commercial and financial business but is incompatible with exercising public functions. **[231]** Economic monopolies can be distinguished from moral monopolies in the sense that the first can be put under competition conditions, namely by offering them for sale by auction and making them concessions of general interest. What could be more appropriate in the case of the railway industry? According to whether the enterprise is to operate at cost price or at the price of maximum net product, the public sale should be an 'inverse auction' [where participants successively make lower and lower bids], or a normal auction [where participants are bidding up]. In the first case, the bids are tariffs and in the second case rent to be paid to the State. The railways, invariably constructed at the expense of the State by means of capital obtained by bonds issued and guaranteed by the State, would then be put in the hands of the railway companies to work them according to their bid at the auction. In the system of operation at cost price, rent paid should be equal to the amount of interest on bonds, and the tariffs should be determined in proportion to this interest and other, general and specific, costs. In the system of exploitation at the price of maximum net product, tariffs should be determined according to the law of supply and demand, and the State should construct railway lines to the extent to which they are able to pay the interest [from rent received]. All this rests on the belief that such companies, placed in normal conditions of industrial enterprise and actually submitted to the regime of free competition, would display the activity and intelligence which have not hitherto been observed in either the State or the companies.

Of course, this solution would not be without complications or problems. If the State is not only the owner of track and buildings, but also of material and movable property, rent would comprise the location of all this, and State inspectors would have to verify with the greatest care whether the tracks, buildings, material and movable property were maintained in conformity with instructions collected in a document comprising very precise and detailed specifications. If material and movable property belonged to the railway companies, specifications would have to stipulate the means and the condition of purchase by the State in case the lease were not renewed. After **[232]** all, this will happen upon the expiry of the contract, unless the companies were asked to be so good as to remain in control of the railways, since the State had no idea what to do with the network. Incidentally, this solution is perhaps the one for which we are being prepared; we admit a preference for our own solution, with all its complications and practical difficulties.

Penetrating into these details is not a matter of science, strictly speaking, but of a more specialist study. In a country where it is believed that good principles are the basis of successful applications, science in a strict sense has done its work having once established those principles. The first that affects the railway industry is that this industry eludes the rule of *laisser-faire, laisser-passer* completely, first because the service of public transport is a public service, and, second, because the service of transport of private interests is a natural and necessary monopoly. The second principle is, therefore, that the railways must be constructed and exploited under conditions of economic monopoly; either at cost price, or at the price of maximum profit; either by the State, or on behalf of the State by concessionary companies. Without these principles there will only be mistakes, confusion and disorder – as the history of railways in the various countries of Europe and the New World amply testifies.

[233] Note

Since this paper was drafted, the following works, among others, have been published that confirm and complete my opinions:

De Labry,[xxvi] Engineer, of the Ponts et Chaussées, *Étude sur les rapports financiers établis pour la construction des chemins de fer entre l'État et les six principales compagnies françaises*. [Première partie, *Des Conventions*, Paris: Dunod, 1875.] (Reprint from *Annales des Ponts et Chaussées*, [2nd semester] 1875 [pp. 56–172].)

Arthur T. Hadley,[xxvii] *Le Transport par les chemins de fer. Histoire, législation*. Translated by A. Raffalovich and L. Guérin [Paris: Guillaumin], 1887.

René Tavernier,[xxviii] Engineer of the Ponts et Chaussées, *Considérations économiques sur les chemins de fer français. De l'exploitation locale des grandes compagnies et de la nécessité de réformes décentralisatrices* [Paris: Dunod, 1888]. (Reprint from *Annales des Ponts et Chaussées*, [April] 1888 [pp. 637–83]).

——*Principes de tarification et d'exploitation du trafic voyageurs* [Paris: Dunod, 1889]. (Reprint from *Annales des Ponts et Chaussées*, [December] 1889 [pp. 595–655]).

——*Économie des exploitations de banlieue sur les grands réseaux de chemins de fer*. Report presented to the Société d'économie politique [et d'économie sociale] de Lyon, session of 21 February 1890 [Lyon: Imprimerie A. Bonnaviat].[xxix]

E. Wickersheimer,[xxx] Chief Engineer of Mines, former Member of Parliament, *Étude sur le rachat des chemins de fer d'Orléans, de l'Ouest, de l'Est et du Midi. Construction de 20.000 kilomètres de chemins de fer économiques* [Paris: Imprimerie de Chaix], 1892.

Both Mr Hadley and Mr Tavernier have mastered the scientific theory of operation under monopoly. Both even expound this theory mathematically, and it is indeed mathematical. The latter writer is wrong in attributing the theory not to Cournot, from whom it originates, but to Dupuit. He is likewise wrong in adopting Dupuit's far-fetched point of view. He is to be praised, however, for completing the theory in question by serious study of [the notions of] gross product and maximum net product, multiple tariffs, etc., and carrying out a rigorous application to the operation of railways. His publications do not take the form of a critique of French companies, but, in my opinion, this critique follows in full measure from the simple statement of what all the companies could have done and did not do, in particular as far as **[234]** passenger traffic is concerned: distinction between the clients from the suburbs and those in transit, train-tramways, regional tariffs, local services. In this respect, I dare say that a more detailed and extended analysis of the management of our companies would suggest no reason to modify my 1875 judgement. Nevertheless, I must mention that because of recent events there is a distinction to be drawn between the companies.

Due to the agreements reached in France between the State and the railway companies, especially those of 1858–9 and 1868–9, the State has made the commitment to subsidize, if necessary, the payment of interest and redemption of bonds issued for the six companies, as well as the payment of a minimum dividend on the shares. In exchange the companies receiving these subsidies, and only those companies, must share the dividend with the State when it rises above a certain maximum. From that time on, the six French companies have been divided into two groups. On the one hand the Nord and the Paris–Lyon–Méditerranée, with their magnificent main lines, found it possible to construct and operate their secondary networks as active monopolists without appealing for subsidies from the State, so that they are not obliged to share the surplus of the maximum dividend with the State. On the other the Est, the Midi, the Orléans and the Ouest, resigning themselves to appealing for subsidies (which have never been repaid) satisfy themselves with the minimum dividend and exploit their companies as lethargic monopolists. My criticism is therefore upheld, in so far as the latter four companies are concerned. Moreover, the position of the State, unable to make anything out of the richer companies and losing everything with the poorer ones, was perfectly characterized by Mr Hadley depicting the French railway companies as playing the game of pitch-and-toss with the French State, according to the rule: *Heads, we win; tails, you lose*.

How can the State get out of this situation? Obviously, by purchasing the networks – not only that of those four companies burdened with debt[xxxi] but of all six companies, under the conditions provided for in the contracts, with a view to abolishing those contracts and setting up a rational operation, either by the State itself, or by companies acting on their behalf. As Mr Wickersheimer has suggested, a cheaper network of railway lines of more modest construction, **[235]** run more simply and productively, should be built, and the sooner the better.

At the meeting on 5 June 1890 of the Société d'économie politique de Paris, M. de Labry, while using his own 1875 paper on the relation between the State and the companies, indicated the ways and means for the purchase, which could be carried out at about this time: an introduction as receipts into the

[State] budget of 810 million gross receipts and 850 million expenses, of which 410 million are exploitation costs and 440 million are annuities payable to the companies until the expiry of their concessions (1954–60); the surplus of 40 million in expenses corresponds to the yearly subsidies advanced at the time by the State to aid the indebted companies; finally, 550 million should be paid as the surplus of the value of the material and movable property of the companies over and above the sum owed because of the subsidies.[xxxii] But since then the 1883 conventions have taken place, increasing the concessions for secondary networks and State commitment to guarantee interest payment; these conventions considerably increased the amount of annuities to be paid. The longer the wait, the more billions will be buried in the railways by the State to the delight of the shareholders, who, by means of State advances to the sum of 50 million per year, receive on average more than 10 per cent on their capital invested without the slightest effort. Here an enormous objection, of a practical rather than theoretical nature, appears: the French State is quite incapable of either running the railways itself or getting them run by concessionary companies.

The report of the 5 June session to which I referred above, ends as follows:

> Mr Joseph Garnier, member of l'Institut, believes that he may say, after all he has read and heard, that the problem of French railways has not been sufficiently elucidated to formulate a scheme of general reorganization.
>
> Rightly or wrongly, Parliament has agreed to purchase the lines of Charentes and the Vendée, which are in disorder. By this fact, the State has become an interim manager of those lines and recommenced the experiment of administrative operation. As a result it was necessary to buy some lines from the Orléans network to manage an exploitable network....
>
> At present, it is not possible to go further. Buying the **[236]** whole Orléans network would be imprudent, because it is not known how to run it.
>
> Buying all the lines would be even less wise, not because financially it would be impossible because of the stipulations in the contracts but also because there are no clear ideas, either about the financial companies to replace the present ones, or about the system of tariffs to be imposed on them.
>
> The operation of these enormous enterprises by the State is altogether out of the question. The State would run them much worse, more expensively and more autocratically than the present companies. On the other hand, the public would be unreasonably exacting and would want transport for nothing. The waste would soon be extensive. Bureaucracy would increase and it would not be long before the employees became electoral agents. Operation by the State would mean a political mess.[xxxiii]

> These lines contain the core of what all people say and write against reform of our railways. It could well be transcribed: We cannot or we do not know how to develop pure science on the subject of social wealth or society. First, it therefore follows that neither the construction and running of the railways nor the organization and the administration of the State can be derived from applied science; second, it follows that our railways are badly run and our State badly governed. We are incapable of reforming the railways since, first, we have no blueprint for normal operation, and, second, if we had and needed State intervention, we do not have the State needed for that either.

Well, so be it! This reasoning is rigorous in the sense that, once its starting point is admitted, its conclusion should be accepted. In heaven's name, however, protect us from being forced to accept this theme as the expression of the 'principle of the freedom of trade'.

Notes

i See the nine unsigned articles published under the title 'Chemins de fer' in the *Nouvellist vaudois et Journal national suisse* (Lausanne), 51st year, from no. 232 (1 October 1875) to no. 250 (22 October 1875).

ii At the beginning of February 1897, probably, Walras did not yet envisage writing a 'Final note'. The original text of the first footnote of this article was then as follows:

> This memoir was composed in the summer of 1875, when the question of the purchase [by the State] of the railways, still live at present in Switzerland, had been asked in the Vaud canton by two members of the State Council of Vaud. One of these, Mr Delarageaz, used it and cited it in a series of articles in the *Nouvelliste vaudois* in October 1875. Since then some important technical works have been published on the subject, of which I shall mention the following: 'De l'exploitation locale des grandes compagnies et de la nécessité de réformes décentralisatrices', by M. René Tavernier, engineer of the Ponts et Chaussées (offprint from the *Annales des Ponts et Chaussées*, April 1888); 'Principes de tarification et d'exploitation du trafic voyageurs' by the same author (*Annales*, December 1889); 'Economie des exploitations de banlieue sur les grands réseaux de chemins de fer', report presented to the Société d'économie politique de Lyon, at the session of 21 February 1890 by the same author; 'Theorie der Tarifbildung der Eisenbahnen', by W. Launhardt, professor at the Technishe Hochschule zu Hannover, 1890. Since then modifications have taken place in practice. However, I publish my paper as it stands, in the opinion that the theories exposed in it are still correct and nearly new, and that the data that have been cited still have at least historical value (Walras Archives, Lausanne, F.W. Vb, box 20).

One may observe that in the 'Final note' Walras added references to De Labry, A. T. Hadley and E. Wickersheimer to his list, but that he no longer mentions W. Launhardt.

iii Charles Coquelin and Gilbert-Urbain Gillaumin, *Dictionnaire de l'économie politique*, Paris: Guillaumin, vol. 1, pp. 337–62.

iv In his article (p. 353) Chevalier indicates that certain persons

> concluded that the English railways were run in a way not much in conformity with public interest. In line with this idea a brochure published in 1843 in London aroused some sensation. Its title is *Railway Reform*. The author shows how an immense force was lost in transporting empty wagons, while poor people plodded wearily along the railway track. He argued that by attracting people for whom the railways are now beyond their means by reduced prices, one could fill the wagons as well as the companies' funds.... The author of *Railway Reform* concluded that the State should acquire the railways and run them at reduced rates, just as the Belgian government does.

The name of the author to whom Chevalier alludes is William Galt.

v Wolowski inserted this letter in his book mentioned by Walras in footnote 3 and he added his response in the same book on pp. 250–92.

vi In the original manuscript Walras wrote in the first instance 'free competition' (Walras Archives, Lausanne, F. W. Vb, box 20, p. 5).

*vii Walras's meaning of the word 'utility' (*utilité*) here, in applied economics, is different from its meaning in pure economics. As follows from the text, the word is used here in the sense of 'usefulness', or, perhaps better, 'efficiency'. When confusion is not to be expected, we shall use the word 'utility' in both meanings, leaving it to the reader to observe whether Walras is dealing with pure economics or applied economics.

*viii Walras was probably thinking of the 'basic laws' (maybe his well known *droit natural*) that underlie written laws.

*ix Quotation marks added.

*x Here Walras has disregarded complications caused by fixed costs.

*xi Presumably, Walras meant here that enterprises interested in the production and distribution of some product (gas, for instance) under monopoly in some city meet in an auction to try to get the concession. This auction might be organized as follows. The interested parties are invited by the auctioneer to propose a price at which they will supply the product. The price proposed by the first bidder, will perhaps exceed the cost price of one or more of the parties. Then the auctioneer tries to solicit a lower selling price. Let us suppose that somebody makes such a bid, possibly still above one or more cost prices. A third selling price might then be proposed, and so forth. Under certain conditions, this process might converge to a bid equal to the cost price of the most efficiently producing party. Here we cannot speak of a Dutch auction, where the auctioneer starts with a high, unacceptable price and then proposes prices gradually lower and lower and where the first participant who calls 'mine' at a certain price proposed is bound by it. In an 'English auction' the auctioneer tries to solicit higher and higher bids from the participants, till nobody wants to make another bid. The highest bidder is then bound by his bid. Both systems are aimed at the achievement of a final price as high as possible. The procedure indicated above in the case of Walras might perhaps be called an 'inverse English auction'.

xii The paper was reprinted in Jules Dupuit, *De l'utilité et de sa mesure*, papers selected and edited by Mario de Bernardi, Turin: La Riforma Sociale, 1933 (pp. 97–162).

xiii Page 248 in *Annales des Ponts et Chaussées* of March–April 1849 and p. 162 in *De l'utilité et de sa mesure*.

xiv Adam Smith, *Wealth of Nations*, Book V, chapter I, Part III, article 1, London: Oxford University Press, 1976, pp. 724–5.

xv From February 1838 onwards, the Chambre des Députés discussed a government proposal of a law for the construction by the State of several railway lines that were considered as having high priority. The director-general of the Ponts et Chaussées et de Mines, Legrand, who had been charged with the laying out before the Chamber the grounds for the proposal, insisted upon the strategic and military implications of the new mode of transport, and the principal spokesmen did the same. Two applications were particularly remarkable: that by Berryer, supporter of the construction of the railways by private industry, and that of the poet Lamartine, supporter of construction by the State. The government's project was eventually rejected with a considerable majority. However, the debate continued till 1842 when the *deputés* accepted a Bill that fixed the lines to be constructed as a priority and that distinguished clearly the State's role from that of the companies: the State would construct the infrastructure (bridges, tunnels, etc.), the private companies concessionaires would construct the superstructure (track, etc.) and would operate the railways (law of 11 June 1842). On these questions one may consult L. Grippon-Lamotte's work, *Historique du réseau des chemins de fer français. Les six grandes compagnies; le réseau 'État'*, Issoudun: Gaignault, 1904, pp. 12–81.

xvi Arsène-Jules Dupuit, 'Péage', in Charles Coquelin and Gilbert-Urbain Guillaumin (eds), *Dictionnaire de l'économie politique*, Paris: Guillaumin, 1853, vol. 2, pp. 339–44.

xvii Gustave Marqfoy, *De l'abaissement des tarifs de chemins de fer en France* (Of the reduction of railway tariffs in France), Paris: Librairie nouvelle, 1863.

xviii Ibid., p. 166.

*xix Ibid., p. 168. Marqfoy made the mistake of transposing the prices of the second and third class. Walras corrected it.

xx Ibid., pp. 11–12. For merchandise the first class applies to liquor and to manufactured products, the second class to corn, metals, etc., and the third class to coal, stone, etc.

xxi Ibid., pp. 25–6.

xxii Cited by Ernest-Jules Lamé-Fleury; see below. Henri comte de Ruolz-Montchal was inspector-general of the railways at the time of Second Empire. We could not find the report concerned.

*xxiii The French original of the term 'sales curve' is *courbe de débit*, Cournot' term for 'demand curve'; see his *Recherches sur les principes mathématiques dee la théorie des richesses* (1838), chapter IV. Although Walras mostly uses the term 'demand curve', he preferred to use Cournot's term when dealing with (the theory of) monopoly.

*xxiv See Chapter 15.

*xxv In France, certainly in Walras's time, an *ingénieur* would have graduated from an *haute école* and therefore enjoyed (in others' and their own opinion) much more status than people with a normal university education. Accordingly, the English word 'engineer' is not an adequate translation because it indicates a job, while *ingénieur* is more of a title. Many *ingénieurs* fulfil(led) senior positions in the French administration. In spite of this, not having been able to find a better word, I sometimes use the term 'engineer' for *ingénieur*; I ask the reader to deduce from the context what is meant.

xxvi In his paper 'De l'esprit communal et de la routine administrative' (1863) Walras discussed another book by Félix-Jacques Olry, comte de Labry, *Utilité de l'ouverture permanente des villes fortifiées. Étude sur la routine administrative* (Paris: Dumaine, 1863). See on this subject L. Walras, *Mélanges d'économie politique et sociale*, vol. VII of *Œuvres économiques complètes*, Paris: economica, 1987, p. 160 f. De Labry is also the author of the article 'Surveillance par l'État de la gestion financière des chemins de fer en France', *Journal des économistes*, 3rd series, 11th year, no. 129, September 1876, pp. 350–8.

xxvii Arthur T. Hadley is the author of *Railroad Transportation: Its History and its Laws*, New York and London: G. P. Putnam's Sons, 1885, translated into French by A. Raffalovich and L. Guérin, under the title *Le transport par les chemins de fer. Histoire, législation*, with a foreword by Arthur Raffalovich (Paris: Guillaumin, 1887). For more on Hadley's work see Melvin Cross and Robert B. Ekelund Jr, 'A. T. Hadley on monopoly theory and railway regulation', *History of Political Economy*, vol. 12, no. 2, pp. 214–33.

xxviii On the two studies by Tavernier published in the *Annales des Ponts et Chaussées*, see François Etner, *Histoire du calcul économique en France*, Paris: economica, 1987, pp. 171–2, 189 and 219–34.

xxix See also *Société d'économie politique et d'économie sociale de Lyon* (25th year), sessions of 1889–90, eighth meeting, 21 February 1890, 'Rapport par M. R. Tavernier', pp. 240–83, 'Discussion', pp. 283–91. In a letter dated 31 May 1890 Tavernier gave Léon Walras notice of the dispatch of his three brochures, evoking 'Dupuit's theories, so forgotten and yet so brilliant', and he adds, 'I believe that nobody at the Société d'économie politique of Lyon ever heard of it, and during the conference that I held I thoroughly avoided introducing in my subject even the name of Mathematics, though it was rather difficult to do without it.' (*Correspondence*, II, letter 1013). In his answer Walras indicated particularly that he had found in these papers 'that theory of the government of the railways that I profess in my lectures on applied economics and that I deduced fifteen years ago from the theories of Cournot and of Dupuit on monopoly. For instance, I found it [your exposition] enriched by empirical evidence which I shall not hesitate to borrow from you, indicating, of course, my source' (ibid., letter 1014, 2 June 1891).

xxx Émile-Charles Wickersheimer's book, *Étude sur le rachat des chemins de fer d'Orléans, de l'Ouest, de l'Est et du Midi. Construction de 20.000 kilomètres de chemins de fer économiques*, preface by Camille Pelletan (Paris: Imprimerie de Chaix) came into Walras's hands at the moment that he was on the point of drafting the 'Note finale' (Walras to E.-C. Wickersheimer, *Correspondence* II, letter 1302, 25 February 1897). Later, Wickersheimer would publish a brochure, *Industries d'État, administrations privées*, Paris: H. Dunod & E. Pinat, 1906.

xxxi In the second draft of the manuscript Walras wrote at this point, 'as proposed by Mr Wickersheimer' (Walras Archives, Lausanne, F. W. Vb, box 20, p. 1).

xxxii Walras was referring to the following passage of the presentation by F.-J. Olry de Labry (*Journal des économistes*, 1880, pp. 466–7):

> According to the operating accounts for 1877, the most recent ones that have been fully published after verification by the Ministry of Public Works, one may assess as follows all the consequences for the public purse of the comprehensive operation of purchasing the six large railway companies in France, allowing all reservations for contentious points. The gross product of the networks of the six companies amounts to 809 million in 1877; 406 million of this amount have

been absorbed by the running costs and 403 million formed the net product. Total subsidies under the State guarantee were 40 million. The additional sum to be paid by the State for the *matérial* and the network might be 500 million. Hence, due to the purchase of the networks of the six large companies by the State, or by its delegates, the State budget should be augmented by the following round figures: (1) yearly receipts of 800 million gross product of the railways, (2) yearly expenses of 400 million operating costs, 450 million paid to the companies annually to make up their actual revenue, and, finally, half a billion, once only, for supplementary indemnity.

xxxiii Ibid., pp. 475–6.

www.ingramcontent.com/pod-product-compliance
Lightning Source LLC
Chambersburg PA
CBHW061149220326
41599CB00025B/4410
* 9 7 8 1 0 4 1 2 7 5 4 1 1 *